Pocket PC
Developer's Guide

About the Author

Dr. Bruce E. Krell is a software developer, author, graduate-level software engineering course teacher, industrial course developer and teacher, and a Certified Microsoft Instructor.

He has developed software for a wide range of applications, including auto and chip manufacturing, electrical vehicle control, laser system operations and control, cardiology, financial and tax accounting, and large, distributed databases. Over the years, Dr. Krell has performed development for customers such as General Motors, Delco Electronics, InfoVision Medical Systems, KLA-Tencor Instruments Corporation, RAM Optical Instrumentation, NanoScan, Inc., ACTA, Inc., 32X Corporation, ATX Forms, Inc., and InfoLink Screening Services, Inc.

Dr. Krell has developed several Pocket PC–based applications. His most recent Pocket PC product is MOA Master™ by ShootRite, Inc. This product enables police and military snipers to improve the accuracy of their long-distance shots by performing accurate predictions of downrange bullet trajectory. An ongoing project involves the development of a mobile Pocket PC application that uses the latest features of .NET support on the Pocket PC.

Prior to founding SWA Engineering, Inc., Dr. Krell was a senior scientist for Hughes Aircraft Company. During his sojourn with Hughes, Dr. Krell worked on a variety of systems, including air traffic control, distributed document and image-processing, night vision, smart missiles, and missile-control. As the lead software engineer for this wide range of systems and applications, Dr. Krell was responsible for all aspects of the design and development of the application software, usually including the actual coding and debugging of critical pieces of software.

His educational background includes a B.S. in Math from Tulane University, an M.B.A. from the University of New Orleans, and a Ph.D. in Management Science from the University of Houston and Rice University.

You can reach Dr. Krell at SWA Engineering, Inc.:
http://www.SWA-Engineering.com
BKrell@SWA-Engineering.com

About the Reviewer

Ken Miller is chief technology officer of 32X Tech Corporation (http://www.32X.com). His interest in Windows CE was inevitable given his years of design experience as an electrical engineer working on embedded hardware and software. Ken's most recent project was the co-development (with Dr. Krell) of a handheld ballistics computer for use by Marine Corps snipers.

Pocket PC
Developer's Guide

Bruce E. Krell, Ph.D.

McGraw-Hill/Osborne

New York   Chicago   San Francisco
Lisbon   London   Madrid   Mexico City   Milan
New Delhi   San Juan   Seoul   Singapore   Sydney   Toronto

McGraw-Hill/Osborne
2600 Tenth Street
Berkeley, California 94710
U.S.A.

To arrange bulk purchase discounts for sales promotions, premiums, or fund-raisers, please contact **McGraw-Hill**/Osborne at the above address. For information on translations or book distributors outside the U.S.A., please see the International Contact Information page immediately following the index of this book.

Pocket PC Developer's Guide

1234567890 CUS CUS 0198765432

ISBN 0-07-213150-0

Publisher	Brandon A. Nordin
Vice President & Associate Publisher	Scott Rogers
Editorial Director	Wendy Rinaldi
Project Editor	Janet Walden
Acquisitions Coordinator	Timothy Madrid
Technical Editor	Ken Miller
Copy Editor	Bart Reed
Proofreaders	Pam Vevea, Pat Mannion
Indexer	David Heiret
Computer Designers	Tabitha M. Cagan, Lucie Ericksen
Illustrators	Jackie Sieben, Lyssa Wald
Series Designer	Roberta Steele
Cover Designer	Greg Scott
Cover Illustration	Eliot Bergman

This book was composed with Corel VENTURA™ Publisher.

Dedicated to my wife, Michiko,
watashi no kawaii tsuma desu.

Contents at a Glance

Contents

Part III User-Friendly Applications in Small Spaces

Chapter 7 Using an Effective Software Design 233

Chapter 8 Using Intrinsic Controls in a Graphical User Interface 281

Acknowledgments

During the gestation period for a book, a number of individuals typically participate in its development. These individuals are highly instrumental in bringing a book to fruition in ways that are not often known publicly. This book is no exception in this regard. Therefore, I would like to thank a number of individuals who really contributed to the success of this book:

▶ Michiko Krell, my wife, who provides encouragement in the face of every seemingly impossible task that I face.

▶ Wendy Rinaldi, editorial director at McGraw-Hill/Osborne, for her bottomless patience through the trials and tribulations of delivering the draft chapters.

▶ Tim Madrid, acquisitions coordinator at McGraw-Hill/Osborne, for his efforts in making sure I had all the resources necessary to generate the manuscript.

▶ Janet Walden, executive project editor at McGraw-Hill/Osborne, for her excellent and careful management of the copyediting process.

▶ Bart Reed, copy editor for McGraw-Hill/Osborne, for his thorough reading and review of the contents of the draft chapters.

▶ Ken Miller, president of 32X Corporation, for his technical review and his substantive comments that improved the readability of the draft chapters.

▶ Mike Meltzer, Pocket PC Group, Microsoft Corporation, for hooking me up with the right people so I would be invited to write this book.

▶ Norm Chandler, Sr., and Norm Chandler, Jr., who encouraged me to learn enough about a police and Marine Snipers to actually develop a commercially viable Pocket PC program.

▶ First Sergeant Bill Skiles, USMC, for providing me with the opportunity to gain the actual experiences to understand the needs of real Marine snipers in the field.

▶ Last but not least, I would like to expressly thank all those individuals at McGraw-Hill/Osborne who performed the hundreds of tasks behind the scenes that are necessary to publish a book.

Preface

Read Me First!

Perhaps the most unread part of any book is the preface. However, this preface contains some very useful tidbits of information. Therefore, the name of this section is an attempt to attract you, the reader, in hopes you will actually read this section.

Who Is This Book For?

This book is for any programmer who would like to learn how to develop programs for the Pocket PC. Additionally, the reader should also have an interest in effective software design and tools and techniques for delivering a quality product on cost and within schedule.

What Is Special About This Book?

This book about Pocket PC programming differs significantly from other books on this topic. Some of the reasons why include the following:

▶ stresses good software-design principles in addition to the programming libraries.

▶ addresses user-interface design issues associated with the small screen space.

▶ provides reusable libraries and tools for quickly implementing complex features.

▶ lists steps to follow in order to efficiently incorporate libraries into a program.

▶ demonstrates and clearly explains examples in each step of the listed steps.

▶ provides complete, realistic working programs to demonstrate library usage.

▶ develops a software framework that enables debugging on the desktop and that ports the program to the Pocket PC by the modification of a single software flag.

Every line of code included in this book has been used on working, commercial Pocket PC programs developed by the author. This code has been developed over years of design and testing on desktop PC programs and then ported to the Pocket PC.

In addition to all these features, this book is filled with hundreds of hidden implications, limitations, and workarounds for programming the Pocket PC. These pearls of wisdom have been gleaned from thousands of hours of debugging programs on the Pocket PC.

Armed with the tools, techniques, and knowledge distilled in this book, you will be able to deliver your Pocket PC programs to the user market on schedule and on cost.

What Are the Prerequisites for Using This Book?

Almost every program in this book uses the C programming language. Programs in Chapter 12, about the Component Object Model, are written in C++. You do not need to be an expert on the C++ programming language in order to understand these programs. The amount of C++ is minimal and generally will not obscure the meaning and intent of the implemented code.

Although Visual Basic is available for the Pocket PC, the maturity of Visual Basic for the Pocket PC is far less than that of the C programming language, so Visual Basic is not used in this book. In order to simplify programming tasks, Visual Basic hides much of the details from the programmer. This hiding significantly restricts the power of the programmer.

This book also assumes that you are familiar with Embedded Visual Studio 3.0 IDE. If you worked with Visual Studio 6.0 in the past, you will have no problems using Embedded Visual Studio 3.0. This book does not contain any tutorials regarding Embedded Visual Studio 3.0, except where necessary to demonstrate specific, relevant programming features.

What Are Notes?

Throughout this text, you will find special formatted areas called *notes*. An example of a note follows:

NOTE

A note contains something of special importance that requires careful attention on your part.

Notes are typically important points I want you to remember or to understand. You'll also find similar *tips* and *cautions*.

What Is the Target Test Platform?

All the sample programs and libraries in this book were fully tested on a desktop PC using Visual Studio 6.0 and on a Casio Cassiopeia EM-500 (nicknamed "The Grape"). During the Pocket PC testing, Embedded Visual Studio 3.0 was used along with the Pocket PC 2002 SDK as the target library.

NOTE

Although the programs worked correctly on the Pocket PC used for testing, the programs may not work on your Pocket PC. Every hardware vendor uses a program called Platform Builder to tailor the Windows CE operating system. Part of this process includes tailoring the SDK for applications.

During the testing for this book, I found numerous examples of SDK methods that were supposed to work on the Pocket PC but did not even link properly. This situation occurred because the vendor, Casio, chose to remove some of these methods from the support system during the tailoring process.

During the development of the libraries and sample programs in this book, I made every effort to limit development to features and capabilities that are most likely to be available. However, some aspects still may not work on your target platform.

What Is Special About the Accompanying Programs?

At the end of each chapter, you'll find a complete set of instructions for each program. This set of instructions covers building, installing, and executing all programs and establishing all support requirements. Every effort has been made to be as complete as possible. These instructions were tested from scratch in order to verify that everything is included.

Every program that you can download from the web site for this book, http://www.osborne.com, appears in folders. Each folder has a name that describes the purpose of the program. This approach is far easier to navigate than the traditional approach, which names folders after chapters and sections of chapters.

NOTE

Although every effort has been made to assure the correctness of the textual and illustrative materials of this book, some errors typically occur in a book of this size. Ultimately, the author is responsible for these errors, so allow me to apologize in advance for any errors that you may encounter.

How Do I Contact the Author?

If you want to contact me with questions, feel free to send me e-mail at
BKrell@SWA-Engineering.com. I will be happy to answer technical questions
to the best of my ability.

PART

The Fundamentals

OBJECTIVES

- ▶ Describe the architecture of Windows CE

- ▶ Understand the subsystems of Windows CE

- ▶ Learn unique features of a Pocket PC program

- ▶ Design an easily tested Pocket PC program

- ▶ Review the implementation of the program

- ▶ Describe the steps to use the program

- ▶ Define the steps to convert the program

- ▶ Analyze the design of the program

Overview of the Pocket PC Environment

Windows CE manages every version of the Pocket PC (PPC). Elements of Windows CE display the windows, service the mouse clicks implemented as stylus taps for the Pocket PC, and update the display. However, a program written by a developer performs all the work to coordinate these activities by the elements of Windows CE. This chapter introduces the elements of Windows CE and describes the manner in which a program operates to interact with those elements.

NOTE

Windows CE is the most underappreciated operating system today.

The Windows CE operating system possesses a number of important and very impressive features. This operating system is a scaled down version of Windows 2000! The primary elements of Windows 2000 are the same elements that appear in Windows CE. Moreover, a Pocket PC application interacts with these elements in the same way that a desktop application interacts with Windows 2000. Windows CE offers the richest array of reusable interface components of any other embedded operating system, including the Palm OS and embedded Unix (which offers exactly none). This array of components is absolutely necessary to compensate for the smaller physical real estate of the Pocket PC display screen. Most real applications require reliable multithreaded applications. Within Windows CE, a program can easily spawn new threads and can ensure reliable access to shared data through the proper usage of provided synchronization primitives. Palm OS does not support multiple application threads. The various flavors of embedded Unix support multiple processes, not threads, that consume excessive overhead and significantly degrade the performance of an application. And, for all this capability, the memory footprint of Windows CE is fairly small—around 4MB of memory. So, for a typical Pocket PC, an application has available a large amount of memory, typically 8MB, for both the program executable code and its attached data. Many full-featured Pocket PC applications consume as little as 64KB of memory. All of the operating system support is memory efficient, enabling an application to exhibit extremely high levels of performance. A carefully constructed Pocket PC application just zips along without any perceptible delay in user response times.

TIP

Techniques and reusable software presented in the chapters of this book help an application to obtain the smallest memory footprint and the best possible performance.

The Basic User Interface

This section introduces the basic elements of the user interface that an application provides when executing on the Pocket PC. One purpose of this section is to introduce some basic elements of user interfaces that appear throughout this book. Another purpose is to provide an initial justification for the proper usage of these basic elements that compensate for the limited screen space of the Pocket PC.

NOTE

As with any programming capability, hundreds of various approaches may be used to construct a user interface. The simple concepts introduced in this section are the result of implementing dozens of programs under Windows CE and have proved to be most effective in utilizing the limited available screen space.

When any application executes under Windows CE, the user sees a specific interface. The basic element of this interface is a window. An example of a very simple user interface and window appears in Figure 1-1. Each of the fundamental elements of a window appears in this figure: the caption bar, the menu bar and associated menu items, and the client area.

Starting at the top of the window appears the caption bar. In the caption bar, the program places a text string that characterizes the purpose of the program. Another use of the caption bar is to serve as a navigation aid. As the user traverses through a complex user interface, the application modifies the text that appears in the caption bar to reflect the relative location within the user interface hierarchy. With a Pocket PC application, the user interface must necessarily be a complex hierarchy due to the limited real-estate of the display device. If the caption area is not used as a navigation aid in the manner described previously, the user is likely to rapidly become lost during program usage.

Below the caption bar is the menu bar. This menu contains menu items. In Figure 1-1, a single menu item appears. This menu item contains the caption Quit. When the user taps this menu item with the stylus, the response of the program is to terminate execution and to remove the window from the physical display. Using a menu item as the only element for exiting the program minimizes the screen space lost to this important feature. For the most part, in the programs in this book, the menu bar serves only to support transitions through a hierarchically organized user interface. Again, this approach minimizes the usage of the limited screen space.

The major portion of the window appears below the menu bar. This client area is the portion of the window that a program manages and utilizes. An application can

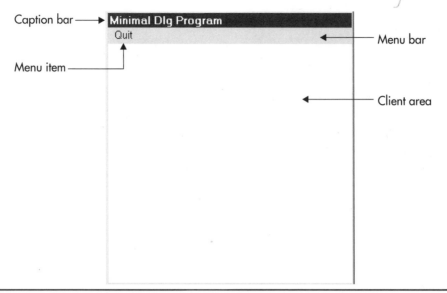

Figure 1-1   *A minimal Pocket PC application graphical user interface*

display controls, such as buttons, in this area. This area is also the portion of the window in which all drawing operations occur. Bitmap images also appear within this area when displayed by a program. Typically, the client area of a program is 145 pixels wide by 145 pixels high. When compared with a standard desktop display size of 1,024 pixels by 760 pixels, this drawing area is very small indeed!

TIP

Using owner-drawn controls, tab pages, and other controls, a program can provide a hierarchical user interface that can prove to be very effective. Chapter 8 provides examples and reusable code for constructing just such an interface.

The Architecture of Windows CE

This section describes the overall architecture of the Windows CE operating system. A description of each of the components of the operating system appears. A demonstration of the interaction of these components assumes the form of a file-creation example. This section also clearly describes the connection between the construction of Windows 2000 and Windows CE.

The layered design approach that Windows CE implements appears in Figure 1-2. This figure shows three important layers. The Applications layer represents any PPC client application written by a developer. Of course, an application client provides a specific set of capabilities and features of interest to a particular user, such as an analysis and database program for evaluating defects in a manufacturing process. Every client application interacts with the primary element of the next lower layer, the Graphics, Windowing, and Event Subsystem (GWES). GWES appears as a protected subsystem in Figure 1-2. A protected subsystem provides a controlled interface between all applications and the underlying operating system features. Consistent with this interface role, the GWES subsystem performs two important functions: relaying user input to the application and translating client program output to the display hardware and to the Windows CE operating system. GWES accomplishes these functions through interaction with the various elements at the next lower layer of the operation system, the CE Executive.

In fact, the CE Executive consists of a number of primary components, some of which interact with each other during normal operations. These elements also appear in Figure 1-2 within the CE Executive box: Object Manager, Process Manager, Memory Manager, Input/Output (I/O) Manager, and the ubiquitous Kernel.

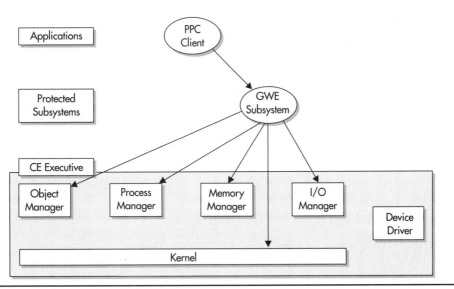

Figure 1-2   *The Windows CE architecture*

TIP

The CE Executive elements that appear in Figure 1-2 are not the only elements of the Windows CE operating system. These elements are simply those that perform the primary work of the operating system.

Windows CE is, in fact, an object-based operating system. Every resource, such as a process, thread, or file, that a program creates or accesses appears as a translucent object to the application. The Object Manager performs the crucial task of relating the data structures in the operating system memory to a translucent object handle or identifier. In this way, a client application can only access the resource through a set of controlled methods that require the object handle and that validate input. Additionally, the client application cannot directly modify the operating system data structures. The ultimate result of all these object-based protections is to impart a greater reliability to the client application and to the operating system itself.

When a user initiates the execution of a client application, the Process Manager comes into play. This component of the operating system creates an initial thread for the application, called the *primary thread*, and establishes a number of important data structures for the application, such as the initial memory heap. In fact, the Process Manager creates these resources through interactions with other components: the Kernel and the Memory Manager.

The allocation, deallocation, and tracking of all available physical memory are the functions that the Memory Manager performs. When the Process Manager or a client application requests memory, the Memory Manager finds the available memory, marks the memory as being allocated, and assigns the memory to the application. Upon release of the memory, this component simply reverses the processes, releasing the memory for use by other client applications.

All input and output resources and operations to physical devices, such as files, the serial port, and the network port, are under the control of the Input/Output Manager. When a client requests access to a file, the I/O Manager performs a set of operations similar to those performed by the Memory Manager. For the Pocket PC, the file space comes from the available memory inside the Pocket PC rather than an external device. Therefore, the File Manager interacts with the Memory Manager to allocate the memory and then creates the data structures to manage the file, such as the pointer to the current location being accessed in the file.

The most important member of the Windows CE operating system is the Kernel. The primary job of the Kernel is to manage and schedule the set of existing executing threads. When the Process Manager requests the creation of an application's primary thread, the Kernel actually establishes the thread and creates the necessary data structures. Of course, allocation of the data structures occurs by interaction with the Memory Manager. Two sets of data structures are necessary for each thread. One data structure enables the Kernel to maintain the state of the executing thread during CPU sharing by maintaining values such as the program counter of the thread code. The other primary data structure is the stack that the thread uses to allocate and manage local variables.

Also a part of the Kernel is the thread scheduler. This nifty little piece of code ensures that each thread receives a fair share of the available CPU cycles according to the priority of the thread. After a thread receives a specific number of CPU cycles, called a *time slice*, an interrupt handler transfers control to the thread scheduler inside the Kernel. The Kernel decides the next thread to execute and transfers control to that thread after saving the current thread state to the thread's data structure, which is managed by the Kernel.

NOTE

The components described previously and depicted in Figure 1-2 are the same components that appear in the Windows 2000 Executive. These CE Executive objects are scaled-down versions of the exact same code that appears inside Windows 2000.

By placing these scaled versions inside Windows CE in the memory of a Pocket PC, Microsoft provides a fully functioning, very powerful operating system for program support.

File creation by a client application provides an example of the typical interactions among the components of the Windows CE layered operating system design. An operational trace of these component interactions appears in Figure 1-3. Each row in this figure represents an interaction between two elements of the layered design. The Source column initiates the interaction. The respondent to the interaction appears in the Destination column. Informative details about the interaction are in the Description column.

Initially, a Pocket PC client application starts the ball rolling by executing the CreateFile method of the Win32 Application Programming Interface (API). Inside this API method call is an interaction with the GWE Subsystem. In response, the GWE Subsystem passes the request to the I/O Manager of the Windows CE Executive. GWES simply validates and passes the necessary arguments to the IOCreateFile method supported by the I/O Manager. The I/O Manager has to accomplish two tasks. Initially, the I/O Manager interacts with the Object Manager to create a specific file resource object. Creating the file object results in the file object entering into the global namespace managed by the Object Manager. After the I/O Manger receives the handle to the file object, the next task consists of requesting physical memory

Source	Destination	Description
PPC Client	GWE Subsystem	Create file
GWE Subsystem	I/O Manager	I/O create file
I/O Manager	Object Manager	Create file object
Object Manager	I/O Manager	File object handle
I/O Manager	Memory Manager	File data structures
Memory Manager	I/O Manager	Memory object pointer
I/O Manager	GWE Subsystem	File object handle
GWE Subsystem	PPC Client	File object handle

Figure 1-3   *An operational view of file creation*

for storing the file contents. Memory allocation is the responsibility of the Memory Manager, so the I/O Manager interacts with the Memory Manager to accomplish this task.

The remaining interactions inside Figure 1-3 consist of the return of the file object handle up the call chain to the client application. All subsequent operations on the file, such as reading, writing, and testing for end to file, utilize the returned file handle. This file handle clearly identifies the open file to the components of the CE Executive. The client application can only perform operations on the file that are supported by methods that accept this file handle as the first argument.

Inside the GWE Subsystem

A Pocket PC client application interacts with the Windows CE operating system through the Graphics, Windowing, and Event (GWE) Subsystem. An understanding of the internal organization and operation of this subsystem enables the application programmer to effectively design the client program. Figure 1-4 illustrates an architectural characterization of the internals of the GWE Subsystem. The important elements of this architecture are the queues and the GDI, WINDOW, and USER components.

The first important element that appears within GWES is the System Queue. All device drivers place a message into this queue that contains information characterizing a specific user interaction. The USER component of the GWE

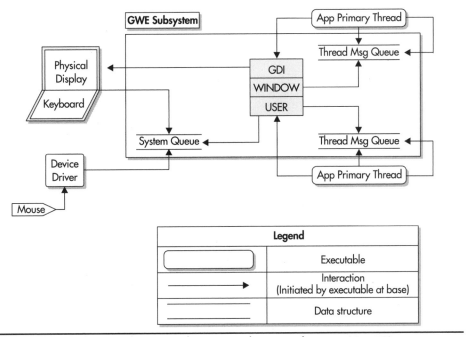

Figure 1-4 *Inside the Graphics, Windowing, and Event Subsystem (GWES)*

Subsystem conveys this message into a thread message queue. Embedded within the USER component executes a special thread named the Raw Input Thread (RIT). This thread simply monitors the System Queue for input messages. Whenever a message appears in this queue, the RIT retrieves the message, identifies the destination thread message queue, and transfers the message to this destination queue.

Recall that the Kernel component of the Windows CE Executive creates a primary thread for an application; this thread receives a dedicated thread message queue. Based on a window handle embedded within the message by the device driver, the RIT of the USER component can easily determine the destination thread message queue.

Code within the client Pocket PC application retrieves the message from the thread message queue. This code then performs an appropriate response for the application. If the response involves updating a window or any controls displayed by the window, the code executes methods supported by the WINDOW component of GWES. Responses that constitute drawing operations interact with the Graphics Device Interface (GDI) element within GWES.

TIP

A detailed discussion of the features and capabilities of GDI appears in "Reviewing The Graphics Device Interface," later in the chapter.

Figure 1-5 provides an example of the interaction among the various elements of the GWES and a Pocket PC client application. This sample operational flow begins with a mouse click by the user inside a window displayed by the client application.

When an actual application user clicks the mouse button, an interrupt occurs within the Windows CE operating system. This interrupt transfers execution control to the mouse device driver. Upon initiation, the mouse driver determines the current window with the input focus. The driver composes a message containing the receiving window handle, the location of cursor in the client area of the window, and the date and time of the mouse click. With all the data packaged into a message, the driver then enters the message into the System Queue. Now, the Raw Input Thread in the USER component of GWES enters the action. Eventually, the scheduler inside the Kernel transfers control to the RIT. This thread sits in a loop that simply monitors the System Queue. The RIT processes messages from this queue on a first-come, first-served basis. Eventually, the mouse message traverses to the head of the System Queue. When this condition occurs, the RIT removes the mouse message from the head of the System Queue.

Upon removing the message from the System Queue, the RIT parses the message, extracts the target window, determines the thread message queue using the window handle, and transfers the message to the receiving thread message queue. The primary thread of the Pocket PC client application also sits in a loop that removes and processes messages from its thread message queue. When the mouse message appears at the head of this queue, the client Pocket PC application removes the

Source	Destination	Description
Mouse Device Driver	System Queue	User clicks on mouse
System Queue	USER Component	Raw input thread in USER reads
USER Component	Thread Msg Queue	Raw input thread in USER writes
Thread Msg Queue	App Primary Thread	Application reads and processes
App Primary Thread	GDI Component	Application draws to client area

Figure 1-5 *An operational view of user interaction*

message and performs application-specific processing. This processing may consist of drawing a line from a start location to the location clicked by the user or any number of other responses, obviously dependent on the features and capabilities supported by the client application.

In order for a client Pocket PC application to successfully interact within the context of operations just described, a specific design approach is necessary for each and every application. The logic for this design approach is as follows:

```
display the main window ;
while not finished
{
    get message from thread message queue ;
    process message retrieved from thread message queue ;
}
```

This special design approach is known as *event-oriented programming*. A Pocket PC client application responds to events, usually in the form of user interactions. Key presses, mouse clicks, and a whole range of events can occur and cause messages to appear in the application's thread message queue.

Reviewing the Graphics Device Interface (GDI)

When a client application chooses to render graphics into the client area, GDI services the graphics command. Elements associated with GDI services appear in Figure 1-6.

When the services of GDI are used, a major distinction exists between *graphics drawing* and *graphics displaying*. Graphics drawing consists of issuing commands to draw an object within a virtual drawing space using a specific set of drawing tools. Initiating these actions is the domain of the program. On the other hand, graphics displaying is the province of GDI. Graphics displaying consists of the actual activity performed by Windows CE and the underlying device drivers to physically display the image described in a virtual drawing space.

Graphics drawing involves a number of important concepts, such as a virtual drawing space, drawing operations, and drawing tools.

A client program performs all drawing in a virtual or logical drawing space. This drawing space is quite large. Arguments to the various drawing commands are 32-bit integers, providing a range along each coordinate system from approximately -2^{31} to $+2^{31}$. Large numbers indeed!

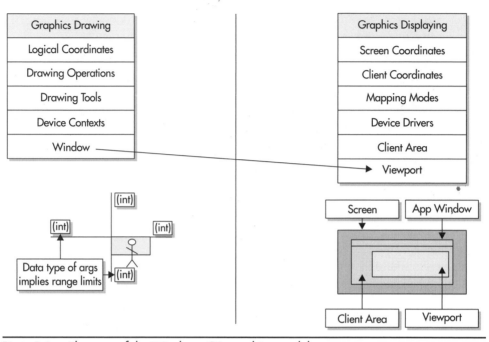

Figure 1-6 *Elements of the Windows CE graphics model*

Available to a program through GDI is a set of drawing operations or commands, such as line, rectangle, ellipse, and rounded rectangle. Also accessible is a nice set of drawing tools, such as pens and brushes, that possess a wide range of attributes under program control.

When performing a drawing operation, the program first collects together a set of drawing tools into a toolbox. This toolbox possesses a rather stuffy formal name—*device context*. Submitting a drawing command consists of packaging together the toolbox, the drawing operation, and any other arguments necessary for the drawing operation. The application submits this information to GDI through a specific set of methods that provide the available drawing operations.

Typically, a Pocket PC client program issues a sequence of these drawing commands. As the program issues these commands, GDI enters them into an internal cache or buffer. When the program signals that all commands have been issued, the actual display activity begins. A sequence of mapping and clipping operations transforms the drawing commands from inside the logical drawing space into the client area inside the physical space of the application window.

Assuming drawing commands survive all the mapping and clipping activities, GDI then performs the drawing commands in the video hardware's frame buffer. However, GDI does not perform the actual drawing. In reality, GDI negotiates with the video device driver to have the actual drawing commands translated into pixels inside a video frame buffer. The device driver translates the individual pixel colors into a color combination that the hardware can display and then transfers the pixels into the video frame buffer. The display hardware accesses the pixels in the video frame buffer, causing the results to display on the physical screen inside the client area of the window.

Using a virtual display space as the arguments to all drawing methods enables a client application to be totally independent from any knowledge regarding the physical display characteristics of the hardware. When a client application moves to another manufacturer's Pocket PC, the developer may not need to modify the program to incorporate the new display sizes or colors. This translation usually occurs within the device driver, enabling application developers to target multiple Pocket PCs without significant rewrite.

CAUTION

If the physical size of the display area changes, the client application developer must resize the display and drawing arguments to consume the smaller or larger space available. However, if the application moves from a black-and-white display to a color display, changes to the drawing code of the application are usually unnecessary.

As described a few paragraphs ago, a device context is really a toolbox containing the current set of tools to be used by GDI in processing a particular drawing operation. Figure 1-7 contains a nominal list of the tools maintained in a device context for GDI. These tools consist of pens, brushes, fonts, and a host of other drawing resources and parameters.

In addition to the toolset maintained in the device context, this figure provides the default values associated with each tool in the toolset. However, an application's user interface would likely be pretty boring if all text and graphics were drawn with a black pen.

Therefore, for each of these tools, a wide range of options is available to the programmer. When an application wants to use some version of a tool or resource other than the default, a simple method call replaces the default tool description with a new tool characteristic. For instance, a client application might indicate that drawing operations should use a red pen rather than a black pen. After drawing operations are completed with the red pen, the client application then restores the

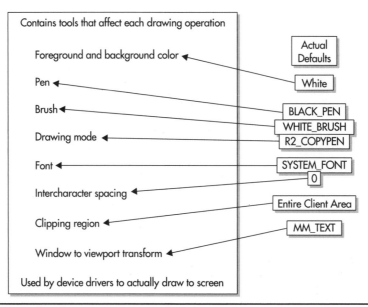

Figure 1-7 *Virtual tools maintained in a device context*

drawing pen in the device context to its default value. This restoration is necessary because a limited number of these device contexts are maintained for the users of GDI, so the device contexts are reused across applications.

TIP

If an application fails to return the tools in the device context to their original configuration, the next user of the device context receives the modified default tool definitions. These modified tools then cause other programs to display differently, which could impact other program users adversely.

Another important facet of tools inside the device context toolbox is that the tools are virtual tools, because the device driver gets to decide the exact meaning of each requested tool.

Suppose for a moment that an application replaces the black pen with a red pen. In this case, a red drawing may not actually appear on the screen. This effect results from the hardware-independent nature of GDI. GDI and the device driver work together to determine the meaning for red based on the capabilities of the video display hardware. If it is a monochrome display, a black line appears. Therefore, in this situation, a virtual red pen is in reality a black pen. However, the client program still executes without breaking and without changes, although the video hardware fails to support red pixels. Without this hardware-independence support by Windows CE and the GDI, an programmer would have to change all the red drawing commands into black drawing commands or drawing commands supported by each Pocket PC's video display hardware.

Logical Design of a Windows Program

Recall that a Pocket PC client program uses a specific program design. The general logic of this program is quite simple:

```
display the main window ;
while not finished
{
    get message from thread message queue ;
    process message retrieved from thread message queue ;
}
```

If responding to a message involves the services of GDI, the application packages the necessary drawing tools into a device context and issues the appropriate drawing commands in virtual space.

In concept, this logic appears to be quite simple. Unfortunately, a client application implements this simple logic in real software. In order to implement this simple logic, an program employs a specific programming dance. General API functions supporting this logic appear in Figure 1-8.

Especially important to correctly implement are the interactions with USER, the primary thread message queue, and the message switch that must be coded into the program.

When constructing the Pocket PC client application, two specific components are necessary:

- ▶ **WinMain**   Includes the message input support for your application
- ▶ **WndProc**   Serves as the response handler for individual messages

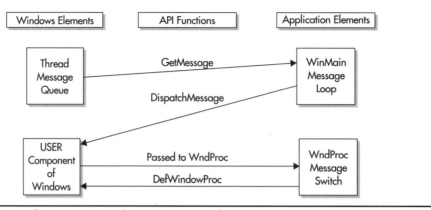

Figure 1-8 *Implementing event/message-oriented programs*

The design requirements for any Pocket PC application indicate that each application must explicitly include these two elements. Moreover, these programs use a required signature. The signature of a function involves its name, return data type, and formal argument list. A Windows CE program fails to compile if either of these elements is absent. Compilation also fails if these pieces do not satisfy the required signatures.

Initialization of the application involves the registration of the window procedure named WndProc. In the WinMain component, a message loop invokes the API function named GetMessage. This method actually asks USER for the next message in the primary thread message queue. Inside the loop, WinMain simply passes the retrieved message to the API method called DispatchMessage. For the most part, this small function unpacks the message and passes the message data to the registered WndProc procedure.

Processing Messages Within a Program

Inside the WndProc, a switch statement routes execution to a message-specific handler. The code written inside the message handler invokes the API functions necessary to communicate with GDI. All messages to an application's main window appear in your primary thread message queue. Many of these messages involve default behavior enforced by USER. Placing the message in the message queue enables a program to override this default behavior. If the client application chooses to stay with default processing, the default case in the switch statement uses the method DefWindowProc to pass the message back to USER for nominal processing.

TIP

According to the online documentation, DispatchMessage causes USER to invoke the registered WndProc. Supposedly, USER wants to save the program the effort of unpacking message arguments and finding the address of the registered WndProc. However, this explanation from the on-line documentation fails to state the real reason for forcing the client application to execute DispatchMessage. Subsequent to calling the registered WndProc, DispatchMessage checks to make sure that the client program has handled the mechanics of painting correctly. If the program mishandles painting, DispatchMessage does the job correctly.

Every interaction with a client program, either by the application user or by the Windows CE operating system itself, involves sending a message to the client program. Literally, USER supports several hundred messages. To simplify the task of using messages, Figure 1-9 includes the most common messages processed by a Pocket PC client application.

Message codes (or *symbols*) appear along the left side of Figure 1-9. Each message enters into your primary thread message queue under specific conditions. The right side of the figure gives the message initiation conditions for these messages.

Most of the messages represent hardware- or display-level activity. The most interesting of these messages are those representing user interaction: WM_COMMAND and WM_NOTIFY. These messages indicate user activity

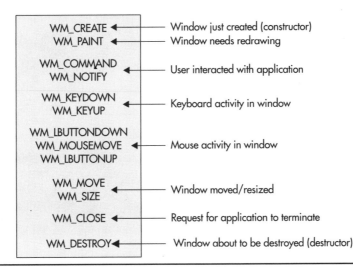

Figure 1-9   *Representing common events as messages*

with a specific component of the graphical user interface. For example, when the user selects a specific menu item from a pop-up submenu, this message enters the rear of the primary thread message queue. Eventually, this message arrives at a specific message handler encoded in the registered WndProc. Code inside the message handler responds to the indicated submenu item.

In essence, the message stream processed by the WndProc exhibits a clear lifecycle pattern. Upon initiation, the client application receives a WM_CREATE message. User interactions during actual program execution result in messages involving changes in the state of the main window (WM_MOVE and WM_SIZE) or messages that signal specific user interactions (WM_COMMAND, WM_KEYDOWN, and WM_LBUTTONDOWN). Immediately prior to termination of the program, the WndProc receives a WM_DESTROY message. WM_CREATE and WM_DESTROY are particularly useful in enabling the client application to acquire and release resources, such as access to hardware, files, and databases.

Updating the Client Area of Your Window

Under this event- or message-oriented mode of developing Pocket PC programs, a specific programming paradigm forms the basis for updating the client area of the main application window. Figure 1-10 illustrates the mechanics involved in updating the window client area.

Updating the window client area usually involves servicing multiple messages with explicit signaling by the client application. A special method, named InvalidateRect, provides the signal to update the client area based on the results of processing a specific message.

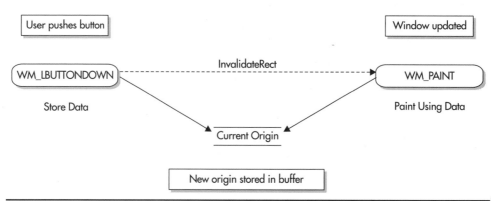

Figure 1-10   *Event-driven approach to updating the client area*

Consider the example in Figure 1-10 in which a user presses the mouse button. Eventually, the WndProc receives the WM_LBUTTONDOWN message. The message handler in the WndProc extracts the mouse cursor location from the message and then caches this location into a buffer for later retrieval. Prior to exiting the handler, the WndProc signals that a window update is necessary. A special API function, InvalidateRect, provides this capability. Eventually, the WndProc receives a WM_PAINT message, indicating that a painting signal was generated. The paint message handler inside the WndProc retrieves the mouse location from its cache, using the location values as arguments in drawing commands to GDI.

Summary

This chapter explains the basic organization and operation of Windows CE and the design requirements for an application to operate within that architecture. Knowledge of the concepts discussed is crucial to understanding the discussions in the following chapters. Here are the specific concepts of importance:

► Windows CE is simply a scaled-down version of Windows 2000.

► Programs receive messages as abstractions of input processing.

► Programs issue virtual drawing commands using boxes of virtual tools as generalizations of output processing.

► Abstractions of input and output processing enable the writing of platform-independent programs.

► Pocket PC client applications require a WinMain and a WndProc with message handlers.

► Message processing often requires processing across multiple events with explicit signaling.

A Typical Pocket PC Program

Τhis chapter introduces the basic implementation mechanics for writing programs to execute on the Pocket PC. A typical implementation of a simple program demonstrates all the implementation requirements. After exposing the typical approach to converting a desktop Windows program into a Windows CE program, an analysis shows the problems and issues associated with this typical implementation. This analysis exposes the flaws associated with the typical approach and establishes the basis for the framework to be introduced in the next chapter.

The features introduced with this simple application are relatively simple to implement. For the most part, these features represent the basic implementation steps necessary to initiate and terminate a Windows CE application. This application employs a WinMain and WndProc, as described in the previous chapter. Additionally, a single button control enables the user to signal the desire to terminate the program. Upon initiation, the program creates the button control by programmatically executing a Windows API method. When the user taps the button, a message handler causes the application to terminate.

Unique Features of a Windows CE Program

Every program that executes under Windows CE requires some special programming considerations over and above the requirements described in the previous chapter. These requirements stem from the fact that Windows CE is a scaled-down version of Windows 2000. Out of necessity, scaling down of the features results in some important limitations in the specifics of developing a program.

The unique considerations that a program must additionally satisfy include the following:

▶   Only a subset of the Win32 API is available for access by an application.

▶   Only a subset of the ANSI C Runtime libraries is available for application use.

▶   Some capabilities may require completely different functions from the Win32 API.

▶   Some methods of the Win32 API behave differently when invoked.

▶   All programs must manage strings as Unicode strings rather than ASCII strings.

Although these limitations may appear daunting, once you learn to incorporate them into a program implementation, these accommodations actually become second nature.

TIP

The library framework in the next chapter introduces an approach that hides most of the special considerations and enables a program to execute on both the desktop and the Pocket PC.

The Win32 Application Programming Interface (API) supports approximately 4,000 methods under Windows 2000. With Embedded Visual C++ version 3.0, approximately 2,000 of these methods are available for use within a Pocket PC program. Moreover, as the remaining chapters of this book clearly demonstrate, the selected API methods provide a feature-rich set of capabilities to be offered by any Pocket PC application.

Some features are noticeably absent from the Embedded Visual C++ version of the Win32 API, including support for console applications, support for security, and the inclusion of services executing in the background. Additionally, specific methods do not appear within the supported subset of the Win32 API. For instance, the method SetWindowPos does not appear within the supported subset. Because moving application and dialog windows is not a part of the Windows CE graphical user interface, the deletion of this method makes a lot of sense. Consuming valuable memory for the object code of a method that implements a capability unsupported by the graphical user interface of all programs would simply result in a waste of valuable, limited memory space.

NOTE

Microsoft provides an initial configuration for the feature set supported by the Win32 API under Windows CE. However, platform vendors, such as Casio, may choose to further modify that support. Platform Builder by Microsoft enables an individual platform vendor to further configure Windows CE. Reconfiguration may include the modification of the underlying API support.

The ANSI C Runtime libraries supported by Embedded Visual C++ also exhibit the same kinds of omissions in support. The most obvious omission is the set of methods provided by stdio.h. This omission appears to be quite logical. The methods provided by this header file deal with console input and output, which Windows CE fails to support. Furthermore, a number of methods of stdlib.h are not available within Embedded Visual C++. Specific omitted methods that might be useful include atof (for converting from ASCII values to float values), calloc (for allocating arrays), and bsearch (for performing binary searches). However, if needed, these methods are easily accomplished by other supported methods or by finding reusable code on the Web.

Another impact on the implementation of an application is the occurrence of completely different methods to implement a specific feature. The most immediate examples of this are the methods used to display a menu. Under the desktop version of Visual C++, the pair of methods LoadMenu and SetMenu cause the menu to display at the top of the client area. In order to obtain the same effect under Windows CE, two different methods are necessary: CommandBar_Create and CommandBar_ InsertMenubar. This difference results from the fact that the menu appears within a command bar that can contain other controls, such as buttons and list boxes. Using a command bar in this way enables a much more complex and capable set of control features to appear at the top of the client area. However, the cost of this flexibility and complexity is a different set of commands to display a simple menu at the top of the client area of an application window on the Pocket PC.

A number of supported methods change behavior when used within the context of Windows CE. The most obvious example of this is the support for the file input/output methods ReadFile and WriteFile. When an application writes a string to a file using WriteFile under the desktop version of the Win32 API, the ASCII codes appear directly within the file. Any text editor, such as Notepad or WordPad, can directly open the file and display the ASCII characters. When a string is written to a file with WriteFile using the embedded version of the Win32 API, the file appears to be gibberish. In fact, the file contains the Unicode version of the string. Prior to writing to the file, a Pocket PC application must convert the string into ASCII and then write the converted string to the file using the WriteFile method.

Perhaps the greatest difference between desktop and embedded Windows programs is the requirement to deal with text strings as Unicode. Unicode is a 2-byte character set. Using 2 bytes for each character significantly extends the range of characters that may be represented by the underlying encoding scheme. By comparison, the ASCII character set employs 1 byte (or 8 bits), which yields a maximum of 256 characters. Although this number of characters easily allows representation of the English character set, other character sets, such as Japanese Kanji, which has over 5,000 characters, simply are not available. By using 2 bytes (or 16 bits), over 65,536 character mappings are available.

Each character represents a *code point* in the Unicode character mapping. Various ranges of code points represent specific languages. For instance, the first 256 code points and the last 256 code points represent the ASCII codes of English characters. Other languages appear within other ranges of the code points. Currently, approximately 50 percent of the code points are available for assignation to other languages.

NOTE

Inclusion of methods that only support Unicode text strings represents further proof that Windows CE is a scaled-down version of Windows 2000. All the text processing within Windows 2000 is actually Unicode processing. When an application executes a Win32 API method with ASCII strings as arguments, Windows 2000 first converts the input strings to Unicode, processes the Unicode, and then converts the output strings to ASCII.

When you're writing programs that use character strings for Windows CE, two sets of methods and macros are available. One set uses strictly Unicode strings as arguments. The primary data type for the Unicode-only methods is the WCHAR character data type. In this data type declaration, the first character, W, stands for *wide*. Therefore, a wide character employs 2 bytes and is strictly Unicode. The other set of methods and macros utilizes environment-portable methods and macros. For this second approach to character representation and manipulation, the fundamental character data type goes by the name *TCHAR*. By definition, a TCHAR data type maps to either the ASCII character data type char or the Unicode character data type WCHAR, *depending on the target platform*. By virtue of the target platform designation, Visual C++ determines the exact character representation to use. When using the portable-character representation, a program automatically receives the appropriate representation during compilation.

TIP

In support of the cross-platform testing capability introduced in the next chapter, all sample programs in this book utilize the TCHAR character data type, methods, and macros.

Using Machine-Portable
String Processing with TCHAR

Unfortunately, using machine-portable string processing requires a bit a work. The specific steps used to convert an ASCII string-processing program into a TCHAR string-processing program are as follows:

1. Include the header file <tchar.h>.
2. Declare all string variables with the data type TCHAR.
3. For pointers to character strings, use either TCHAR * or LPTSTR.
4. Surround string literals with the macro __TEXT( ).
5. Use the portable string-processing functions, such as _tcscpy instead of strcpy.
6. Multiply all calculations that determine required memory sizes for character variables by sizeof(TCHAR).

An area that might be affected by the automatic mapping to an underlying character set is pointer arithmetic. Many programs employ pointer arithmetic to scroll through buffers. Actually, mapping to a specific character set during compilation does not affect pointer arithmetic. All calculations on pointers compute correctly based on the target platform and the selected underlying character representation.

A simple code segment suffices to illustrate the conversion process. The following code utilizes strictly ASCII-based string processing:

```
#include <string.h>

char   String1[50] ;
LPSTR String2 ;

String2 = (LPSTR) malloc( 20 * sizeof(char) ) ;

strcpy( String1 , "abcdef" ) ;
strcpy( String2 , "xxyyzz" ) ;

free( String2 ) ;
```

After the conversion steps, the code looks like the following:

```
#include <tchar.h>                                        // Step 1

TCHAR  String1[50] ;                                      // Step 2
LPTSTR String2 ;                                          // Step 3

String2 = (LPTSTR) malloc( 20 * sizeof(TCHAR) ) ;         // Step 6

_tcscpy( String1 , __TEXT("abcdef") ) ;                   // Steps 5, 4
_tcscpy( String2 , __TEXT("xxyyzz") ) ;                   // Steps 5, 4

free( String2 ) ;
```

At the end of each line of this converted code appears a command with one or more numbers. Each number (or numbers) indicates the conversion rule or rules applied to the individual line of code. For instance, consider the first line that begins with _tcscpy. Applying conversion rule 5 transforms the ASCII string method strcpy into the portable string method _tcscpy. By using conversion rule 4, the string literal "abcdef" becomes platform portable when surrounded by the macro __TEXT.

TIP

Although Windows CE supports primarily Unicode methods, some ASCII string-manipulation methods are available. When using these methods, an application can declare variables that store ASCII characters by using the char data type. For instance, prior to writing a string to a file, you can convert the Unicode string into an ASCII string using the method wcstombs. This method takes a Unicode string as input and returns an ASCII string into a previously declared char buffer. However, methods such as strcpy, for copying ASCII strings, are unavailable and do not compile.

Overview of a Simple Windows Program

This section introduces the features of a simple Windows program at a conceptual level. A number of implementation-specific details appear that were not discussed earlier: the specific graphical user interface, a set of tables/data structures maintained for each application that executes under Windows, the format of Windows messages sent to the application, and the binary signature of the program. All these concepts are necessary for understanding the implementation and operation of all Windows CE programs.

Figure 2-1 contains the graphical user interface of the simple program implemented for this chapter.

This program displays a caption bar containing the descriptive caption "HelloWorld Program." In the upper-left corner of the client area for the window, a button control appears. This button enables the user to signal termination of the program. Although many desktop Windows programs employ other icons in the

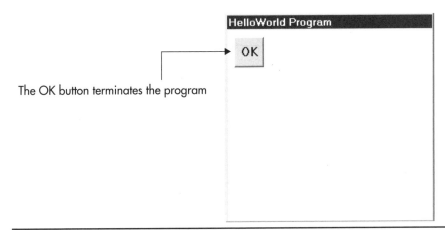

Figure 2-1 *Graphical user interface of a simple program*

upper-right corner of the caption bar to control minimization and maximization, this program does not use such features. These features are available to Windows CE programs, but as a matter of programming style, the applications in this book avoid such features. By avoiding features such as minimization and maximization, the applications in this book provide greater discipline and control to the user interface. The user must utilize the program or exit from the program. Minimization and maximization features apply primarily to desktop environments where a user employs multiple programs simultaneously. However, in the embedded environment of Windows CE, users typically focus on a single task supported by executing one application at a time. Therefore, minimization and maximization are generally unnecessary for most Windows CE applications.

An additional side effect of using the minimization feature is that minimized programs can leave resources such as files and serial ports in an uncertain state. On the Pocket PC, due to the small screen space, a user can easily minimize the program and then forget the program is still executing. During minimized execution, any files remain open and any resources fully committed. Other applications can experience failure because the resources remain committed. If the battery charge expires, the open files could conceivably be in an uncertain state relative to the application, resulting in lost data when the program is reloaded and restarted. These potentially hazardous side effects are not an issue if minimization is not supported by the application.

When developing a Windows application, a number of important data structures come into play. Relevant structures include defining and instantiating a window class and processing message fields. At the native API level, entering data into tables defines a window class.

TIP

Placing data into tables significantly shortens development time versus writing code. When you enter data into tables, debugging is usually unnecessary. Debugging software logic, pointer dereferences, and all the tedious programming details easily consume development hours.

The first data structure uses the type name WNDCLASSEX. Figure 2-2 shows the specific components in this data structure.

The WNDCLASSEX structure defines generic features of a window class. The two most important elements in this data structure appear at the top of the list. The field at the top of the list, ClassName, enables you to define a specific name for the application class. This field is important because this name is the name used throughout Windows

Figure 2-2 *Class, window, and application data structures maintained by Windows*

to reference the application's window class. As the second entry in the list, WindowProcedure points to a specific function that processes all messages routed to a window of the application's class. A discussion of the other entries in the list appears in the actual code discussion that follows.

Once the characteristics of a general application window class are defined, the program creates a specific instance of the class. Creation of window objects or instances occurs by filling a second table. Entries for a table to define a specific window object also appear in Figure 2-2. As the first entry in this structure, the class name refers to the application class defined earlier. This entry allows Windows to connect the general characteristics with this specific window object. Other entries in this table are specific to the individual window object being defined. Clearly, defining a location and a size is specific to an individual window instance.

At the level of the native Windows API, an application window procedure processes messages. Each message presented to a window procedure follows a fixed format. Figure 2-3 describes the standard Windows message format and demonstrates the use of this format for a WM_COMMAND message.

A message code identifies the specific message. One of the Windows header files defines a set of messages that may be sent to any application and that may need to be processed by the application. The numeric message codes for these messages appear as predefined symbols, such as WM_COMMAND, in the header file.

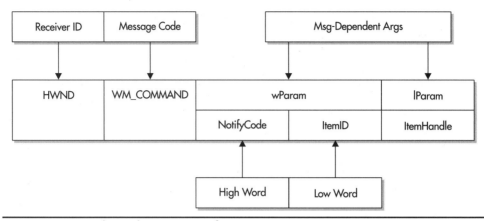

Figure 2-3   *Typical Windows message format*

TIP

Every message associated with a window passes through an application's window procedure. This procedure processes the messages that are important to the application. If the application does not need to process a message, the window procedure must return the message to the system for potential default processing.

If the message is not processed and not submitted for default processing, strange effects can occur. For instance, one series of messages causes Windows to paint the caption bar of the application window. When these messages fail to return for default processing, the caption bar does not appear. In this situation, the resulting window looks strange to the user.

In addition to a message code, each message contains two parameters, commonly called wParam and lParam. These names result from the early days of Windows, when the first parameter was a 16-bit *WORD* and the second parameter filled a 32-bit *LONG*. These days, both arguments are 32 bits, but changing all the API documentation is an onerous task. So, the original names still stick.

Interpretation of these parameters depends on the value of the message codes. Every message code uses the arguments differently. The application window procedure has the responsibility for parsing these message parameters appropriately. You have several options for determining how to parse these incoming arguments. One way to determine how to parse the parameters is to read the online documentation. For instance, in Figure 2-3, the wParam parameter actually contains two important values. In the high word, a special notification indicates a pending operation to be performed by the control, such as when an edit control sends an EN_CHANGE notification code to indicate that the text contents have been modified. Another value appears in the low word of the wParam. This value indicates the numeric identifier of the item, such as a button control, that has sent the WM_COMMAND message to the application window procedure. Several macros are available for parsing these values out of the wParam parameter, among which are HIWORD and LOWORD. Usage of these macros appears in the sample code listings that follow later in this chapter.

One last important piece of information is necessary prior to showing the first Windows program. Many of the Win32 API method calls require an argument called an *instance handle*. Figure 2-4 illustrates the concept of an instance handle in a simple manner.

When a Windows program is loaded into memory, an application needs a way to identify the loaded program object to Windows. One option might be to use a string that completely represents the executable name. However, this approach is much too time consuming. Every time an application needs to refer to its own loaded instance in memory, the same string name would appear as an argument. Therefore, the Win32 API provides a simple integer to identify a loaded program. This unique integer identifier is the instance handle. Windows automatically creates this identifier for a program and passes it to the program upon initiation.

Another important concept also appears in Figure 2-4. Every Windows API loaded into memory contains two elements. Of course, the binary object code is a part of the loaded program. However, a second component includes a set of binary resources that have been defined. Binary resources include menus, dialogs, toolbars, icons, bitmaps, and strings as resources. In essence, when an application declares these binary resources, the resource descriptions enter into a resource descriptions table. During program execution, an application obtains access to these loaded binary resources and uses them to interact with users.

General Windows Program Logic

Based on the discussions from the previous chapter and this chapter, a WinMain program must conform to the following logical organization:

1. Register a new window class by entering data into the required data structure.

2. Create a window object in the new window class by entering data into the required data structure.

3. Show the window object to the user.

4. Retrieve messages from the message queue.

5. Dispatch messages to the window procedure for processing.

Figure 2-4   *Binary signature of a Windows program*

The code example of a WinMain that appears in Listing 2-1 in the upcoming section "The Complete WinMain Listing" follows this exact logic.

Internally, a WndProc also exhibits a specific design. The specific logical organization of this element of a Windows program is as follows:

1. Implement a switch using the received message code.

2. For each message of interest to the application,

   ▶ Parse the message parameters

   ▶ Take appropriate action

3. Return unhandled messages to Windows for default processing.

The code description that appears in Listing 2-2 in the upcoming section "The Complete WinProc Listing" contains a sample implementation of the WndProc that conforms to this internal logical organization.

A Typical Windows Program

The general approach to presenting code in this book consists of first showing the complete code listing and then presenting a line-by-line analysis of the code. Showing the complete listing demonstrates the overall organization and behavior of the code element. An individual discussion of each line of code helps you understand the exact construction of each line.

TIP

For the sake of conserving space, the declarations of variables of standard data types, such as integer and float data types, do not usually appear in the code listings. However, the actual declarations for these variables do appear in the code listings on the web site (http://www.osborne.com) for this book.

The Complete WinMain Listing

Listing 2-1 shows the complete code for the WinMain element of the desktop version of the simple Windows program.

Listing 2-1:   *The complete WinMain listing*

```
/************************************************
 *
 * File: WinMain.c
 *
 * copyright, SWA Engineering, Inc., 2001
 * All rights reserved.
 *
 ************************************************/

#include <windows.h>
#include <windowsx.h>
BOOL CALLBACK WinProc(HWND hWnd,UINT message,WPARAM wParam,LPARAM lParam);

int WINAPI WinMain(     HINSTANCE hInstance, HINSTANCE hPrevInstance,
                    LPTSTR lpCmdLine, int nCmdShow)
{
    HWND        hwnd;
    HICON       hicon ;
    HCURSOR     hcursor ;
    HBRUSH      hbrush ;
    WNDCLASSEX  wclass ;

    MSG         msg ;

    hicon   = LoadIcon( NULL , IDI_APPLICATION ) ;
    hcursor = LoadCursor( NULL, IDC_ARROW ) ;
    hbrush  = GetStockObject( WHITE_BRUSH ) ;

    wclass.cbSize           =   sizeof(WNDCLASSEX) ;
    wclass.style            =   CS_HREDRAW | CS_VREDRAW  ;
    wclass.lpfnWndProc      =   (WNDPROC)WinProc ;
    wclass.hInstance        =   hInstance ;
    wclass.hIcon            =   hicon ;
    wclass.hCursor          =   hcursor ;
    wclass.hbrBackground    =   hbrush ;
    wclass.lpszMenuName     =   NULL ;
    wclass.lpszClassName    =   "HelloWorld Class" ;
    wclass.hIconSm          =   hicon ;
    wclass.cbClsExtra       =   0 ;
```

```
        wclass.cbWndExtra       =   0 ;

        RegisterClassEx( &wclass ) ;

        hwnd = CreateWindowEx( 0 , "HelloWorld Class" , "HelloWorld Program" ,
                        WS_OVERLAPPED ,
                        0, 0 , 288,375,
                        NULL , NULL , hInstance , NULL ) ;

        ShowWindow( hwnd , nCmdShow )
        UpdateWindow( hwnd ) ;

        while ( GetMessage( &msg, NULL , 0 , 0 ))
        {
            TranslateMessage( &msg ) ;
            DispatchMessage( &msg ) ;
        }

        return msg.wParam ;
}
```

This program follows the required general logic of an application's main program that executes under Windows. First, the definition, generation, and display of the main window occur. Then, a message loop processes messages through the registered window procedure.

The Line-by-Line Analysis of WinMain

Now comes the line-by-line analysis. Performing this analysis does not include obvious elements, such as the declaration of variables of relatively common data types and the use of code block begin and end delimiters.

```
#include <windows.h>
#include <windowsx.h>
```

In fact, these files include a large number of other header files that contain the actual declarations for the data types and methods. For example, one of the files included within windows.h is the header file winuser.h. The selection of the name for this header file indicates that this file contains the data types and methods used to access the features provided by the USER component of Windows 2000 and Windows CE.

```
BOOL CALLBACK WinProc(HWND hWnd,UINT message,WPARAM wParam,LPARAM lParam) ;
```

This declaration describes the required signature for the window procedure provided by each application. A signature consists of the return data type, the name of the method, and an argument list. This declaration also contains a special element specific to Windows programming. The element of the signature named CALLBACK is know as an *adornment*, which consists of any compiler-related information necessary to establish special code-generation mechanics. In this case, the CALLBACK adornment indicates the order in which arguments are placed on the stack prior to transfer of control to the method.

For the WinProc, the signature is somewhat flexible. The name of the procedure and the name of the arguments may be different from those declared previously. However, the return data type, the adornment, and the data types of the arguments must be exactly the same as these declarations. These constraints are necessary to ensure that the space allocated for the method arguments matches exactly the space and data type declarations expected by Windows. If these elements do not match, some rather interesting side effects may occur. Windows places the correct incoming values into the allocated memory. However, the receiving window procedure interprets these values as different data types, causing the message switch to work incorrectly and resulting in inappropriate and unreliable responses.

```
int WINAPI WinMain(     HINSTANCE hInstance, HINSTANCE hPrevInstance,
                   LPTSTR lpCmdLine, int nCmdShow)
```

This method heading shows the required signature for the WinMain method that every application provides to Windows. A new adornment, WINAPI, appears in this heading. This adornment has the same effect as the CALLBACK adornment defined previously. The first argument, named hInstance, is the unique integer identifier for the binary program loaded into memory. As the second argument, Windows provides the hPrevInstance instance handle, which always receives the value 0. Inclusion of this argument is strictly for compatibility with earlier versions of Windows and is absolutely useless for current programs. However, if this argument were omitted, a large number of existing Windows applications would break. For the next argument, the variable lpCmdLine contains a pointer to a string containing the command-line arguments presented at the initiation of the program. For most programs, this argument points to an empty string. In the last argument, named nCmdShow, a value indicates the initial display status of the window. For almost every program, this initial value is SW_SHOW, indicating that the window is to be visible when first displayed to the user.

With this method heading, only the names of the arguments may be different. If anything else differs from the preceding heading, the program simply does not compile or work correctly. In fact, Windows and Visual C++, working together, map the address of the WinMain as the entry point to the program. If the program does not contain a WinMain with this name and signature, Visual C++ complains loudly that a WinMain is missing.

```
HWND         hwnd;
HICON        hicon ;
HCURSOR      hcursor ;
HBRUSH       hbrush ;
WNDCLASSEX   wclass ;
MSG          msg ;
```

These variable declarations enable the WinMain to store a number of important values used throughout the program. The data types appearing on the left are unique to Windows programming. For instance, the data type HWND indicates a handle to a window object. In Windows parlance, a *handle* is a unique integer identifier used as a key to access an internal data structure. Anytime an application desires to manipulate the data structure, this handle is the first argument to a specific method that manipulates the underlying data. A program never touches an actual data structure but rather uses a handle and a method. This approach enables Windows to ensure the reliability and integrity of the operating system by standing guard and validating all attempts to manipulate internal data structures.

A few other data types in this declarative segment are interesting. The WNDCLASSEX structure serves as a temporary holding place for the arguments that define an application-specific window class. When processing messages from the primary thread message queue, the MSG variable hosts the current message returned from the message queue.

```
hicon   = LoadIcon( NULL , IDI_APPLICATION ) ;
hcursor = LoadCursor( NULL, IDC_ARROW ) ;
```

These lines of code retrieve handles to specific resources associated with an application. Each method expects two arguments. The first argument indicates the loaded binary object that contains the resource. Typically, this argument receives an instance handle. However, using the value NULL for the instance handle signals to Windows that the owner of the resource is Windows.

CAUTION

For Windows CE applications, the instance handle value must be NULL. If the instance handle for the application is used instead of the value NULL, the return handles have the value NULL. When used to register the application class and window as arguments to RegisterClassEx later in this chapter, the application fails to initialize and the application window never displays at all.

As the second argument, each function expects to receive a numeric identifier for a specific resource. The preceding code uses predefined identifiers for system resources. The handle requested by the LoadIcon method is for the code IDI_APPLICATION, which is the system default application icon. In the arguments for LoadCursor, the code IDC_ARROW represents the system cursor.

```
hbrush  = GetStockObject( WHITE_BRUSH ) ;
```

A number of stock objects are available through the Graphics Device Interface (GDI). These objects represent various drawing tools. This line of code requests the drawing tool that acts as a white brush. A number of other brushes are available, such as DKGRAY_BRUSH and LTGRAY_BRUSH. By definition, GetStockObject assumes that the owner of the resource is GDI and that the resource is a drawing tool.

```
wclass.cbSize        =  sizeof(WNDCLASSEX) ;
```

With this line of code, initialization of the arguments defining an application-specific window class begins. Windows requires the program to explicitly fill the size of the WNDCLASSEX structure that holds the arguments. When Windows processes the arguments, the value of the size argument tells Windows the version of the data structure that is being used.

```
wclass.style         =  CS_HREDRAW | CS_VREDRAW  ;
```

Using these two manifest constants to initialize the style of the application window class indicates that all windows in the class are to be automatically redrawn if the window is moved or resized.

```
wclass.lpfnWndProc   =  (WNDPROC)WinProc ;
wclass.hInstance     =  hInstance ;
wclass.hIcon         =  hicon ;
wclass.hCursor       =  hcursor ;
wclass.hbrBackground =  hbrush ;
wclass.lpszMenuName  =  NULL ;
```

These arguments initialize various features for all windows created in the application window class. Every window created in this application class has messages routed to the same window procedure WinProc, declared earlier. If the name of the application window procedure changes, the new name appears here. The brush with which GDI paints the background of the window goes into the hbrBackground field of the structure. Generally, the lpszMenuName component is always set to the value NULL. Setting the menu name here would statically set the same menu for all windows created in the application window class. Initialization of menus typically occurs programmatically during window initialization in the window procedure.

```
wclass.lpszClassName   =   "HelloWorld Class" ;
```

This name is the specific name of the application window class. Windows maintains a list of all windows created in this class. Many of the Win32 API methods enable a program to search through the list of windows in a specific class. For these methods, the class name declared in the preceding line of code is the key used to search through the list of window instances or objects.

```
wclass.hIconSm         =   hicon ;
wclass.cbClsExtra      =   0 ;
wclass.cbWndExtra      =   0 ;
```

When the user minimizes the window of an application, Windows displays the icon indicated in the hIconSm field.

TIP

Because Windows CE does not support the minimization of windows in the same way as desktop windows, this field disappears in the Windows CE version of this program.

```
RegisterClassEx( &wclass ) ;
```

Once all the fields of the WNDCLASSEX variable are filled, this method submits the class definition to Windows. Upon receipt of the class declaration, Windows copies the entries into an internal system data structure. Subsequent references to this class and its features occur using the class name inside the data structure.

```
hwnd = CreateWindowEx( 0 , "HelloWorld Class" , "HelloWorld Program" ,
              WS_OVERLAPPED ,
              0, 0 , 288,375,
              NULL , NULL , hInstance , NULL ) ;
```

Now that the application class has been declared, this line of code creates a window instance or object of this class. Arguments to this method include the name of the class and a group of other features unique to a specific window. In addition to these window-specific features, the window object inherits all the features associated with the application-specific window class. The most important of these features is the window procedure that processes messages for every window in the class.

The first argument provides one or more extended style constants. These constants enable a specific window to stay on top of all other windows and exhibit various other features. When a window receives the WS_OVERLAPPED style, the window shows only a caption bar and a frame around itself. Other styles are available but are not particularly relevant for Windows CE applications. Every window needs an origin and a size. The first pair of arguments (0, 0) indicates the location of the upper-left corner of the window relative to the upper-left corner of the physical display. After these arguments appear the window width (288) and the window height (375). These sizes are appropriate to almost fill the physical screen of a Pocket PC. The remaining parameters are necessary for the creation of child windows and for declaring additional initialization data. An example of using these parameters appears in the analysis of the application window procedure that appears later in this chapter.

When Windows receives the information provided in the arguments, the values are placed into a new entry in a system data structure. This data structure tracks the properties of each specific window created in the application window class. The method returns a handle to this entry in the system structure.

```
ShowWindow( hwnd , nCmdShow )
UpdateWindow( hwnd ) ;
```

These methods cause the application window to be displayed to the user. By receiving the window handle to the specific entry in the system data structure as the first argument, Windows can use the data stored in the structure to actually display the window. For instance, Windows uses the location and size information in this entry to place the actual window into the physical display screen. If the program does not execute these methods, the window does not display.

When the ShowWindow method executes, the window border and caption area appear on the screen. Then, Windows schedules a WM_PAINT message for the application to paint the contents of the client area. UpdateWindow moves the WM_PAINT message to the head of the primary thread message queue and actually executes the window procedure with this message, causing the initial drawing of the client area.

```
while ( GetMessage( &msg, NULL , 0 , 0 ))
{
    TranslateMessage( &msg ) ;
    DispatchMessage( &msg ) ;
}
```

After the initial display of the application window and drawing of the client area, this message loop processes messages from the primary thread message queue. At the head of the loop, the method GetMessage executes. This method performs two basic operations. It copies the message at the head of the primary thread message queue into the argument named msg. If the message is a WM_QUIT message, the method returns a FALSE value, causing the loop to terminate. On the other hand, a TRUE return value results in the execution of the loop body. Other arguments enable the program to look for a range of messages and are inappropriate here.

If the GetMessage method finds that the primary thread message queue is empty, the primary thread suspends. This voluntary suspension enables the Kernel scheduler to initiate execution of a waiting thread. The primary thread for this application remains in a suspended state until a message appears in the primary thread message queue. At this time, the primary thread of the application enters the wait queue until CPU cycles are assigned by the Kernel scheduler.

When execution enters the loop body, the TranslateMessage method determines whether the message is a hardware-specific key message and places a WM_CHAR message at the head of the primary thread message queue. The next access by GetMessage to the queue retrieves this message, enabling the window procedure to process individual characters in a keyboard hardware–independent manner. After processing by TranslateMessage, the message passes to the DispatchMessage method. This method further passes the message to the window procedure WinProc that was registered with the application-specific window class.

```
return msg.wParam ;
```

Upon exiting from the message loop, the msg variable contains a WM_QUIT message. The wParam field of this structure is an argument passed to the method that actually submitted the WM_QUIT message to the primary thread message queue. This value returns to Windows as an error code. Usually, this value is 0, indicating that window processing terminated successfully.

The Complete WinProc Listing

Listing 2-2 shows the complete code for the WinProc element of the desktop version of the simple Windows program.

Listing 2-2:   *The complete WinProc listing*

```
/*************************************************
 *
```

```
 * File: WinProc.c
 *
 * copyright, SWA Engineering, Inc., 2001
 * All rights reserved.
 *
 ***********************************************/
#include <windows.h>
#include <windowsx.h>

BOOL CALLBACK WinProc(HWND hWnd,UINT message,WPARAM wParam,LPARAM lParam )
{
    HINSTANCE        Instance ;
    int              iID ;

    HDC              DeviceContext ;
    PAINTSTRUCT      Paint ;
    RECT             Rectangle ;
    HBRUSH           Brush ;
    switch (message)
    {
    case WM_CREATE:
        Instance = GetWindowInstance(hWnd) ;
        SetWindowPos(hWnd,NULL,0,0,0,0,SWP_NOSIZE | SWP_NOZORDER) ;
        CreateWindowEx(0,"BUTTON","OK",WS_CHILD|WS_VISIBLE|BS_PUSHBUTTON,
                       10,10,40,40,
                       hWnd,(HMENU)IDOK,Instance,NULL) ;
    return TRUE ;
    case WM_COMMAND:
        iID = LOWORD(wParam) ;
        switch( iID )
        {
        case IDOK:
            PostQuitMessage(0)  ;
        break ;
        }
    return FALSE ;
    case WM_PAINT:
        DeviceContext = BeginPaint(hWnd,&Paint) ;
        GetClientRect(hWnd,&Rectangle) ;
        Brush = (HBRUSH)GetStockObject(WHITE_BRUSH) ;
        FillRect(DeviceContext,&Rectangle,Brush) ;

        EndPaint(hWnd,&Paint) ;
    return FALSE ;
    case WM_MOVE:
        SetWindowPos(hWnd,NULL,0,0,0,0,SWP_NOSIZE | SWP_NOZORDER) ;
    return FALSE ;
    case WM_CTLCOLORSTATIC :
```

```
    return ((DWORD) GetStockObject(WHITE_BRUSH)) ;
    }

    return DefWindowProc(hWnd,message,wParam,lParam) ;
}
```

This program follows the required general logic of an application window procedure that executes under Windows. A switch statement routes the incoming message to a specific message handler, if the application needs to process the message. Otherwise, the message passes to the method that performs default processing.

The Line-by-Line Analysis of WinProc

This analysis works on multiple lines of code rather than individual lines whenever possible. In the previous line by line analysis, a number of important concepts and definitions were necessary. Since many of these concepts and definitions do not bear repeating, analysis can occur around groups of lines.

```
BOOL CALLBACK WinProc(HWND hWnd, UINT message, WPARAM wParam, LPARAM lParam )
```

Recall that this signature constitutes the required signature for a registered window procedure. When the WinMain executes the method DispatchMessage, this method parses the contents of the submitted messages and passes them as the preceding arguments. The hWnd identifies the row in the system data structure that contains the properties of the window that generated the message. In the message argument is a numeric code that uniquely identifies the specific message. Each of the remaining arguments contains additional information about the context of the message. Individual message handlers parse this information appropriately and utilize the information to correctly perform the application-specific response.

```
    HDC             DeviceContext ;
    PAINTSTRUCT     Paint ;
    RECT            Rectangle ;
```

Of the variables declared, only these variables need discussion. The variable DeviceContext of data type HDC is a unique integer identifier for a device context. As described previously, a device context consists of a set of drawing tools for a specific display device. This identifier enables Windows to control program access to the underlying system data structures that manage the drawing tools. A PAINTSTRUCT contains detailed information regarding the client area that needs painting. The RECT data structure stores the left, top, right, and bottom parameters associated with any rectangle. These three variables play key roles during the message processing that handles the updating of the client area of an application window.

```
switch (message)
```

Using the message code provided as an argument to the application window procedure, this line of code routes the message to an application-specific message handler.

```
case WM_CREATE:
    Instance = GetWindowInstance(hWnd) ;
```

When an application executes the CreateWindowEx method, this message appears at the head of the primary thread message queue. The intent of providing this message is to allow a program to perform any application-specific initialization.

In this application, application-specific initialization consists of two important steps: fixing the initial window position and creating the button control inside the client area of the window.

In order to create a button control, the instance handle of the parent application is necessary. Prior to these steps being performed, the handler retrieves the instance handle for the parent window using the macro GetWindowInstance. This macro uses the window handle to retrieve the instance handle from a system data structure without allowing the program to directly manipulate the structure. When the window procedure includes the header file windowsx.h, this macro becomes visible for use.

```
SetWindowPos(hWnd,NULL,0,0,0,0,SWP_NOSIZE | SWP_NOZORDER) ;
```

This method fixes the initial position of the window to physical screen location 0,0, which is the upper-left corner of the physical display. Three actual window operations are available through this method. An application can use this method to set the window position, set the window size, and/or set the window z-order. The z-order determines the order in which application windows stack on top of each other on the physical display device. Those flags in the last argument indicate that the size arguments and the z-order arguments are to be ignored. By implication, only the position arguments are of interest. Windows uses the first two numeric arguments after the NULL value to set the location of the upper-left corner of the window relative to the upper-left corner of the physical display.

```
CreateWindowEx(0,"BUTTON","OK",WS_CHILD|WS_VISIBLE|BS_PUSHBUTTON,
               10,10,40,40,
               hWnd,(HMENU)IDOK,Instance,NULL) ;
```

Referring back to Figure 2-1, the graphical user interface shows a button control. The user taps this button with the stylus to signal that termination is desired. With this line of code, the creation, styling, and display of the button control occurs.

The second argument indicates that the button control, which is just another window, inherits a predefined set of properties from a "BUTTON" class. The Win32 API provides this class. Following the class indicator, a caption string specifies that "OK" displays on the face of the button. A specific set of styles appears as the next argument. Specifically, this window is a visible child window that utilizes a predefined push button graphical user interface. After the styles, the numbers indicate the location and the size of the button control. In this situation, these numbers are relative to the upper-left corner of the client area of the window. Windows refers to these numbers as *client area coordinates*. By indicating a WS_CHILD style, this method signals Windows to interpret these arguments as coordinates relative to the upper-left corner of the client area.

Because this control is a child window, the next two arguments identify the parent/child relationship. The parameter hWnd identifies the parent window of the control. This parent is simply the main application window. Next follows the integer identifier for the button child window—the integer identifier IDOK. Somewhere in the file windows.h, this identifier appears as a symbolic constant declared by a #define compiler directive. The cast conversion to type HMENU is necessary to defeat the type mismatch detected by the compiler. Unfortunately, the Win32 API chooses to have this argument perform double duty as a means to provide the identity of a child window or to indicate a handle to a menu. Again, the WS_CHILD style ensures that this argument is interpreted as a child window identifier. The instance handle Instance indicates the loaded binary module of the program. As the final argument, the program may provide a pointer to memory that contains additional initialization data. In this case, the NULL value indicates the absence of any extra data.

```
return TRUE ;
```

When the application window executes the method CreateWindow in order to create the main application window, the window procedure receives the WM_CREATE message. However, additional processing by Windows is necessary. By returning a TRUE value, this message handler signals to Windows to complete this extra processing. If the message handler returns a FALSE value, the application window does not display because the window-creation mechanics are not completed.

```
case WM_COMMAND:
    iID = LOWORD(wParam) ;
    switch( iID )
```

```
        {
        case IDOK:
              PostQuitMessage(0)  ;
        break ;
        }
     return FALSE ;
```

Immediately after the user taps the button to signal program termination, a WM_
COMMAND message enters into the primary thread message queue. Unfortunately,
any of the button controls in the GUI of an application can also generate these messages.
Therefore, this application must determine the source of the message in order to
respond appropriately. In order to identify the source, the message handler first
parses the appropriate message arguments. According to the Win32 API documentation,
the low word of the wParam contains the integer identifier for the child control that
generated this message. Available in the Win32 API is the LOWORD macro, which
extracts the integer identifier into a local variable. After parsing takes place, a switch
statement further routes execution control to a command handler that specifically
responds to this signal from the source—the button with the IDOK identifier.

In response to a click of this button, the command message handler invokes the
PostQuitMessage method. This method submits a WM_QUIT message into the
primary thread message queue. The argument to this method is a termination error
code, usually 0, that appears in the wParam of the WM_QUIT message. Eventually,
the message appears at the head primary thread message queue, causing an exit from
the message processing loop of the main program, as explained earlier.

By comparison with the WM_CREATE message handler, the WM_COMMAND
handler returns a FALSE value. This value signals to Windows that further processing
of this message is unnecessary. Otherwise, Windows would continue processing this
message, which might result in some interesting, unpredictable side effects.

```
     case WM_PAINT:
          DeviceContext = BeginPaint(hWnd,&Paint) ;

          GetClientRect(hWnd,&Rectangle) ;
          Brush = (HBRUSH)GetStockObject(WHITE_BRUSH) ;
          FillRect(DeviceContext,&Rectangle,Brush) ;

          EndPaint(hWnd,&Paint) ;
     return FALSE ;
```

Redrawing the client area is the responsibility of the program. The WM_PAINT message handler performs the drawing operations, reflecting the result of user interaction with the application. Redrawing operations must conform to a specific protocol. This protocol involves a specific design that employs two methods: BeginPaint and EndPaint. The purpose of the BeginPaint method is to reserve and obtain a handle to a device context of default drawing tools for the window and to mark a flag indicating that the client area has been successfully updated. After update operations have occurred, the execution of EndPaint frees the device context for use by other applications. The paint structure filled by BeginPaint contains a copy of the device context handle and need not be provided as an argument to the EndPaint method. Within Windows, the GDI component maintains a limited number of device contexts. Reserving and freeing device contexts is critical to correct behavior of a program.

CAUTION

If the WM_PAINT handler fails to first execute BeginPaint, Windows thinks that the client area needs repainting. As a result, the application enters an infinite paint loop, causing the program to essentially hang and the window to flicker continuously. Failing to invoke EndPaint also causes an interesting side effect. Eventually, all the available device contexts are consumed, resulting in aberrant drawing behavior by the application and by all other applications. A typical weird behavior is for all applications to begin drawing with a black pen only, regardless of the colors requested by the paint handler.

This paint handler performs a very simple task. The goal is to paint the background of the client area with a white brush. In order to accomplish this task, the handler fills a rectangle structure that includes the bounds of the client area using the method GetClientRect. Next, the handler obtains a white brush using the GetStockObject method. Finally, both the white brush and the painting area are passed as arguments to the FillRect drawing method, causing the background to be painted with the white brush. Any other application-specific required drawing operations must follow the background painting so that these drawings appear on top of the background.

Painting the client area with a white brush causes the menu bar to appear distinct from the client area. If the application does not paint the client area white, the menu bar and the client area appear to merge. Aesthetically, the user reacts better to having the menu bar and the client area appear as distinctly separate entities. Additionally, studies of Web site design demonstrate that a white client area provides the easiest burden on the human eye, enabling the user to concentrate on the user interface for longer periods of time without tiring.

```
case WM_MOVE:
    SetWindowPos(hWnd,NULL,0,0,0,0,SWP_NOSIZE | SWP_NOZORDER) ;
return FALSE ;
```

A window procedure receives this message when the user moves the application window by depressing the stylus on the caption bar and dragging the window to a new position. This handler always returns the application window to the physical screen origin. For most desktop applications, enforcing this behavior is unnecessary. However, this simple application intentionally enforces this behavior. The manner in which an application enforces this behavior under Windows CE differs in an important way. When this application is converted to Windows CE later in this chapter, the discussion clearly identifies the difference in approach.

Additionally, on the Pocket PC, window dragging is aesthetically displeasing to a typical user. The small physical display space of a Pocket PC looks very confusing to a user when windows are partially exposed. Applications that force a user to focus on a single window at a time exhibit a much greater sense of user friendliness than a small, cluttered display of partially exposed application windows.

```
case WM_CTLCOLORSTATIC :
    return ((DWORD) GetStockObject(WHITE_BRUSH)) ;
```

Prior to painting any static text field, Windows sends this message to the parent window procedure. This message enables the window procedure to paint the background around the static text to match the color of the background of the client area.

CAUTION

If this message is not processed in this way, the text fields have a different background color from that of the client area, making the text look as if embedded in a box.

Because the WM_PAINT handler used a handle to a stock white brush provided by the GDI component of Windows, this handler must also provide the same kind of brush. Otherwise, the text background simply does not match the client area background.

Oddly enough, Windows expects the return value to be a handle to a brush that will be used to paint the background around the static text. This return value differs significantly from the normal message handler, which returns a Boolean value of TRUE or FALSE. Returning such a Boolean value causes the text background to not be painted. Notice that the brush handle is first cast-converted into a DWORD data type. Failure to perform the conversion also causes the text background painting to not happen.

```
return DefWindowProc(hWnd,message,wParam,lParam) ;
```

Every operation performed on an application window causes Windows to submit a message to the application window. For instance, one series of messages signals that the non-client areas, such as the caption bar, are about to be drawn. The application window procedure must ensure that these messages continue back to Windows for default processing. In the code for the window procedure, any message that is not processed by one of the case alternatives causes execution to move to this return statement. This statement passes the message arguments to the method DefWindowProc, which performs all the required default processing. The return value of this method then reflects back to Windows to indicate that all processing of the message is complete.

CAUTION

Failure to pass unprocessed messages to DefWindowProc usually causes one of two side effects. The client area may display properly but without the window frame and caption bar. Another result may be that the window does not display at all but the program exists in an executing state. If this situation occurs, an operator must use the Windows Task Manager to kill the application.

Converting the Program to Execute Under Windows CE

This section describes all the changes necessary to support the unique Windows CE characteristics described earlier in this chapter. A specific list of changes appears for each of the two program elements.

Modifications to the WinMain Element

The steps that follow describe the mechanics necessary to convert WinMain from a desktop Windows application into a Windows CE application:

1. Declare the global variable Instance to store the instance handle for the program.

2. Convert the lpCmdLine argument of WinMain to use the target platform–independent string data type LPTSTR.

3. Replace the WNDCLASSEX data structure with the WNDCLASS data structure.

4. Insert a line of code after the variable-declarative section that stores the argument instance handle hInstance in the declared global variable Instance.

5. Replace the system resource identifiers for the icon and cursor with the identifier 0.

6. Surround the class name string literal with the __TEXT macro.

7. Remove the cbSize and hIconSm field-initialization statements.

8. Replace the RegisterClassEx method with the RegisterClass method.

9. Surround the string literal arguments of CreateWindowEx with the __TEXT macro.

If any of these steps is not performed, the program either fails to compile or fails to initialize. Generally, the data type conversions and method replacements are necessary to ensure compilation. Remaining changes cause the program to initialize correctly, leading to correct initial display.

NOTE

Just because a program compiles correctly, do not assume that the program will execute properly. Worse yet, when a program fails to execute correctly, little or no information is available to indicate the reason. Finding the solution may require some remote debugging. However, the framework that appears in the next chapter goes a very long way toward avoiding these kinds of problems.

Discussion of WinMain Modifications

Some of the modifications bear further discussion. In the desktop version of this program, a macro is available for windowsx.h that enables the program to programmatically retrieve the instance handle from the system data tables. For Windows CE, this macro and the underlying symbolic constants are unavailable. This elimination is somewhat surprising given the large number of methods throughout the Win32 API that require this value. Therefore, the main program declares a global variable to maintain this value. Immediately upon entry, the main program saves the incoming program argument into this global variable.

Windows CE does not support the WNDCLASSEX structure. This structure contains two extra parameters: the size of the structure and a handle to an icon resource that Windows displays when the application window is minimized. Because Windows CE does not display a small icon when the window is minimized, this information is unnecessary. Moreover, the method used to submit the WNDCLASS structure differs from the method that an application employs to submit the WNDCLASSEX structure.

The code from that desktop version of this program uses the resource icon identifier IDI_APPLICATION and the resource cursor identifier IDC_ARROW. Apparently, Visual C++ for Windows CE does not support either of these identifier constants. The only way to obtain these defaults is to replace them by the value 0.

All remaining steps deal with the issue of converting from ASCII strings to platform-independent, portable strings. Sufficient discussion was given to these issues earlier in this chapter.

The Annotated Code Listing for the Modified WinMain Element

Because the detailed code for the WinMain element was discussed previously, a slightly different approach appears in this section. Listing 2-3 contains annotations indicating the conversion steps applied.

Listing 2-3:   *The annotated code listing for the modified WinMain element*

```
/***********************************************
 *
 * File: WinMain.c
 *
 * copyright, SWA Engineering, Inc., 2001
 * All rights reserved.
 *
 ***********************************************/

#include <windows.h>
#include <windowsx.h>

BOOL CALLBACK WinProc(HWND hWnd,UINT message ,WPARAM wParam ,LPARAM lParam);

HINSTANCE Instance ;                                        // Step 1

int WINAPI WinMain(    HINSTANCE hInstance, HINSTANCE hPrevInstance,
               LPTSTR lpCmdLine, int nCmdShow)               // Step 2
{
    HWND        hwnd;
    HICON       hicon ;
    HCURSOR     hcursor ;
    HBRUSH      hbrush ;
    WNDCLASS    wclass ;                                     // Step 3

    MSG         msg ;
    Instance = hInstance ; ;                                 // Step 4

    hicon   = LoadIcon( NULL , 0 ) ;                         // Step 5
    hcursor = LoadCursor( NULL, 0 ) ;                        // Step 5
    hbrush  = GetStockObject( WHITE_BRUSH ) ;
```

```
    wclass.style           =    CS_HREDRAW | CS_VREDRAW  ;
    wclass.lpfnWndProc     =    (WNDPROC)WinProc ;
    wclass.hInstance       =    hInstance ;
    wclass.hIcon           =    hicon ;
    wclass.hCursor         =    hcursor ;
    wclass.hbrBackground   =    hbrush ;
    wclass.lpszMenuName    =    NULL ;
    wclass.lpszClassName   =    __TEXT("HelloWorld Class") ;   // Step 6
    wclass.cbClsExtra      =    0 ;
    wclass.cbWndExtra      =    0 ;
    // Deleted Items cbSize, hIconSm                          // Step 7
    RegisterClass( &wclass ) ;                                // Step 8
    hwnd = CreateWindowEx( 0 , __TEXT("HelloWorld Class") , // Step 9
                    __TEXT("HelloWorld Program") ,    // Step 9
                    WS_OVERLAPPED,
                    0, 0 ,  288,375,
                    NULL , NULL , hInstance , NULL ) ;

    ShowWindow( hwnd , nCmdShow ) ;
    UpdateWindow( hwnd ) ;

    while ( GetMessage( &msg, NULL , 0 , 0 ))
        {
        TranslateMessage( &msg ) ;
        DispatchMessage( &msg ) ;
        }

    return msg.wParam ;
}
```

Compare the annotated steps in the preceding listing with the description of the steps that appears previously. The changes will be obvious and easy to understand.

Modifications to the WinProc Element

The WinProc element also requires a number of specific modifications in order to execute under Windows CE. The necessary steps are as follows:

1. Declare an external reference to the global variable Instance, which caches the instance handle for this application.

2. In the declarative section, add a variable named Style of data type LONG to temporarily store the value of the window style.

3. Add code to the WM_CREATE handler to set the extended window style so that dragging is disallowed.

4. Surround the string literal arguments of CreateWindowEx with the
    __TEXT macro.

5. Delete the code inside the WM_MOVE message handler.

Although the number of changes here is smaller, these changes do exhibit some
important differences in the Windows CE version of the WinProc.

Discussion of WinProc Modifications

The major new change that warrants discussion deals with the manner in which a
program disables dragging under Windows CE. Recall that with the desktop version
of this program, the WinProc captures the WM_MOVE message and resets the
location of the upper-left corner of the application window. This method actually
does not work under Windows CE. The reason for this lack of support is because
the method SetWindowPos is unavailable under Windows CE.

In order to freeze the location of the application window, this program uses a
radically different approach. This approach involves setting an extended window
style to ignore any attempts by the user to drag the window. Moreover, the application
sets this value only once in the WM_CREATE handler, as opposed to handling
every WM_MOVE message that arrives into the WinProc.

The following code contains the steps necessary to initially disable window dragging:

```
Style = GetWindowLong(hWnd,GWL_EXSTYLE) ;
Style = Style | WS_EX_NODRAG ;
SetWindowLong(hWnd,GWL_EXSTYLE,Style) ;
```

This approach retrieves the style value for the window that is stored in the system
data tables. The method GetWindowLong retrieves a value from the table when given
the window handle that identifies the table entry and the integer code that defines the
specific field in the entry. The windows.h file contains a number of symbolic constants
that identify specific fields, such as the GWL_EXSTYLE identifier, utilized in this
code fragment.

After retrieving the value, the application must flip the specific bit that represents
dragging control. In fact, the style value contains a set of bits that represent the status
of 32 specific styles that may apply to an application window. Via the use of the "|"
bitwise operator and the WS_EX_NODRAG mask defined in windows.h, the bit flip
occurs. Using SetWindowLong, the application replaces the updated style status value
into the system data table. Prior to performing any operation on this application
window, Windows consults these style bits. Because the WS_EX_NODRAG bit is

now set, Windows ignores any attempt by the user to drag the window by the caption bar.

Because the WM_MOVE processing no longer serves as the basis for inhibiting window dragging, the code segment inside the WM_MOVE handler needs to be deleted. Leaving the framework in here may be valuable at some later step of development, so the handler case remains within the switch statement.

The Annotated Code Listing for the Modified WinProc Element

As with the WinMain listing, Listing 2-4 includes annotated comments that indicate the modification steps applied.

Listing 2-4:   *The annotated code listing for the modified WinProc element*

```
/************************************************
 *
 * File: WinProc.c
 *
 * copyright, SWA Engineering, Inc., 2001
 * All rights reserved.
 *
 ************************************************/
#include <windows.h>
#include <windowsx.h>

extern HINSTANCE Instance ;                                    // Step 1

BOOL CALLBACK WinProc(HWND hWnd,UINT message,WPARAM wParam,LPARAM lParam )
{
    HINSTANCE       Instance ;
      int           iID ;
    HDC             DeviceContext ;
    PAINTSTRUCT     Paint ;

    RECT            Rectangle ;
    HBRUSH          Brush ;
    LONG            Style ;                                    // Step 2

    switch (message)
    {
    case WM_CREATE:
        Style = GetWindowLong(hWnd,GWL_EXSTYLE) ;    // Step 3
        Style = Style | WS_EX_NODRAG ;               // Step 3
        SetWindowLong(hWnd,GWL_EXSTYLE,Style) ;      // Step 3
```

```
            CreateWindowEx(0,__TEXT("BUTTON"),            // Step 4
            __TEXT("OK"),                                 // Step 4
            WS_CHILD|WS_VISIBLE|BS_PUSHBUTTON,
            10,10,40,40,
            hWnd,(HMENU)IDOK,Instance,NULL) ;
        return TRUE ;
      case WM_COMMAND:
            iID = LOWORD(wParam) ;
            switch( iID )
            {
            case IDOK:
                PostQuitMessage(0)  ;
            break ;
            }
        return FALSE ;
      case WM_PAINT:
            DeviceContext = BeginPaint(hWnd,&Paint) ;

            GetClientRect(hWnd,&Rectangle) ;
            Brush = (HBRUSH)GetStockObject(WHITE_BRUSH) ;
            FillRect(DeviceContext,&Rectangle,Brush) ;

            EndPaint(hWnd,&Paint) ;
        return FALSE ;
       case WM_MOVE:                                      // Step 5
        return FALSE ;
       case WM_CTLCOLORSTATIC :
         return ((DWORD) GetStockObject(WHITE_BRUSH)) ;
     }

    return DefWindowProc(hWnd,message,wParam,lParam) ;
}
```

Because of these changes to the WinProc element of the application, this simple Windows program now compiles under Embedded Visual C++ and executes on the Pocket PC under Windows CE.

Analyzing the Design of the Simple Windows Program

The sample program is typical of the programs that appear in most books about programming for Windows CE. From the standpoint of developing real-world applications, the design of this program leaves much to be desired. Organizing a real Windows CE application that plays a central role in the revenue stream or operations of a company is likely to encounter real problems when the application is designed with this approach.

In order for a Windows CE program to play a key role in a business operation, the overall design of the program should meet certain criteria:

▶ **Productivity**   Quickly implementing a complete working application to minimize the delivery time to market

▶ **Extensibility**   Easily adding features to the application with minimal debugging and testing

▶ **Performance**   Repeatedly exhibiting high reliability, low memory occupancy, and fast response times

▶ **Reusability**   Usually enabling multiple products to be easily generated

Frankly, the design approach illustrated earlier rates very poorly in each of these areas. Changing the impact of this approach is next to impossible after a large number of lines of code have been written and delivery deadlines are missed. Prior to coding is the proper time for choosing a basic program design approach that meets these criteria.

Relative to productivity, several issues emerge when reviewing the current program design. Developer productivity is usually higher when an embedded application can be tested first on the desktop prior to testing on the Pocket PC. Remote debugging is tedious and time consuming, significantly reducing programmer productivity. As the preceding example demonstrates, the design approach that is employed requires a healthy number of steps to convert from the desktop version to the embedded version. Multiply this number by a factor of perhaps a thousand to estimate the number of changes required to port a complex, real application. This conversion can take weeks or months. A design that enables easy transition from desktop to a Pocket PC with as few changes as possible leads to significantly greater productivity. If easy transition is available, desktop testing often completely eliminates the need for embedded debugging.

Another productivity issue relates to the generation of controls on the face of the graphical user interface. Higher programmer productivity results when a developer can use a drag-and-drop editor to place controls on the face of the GUI. In the previous examples, a button control appears on the GUI by programmatically generating the button using CreateWindowEx. When this method is used, the application supplies location and size data. For a complex GUI, placing controls with this method is an iterative, very time-consuming process that significantly reduces programmer productivity. Initially, the programmer supplies a guess as to location and size. Then, program compilation and execution reveal the actual display of the control. If the control does not appear at an appropriate location, a revised guess shows a new location. Sometimes, ten or more iterations occur before the location and size of a single control is obtained. For a complex application, this iterative process can consume days. Changes can even consume more time. By employing a design approach that uses a drag-and-drop editor for control placement, a developer can see the exact placement of controls. This immediate feedback completely eliminates the time-consuming, productivity-reducing iterative process.

Extensibility usually results when a program is well structured. The program design of the examples that appear in this chapter completely fails to exhibit an extensible structure. As the complexity of this application grows, the WinProc will become more ugly, more messy, and extremely difficult to modify and debug. A well-structured WinProc would have each message handler as a unique function called from the switch statement. The modification to existing message responses is easy to accomplish within the single method that handles the message. Adding a response for a new message simply requires declaring the new message handler, executing the method handler within the switch statement, and programming the body of the message handler.

From an extensibility perspective, using global variables and external declarations constitutes a very poor approach. Under this scheme, accessing globally shared variables requires some searching around in the source code in order to find both the existence and the declaration for the variables. Finding this information is necessary to be able to make the external declarations. A better approach is to employ a global data manager class. This class maintains all shared variables and enables read and write access through a set of access methods. The sample code in this chapter uses a global variable to enable the WinMain and the WinProc to share the instance handle of the loaded program.

An additional structuring issue deals with the parsing of message parameters. An effectively structured program embeds the parsing into program code in a manner that automates and hides the messy details of parameter parsing. Automating the message-parsing activities in this manner ensures that adding new messages becomes a part of the structuring rather than requiring a bunch of tedious, extra coding. In the preceding coding example, the message parsing for the WM_COMMAND message handler appears as explicit code within the handler itself. A developer should not have to deal with these details when adding new message handlers. Parameter parsing is an automatic process that should be easily programmed in a reusable manner so that no extra work is necessary to extend the program with additional message handlers.

Proper structuring of a design results in better performance without any additional effort on the part of the programmer. A well-structured design is likely to be highly reliable. Once the specific implementation details within a method have been debugged, the application can repeatedly invoke the method from various locations and can expect the method to work correctly every time. An effective use of structuring can completely eliminate the infamous memory leak problem associated with C and C++. With an appropriately structured design, memory control becomes more immediate. Memory allocation occurs when needed. When the memory is no longer necessary, memory deallocation happens. Effective structuring yields a small number of reusable elements or methods, thus reducing memory occupancy and significantly improving performance, even when the extra method overhead is included in user response times. As the program demonstrated grows to add the real-world features, the resulting implementation is likely to experience code bloat, yielding poor reliability, high memory occupancy, and slower user response times. The lack of structuring encourages a programmer to copy and paste code rather than to create an executable method that receives parameters. As a result, the program grows larger and larger. Memory management is ineffective and causes memory leaks, which is a real problem for a Pocket PC application with limited memory. The larger program size occupies more memory and takes longer to execute a single response to a user interaction.

Using a global data manager class with access methods, as described earlier, goes a long way toward ensuring the reliability of a software application. If the shared data possesses special memory requirements, these requirements can be met in a controlled manner within the access methods. Moreover, if an application is multithreaded, using access methods enables the application to rigidly synchronize access to shared data in an uncorrupted way. Of course, the global variable approach demonstrated in the sample program would require synchronization control at every location that accesses the global variable. In a real application using the global variable approach, all accesses would have to be found and synchronization control placed in all these locations.

Structuring also encourages reuse. By establishing reusable elements and components, a set of methods emerges that a developer can reuse within a single application and across multiple applications. The application design approach that the examples utilize does not really admit to anything reusable.

In order for an application design to support productivity, extensibility, performance, and reusability, this design should exhibit the following characteristics:

- ▶ An easy transition is made from desktop to Pocket PC with as few changes as possible.
- ▶ A drag-and-drop editor is used to place controls on the face of the GUI.
- ▶ Message handlers as unique functions are called from the switch statement.
- ▶ The messy details of parameter parsing are automated and hidden in a structured manner.

▶   A global data manager with access methods is used to maintain shared data.

▶   Reusable methods that reduce the size of the source program are defined.

The sample program that appears earlier in this chapter simply does not meet any of these criteria. Yet, this program provides the basis for most books on developing Windows CE applications.

NOTE

The primary focus of the next chapter is to provide an implementation approach with reusable components that specifically addresses each of these issues.

Summary

This chapter illustrates the mechanics of implementing a simple desktop Windows program and converting the program to execute under Windows CE and the Pocket PC. It also reveals the flaws in the design approach used in most books on Windows CE programming. Here are some specific concepts of importance:

▶   Windows CE programs use either WCHAR or TCHAR data types, further demonstrating that Windows CE is a scaled-down version of Windows 2000.

▶   WinMain defines an application window class and then creates a window object in this class.

▶   WinMain contains a message loop that monitors the primary thread message queue and processes the messages on a first-come, first-served basis.

▶   WinProc employs a switch statement that routes incoming messages to application-specific message handlers.

▶   Most Windows CE books use a program design that exhibits poor productivity, extensibility, performance, and reusability.

Sample Programs on the Web

The following programs are available at http://www.osborne.com:

Description	Folder
Desktop Simple Window Program	HelloWorld
Pocket PC Simple Window Program	HelloWorldPPC

Execution Instructions

Desktop Simple Window Program

1. Start Visual C++ 6.0.

2. Open the project HelloWorld.dsw in folder HelloWorld.

3. Build the program.

4. Execute the program.

5. Attempt to drag the window by the caption bar. Although a bit messy looking, the application window should remain fixed at the upper-left corner of the physical display screen.

6. Click the OK button.

7. The application window disappears because the application has terminated.

Pocket PC Simple Window Program

1. Attach the Pocket PC cradle to the desktop computer.

2. Insert the Pocket PC into the cradle.

3. Tell ActiveSync to create a guest connection.

4. Make sure the status is connected.

5. Start Embedded Visual C++ 3.0.

6. Open the project HelloWorldPPC.vcw in folder HelloWorldPPC.

7. Build the program.

8. Make sure the program successfully downloads to the Pocket PC.

9. On the Pocket PC, open the File Explorer.

10. Browse to the MyDevice folder.

11. Execute the program HelloWorld.

12. Attempt to drag the window by the caption bar. The application window remains fixed at the upper-left corner of the physical display screen.

13. Tap the OK button.

14. The application window disappears because the application has terminated.

CHAPTER 3

A Minimal, Easily Tested Pocket PC Program

Because the last chapter describes the flaws in the typical approach to developing programs for Windows CE and the Pocket PC, this chapter provides an alternative approach. The graphical user interface of a minimal, easily tested Windows CE program illustrates a standard user interface that compensates for the small physical screen display. A structured design enables the implementation to meet the goals identified in the previous chapter. A tool—the Message Cracker Wizard—provides the capability to easily incorporate new message handlers into the structured design. A step-by-step procedure demonstrates the way in which the structured approach enables a developer to get an initial application with a complex user interface up and running fairly quickly. Finally, a detailed analysis demonstrates that the suggested design approach meets the design criteria outlined in the previous chapter.

User Interface of the Minimal Pocket PC Program

This section introduces the graphical user interface of the minimal Pocket PC program. The key purpose of this interface is to establish a standard interface design that compensates for the small physical screen display. Figure 3-1 shows the user interface of the minimal Pocket PC program.

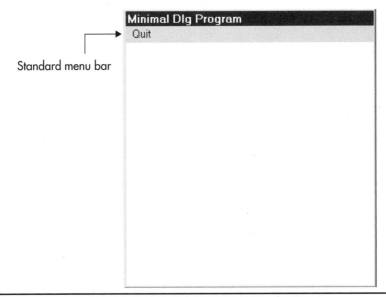

Figure 3-1 *Graphical user interface of the minimal Pocket PC program*

At first glance, this interface may appear to be no different from the interface in the previous chapter. But, take a closer look. In this interface, a menu bar appears. This menu bar provides the Quit menu item, which is the only means for the user to signal the termination of the program.

Using a menu bar is a conscious choice here. A menu bar minimizes the consumption of physical screen space. Employing a button, as the program in the previous chapter did, is an incredible waste of physical screen space. Compare the size of the button (refer to Figure 2-1 in the previous chapter) with the size of the menu bar. An additional consideration is the fact that the Quit operation is only performed once during any specific use of the program. By placing the Quit operation on a small menu bar, more valuable physical screen space is available to support the real features of the program.

Standardization results from the decision to always place the Quit menu item as the first entry in the menu bar. The user always knows to go to the same exact position to leave the program (or later to leave a lower level in the user interface using the Return menu item). Many programs place this entry on the right side. Because the number of menu items may vary from application to application or within an application at different levels in the user interface, the location of the Quit or Return item appears to float around. Always placing this operation at the far left fixes the location in a manner that is more friendly to the Pocket PC user.

NOTE

The implication here is that a Pocket PC application is providing only one way in which a user can accomplish a specific task. This theme recurs throughout this book. Frankly, allowing a user to have a single way in which to accomplish a task goes against the current philosophy for designing user interfaces. Books today on user interface design flatly state that a user should have several ways in which to accomplish any give task. That approach works fine if a user has a large screen, a mouse, and a full-size keyboard. With a Pocket PC, the user has a small screen, a stylus, and a very awkward, marginally useful keyboard. These conditions radically differ and therefore the typical desktop principles simply do not apply here.

During the development process, design of the graphical user interface presents a special challenge for a Pocket PC application. Every effort is necessary to efficiently use the physical screen space.

Design of the Minimal Pocket PC Program

The basis for the minimal program presented in this section is a dialog. From a user perspective, no difference exists between a window and a dialog. In fact, a dialog is simply a window. However, as far as a program developer is concerned, using a dialog brings to bear a host of tools and assumptions that make the development task quite a bit easier.

Figure 3-2 shows the design of the minimal dialog program. This design chart shows primarily the key elements of the design.

Each box in the design diagram represents an individual method or element of the design. At the top of each box appears a name that represents the name of the method or element. Some of the boxes contain smaller boxes that extend beyond the boundary of the parent boxes. These smaller boxes demonstrate specific software methods that are provided by the element. Interactions among various elements also appear on the diagram.

Characterizing an interaction involves two important features: the initiator of the interaction and the flow of data during the interaction. A heavy arrow indicates a specific interaction between two elements in the design. The element at the base of the interaction arrow specifies the element that initiates the interaction. On top of each interaction arrow is a data-flow arrow. These arrows have a circle at their base to distinguish that they represent data flow. When data flows in a particular direction, the data-flow arrow points in that direction.

Another feature used in the diagram is the connector indicator. Occasionally in diagrams of this type, interaction arrows cause the diagram to look cluttered.

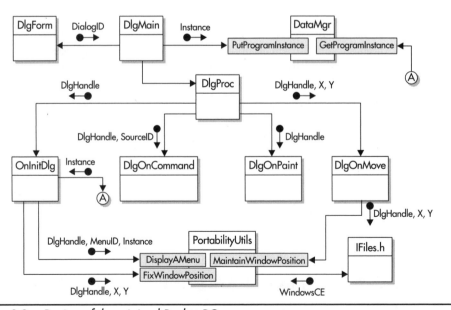

Figure 3-2   *Design of the minimal Pocket PC program*

A connector indicator enables the diagram to temporarily terminate an interaction and to resume the interaction later. These connectors appear as circles with a contained letter. Obviously, two connector indicators with the same letter imply the temporary suspension and resumption of an interaction for diagramming purposes only.

The design in Figure 3-2 contains a number of specific software elements, as detailed in the following list:

▶ **DlgForm** A resource script containing a dialog template that defines the user interface

▶ **DlgMain** A simple main program that launches the dialog in the resource script

▶ **DlgProc** A dialog procedure that is highly structured around message handlers

▶ **OnInitDlg (and others)** Specific methods that implement message handlers for a specific Windows message

▶ **DataMgr** A repository for shared data that exercises access control through methods

▶ **PortabilityUtils** A set of methods that map specific operations to the API methods for specific hardware platforms

▶ **IFiles.h** A file that contains a flag used to retarget the portability methods to a specific target platform

At first glance, this list may appear to be overkill for a simple application. After all, the simple programs in the previous chapter only used a WinMain and a WinProc. However, at the end of this chapter, a detailed analysis demonstrates that this approach is necessary to satisfy the features associated with productivity, extensibility, performance, and reusability.

When initiated, this program executes the WinMain program found in the file DlgProc. This program stores the instance handle Instance into the DataMgr using the access method PutProgramInstance. Then, the program obtains the DialogID from the DlgForm and launches the dialog. As messages climb to the front of the primary thread message queue, the DlgProc receives these messages and dispatches them to the appropriate message handler, such as DlgOnCommand. Individual message handlers respond to a message in a manner appropriate to the application. Some of these responses require that the handler perform operations using one of the methods provided by PortabilityUtils, such as DisplayAMenu. With the flip of the software switch in IFiles.h, this method executes correctly on either the desktop version of Windows or Windows CE for the Pocket PC.

From the diagram, the necessity for the DataMgr repository becomes evident. This common data store enables the program to maintain the instance handle of the program in a central area. Moreover, the data store ensures that the data value persists across separate executions of method handlers that may occur literally minutes apart. The WinMain in DlgMain installs the value of the instance handle using the access method PutProgramInstance. Notice the data flow arrow on this interaction—it points in the same direction as the interaction arrow from the DlgMain element to the PutProgramInstance method of the DataMgr element. Later, when the WM_CREATE message appears at the head of the message queue, the OnInitDlg message handler retrieves this method from the DataMgr element. An interaction arrow (using a connector indictor) reveals the OnInitDlg method initiating an interaction with the GetProgramInstance method of the DataMgr. As a result of this interaction, the instance handle Instance returns to OnInitDlg. Therefore, the data-flow arrow points in the opposite direction from the interaction arrow.

NOTE

Using a data manager element is like imposing a C++ class on a C program. The persisted data acts like a private data member of a C++ class, although implemented somewhat differently. Obviously, the access methods serve the same role as public member methods in a C++ class. An important theme of this book is the use of abstraction in this way.

The diagram omits some minor details of the design but does emphasize its key elements. When generating this kind of diagram, discerning between key drivers and minor details is important to the clarity of the diagram. If this diagram had included every detail possible, the result would have been noisy and cluttered, reducing the ability to use the diagram to really communicate the organization and the operation of the design.

The design diagram in Figure 3-2 exhibits another important characteristic. Elements of the design form into cohesive layers. A characterization of the layers is as follows:

▶ **Control and sequencing layer**   The DlgMain and DlgProc elements manage the flow of messages through the application.

▶ **Functional processing layer**   Message handlers, such as OnInitDlg, perform responses to specific messages.

▶ **Data and interface management layer**   This layer controls access to shared data and to specific interfaces, such as hardware and platform targeting.

Layering of structured designs is a key theme of this book. Many of the sample programs in later chapters illustrate structured design-layering techniques to promote all the design criteria defined in the previous chapter.

NOTE

Structuring a design is a necessary condition to obtain productivity, extensibility, performance, and reusability. However, a sufficient condition is that the structured elements be organized into tight layers. Establishing layers of software elements with limited interactions significantly reduces the complexity of the design. Obtaining a powerful feature set with minimal complexity that tightly restricts interactions of elements ensures the benefits of productivity, extensibility, performance, and reusability.

Introducing the Magic of Message Crackers

One important detail does not appear in the previous discussion. This detail relates to the mechanics of translating the inputs to the dialog procedure in DlgProc into the execution of a message handler. Two activities compose the translation process. The dialog procedure has to parse the wParam and the lParam into the appropriate message parameters. Then, the handler execution must marshal these parameters into the appropriate message handler signature. Both of these activities occur through the magic of message crackers.

Prior to looking at message-cracking specifics, consider the overall architecture of the message-cracking process that appears in Figure 3-3.

This diagram uses the same techniques as the previous design diagram. Appearing in the top area of this diagram are the various pieces that contribute to the message-cracking process. The bottom portion simply repeats the message handlers themselves and characterizes the interactions with the dialog procedure in DlgProc.

When developing the Pocket PC application, the program developer uses a special tool called the Message Cracker Wizard. This tool generates the specific lines of code that are necessary to implement the message cracker for a specific message handler.

NOTE

This tool is not a Microsoft product. This tool exists because I needed an automated approach to generate the message-cracking implementation for a number of Pocket PC applications.

This tool generates a signature declaration for the message handler, a switch case based on the macro HANDLE_DLG_MSG, and a skeleton for the handler body. As shown in Figure 3-3, HANDLE_DLG_MSG comes from the element windowsy.h.

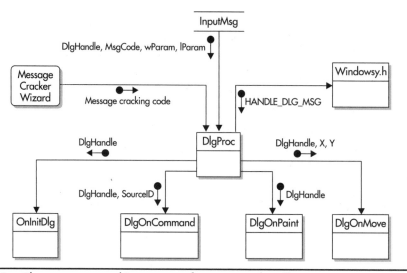

Figure 3-3   *The message-cracking process for message handlers*

NOTE

This header file is also not a Microsoft product but is derived from the header file windowsx.h. The windowsx.h file contains a set of message crackers for window procedures. However, the arguments and return values for a dialog procedure significantly differ from those of a window procedure. As with the Message Cracker Wizard, the header file is available due to my modifications in support of this method-cracker system.

When a message enters the dialog procedure, the arguments appear in the form of a wParam and an lParam, as with any window procedure that conforms to the requirements for interacting with Windows. Within the message-routing switch of the dialog procedure, the HANDLE_DLG_MSG macro cracks the message by performing the following steps:

1. Providing the case statement for the message code.

2. Parsing the message parameters wParam and lParam into the appropriate parameters for the specific message handler.

3. Marshaling the parameters into a statement that executes the message handler with the parsed arguments.

4. Implementing the return statement with the desired return value.

Every instance of the message-cracking macro HANDLE_DLG_MSG accomplishes these same steps. However, the macro actually tailors the steps to the specifics of an individual message.

TIP

The actual details of the internal workings of a message cracker appear in "Typing and Echoing Characters" in Chapter 5, which addresses the implementation of a message cracker for a user-implemented message.

The following code fragment shows the necessary elements of a message cracker. This code includes the handler prototype, the message cracker, and the handler body for a WM_COMMAND message:

```
// Access To The Message Cracker Macro
#include "windowsy.h"
// The Handler Declaration
void   DlgOnCommand(HWND  hDlg,int  iID,HWND  hDlgCtl,UINT  uCodeNotify);
// The Message Cracker For The Switch In The Dialog Procedure
HANDLE_DLG_MSG( hDlg , WM_COMMAND , DlgOnCommand ) ;
// The Handler Body
void  DlgOnCommand(HWND  hDlg,int  iID,HWND  hDlgCtl,UINT  uCodeNotify)
{
}
```

Including the header file windowsy.h provides access to the message-cracking macro. The DlgOnCommand handler declaration shows the exact arguments to the command message handler. When inserting the HANDLE_DLG_MSG macro into the message-processing switch of the dialog procedure, the application substitutes the handle to the dialog window hDlg, the message code WM_COMMAND, and the name of the handler method DlgOnCommand. Of course, the entry point to the message handler body conforms to the signature of the previous declaration.

TIP

Inside the header file windowsy.h appear comments that reveal the required method signature for each handler. By using the comments in this header file as a guide, a developer can manually add these elements to the DlgProc file.

Oddly enough, the message parameters wParam and lParam do not appear as arguments to the message-cracking macro. In fact, hidden inside the macro expansion is code that parses these parameters and constructs the handler-execution code with the results of the parse. Because the compiler expands the macros to actual code prior to execution, the variables wParam and lParam can appear inside the body of the macro and will appear in the expanded code. After being inserted into the expanded code, access to the values of these parameters compiles correctly because the resultant expanded code is within the scope of the dialog procedure that receives the parameters as input arguments.

Using the Message Cracker Wizard

The Message Cracker Wizard is an easy tool to learn to use. The user interface is simple and requires only a few mouse clicks. This section takes a programmer through the steps necessary to use the wizard in order to generate the message-cracking code for a specific message. In addition, the Message Cracker Wizard generates some of the detailed requirements of the message handler code body for a few of the messages.

Figure 3-4 shows the primary interface of the Message Cracker Wizard. This interface exhibits additional annotations that characterize the sequence of user interactions for generating the actual message-cracking code.

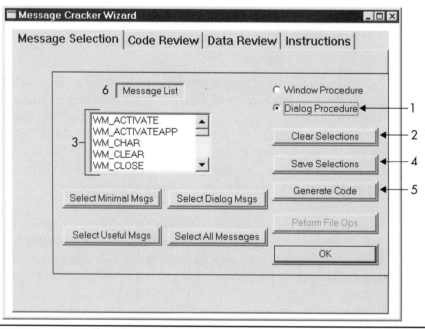

Figure 3-4   *Primary interface for the Message Cracker Wizard*

The user interface consists of a set of tab pages that control the primary interactions with the user. As indicated by the static labels on the tab pages, the individual pages provide the following support:

▶ **Message Selection**   Allows the user to choose one or more specific messages

▶ **Code Review**   Performs the actual message-cracking code generation for the selected messages

▶ **Data Review**   Demonstrates the message handler signature information for the selected message

▶ **Instructions**   Provides the online usage sequence for the wizard

For most users, the first two tabs are the tabs of primary interest. These tabs provide the basic capability to generate all the message-cracking code.

In order to select a set of one or more specific messages for input into the code-generation process, perform the following sequence of operations (refer to corresponding numbered annotations in Figure 3-4):

1. Click the Dialog Procedure radio button to ensure that the HANDLE_DLG_MSG message cracker is used.

2. Click the Clear Selections push button to clear the internal list of selected messages.

3. From the message list, click one or more messages to be copied to the list.

4. Click the Save Selections push button to enter the selected message codes into the list of selected messages.

5. Click the Generate Code button to cause the internal list to be processed.

6. Click the Code Review tab page to review and to copy the generated code.

Other buttons at the bottom of the interface represent various combinations of messages that are automatically entered into the list of selected messages as a result of clicking these buttons. For instance, clicking the Select Dialog Msgs button causes the Message List items representing the WM_INITDIALOG message and the WM_COMMAND message to be highlighted. An added result is that these items appear in the internal list of selected items. Another combination occurs in response to clicking the button labeled Select Useful Msgs. This button enters the WM_CREATE, WM_COMMAND, WM_PAINT, and WM_DESTROY messages into the internal list of selected messages.

Once these steps have been completed, the user sees the interface displayed in Figure 3-5.

To review and copy the generated code, perform the following steps (refer to the corresponding numbered annotations in Figure 3-5):

1. Scroll through the top window to review the list of generated handler method declarations.

2. Scroll through the middle window to review the dialog procedure with embedded message crackers.

3. Scroll through the bottom window to review all the message handler bodies.

4. Click the Copy All Text button to place the contents of all three windows into the Windows Clipboard.

Once the generated code moves into the Windows Clipboard, the developer can paste the contents into a text window inside Visual Studio C++. Some additional cutting and pasting is then necessary to place the generated code into the proper locations inside the DlgProc element so that compilation is successful.

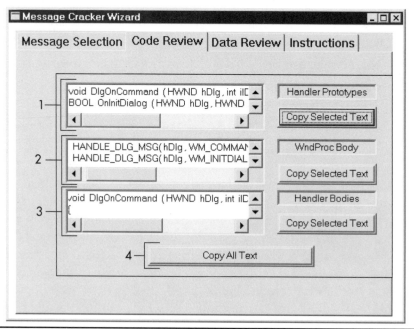

Figure 3-5   *Code review for the Message Cracker Wizard*

Several copy alternatives are available when using this tool. For instance, the buttons on the right side of the tab page enable the developer to copy the contents of a single window. In addition, the keyboard and mouse enable the developer to copy anything in any of the three code-generation windows to the Windows Clipboard. Sometimes, copying and pasting one element at a time from the window on the tab page to the window containing DlgProc in Visual Studio C++ is a far easier alternative.

A certain amount of native intelligence is built into the code-generation portion of the Message Cracker Wizard. An include statement for windowsy.h appears in the top window containing the message handler prototypes. A complete dialog procedure, including the switch statement and message crackers for all selected messages, appears in the middle window. Finally, a number of the message handler bodies contain actual code that the user would have to type. Messages that generate initial code bodies include the WM_INITDIALOG, WM_COMMAND, and any of the WM_CTLCOLOR messages, such as the WM_CTLCOLORSTATIC and WM_CTLCOLORBUTTON messages as well as the WM_PAINT message. Of course, some of the default code may need modification for a specific application. However, including some of the required code clearly improves the productivity of a developer.

As an example, the following code demonstrates the code body generated by the wizard for the WM_PAINT message:

```
void  OnPaint  ( HWND  hDlg )
{
    HDC          hdc ;
    PAINTSTRUCT ps   ;

    hdc = BeginPaint(hDlg , &ps )  ;
    EndPaint(hDlg , &ps)   ;
}
```

In the previous chapter, a discussion about the message handler for this message explained the reasons for actually including this minimal code segment. By having the wizard automatically generate this code body, the developer simply has to fill in the application-specific details between the BeginPaint and the EndPaint method calls.

Another tab page, Data Review, enables the developer to gain a quick review of the information about each message handler method. The interface for this tab page appears in Figure 3-6.

To fill the window on this tab page, the user must first go through the code-generation process at least to the step that saves the selections, as described earlier in Figure 3-4. Once the "save selections" step enters the selected message into the internal selection list, the wizard can insert the data into the table on this tab page.

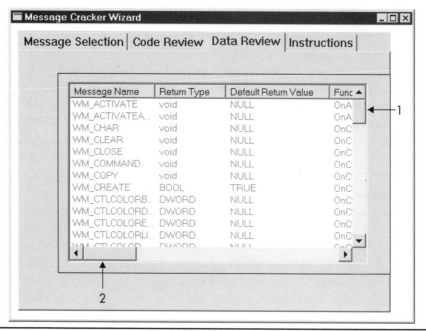

Figure 3-6 *Data review for the Message Cracker Wizard*

Browsing the information involves two fairly simple steps (refer to the corresponding numbered annotations in Figure 3-6):

1. Use the vertical scroll bar to scroll to the row that represents the specific message of interest.

2. Use the horizontal scroll bar to scroll through the columns that contain the data that describes the signature of the message handler.

Each row contains extensive detailed information about the specific message handler.

In the first column of the message-specific row appears the message name, such as WM_COMMAND. A return data type and a default value appear in the next two columns. The next column provides the function name of the handler method, followed by a column indicating the number of arguments in the argument list. Remaining columns contain the argument list for the message handler. Each argument receives two columns—one for the data type of the argument and another for the formal parameter name of the argument.

The Implementation of the Minimal Dialog Program

This section submits each of the elements of the minimal dialog program to a detailed review. As with previous discussions, a complete listing of each element precedes the detailed, line-by-line analysis. The elements that this section reviews include the dialog template, the WinMain program, the dialog procedure and the message handlers, and the portability utilities in PortabilityUtils.

Reviewing the Dialog and Menu Resource Templates

One of the reasons for using a dialog-based application is that the resource editor can be used to construct the user interface and the menu that appear on the face of the dialog. This resource editor provides a drag-and-drop facility. The developer simply drags the controls off a control resource bar and drops the control onto the face of the dialog. After the dialog is saved, the resource editor creates a dialog template that is compiled into the executable of the program.

This listing exhibits a complete dialog template as generated by the resource editor of Visual C++:

```
// From File: resource.h
#define IDD_DIALOG1  101
// From File: DlgForm.rc
IDD_DIALOG1 DIALOG DISCARDABLE  0, 0, 155, 157
STYLE DS_MODALFRAME | WS_POPUP | WS_CAPTION
CAPTION "Minimal Dlg Program"
FONT 8, "MS Sans Serif"
BEGIN
END
```

Actually, defining a resource template involves two specific files. The file resource.h contains a symbolic constant that represents the unique resource identifier of the dialog. For this application, the dialog identifier is IDD_DIALOG1. When generated by Visual C++, all developer-defined symbols exist in the header file resource.h. Moreover, when the programmer creates a new dialog with the resource editor in Visual C++, the resource editor automatically creates this identifier. Visual C++ stores the dialog template in a second file, the resource script file. For this application, the script file possesses the name DlgForm.rc. This file represents the DlgForm element that appeared in the design diagram of Figure 3-2.

In the dialog template just shown, the dialog identifier precedes the DIALOG DISCARDABLE keywords, followed by the location of the upper-left corner of the dialog and the width and height of the dialog frame. Location and size units in this declaration represent dialog box units. These units represent a screen-independent location translated into physical pixels by Windows.

TIP

The width of 155 and the height of 157 in dialog box units approximately fill the physical screen space of the Pocket PC. Filling the physical screen is consistent with the interface design goal of forcing the user to focus on one simple task at a time. When using the minimal dialog program to create an application program, the developer may have to modify these values. However, for most Pocket PCs, these values should be acceptable.

A dialog in the resource editor allows the developer to set the style parameters. Here, options indicate that the dialog is a modal dialog with a frame (DS_MODALFRAME), is a pop-up window (WS_POPU), or possesses only a caption bar (WS_CAPTION). For the contents of the caption bar, the dialog displays the label Minimal Dlg Program. Any controls added to the face of the dialog form appear inside the BEGIN .. END clause of the template.

When compiled, this template becomes a data structure included into the loaded executable program. Access to this template/data structure occurs through the use of the instance handle for the loaded application and the dialog identifier—in this case, IDD_DIALOG1.

Creating a menu also generates a resource template—the menu template. The specific menu template for the main menu in this dialog application appears as follows:

```
// From File: resource.h
#define IDR_MENU1   102
// From File: DlgForm.rc
IDR_MENU1 MENU DISCARDABLE
BEGIN
    MENUITEM "Quit", IDOK
END
```

In the resource.h file, the symbolic constant IDR_MENU1 uniquely identifies the resource template. When the menu is created and saved, the resource editor within Visual Studio automatically creates this name. When used by an application, a menu resource template always resides in the file DlgForm.rc. Initially, the menu declaration states the unique integer identifier and the keywords MENU DISCARDABLE. Following the menu declaration, a BEGIN .. END clause contains a series of one or more MENUITEM declarations. Each item declaration begins with the MENUITEM keyword, followed by the text label for the time and the resource identifier for the menu item.

NOTE

This unique integer identifier for the menu item is the value that returns with the WM_COMMAND message when the program user clicks the menu item with the mouse.

The symbol IDOK is often a part of every user interface. As a result of this frequent usage, the header file windows.h predefines this symbol. For this reason, the symbol IDOK is not a member of the file resource.h.

Reviewing the WinMain Method in DlgMain

Because the WinMain method comprises the primary entry point of the program, this section introduces and analyzes this method. This listing contains the WinMain method for the minimal dialog application:

```
/************************************************
 *
 * File: DlgMain.c
 *
 * copyright, SWA Engineering, Inc., 2001
 * All rights reserved.
 *
 ************************************************/
#include <windows.h>
#include <windowsx.h>

#include "resource.h"
#include "DataMgr.h"

BOOL CALLBACK DlgProc(HWND hDlg,UINT message,WPARAM wParam,LPARAM lParam) ;

int WINAPI WinMain(    HINSTANCE hInstance, HINSTANCE hPrevInstance,
                LPTSTR lpCmdLine, int nCmdShow)
{
    PutProgramInstance(hInstance) ;

    DialogBox(hInstance,MAKEINTRESOURCE(IDD_DIALOG1),
            HWND_DESKTOP, (DLGPROC)DlgProc ) ;

    return 0 ;
}
```

Compare this WinMain with the corresponding program in the previous chapter. In the body of this method, only three lines of code are necessary. In the first line, executing the method PutProgramInstance enters the instance handle hInstance into the shared data store managed by the DataMgr. Executing the method DialogBox in the second line causes the dialog window to display.

Several key elements appear to be missing: registering the application class with the dialog procedure, creating the main window as an object in the window class, and cycling in the message-processing loop. Actually, these elements do exist. The Win32 API provides these for the application for free inside the DialogBox method. A programmer does not have to code these elements at all!

NOTE

By not having access to the message loop, the program does lose something—the ability to support accelerators. An accelerator is a combination of keyboard keystrokes that shortcut a sequence of menu items. The likelihood that accelerators are an element of a user interface on a Pocket PC is pretty slim. Using accelerators requires that the operator simultaneously press some combination of keys on the keyboard. The "keyboard" on the Pocket PC appears on the physical display screen with the stylus being used to "press" keys. Very limited support is available to simultaneously press a combination of keys. Therefore, losing the accelerator support does not comprise a serious feature loss for the Pocket PC.

In the WinMain method, the most important line of code is the specific line that launches the dialog window:

```
DialogBox( hInstance, MAKEINTRESOURCE(IDD_DIALOG1),
          HWND_DESKTOP, (DLGPROC)DlgProc ) ;
```

Each of the arguments provides important information to the method. As the first argument, this method receives the instance handle hInstance of the loaded application. This handle enables the method to retrieve the specific dialog resource template. After this value, the next argument identifies the specific dialog resource. In this line of code, the macro MAKEINTRESOURCE surrounds the symbol for the dialog template identifier IDD_DIALOG1. The application obtains access to this macro through the windows.h header file. Because the identifier is surrounded with this macro, the integer identifier transforms into a string representation, as required by the DialogBox method. In the third argument position is the handle of the parent window. Because this dialog box is the main application window, the parent window is the desktop window, indicated by the predefined symbol HWND_DESKTOP.

Finally, the method requires a pointer to the dialog procedure DlgProc, which processes the message for the dialog window.

Once this element is created and included in the application, the developer can simply ignore it. When features are added to the program, new code insertion begins with the DlgProc.

Reviewing the DlgProc Method

As with any Windows program, the workhorse of the application is the element that processes messages. The DlgProc in this application significantly differs from the WinProc of the previous chapter. This difference results from the use of message crackers to dispatch messages and not from the fact that a dialog is the basis for the application. Here's the complete listing of the dialog procedure DlgProc:

```
/***********************************************
 *
 * File: DlgProc.c
 *
 * copyright, SWA Engineering, Inc., 2001
 * All rights reserved.
 *
 ***********************************************/
#include <windows.h>
#include <windowsx.h>

#include "resource.h"
#include "windowsy.h"

BOOL  OnInitDialog ( HWND  hDlg , HWND  hDlgFocus , long  lInitParam ) ;
void  DlgOnCommand (HWND hDlg,int  iID,HWND  hDlgCtl,UINT  uCodeNotify);
void  DlgOnPaint(HWND hDlg) ;
void  DlgOnMove( HWND  hDlg , int  x , int  y ) ;
DWORD DlgOnCtlColorStatic(HWND hDlg,HDC hDC,HWND hDlgChild,UINT msgCode);

#include <tchar.h>
#include "IFiles.h"

#include "DataMgr.h"
#include "PortabilityUtils.h"

BOOL CALLBACK DlgProc(HWND hDlg, UINT message, WPARAM wParam, LPARAM lParam )
{
    switch (message)
    {
```

```
        HANDLE_DLG_MSG ( hDlg , WM_INITDIALOG , OnInitDialog ) ;
        HANDLE_DLG_MSG ( hDlg , WM_COMMAND , DlgOnCommand ) ;
        HANDLE_DLG_MSG ( hDlg , WM_PAINT , DlgOnPaint ) ;
        HANDLE_DLG_MSG ( hDlg , WM_MOVE , DlgOnMove ) ;
        HANDLE_DLG_MSG ( hDlg , WM_CTLCOLORSTATIC , DlgOnCtlColorStatic ) ;
    }
    return FALSE ;
}
```

Again, compare this implementation with that of the WinProc of the previous chapter. This version is clean, simple, easy to read, and well structured. All the message parsing of the message parameters occurs within the HANDLE_DLG_MSG message-cracking macros. Another benefit of this approach is that the details for processing individual messages are structured into isolated handler methods and do not clutter up the DlgProc. Structuring the handlers in this manner isolates the behavior of each message handler from the other handlers, thus resulting in a much shorter debugging period.

The only element of this dialog procedure not previously discussed is the header for the dialog procedure:

```
BOOL CALLBACK DlgProc(HWND hDlg,UINT message,WPARAM wParam,LPARAM lParam)
```

This procedure declaration has some similarities and differences with the window procedure WinProc presented in the previous chapter. The similarities should be obvious. All the arguments are essentially the same for both DlgProc and WinProc. The first argument is the same data type, just renamed to reflect that the source is a dialog window.

The primary differences occur in the return value and the adornment. Dialog procedures return a BOOL value of TRUE or FALSE. However, when using this approach, a programmer need not worry about the return value because the message cracker macro HANDLE_DLG_MSG generates the correct value for the message.

TIP

In the file windowsx.h, the message macros return a long value. For this reason, this header file does not provide useful message crackers for use in dialog-based applications. In order to support dialogs, the header file windowsy.h (written by the author) provides the correct BOOL return values to support dialog procedures.

This header for the dialog procedure uses the CALLBACK adornment. In fact, the header file windows.h redefines this to the symbol WINAPI—the same adornment used in the window procedure WinProc. Recall that WINAPI simply informs the compiler as to the calling convention for placing an argument on the stack prior to transferring control to the called method. A developer could easily substitute the WINAPI symbol for the CALLBACK symbol without any serious side effects.

Studying the Message Handler Bodies

The message handlers perform the functional processing of the application. Each handler method focuses on processing a simple message. Handling a message consists of a combination of specific sequencing and control logic combined with method calls to elements in the data management and interface layer. For this minimal program, the sequencing and control logic is usually linear, indicting a simple, ordered sequence of steps.

As the first message handler method, consider the handler for the WM_INITDIALOG message, the body of which appears listed here:

```
BOOL  OnInitDialog ( HWND  hDlg , HWND  hDlgFocus , long  lInitParam )
{
   HINSTANCE Instance ;
   Instance = GetProgramInstance() ;
   FixWindowPosition( hDlg, 0, 0 ) ;
   DisplayAMenu( hDlg, IDR_MENU1 , Instance) ;
   return TRUE ;
}
```

Inside this handler, the control and sequencing logic is definitely linear: a simple sequence of method calls performed in order, from beginning to end. For purposes of this analysis, the primary argument of interest is the first parameter, hDlg. This parameter contains the handle for the dialog window that represents the main window of the application.

The dialog procedure receives a WM_CREATE message from Windows when the DialogBox method executes a CreateWindow statement to generate the application's main window. This message handler initializes the window position using the method FixWindowPosition. Then, the handler displays the menu for the window using the method DisplayAMenu. Both methods are available from the lower-layer element named PortabilityUtils. These methods target the specific operations to either desktop Windows or Windows CE on the Pocket PC.

In order to execute the method that initializes the menu for the primary application window, this method handler needs the instance handle for the application. In the WinMain, using PutProgramInstance passes this instance handle to the data cache provided by the lower-level DataMgr element. Therefore, the OnInitDialog message handler simply asks the DataMgr for a copy of the handle, using the method GetProgramInstance.

When the user taps the Quit menu item, a WM_COMMAND message passes to the dialog procedure. The code body of the handler for this message is as follows:

```
void DlgOnCommand(HWND hDlg ,int iID,HWND hDlgCtl,UINT uCodeNotify )
{
  switch( iID )
  {
    case IDOK:
      EndDialog(hDlg , 0)  ;
    break ;
 }
}
```

With this message handler, the second argument is of the most interest. This argument, named iID, represents the unique integer identifier for the source of the WM_COMMAND message. A switch statement inside the body of the handler routes execution control to a code segment that knows how to respond appropriately.

Because a dialog composes the application, a different method signals the termination of the application. For the WinMain of the previous chapter, the method PostQuitMessage performs the termination signal. However, with dialog-based applications, the EndDialog method accomplishes the same result. Just like the PostQuitMessage method, this method places a WM_QUIT message into the primary thread message queue. As a result, the message loop inside the DialogBox method exits the message loop.

All windows, no matter how they are created, require that the application draw the specifics of the client area. The WM_PAINT message handler performs the client area refresh, as follows:

```
void  DlgOnPaint(HWND hDlg)
{
     HDC           DeviceContext ;
     PAINTSTRUCT   Paint ;
     RECT          Rectangle ;
     HBRUSH         Brush ;

     DeviceContext = BeginPaint(hDlg,&Paint) ;
     GetClientRect(hDlg,&Rectangle) ;
     Brush = (HBRUSH)GetStockObject(WindowBGColor) ;
     FillRect(DeviceContext,&Rectangle,Brush) ;
     EndPaint(hDlg,&Paint) ;
}
```

The single argument to this message handler is the window handle for the dialog. All the code in this handler is exactly the same as the painting commands from the WinProc of the previous chapter. For structuring purposes, this same code now exists inside the handler, rather than in the body of dialog procedure.

One difference does exist in the code body. In creating a brush to paint the background area, the identifier for the brush is the symbol WindowBGColor. A definition of this symbol appears in the file IFiles.h. A copy of the exact symbol definition is as follows:

```
#define WindowBGColor WHITE_BRUSH
```

Placing this symbol into the header file enables multiple elements in the software design to access the value from a single location. Another important benefit to centrally locating this symbol is that each usage can be converted to a different color with a single change of the shared symbol.

In the previous chapter, a WM_MOVE message handler forced the application to remain in the upper-left corner of the physical display. The code body for the message handler in this implementation is as follows:

```
void  DlgOnMove  ( HWND  hDlg , int  x , int  y )
{
    MaintainWindowPosition( hDlg, 0, 0 ) ;
}
```

New arguments in this method header include the desired location of the upper-left corner of the window, as embedded into the WM_MOVE message. Nothing obligates the handler to actually use these values in any way.

Only one line of code appears in the body of this message handler. This line of code executes the method MaintainWindowPosition, provided by the PortabilityUtils element. Arguments include the window handle to the dialog window and the desired screen location of the upper-left corner of the window. Because the effect of this handler is to freeze the location of the window to the upper-left corner of the physical display, the input location x,y does not pass to the method that maintains the window location. Instead, the values 0,0 indicate that the window is to stay at the upper-left corner of the physical screen display.

As the final message handler, the body of the WM_CTLCOLORSTATIC messages appears as follows:

```
DWORD DlgOnCtlColorStatic(HWND hDlg,HDC hDC,HWND hDlgChild,UINT msgCode)
{
    return ((DWORD) GetStockObject(WindowBGColor)) ;
}
```

With this header, a number of interesting arguments arrive to the handler. The hDlgChild value is the handle to the child window of the static text control. Using this value, a message handler can actually perform operations on the static text window. Even more useful is the hDC argument. This argument is a handle to a device context for the static text window. Because any of the drawing functions from GDI use this value as the first argument, the body of the message handler can employ this argument to perform any arbitrary drawing operation, such as placing a bitmap image into the static text window.

Just like the window procedure, this message handler returns a handle to a brush used to paint the background of the static text window. Notice that the argument to the method GetStockObject is the same symbol that is used by the WM_PAINT message handler to paint the background of the client area. As a result, the background of every static text window appears the same as the background of the client area. In order to change the background color of both the client area and all static text windows, a single change suffices to the definition of the constant WindowsBGColor in the header file IFiles.h. Making a single change is certainly more productive that finding all the locations where the color is hard-coded and then making all the individual changes.

Evaluating the PortabilityUtils Element

The goal of this element is to provide an interface to Windows system services in a machine-portable manner. This element is necessary because some programming interfaces differ significantly between desktop Windows and Windows CE on the Pocket PC. Methods in this element use a flag named WindowsCE provided by the header file IFiles.h to redirect specific Win32 API method calls for the appropriate hardware target platform.

The code body for the method that displays a menu appears is shown here:

```
void DisplayAMenu( HWND Window, int MenuID , HINSTANCE Instance)
{
#if WindowsCE
    HWND CBar ;
    CBar = CommandBar_Create( Instance, Window, IDCB_MAIN) ;
    CommandBar_InsertMenubar(CBar,Instance,(WORD)MenuID,(WORD)0) ;
#else
    HMENU MenuHandle ;
      MenuHandle = LoadMenu( Instance , MAKEINTRESOURCE(MenuID) ) ;
      SetMenu( Window, MenuHandle ) ;
#endif
}
```

A key feature of this method is the use of the conditional compilation commands based on the flag WindowsCE, acquired from the header file IFiles.h. If this flag has the value 1, the preprocessor emits the WindowsCE code segment for compilation. When the application sets this symbol to the value 0, the preprocessor selects the desktop Windows code segment for inclusion.

NOTE

By changing the value of a software flag named WindowsCE, the complete application retargets between desktop Windows and Windows CE on the Pocket PC.

As the code body clearly shows, WindowsCE uses the methods CommandBar_ Create and CommandBar_InsertMenubar, whereas desktop Windows supports LoadMenu and SetMenu. The value of the flag WindowsCE determines the platform-specific method to execute. Obviously, both the method names and the argument lists are completely alien to each other.

This method requires three input arguments. The window handle Window identifies the parent window of the menu that displays the menu bar. An application may contain more than one menu, each identified by a unique integer identifier. When executed, this method receives the argument MenuID, which contains the unique identifier of the menu. Because the menu template is a resource inside the loaded program, the Instance argument provides the unique integer identifier for the loaded program that will be used to retrieve the menu template.

Because the methods inside the body are all new methods, a complete analysis of each of the lines of code is necessary. Consider the code necessary to display a menu with Windows CE:

```
HWND CBar ;
```

For Windows CE, the menu bar exists within a command bar. No other mechanism is available with which to display a menu in Windows CE. This temporary variable stores a handle to the command bar, which is simply another window. Using the command bar window as a host for the menu bar promotes a more general concept for the bar at the top of the client area. A command bar can host other controls and windows, such as buttons and drop-down lists.

```
CBar = CommandBar_Create( Instance, Window, IDCB_MAIN) ;
```

The method CommandBar_Create actually generates the command bar window. Arguments to this method include the instance handle Instance, which uniquely identifies the loaded program, the window handle Window, which uniquely identifies the hosting window, and the unique integer identifier for the command bar, IDCB_MAIN.

TIP

If the command bar is to reside on the face of the main application window, as is the case here, the application must use the predefined identifier IDCB_MAIN. If the application employs any other identifier, the command bar does not display to the user.

```
CommandBar_InsertMenubar(CBar,Instance,(WORD)MenuID,(WORD)0) ;
```

Once the command bar window is created, the method CommandBar_InsertMenubar attaches the menu to the command bar. The handle to the command bar window CBar is the first argument to this method. Because this method retrieves and translates the menu bar, the instance handle for the loaded program, Instance, passes to this method. A second item of information necessary to obtain the menu template is the unique integer identifier for the menu, named MenuID in the preceding line of code. The final argument enables the program to indicate a previously inserted button that the menu is to follow. For the applications in this book, this value is always 0.

By comparison, the following code performs the operations to display a menu on the desktop version of Windows:

```
HMENU MenuHandle ;
```

The method uses this variable to store a handle to the menu. Because the menu template is a data structure in memory, using a handle to protect access to the data structure is the mechanism for providing reliable access, forcing all manipulations to go through the provided access methods.

```
MenuHandle = LoadMenu( Instance , MAKEINTRESOURCE(MenuID) ) ;
```

This method acquires a handle to the menu template stored as a table in memory. The instance handle Instance identifies the loaded program and informs Windows as to the owner of the menu resource template. In addition to the owner of the menu, the MenuID argument identifies the specific menu of interest. Wrapping the MenuID with the macro MAKEINTRESOURCE converts the identifier into a string representation, as required by the method declaration.

The method name LoadMenu is actually a misnomer. The menu template actually resides within the resource area of the loaded program or binary signature, as described in Chapter 1. An improved name for this method might be GetMenu.

```
SetMenu( Window, MenuHandle ) ;
```

Once the menu handle is obtained, this method attaches the menu to the window. Arguments include the owner and parent of the window Window and the handle of the desired menu MenuHandle. After this command executes, the menu displays inside the menu bar and looks exactly like the command bar/menu bar combination that Windows CE presents to the user.

Freezing the window to a specific location requires two methods. The first method fixes the window into an initial position. A second method holds the window in this same position every time the dialog procedure receives a WM_MOVE message. The code bodies for the method that initially fixes the window are as follows:

```
void FixWindowPosition( HWND Window , int XLocation, int YLocation )
{
#if WindowsCE
    LONG Style ;
    Style = GetWindowLong(Window,GWL_EXSTYLE) ;
    Style = Style | WS_EX_NODRAG ;
    SetWindowLong(Window,GWL_EXSTYLE,Style) ;
#else
    SetWindowPos(Window,NULL,XLocation,YLocation,
                 0,0,SWP_NOSIZE | SWP_NOZORDER) ;
#endif
}
```

Recall from the previous chapter that placing a window on the desktop uses the method SetWindowPos, whereas an extended style bit accomplishes this task under Windows CE. Discussions in the previous chapter describe the workings and variables in all the code. Therefore, a further detailed discussion is unnecessary.

Maintaining the window position in the face of a series of WM_MOVE messages is the goal of the next method, whose code body appears here:

```
void MaintainWindowPosition( HWND Window , int XLocation, int YLocation )
{
#if WindowsCE
#else
    SetWindowPos(Window,NULL,XLocation,YLocation,
                 0,0,SWP_NOSIZE | SWP_NOZORDER) ;
#endif
}
```

Under Windows CE, additional processing is unnecessary. Once the extended style bit for the window disables window dragging, Windows CE does not issue WM_MOVE messages for a window, regardless of the user's efforts to drag the window. Because further processing is unnecessary, setting the flag WindowsCE to target the Pocket PC results in an empty code body. On the desktop, the SetWindowPos method forces the window back to a location indicated by the arguments XLocation and YLocation.

Considering the DataMgr Element

Both WinMain and some of the message handlers require access to the instance handle for the application. Unfortunately, Windows CE does not support access to the application table entry that contains this handle. A DataMgr element serves as a central memory cache for this value. Other applications in this book also use this element to store values that may be needed across various methods in the application.

In the following code listing, the complete implementation of the DataMgr element shows the mechanism for creating a central data cache:

```
/************************************************
 *
 * File: DataMgr.c
 *
 * copyright, SWA Engineering, Inc., 2001
 * All rights reserved.
 *
 ***********************************************/
#include <windows.h>

static HINSTANCE CurrentInstance ;

void PutProgramInstance(HINSTANCE Instance )
{
     CurrentInstance = Instance ;
}
HINSTANCE GetProgramInstance(void)
{
     return CurrentInstance ;
}
```

Creating a central data manager for a specific piece of data requires two important features: a mechanism for persisting the value of the data across the life of an application and a set of access methods for controlling the value.

In the previous code listing, use of the static storage class specifier enables the persistence of the value over the life of the application. Each application that executes receives a static data area that remains allocated and under program control from the initiation until the termination of the application. Moreover, when applied to a variable, the static storage class specifier ensures that the variable is visible only within the body of the file in which the variable is declared. Hiding the existence of the variable from the rest of the application forces all applications to manipulate the data through the access methods, providing compile-time control over the variable and manipulation of any internal data structure.

TIP

Using the static storage class specifier causes the variable to behave like a private data member in C++. Therefore, by using this approach in C, the DataMgr encapsulates the private data. If this data contains a complex data structure, the internal organization of the data structure is invisible to the remainder of the application. As a result, this design approach isolates the remainder of the application from any impact due to the changes in the data structure. Many of the chapters in this book use this form of encapsulation to hide internal data structures.

Only two access methods are necessary for the management of the encapsulated, persistent value of the instance handle. One method, PutProgramInstance, enables any method inside the application to store a value in the hidden variable. The other method, GetProgramInstance, allows for the retrieval of the stored value.

Using the Dialog Program to Initialize a Desktop Program

Only a few easily followed steps are necessary to employ the minimal dialog program of this chapter as the basis for a new application. The needed steps are as follows:

1. Create a project folder with a name that meaningfully describes the project.
2. Copy all the files except the project files (with .dsp and .dsw extensions) from the folder MinimalDlgProgram to the created project folder.
3. Start a new Win32 Application Project in Visual C++. Enter the project folder into the Project Name field of the New Projects tab page.
4. Select Project | Add To Project | Files from the menu bar of Visual C++.
5. Select all the C files and the resource script file DlgForm.rc for entry into the project.

6. Go to the Resource View of the Project Explorer window and expand the resources to reveal the main dialog IDD_DIALOG1.

7. Double-click the dialog form and enter a descriptive caption into the Caption text field of the dialog properties file.

8. Build and execute the program to ensure that a working project was created.

Once these steps are completed, the code provides the basis for incorporating additional features and capabilities into the application. Additionally, a number of tools are available for easily extending the application. Using the floating Tools toolbar, simple drag and drop operations enable the addition of controls to populate the user interface. The Message Cracker Wizard allows for the processing of messages in support of these controls.

Retargeting the Desktop Program to the Pocket PC

After extending the base application and obtaining proper execution on the desktop, the application easily converts to a Windows CE application for the Pocket PC. Use the following steps to accomplish the conversion:

1. Create a project folder with the same folder name as the desktop project with the string "PPC" added to the end.

2. Copy all the files except the project files (with .dsp and .dsw extensions) from the desktop folder project to the created project folder.

3. Start a new WCE Pocket PC Application Project in Embedded Visual C++. Enter the project folder into the Project Name field of the New Projects tab page.

4. Select Project | Add To Project | Files from the menu bar of Embedded Visual C++.

5. Select all the C files and the resource script file DlgForm.rc for entry into the project.

6. Select Project | Settings from the menu bar of Embedded Visual C++ and then select the Debug tab. Set the entry in the Download Directory box to \ (the root directory).

7. Select the Link tab from the Project Settings dialog. Remove the PPC extension from the name of the EXE file in the Output File Name box.

8. Close the Project Settings dialog by clicking the OK button.

9. Edit the header file IFiles.h to change the value of the flag WindowsCE to 1.

10. Build the application to ensure that a complete product correctly transfers. If the program compiles successfully, Embedded Visual C++ automatically downloads the application to the Pocket PC.

11. Execute the program to ensure that a complete and correct transfer occurs.

If the logic of the application works correctly on the desktop and the portability utilities are used correctly, the program usually works on the Pocket PC the first time.

CAUTION

Two of the steps listed are extremely critical. The new project must be a WCE Pocket PC application. If any other project type is used, compilation emits a large number of errors. Failing to flip the WindowsCE flag in the header file also causes compilation errors. Many of the desktop methods in PortabilityUtils do not compile under Windows CE.

If the program fails to execute the first time on the Pocket PC, the remote debugger is usually necessary. Using the debugger may be necessary under the following conditions:

▶ Looking into Unicode character strings to determine differences in processing compared to ASCII character strings

▶ Executing methods that work differently under Windows CE and desktop Windows

▶ Executing methods under Windows CE that do not have corresponding methods within desktop Windows, such as the Windows CE database-access methods

Using the remote debugger can be tedious and time consuming. Most developers use the serial port interface, which consumes quite a bit of transfer time during debugging. A capability does exist to debug through a network interface. However, this approach requires that the development platform has access to a DNS server.

TIP

Using the debugger was only necessary once during the creation of the sample programs for this book. In Chapter 10, a software element involves interfacing to the native Windows CE database manger. The available database-access methods do not possess corresponding methods on the desktop, requiring the remote, embedded debugger to fix problems.

Analyzing the Design of the Minimal Dialog Program

At the end of the previous chapter, an analysis of the program design yielded a set of criteria to ensure that a Windows program provides productivity, extensibility, performance, and reusability. These criteria appear as follows:

▶ Allows easy transition from desktop to Pocket PC with as few changes as possible

▶ Uses a drag-and-drop editor to place controls on the face of the GUI

▶ Implements message handlers as unique functions called from the switch statement

▶ Automates and hides the messy details of parameter parsing in a structured manner

▶ Uses a global data manager with access methods to maintain shared data

▶ Defines reusable methods that reduce the size of the source program

Applying these criteria to the software design that appears in this chapter reveals conclusively that this design obtains the design goals of productivity, extensibility, performance, and reusability.

The design in this chapter obtains easy transition from the desktop to the Pocket PC by simply flipping a single software flag. Employing a single change like this approach utilizes exactly the fewest number of possible changes. Therefore, the design of this chapter satisfies this criteria by using the PortabilityUtils element and the WindowsCE flag in the header file IFiles.h.

Converting to a dialog-based program ensures that the design approach in this chapter enables the use of a drag-and-drop operation to move and place controls on the face of the GUI. A developer can easily identify the proper placement of the controls to maximize the effectiveness of the user interface without the iterative, time-consuming compile and execute sequence.

Using the message cracker HANDLE_DLG_MSG allows the application to employ message handlers as unique functions. Each message handler focuses on performing the appropriate response to a specific Windows message. Additionally, the Message Cracker Wizard automatically generates the necessary code for this approach, enhancing both the productivity of the design as well as the extensibility of the design.

Automating and hiding the messy details of message parameter parsers also occurs under the auspices of the message cracker HANDLE_DLG_MSG. As explained earlier, a sequence of internal macro expansions parses the message parameters into required values and marshals these values into the correct sequence for executing the message handler.

The DataMgr uses an encapsulating technique to control access to shared data. This data enters into the static session and persists throughout the complete execution of the application.

Finally, the whole project consists of elements with reusable methods. The proof of this assertion is that a sequence of steps was provided that enables a developer to rapidly create the basis for a new application from these elements.

Although the introduction to the design may have initially given the impression of overkill, this design, in fact, purposely utilizes the specific elements to obtain the design goals listed previously. After the criteria that support the design goals are applied, the appropriateness of the design is apparent.

Summary

In this chapter, a minimal dialog-based Windows application provides the basis for an optimal design that meets the design criteria to obtain productivity, extensibility, performance, and reusability. Some of the factors that contribute to meeting the design criteria include the following:

- ▶ A layered, structured design tightly controls the interactions among elements to reduce the complexity of the application.

- ▶ Message crackers hide the messy details of message parameter parsing and pass the parsed parameters to message handler methods.

- ▶ Dialogs and menus are stored as resource script templates within the loaded executable of a Windows program.

- ▶ The design of the minimal dialog program forms the basis for any new Windows application and easily ports from the desktop to the Pocket PC.

- ▶ Using the static storage class specifier in C allows an application to obtain the same encapsulation benefits as using private data members in a C++ class.

Sample Programs on the Web

The following programs are available at http://www.osborne.com:

Description	Folder
Desktop Minimal Dialog Program	MinimalDlgProgram
Pocket PC Minimal Dialog Program	MinimalDlgProgramPPC

Execution Instructions

Desktop Minimal Dialog Program

1. Start Visual C++ 6.0.
2. Open the project MinimalDlgProgram.dsw in folder MinimalDlgProgram.
3. Build the program.
4. Execute the program.
5. Attempt to drag the window by the caption bar. Although it's a bit messy looking, the application window should remain fixed at the upper-left corner of the physical display screen.
6. Click the Quit menu item on the window's menu bar.
7. The application window disappears when the application terminates.

Pocket PC Minimal Dialog Program

1. Attach the Pocket PC cradle to the desktop computer.
2. Insert the Pocket PC into the cradle.
3. Tell ActiveSync to create a guest connection.
4. Make sure the status is connected.
5. Start Embedded Visual C++ 3.0.
6. Open the project MinimalDlgProgramPPC.vcw in the folder MinimalDlgProgramPPC.
7. Build the program.
8. Make sure the program successfully downloads to the Pocket PC.

9. On the Pocket PC, open the File Explorer.

10. Browse to the MyDevice folder.

11. Execute the program MinimalDlgProgram.

12. Attempt to drag the window by the caption bar. The application window remains fixed at the upper-left corner of the physical display screen.

13. Tap the Quit menu item on the window's menu bar.

14. The application window disappears when application terminates.

Drawing and Painting

OBJECTIVES

▶ Implement a simple animation program

▶ Demonstrate use of timers for animation

▶ Implement drawing using rubber banding

▶ Support type and echo processing of characters

▶ Rapidly erase and redraw text strings

▶ Develop a library for managing bitmaps

▶ Implement an image processing program

▶ Implement a splash screen program

▶ Implement a bitmap animation program

Drawing Images Using Graphics

IN THIS CHAPTER:

Graphical User Interface for a Simple Animation Program

Drawing Images Using Graphics

Using Encapsulation in an Application Design

The Implementation of the Simple Animation Program

Analysis of the Effectiveness of the Encapsulation

Summary

Sample Programs on the Web

The primary emphasis of the simple example in this chapter is to perform drawing operations in any window using graphic primitives. In other words, this chapter emphasizes output processing from the Windows program utilizing features supported by the Graphics Device Interface (GDI) component of Windows. An initial emphasis on output is preferred because that is the primary means for communication with the user of an application. In the next chapter, the emphasis is providing and servicing user input into the program.

Rather than just listing the drawing primitives and their arguments, the description of drawing activities appears within the context of a simple animation program. In this way, something actually happens in the client area of the application window, providing feedback on the effect of using the drawing primitives. In addition to using the graphics primitives, animating a simple drawing requires the use of timers and the ability to force a repaint of the client area of the application. Another important issue deals with performing the animation in a smooth continuous manner that eliminates image flickering.

The program implemented in this chapter involves drawing and animating a stick figure within the client area of an application window. Using a stick figure helps to minimize application-specific graphic details of the image. This simple figure focuses on the mechanics of graphics drawing without being overly concerned with an accurately detailed graphic image. However, the image portrays sufficient realism to relate the programming mechanics to the animation behavior seen in the client area of the application window.

Graphical User Interface for a Simple Animation Program

Rather than listing all the graphics primitives, this chapter introduces these drawing operations in the context of a very simple animation program. Figure 4-1 demonstrates the user interface for this program.

The key goal of this application is to smoothly move the stick figure around the client area of an application window. A simple stick figure provides a graphic image that reveals the effective use of the graphic primitives without clouding the implementation issues with overly detailed drawing commands. Moreover, using an animation to illustrate graphics primitives reveals more of the issues associated with using graphics operations in a real application.

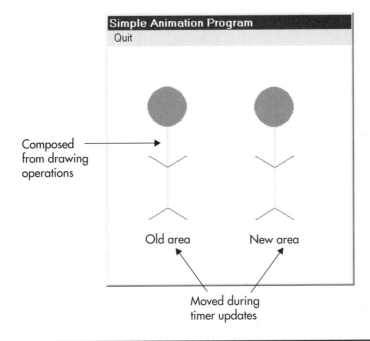

Figure 4-1   *User interface for the simple animation program*

The important features of this simple program appear as callouts in Figure 4-1. Composing a stick figure utilizes basic drawing operations. A circle or ellipse operation displays the head of the human figure. In order to indicate solidity, the application further fills the ellipse that forms the head with a dark color, such as gray. Repeated use of a line-drawing operation provides the body, arms, and legs of the figure.

During program execution, a timer drives the animation. At the elapse of a specific timer interval, the program moves the stick figure. A movement consists of erasing the figure at the current location, computing the new location, and drawing the figure at the new location. Additionally, the program needs to perform this movement in a smooth, flicker-free manner.

If an application simply erases the whole client area prior to a redraw, a flickering appearance results. The key to eliminating flicker in this situation is to limit repainting only to the affected portions of the client area. If effectively managed, the program erases only the rectangle containing the current image (old area) and draws only the rectangle containing the new image (new area). Rather than redrawing the whole client area, the program restricts erasing and drawing only to the immediately affected areas. This form of client area refresh is fast and flicker free.

Drawing Images Using Graphics

Many applications use graphics to display information. For instance, displaying a bar chart involves using line-drawing graphics operations. This chapter introduces the use of graphics within a Pocket PC application. As the primary emphasis, the topics in this chapter describe the detailed mechanics for using the drawing primitives available on the Pocket PC.

All implementations of graphics-drawing capabilities possess certain features in common. Every graphics-drawing environment requires the use of a drawing toolkit. This toolkit contains a set of drawing tools used by all subsequent drawing commands, such as line-drawing operations. The most common types of drawing tools are pens and brushes. These tools are used by the GDI component of Windows when an application performs drawing operations, such as line and rectangle drawing. Finally, GDI provides a scroll window into a virtual drawing space. This window enables the application to clip or remove portions of the image prior to displaying the image.

Using Drawing Toolkits

Figure 4-2 provides a characterization of a drawing toolkit. In Windows, this toolkit goes by the name *device context*. As the name suggests, the drawing toolkit contains tools, such as a pen, a brush, and a font, that are used during all drawing operations.

Using the toolkit necessitates a specific protocol or sequence of operations. The figure also depicts the steps in the protocol.

TIP

The concept of a drawing toolkit is not unique to Windows. This concept initially appeared in X Windows, the windowing system for the Unix operating system. Under X Windows, the drawing toolkit goes by the term graphics context, whose data type is denoted as GC. Pretty much the same protocol or dance is necessary to use a graphics context under X Windows.

Reading across Figure 4-2 from left to right reveals the steps involved in using the toolkit, which are as follows:

1. *Acquire a toolkit object/device context.* When a program acquires a drawing toolkit/device context, this kit comes equipped with a default set of tools. The

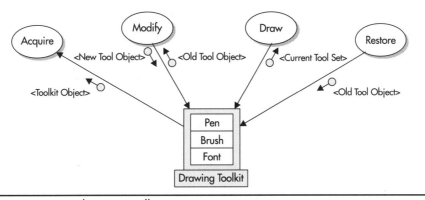

Figure 4-2   *Using a drawing toolkit*

set of tools and the default tool objects contained in a toolkit are specific to the Windows GDI. As a minimum, a drawing toolkit contains a pen, a brush, and a font tool with default objects. The pen is used to draw lines, the brush is used to fill an area, and the font tool provides a means for defining the style of any text written into a window. Other elements also appear in the toolkit but are not discussed here.

2. *Modify the toolkit object/device context by inserting new tool objects.* Sometimes, the default tool is adequate for the specific needs. More often, however, an application needs to replace the default tool object temporarily. For instance, the default pen object is usually a pen that uses black ink. However, the application may need to draw a line using red ink—for drawing a multiline plot, for example. To do this, the application first creates a red pen object. Then, the application inserts the red pen object into the drawing toolkit. When tools are exchanged in this manner, the Windows GDI provides the old tool (in this case, the black pen). The application must cache this old tool for later use.

3. *Perform drawing operations using the current toolkit/device context.* When the application subsequently commands any drawing operation, such as line drawing, the current toolkit object passes as an argument to the drawing command. Inside the Windows GDI, the display engine uses the appropriate tools to perform the appropriate drawing operation.

4. *Restore the toolkit object/device context to its original state.* Subsequent to performing drawing operations, the application should return the default objects to the drawing toolkit. This restoration leaves the toolkit in its original

state for the next user of the toolkit. To restore the toolkit to its pristine state, the application caches the tool objects returned to when installing a new tool object into the toolkit. After the drawing operation is completed, the application restores the cached tool objects to the toolkit.

NOTE

A device context is a GDI resource reused by other application programs. If an application fails to restore the toolkit like a good neighbor, the next user of the toolkit is going to receive a nasty jolt. Imagine an application having to draw with a red pen even though a red pen was not requested.

A number of primary benefits accrue to the practice of using device contexts as drawing toolkits. These benefits more than offset the extra programming effort in the usage protocol just described. The primary benefit is to allow simple method calls for drawing operations. The first argument to any drawing operation is the device context. Rather than having to indicate all the current drawing tools and their attributes, everything resides in a single object—the device context. Furthermore, the toolkit approach enables the application to treat drawing tools as virtual entities that are independent of the features of the hardware display environment. Therefore, any program compiles and executes correctly, regardless of the drawing capabilities of the display hardware.

Available Pen and Brush Styles

The primary drawing tools used in the animation program are pens and brushes. A pen is the tool for drawing lines, and a brush tool fills areas. Figure 4-3 depicts all the wide range of pen and brush styles available from the Windows GDI that are used in the animation program implementations.

Consider the pen styles shown in the figure. As supported by the Windows GDI, three characteristics of a pen are under direct program control: style, color, and width. The pen-drawing style indicates the manner in which the pen traces lines. Line styles include Solid, Dash, DashDot, DashDotDot, and Dot. These style names indicate the effect of the various pen styles. The figure provides examples of lines drawn using these different styles. In addition to the drawing style, an application may set the pen to any color. An application program is also free to indicate a line width in pixels. This pen property or attribute enables an application to draw thin or fat lines.

Brush styles that an application can use also appear in Figure 4-3. For the Windows GDI, brush styles fall into three broad categories: solid, pattern, and hatched. With a solid brush, an application can fill in the result of any graphics-drawing operation, such as a rectangle, with pixels of a uniform color. Pattern brushes use an arbitrary bitmap to fill the pixels of a graphics-drawing operation. Hatched brushes use lines separated by blank space within the body of your graphics object. When an application uses brushes in any of these styles, the application can simultaneously apply any color. When using hatch brushes, the hatch marks appear in the selected color. Moreover, the program can cause the hatch marks to have any arbitrary line width in pixels. By utilizing these features in various combinations, a Pocket PC application acquires considerable flexibility when any of the graphics-drawing operations are performed.

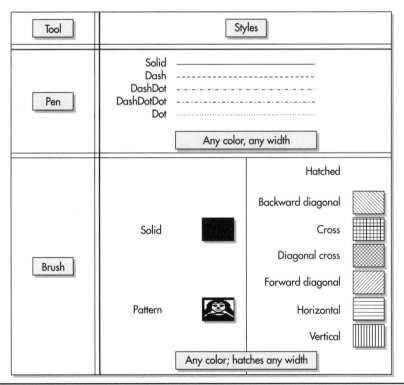

Figure 4-3   *Pen and brush tool styles*

Drawing Operations

After storing the desired pen and brush styles into a drawing toolkit, an application uses the toolkit to perform drawing operations. The drawing operations available to a program from Windows GDI appear in Figure 4-4.

Each drawing operation requires a drawing toolkit and a set of descriptive locations. These drawing commands or operations require endpoints or locations. As a result, most people refer to these drawing commands as *vector-drawing operations*. Endpoints (vector data) and the type of graphic object, such as a line, become the parameters for an algorithm that generates the actual pixel data.

For example, consider the rectangle-drawing command. This command requires an upper-left corner and a lower-right corner that characterize the rectangle. Usually, an application supplies these arguments in terms of offsets from the origin of a virtual drawing space. This drawing space extends a large number of pixels in the X and Y directions. An application has the programming flexibility to command that the rectangle be drawn anywhere in the virtual drawing space. However, clipping

Operations	Graphics	Desktop	Pocket PC
Rectangle	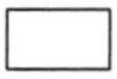	Yes	Yes
Ellipse	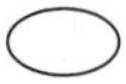	Yes	Yes
Line		Yes	Yes
Polygon		Yes	Yes
Rounded Rectangle	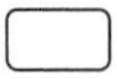	Yes	Yes
Pie		Yes	No
Arc		Yes	No
Bézier Curve		Yes	No

Figure 4-4   *Available GDI drawing operations*

may cause the rectangle to not actually appear. A discussion of clipping operations appears in the next section, "Clipping Operations."

TIP

The range of the virtual drawing space in both the X and Y directions is very large. Arguments that the program provides to the drawing commands are 32-bit, signed integer values. Using these values implies that each axis (X or Y) can have the following range of pixel locations:

Minimum value: −2 ^ 31 + 1

Maximum value: +2 ^ 31 − 1

By using a large virtual space, graphic images can exist that are bigger than the physical display space within the client area of the application window. A simple approach to clipping, described later, simply maps a portion of the image to the client area.

Figure 4-4 clearly indicates some important differences between GDI support in desktop Windows and GDI support in Windows CE on the Pocket PC. A smaller set of drawing primitives is available to the application under Windows CE. Pie, arc, and Bézier curve operations are unsupported on the Pocket PC.

TIP

A large number of books on computer graphics contain algorithms for approximating these kinds of drawing operations. These algorithms generate curves using a large number of very small line segments. Because line drawing is supported on the Pocket PC, a developer can implement these approaches from scratch, if necessary.

Notice that a circle-drawing primitive is missing from the list. This omission is not really a problem. If an application needs to draw a circle, it can use the ellipse method. After all, a circle is, in fact, an ellipse whose bounding rectangle is a square.

Because each of these drawing primitives accepts a drawing toolkit (the device context), an application can apply these primitives using various pen styles, colors, and line widths to draw the boundaries. Additionally, brushes enable the filling of any interior areas.

Clipping Operations

In general, the Windows GDI enables an application to control the portion of an image that appears in the client area of an application window. This control mechanism is the *scroll window*. A more realistic name for this window would be *clipping window*.

All Windows applications draw a graphic image in a virtual drawing space using the drawing commands in Figure 4-4. Any portion of the graphic image in virtual space drawn inside the scroll window (or clipping window) appears within the client area of the application window. Conversely, if a portion of the virtual drawing moves outside the scroll window, that part of the image no longer appears in the client area. In other words, the scroll window clips that part of the virtual image.

The virtual coordinate system defined by Windows GDI has two coordinate axes. In this coordinate system, the X axis is the horizontal axis, and the Y axis is the vertical axis. This orientation differs from a lot of the literature in the graphics field, which uses the exact opposite orientation.

Initially, the upper-left corner of the scroll window into virtual space coincides with the upper-left corner of the client area of the application window. The portion of the graphic image that appears within this area near the virtual space origin appears in the client area of an application window. During the display process, Windows GDI clips every other part of the image. On the desktop, the program possesses the control to actually move the scroll window to reveal and hide other parts of the virtual image.

By moving the scroll window, an application can actually cause an animating effect to occur. This animating effect is explained in Figure 4-5.

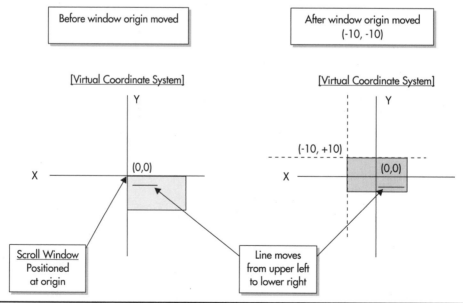

Figure 4-5 *Clipping in desktop Windows*

By moving the scroll window relative to the virtual origin, a graphics object can appear within a different portion of the client area of an application window. Therefore, the application can actually animate any graphically drawn object simply by moving the scroll window.

In Figure 4-5, the before-and-after effect of moving the upper-left corner of the scroll window demonstrates this animation technique. Initially, the scroll window appears positioned at the default location—the upper-left corner of the scroll window coincides with the origin of the imaginary or virtual drawing space. If the scroll window moves to the virtual location (−10,+10), this movement exposes a different portion of the virtual drawing space maintained by Windows GDI. As a result, the simple line appears to move to a different location in the client area.

A single command is capable of moving the scroll window (or clipping window). The graphic image automatically moves to a new location. One command animates a whole graphic image—that's pretty powerful!

Lack of support for moving or scrolling the clipping window around in virtual space is a major difference between Windows CE for the Pocket PC and the desktop version of Windows. A Windows CE application moves the image rather than moving the clipping window. Moving an image is computationally intensive for a complex image that utilizes a large number of drawing operations. The user experiences a slower, less smooth animation under this more manual form of animation.

NOTE

Animating the image manually employs a number of steps. First, the application determines an offset from the origin of the virtual drawing space. Then, each of the arguments in the drawing operation commands receives this offset as an increment to a base set of locations. Finally, the drawing commands are executed with the updated locations. Additional computational overhead results from having to update the arguments to each and every drawing command executed in the drawing of the complex image.

Displaying the Image

An image transfers to the client area of an application window through a process often characterized as a *rendering* or a *viewing pipeline*. An overview of the rendering pipeline appears in Figure 4-6.

Every drawing command processes through this pipeline. Typically, the software inside the GDI component of Windows caches the drawing commands until a bunch of commands are available. Then, drawing operations pass through the pipeline as a batch, thus reducing overhead for accessing hardware device drivers.

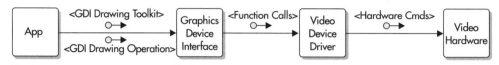

Figure 4-6 *A system view of the viewing pipeline*

Every drawing command issued by an application includes the type of operation (such as a rectangle), a drawing toolkit, and a set of locations in virtual space necessary to characterize the drawing operation. Methods in the Win32 API that support the drawing operations submit the commands directly to GDI to initiate the operation of the rendering pipeline. GDI performs the clipping operations by applying the scroll window to the graphics-drawing commands. After clipping, GDI negotiates with the video device driver using a set of standard, predefined method calls provided by the device driver to associate actual tool styles with the tool styles in the drawing toolkit.

NOTE

The drawing tools in the supplied drawing toolkit are, in fact, virtual (or imaginary) drawing tools. The negotiation between GDI and the video device driver determines the actual appearance characteristics of the drawing tool on the display.

In a sense, this approach achieves hardware independence. If the video hardware and device driver change, the Windows application still works and does not break. Of course, the appearance may be somewhat different. If the video card does not support a specific color, the video driver provides the closest matching color, which becomes the displayed color. A line that originally appears as red on one system may be drawn as black on another system if the only available video display hardware uses monochrome.

TIP

This situation is extremely likely with the Pocket PC. Some of these devices utilize full colors, whereas others only provide monochrome displays. The color displays work best in low light or dark, whereas the monochrome displays provide the brightest picture in direct sunlight. Depending on the ultimate operational context for an application, a program needs to be able to target either of these display technologies.

The manufacturer-supplied video device driver knows all about the physical mechanics of specific video display hardware. Therefore, the device driver uses the drawing commands and the negotiated tools to initiate hardware commands to fill the video hardware frame buffer associated with the client area of an application window.

Forcing a Repaint of Your Application Window

As the user interacts with an application, the program may need to force a repaint of the client area of the application window. The mechanics for forcing a repaint appear in Figure 4-7.

Forcing a repaint of the client area usually occurs in response to a specific user- or system-initiated event. The term *Windows drawing model* identifies this approach to updating the client. This drawing model separates data management from window updating. By using this approach, an application response may require multiple user- or system-initiated events prior to updating the client area.

In an application, when a user- or system-initiated event occurs, embedded within the event fields is some relevant data that characterizes the event. A good example is the inclusion of the mouse cursor location when the user clicks the left mouse button in the client area of an application window. A message handler extracts this data from the message parameters wParam and lParam and applies the data to some cached (permanently stored) fields maintained by the window procedure or by a global data manager—often called a *buffer*. After caching the message data, the application forces a repaint of the client area. Eventually, forcing a repaint results in the execution of the paint event message handler. Inside this paint event message handler, the implemented code extracts the cached or buffered data and uses this data to update the client area.

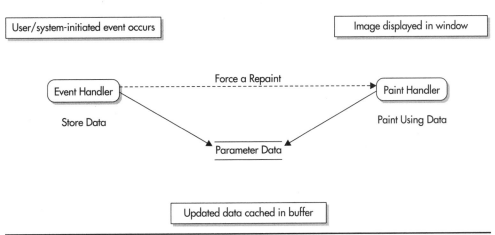

Figure 4-7   *Forcing a repaint of the client area*

The animation program described as the sample program throughout this chapter implements this forced-repaint approach in a specific way. The goal of this modified approach is to limit redrawing of the client area to only the portions necessary to erase the old image and to draw the new image. In this manner, the animation looks smooth and continuous rather than jerky and flickering.

Each animation update results from the firing of a timer at a regular interval. In the timer message handler, the following steps take place:

1. Compute a rectangle that describes the old area containing the stick figure.

2. Force a repaint of the client area that specifically erases only that portion of the client area described by the computed rectangle.

3. Compute an updated origin for the new portion of the client area that is to contain the stick figure.

4. Cache the updated origin into a set of private fields within the window procedure.

5. Force a repaint of the client area that specifically draws only that portion of the client area containing the stick figure at the updated origin.

In the paint event handler, the following actions occur:

1. Extract the updated origin for the stick figure from the cached fields.

2. Draw the graphic image of the stick figure using the extracted origin and the rectangular area that encompasses the stick figure.

By virtue of separating and targeting the redraw to specific old and new areas, the stick figure moves to a different location in the client area in a smooth, continuous manner.

Using Timers in Your Application

As described earlier, timers play an important role in any animation program. In fact, timers play an important role in many other applications. A timer signals that a time period has expired or elapsed. Many applications use timers in this way. For applications that monitor hardware interfaces, timer events signal the need to collect the next sample values from the hardware interface. If an application supports servicing of prescheduled events, a timer event initiates a schedule check for a prescheduled event.

The use of timers in any application, not just a Windows application, requires a program that operates according to the sequencing shown in Figure 4-8.

This figure assumes the form of a state transition diagram (STD). An STD indicates states of a program and the transition among these states when using the timer in the program.

States appear as labeled rectangles in the figure. A *state* is the memory of an application that summarizes everything that has happened to the application up to the current time in its execution history. When timers are used in a program, each state indicates an accumulation of program actions taken over a series of elapsed timer intervals. An arrow represents a transition between two states. Each transition label contains two pieces of important information. At the top of the label appears the event that initiates the transition. Along the bottom of the label is a summary description of the response action taken as a result of the transition.

Initially, a program begins in an "idle" state. Eventually, a user- or system-initiated event causes the program to start the timer firing events according to a specified elapsed time. Thus, the Create Event occurs when the program is in an idle state. The application responds to the Create Event by the action Start Timer Firing. Now, the program transitions to the "firing" state.

At regular timer intervals, a Timer Event fires. Because the program is in the firing state and a Timer Event occurs, the program performs the response Execute

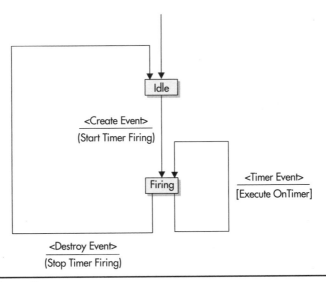

Figure 4-8   *Using a timer*

OnTimer. OnTimer is the timer message handler implemented in the window procedure of a program. Then, the program transitions back to the firing state. Sooner or later, a user- or system-initiated event occurs that signals the destruction of the timer. This situation appears in Figure 4-8 as the event named Destroy Event. An application responds by performing the action named Stop Timer Firing and returns to the idle state.

For the simple animation program in this chapter, elements of this sequence translate into an actual implementation in the following ways:

▶ **Idle state**   The period before application window creation.

▶ **Create Event**   An application window WM_CREATE message.

▶ **Start Timer Firing**   Sets the timer and its elapsed time duration.

▶ **Timer Event**   A WM_TIMER message that arrives at the indicated interval.

▶ **Execute OnTimer**   Implements the body of the OnTimer message handler.

▶ **Destroy Event**   The user decides to terminate the application.

▶ **Stop Timer Firing**   Resets the timer so that timer events no longer occur.

Inside the timer message handler of the window procedure, the program performs the actions necessary to ensure that the stick figure animates correctly. As indicated previously, these steps include erasing the current stick figure, computing the new location for the figure, and forcing a repaint of the client area.

Using Encapsulation in an Application Design

A key theme of this book is to encourage the use of good design approaches. In previous chapters, extensive references describe the uses and benefits of effective structuring. This section introduces a specific example of structuring, referred to as *encapsulation*.

The purpose of encapsulation is to hide or push specific processing details beneath method interfaces. Encapsulation enables an application to provide access control and management of global shared data or to group logically related operations together in a set of methods. A number of important benefits accrue from the hiding of programming details. Programs that effectively use encapsulation to hide messy implementation details are faster to implement and easier to debug. They also perform better and are simpler to extend.

Shortened implementation times result from the fact that a developer can reuse reliable encapsulated code over and over without taking the time to implement and debug a lot of new code. Once typed and debugged, the encapsulating methods act like bricks in a house, forming a foundation upon which to build the overall structure. New features are easily added by executing these rock-solid methods.

Debugging is extremely easy when encapsulation is used effectively. Because methods encapsulate specific implementation details, these methods isolate specific debugging problems from the remainder of the program. If a problem occurs inside the encapsulating method, debugging occurs only within the body of the encapsulating method. Additionally, by using method calls, the logic and any flaws stand out, further easing the pressures of debugging. With proper encapsulation, a piece of code in C or C++ can often be made to look almost as readable as English. This readability is a key factor in enabling a developer to more rapidly debug logic flaws.

By invoking already implemented methods, the actual memory footprint of the program is much smaller. By comparison, many developers just cut and paste code and then modify names of variables instead of using encapsulating methods with arguments. The cut-and-paste approach leads to code bloat, high memory occupancy, and long user response times. With effective encapsulation using methods and arguments, only one instance of a code segment appears within the program body, significantly reducing the size of the actual code implementation.

 TIP

Later in the chapter, the section "Analysis of the Effectiveness of the Encapsulation" includes a specific example of the code bloat that can result from failure to effectively use encapsulating methods.

Extensibility is usually a snap when using a design approach that depends heavily on encapsulation. Adding additional methods to the encapsulation has no effect on the other elements of the encapsulation, or on any of the other parts of the application for that matter. Moreover, expanding the application entails using new or existing encapsulating methods that have already been debugged. Usually, added capabilities require a minimum of time and effort when built on a design that effectively utilizes encapsulation.

An excellent opportunity is available for building a reusable encapsulating set of functionally related methods for the simple animation program in this chapter. Recall that modifying the device context or toolkit of drawing tools requires a special protocol or dance. This protocol involves temporarily replacing and then restoring one or more default tools in the device context.

Performing this tool management dance is the basis for a set of encapsulating methods. Consider the following declaration for an encapsulating method:

```
void DrawLineShapeAt(HDC DC, int x1, int y1, int x2, int y2,
                     int line_width , int line_style , int line_color);
```

This method hides the specific details for drawing a line between two points in virtual space using an arbitrary line, width, style, and color.

As arguments, the program passes a default device context, DC, the start point of the line (x1,y1) in the client area of the window, the endpoint of the line (x2,y2) in the client area of the window, and additional parameters that further characterize the line. Of course, the start and end points of the line are in virtual coordinates, which may cause a portion or all of the line to be clipped by the GDI viewing pipeline. The first of the line-characterization parameters is line_width, which is the number of pixels used to draw any point on the line. Next comes line_style, which indicates any of the legal line styles indicted in Figure 4-4. This value must be one of the predefined constants PS_SOLID, PS_DOT, PS_DASH, or PS_DASHDOT. For line_color, the application provides a red, green, and blue combination, supplying these values through the RGB macro available from windows.h.

Here is an example of using this encapsulating method in a Windows program:

```
DrawLineShapeAt(DeviceContext, 0, 0, 75, 75 , 1 ,
                PS_SOLID , RGB(0,255,0) ) ;
```

Executing this method draws a straight line from the origin of the virtual coordinate system (0,0) to the point (75,75) in the virtual coordinate system. This line is to be a solid line that is 1-pixel wide. According to the RGB macro, green is the color of the line.

In the preceding method execution, the color declaration employs the macro RGB(0,255,0). More accurately, this argument provides a color combination in the form RGB(*RedConcentration*, *GreenConcentration*, *BlueConcentration*). The order of the letters in the macro name, RGB, indicates the order of the color concentrations in the argument list. Each concentration value ranges from 0 to 255. When the concentration is 0, the component color does not contribute to the overall color combination. If the concentration value is 255, the maximum amount of the color component enters into the color combination. For the combination indicated in this example, only green contributes and does so at full concentration. Because these values range from 0 to 255, each component color consumes 8 bits of representation. The RGB macro enters these bits into a 32-bit number that the video driver uses to control the color-generating hardware of the video display subsystem.

Some of the encapsulating methods, such as DrawRectangleShapeAt, use the argument fill_brush. This argument must have a value that uniquely identifies one of the stock brushes. A number of constants in windows.h define unique integer identifiers for each of the stock brushes: BLACK_BRUSH, DKGRAY_BRUSH, GRAY_BRUSH, LTGRAY_BRUSH, and WHITE_BRUSH.

All the protocol steps for modifying the default device context appear within the body of this method. The method creates each of the necessary new drawing tools, stores them in the device context, issues the drawing command, and then restores the default values in the device context. A complex drawing that uses a series of these encapsulating commands is likely to be less cluttered and easier to understand at a casual glance rather than taking hours of reading to decipher.

TIP

The contents of this encapsulating method's body appear in the detailed code analysis in the section "Evaluating The DrawOps Element." The detailed analysis provides a review and discussion of every line of the implemented method body.

In fact, the project element that implements this encapsulating method also provides a number of other methods that encapsulate other drawing operations. The name of this element is DrawOps. Other drawing operations supported by this element include the rectangle, the rounded rectangle, and the ellipse.

The header file for this encapsulating element lists all the related methods that are supplied by the DrawOps element. This header file appears as follows:

```
/***********************************************
 *
 * File: DrawOps.h
 *
 * copyright, SWA Engineering, Inc., 2001
 * All rights reserved.
 *
 ***********************************************/
#include <windows.h>
#include <windowsx.h>

void DrawLineShapeAt(HDC DC, int x1, int y1, int x2, int y2,
                 int line_width , int line_style , int line_color) ;

void DrawRectangleShapeAt(HDC DC, int x1, int y1, int x2, int y2,
                    int line_width , int line_style ,
                    int line_color, int fill_brush) ;
```

```
void DrawRoundRectShapeAt(HDC DC, int x1, int y1, int x2, int y2,
                          int line_width , int line_style ,
                          int line_color, int fill_brush) ;

void DrawEllipseShapeAt(HDC DC, int x1, int y1, int x2, int y2,
                        int line_width , int line_style ,
                        int line_color, int fill_brush) ;
```

Arguments to the last two methods, DrawRoundRectShapeAt and
DrawEllipseShapeAt, differ somewhat in interpretation. These arguments
represent the bounding rectangle of the drawing operation. The shape of this
rectangle forms the basis for the shape of the drawing operation. As indicated
earlier, using a square as the bounding rectangle causes the ellipse to display
as a circle.

The Implementation of the Simple Animation Program

From this chapter forward, all sample program discussions begin with the dialog
window procedure. As mentioned in the last chapter, the WinMain element never
changes from application to application. Therefore, any further discussion of this
element is totally unnecessary.

The following code shows the complete DlgProc for the simple animation program:

```
/************************************************
 *
 * File: DlgProc.c
 *
 * copyright, SWA Engineering, Inc., 2001
 * All rights reserved.
 *
 ************************************************/


#include <windows.h>
#include <windowsx.h>
#include "resource.h"
```

```
#include "windowsy.h"

BOOL  OnInitDialog( HWND  hDlg , HWND  hDlgFocus , long  lInitParam ) ;
void  DlgOnCommand(HWND hDlg,int iID,HWND hDlgCtl,UINT uCodeNotify ) ;
void  DlgOnPaint(HWND hDlg) ;
void  DlgOnMove  ( HWND  hDlg , int  x , int  y ) ;
DWORD DlgOnCtlColorStatic(HWND hDlg,HDC hDC,HWND hDlgChild,UINT msgCode);

#include <tchar.h>
#include "IFiles.h"
#include "DataMgr.h"
#include "PortabilityUtils.h"

#include "DrawOps.h"

#define     HORIZONTAL_DELTA  100
#define     VERTICAL_DELTA    0
#define     HORIZONTAL_MAX    400
#define     VERTICAL_MAX      +400

#define     ID_TIMER          1
#define     TIMER_INCREMENT   250

static int CurrentOriginX = 0 ;
static int CurrentOriginY = 0 ;

void DlgOnTimer(HWND hDlg, UINT id);

BOOL CALLBACK DlgProc(HWND hDlg,UINT message,WPARAM wParam,LPARAM lParam)
{
    switch (message)
    {
        HANDLE_DLG_MSG( hDlg , WM_INITDIALOG , OnInitDialog ) ;
        HANDLE_DLG_MSG( hDlg , WM_COMMAND , DlgOnCommand ) ;
        HANDLE_DLG_MSG( hDlg , WM_PAINT ,  DlgOnPaint ) ;
        HANDLE_DLG_MSG( hDlg , WM_MOVE , DlgOnMove ) ;
        HANDLE_DLG_MSG( hDlg , WM_CTLCOLORSTATIC , DlgOnCtlColorStatic ) ;
        HANDLE_DLG_MSG( hDlg , WM_TIMER,DlgOnTimer);
    }
    return FALSE ;
}
```

Reviewing the DlgProc Method

Most of the code in this listing should be very familiar at this point. Therefore, only the new elements that implement the animation aspects of the program need further detailed discussion. A discussion of each of the new elements appears next.

```
#include "DrawOps.h"
```

This include declaration provides visibility to the encapsulated drawing methods. Usage of these methods appears in the WM_PAINT message handler body, which is discussed a little bit later.

```
#define    HORIZONTAL_DELTA   100
#define    VERTICAL_DELTA      0
```

After every timer interval, the origin of the bounding area of the stick figure increments by these amounts. For horizontal movement, a positive delta indicates a movement to the right, whereas a negative delta causes movement to the left. Because the value of VERTICAL_DELTA currently equals 0, each timer event causes the stick figure to move horizontally to the right. A positive vertical delta results in upward movement. Similarly, downward vertical movement happens when the vertical delta value is set to a negative number.

```
#define    HORIZONTAL_MAX     400
#define    VERTICAL_MAX       +400
```

If not constrained, adding the previous delta movements to the origin causes the stick figure to completely disappear from the client area. When enforced in code, these maximum limits ensure that the stick figure wraps around and reappears in the client area.

```
#define    ID_TIMER           1
#define    TIMER_INCREMENT    250
```

When creating a timer, two important parameters are necessary. A unique integer identifier, ID_TIMER, associates a specific virtual timer with a specific application window, and TIMER_INCREMENT tells Windows the amount of elapsed time in milliseconds between individual WM_TIMER messages. According to the Windows documentation, this value must be at least 50 milliseconds. If an application provides a value smaller than this acceptable lower bound, Windows simply rounds up to this minimum value.

```
static int CurrentOriginX = 0 ;
static int CurrentOriginY = 0 ;
```

These static variables serve as the permanent data fields that cache the current location of the origin of the bounding rectangle for the stick figure. By definition, this origin consists of the upper-left corner of the bounding rectangle. Inside the WM_TIMER message handler, these values update by the delta increments defined earlier. Then, the handler checks these values against the maximum limits described previously. If adding the increments exceeds the maximum limits, these values are set back to the origin of the virtual coordinate system.

```
void DlgOnTimer(HWND hDlg, UINT id);
```

This statement declares the header for the WM_TIMER message handler. When executed by the message handler, this method receives two arguments. The hDlg argument identifies the window that owns the timer. A unique integer identifier ID indicates the specific timer resource that is the source of the WM_TIMER message. A well-behaved WM_TIMER message handler compares this ID with the ID_TIMER declared earlier to ensure that the correct response is performed.

```
HANDLE_DLG_MSG(hDlg,    WM_TIMER,DlgOnTimer);
```

Adding this message cracker to the message switch in the DlgProc element routes the WM_TIMER message to the DlgOnTimer message handler.

Studying the Message Handler Bodies

During operation of this program, message handlers execute in a specific sequence. The sequence revolves around the manner in which the program works, as follows:

1. The program begins and a WM_CREATE message causes the message handler OnInitDialog to execute.

2. OnInitDialog initiates a timer. After each timer interval, the arrival of a WM_TIMER message causes DlgOnTimer to execute.

3. DlgOnTimer erases the old stick figure and draws the new stick figure. Both the erase and redraw operations submit a WM_PAINT message and immediately execute DlgOnPaint.

4.   When the user terminates the program with the Quit menu item, a WM_COMMAND message executes the DlgOnCommand message handler. This handler terminates the timer.

NOTE

Actually, a WM_TIMER message never really appears on the primary thread message queue. When the hardware timer signals that the timer interval has elapsed, Windows sets a Boolean value that signals that a timer event has occurred. When the message loop of DialogBox executes GetMessage, this method checks the bit. If the bit is set, GetMessage returns a WM_TIMER message.

In the following analysis, message handlers appear in this same order to mimic the actual execution sequence. Following the execution sequence in this manner provides clear insight into the detailed operation of the program and illustrates clearly the way in which the elements perform the actual animation.

```
BOOL  OnInitDialog ( HWND  hDlg , HWND  hDlgFocus , long  lInitParam )
{
   // Previously Discussed Lines Omitted
   SetTimer(hDlg,ID_TIMER,TIMER_INCREMENT,NULL) ;
   return TRUE ;

}
```

   In addition to the required initialization code described earlier, this handler initiates the hardware timer. Assigning and initiating a hardware timer uses the SetTimer method. This method requires the owner of the timer hDlg as the first argument. A unique integer, ID_TIMER (defined earlier), identifies the specific timer. Once started, the timer continually initiates a timer event after the elapse of every TIMER_INCREMENT time interval. The final argument allows the program to submit a timer handler procedure to be executed rather than the generation of a WM_TIMER message. Supplying a NULL value here forces the generation of a WM_TIMER message.

NOTE

The TIMER_INCREMENT time interval is the minimum amount of time between the arrival of successive WM_TIMER messages. Once generated, a WM_TIMER message enters the thread message queue and crawls to the head of the queue. This additional time to get to the head of the queue causes actual messages to arrive at greater elapsed time intervals than indicated in the SetTimer method call. If a thread message queue already contains a WM_TIMER message, Windows does not add an additional message to the queue.

```
void DlgOnTimer(HWND hDlg, UINT id)
{
   RECT OldArea ;

   if ( id == ID_TIMER )
   {
         OldArea.left = CurrentOriginX + 50 ;
         OldArea.top = CurrentOriginY + 50 ;
         OldArea.right = CurrentOriginX + 100 ;
         OldArea.bottom = CurrentOriginY + 215;

         // Clean Out The Old Image
         InvalidateRect(hDlg,&OldArea,FALSE) ;
         UpdateWindow(hDlg) ;

         CurrentOriginX = CurrentOriginX + HORIZONTAL_DELTA ;
         CurrentOriginY = CurrentOriginY + VERTICAL_DELTA ;

         if ( CurrentOriginX > HORIZONTAL_MAX )
              CurrentOriginX = 0 ;
         if ( CurrentOriginY > VERTICAL_MAX )
              CurrentOriginY = 0 ;

         // Draw The New Image
         InvalidateRect(hDlg,NULL,FALSE) ;
         UpdateWindow(hDlg) ;
   }
}
```

This WM_TIMER message handler erases the existing stick figure, updates the origin of the bounding rectangle, and displays the new stick figure at the new origin. Because this handler includes a number of important programming issues, the following discussion focuses on specific lines of the handler.

```
   if ( id == ID_TIMER )
```

A window may have any number of virtual timers, each with a separate timer interval and unique identifier. Although the hardware only possesses a single timer, Windows manages this timer to ensure that all the individual timer interval events actually occur as requested. Because all the timer events route to this DlgOnTimer message handler, the handler checks the incoming identifier in the argument ID against known identifiers. In this way, the handler implements a specific response to each executing virtual timer created by the program. The identifier ID_TIMER appears earlier in the discussion of the main body of the DlgProc.

```
OldArea.left = CurrentOriginX + 50 ;
OldArea.top = CurrentOriginY + 50 ;
OldArea.right = CurrentOriginX + 100 ;
OldArea.bottom = CurrentOriginY + 215;
```

In order to erase the current stick figure, the bounding rectangle of this area is necessary. These lines compute the bounding rectangle and store the results in a RECT structure, OldArea, declared upon entry to this timer message handler. The location (CurrentOriginX,CurrentOriginY) represents the upper-left corner of the bounding rectangle in client area coordinates. Added to these values are the precomputed offsets for the bounding rectangle of the stick figure.

```
InvalidateRect(hDlg,&OldArea,FALSE) ;
UpdateWindow(hDlg) ;
```

These two lines of code force the program to immediately erase the bounding rectangle of the stick figure that is stored in the rectangle OldArea. In the first line, the method InvalidateRect adds the bounding rectangle OldArea to the update region of the window hDlg. The update region represents the portion of the client area that must be redrawn. A FALSE value for the last argument limits background repainting to the update region in the bounding rectangle. When the paint message handler executes, all drawing and refreshing occurs only in the area of the bounding rectangle. As a result, this combination of arguments quickly and smoothly erases the current area that contains the stick figure, painting over the area with the white brush.

After executing the InvalidateRect method, the WM_PAINT message enters the primary thread message queue for the window hDlg. By immediately executing the UpdateWindow method, the WM_PAINT message moves to the head of the queue. Windows then forces immediate processing of the paint message handler, causing the erasure of the current stick figure.

NOTE

Although the execution of the program behaves as if a WM_PAINT message appears in the message queue, no such message actually exists. Windows controls all painting through a special Boolean value maintained for each application window. InvalidateRect sets the bit, GetMessage checks the bit, and BeginPaint resets the bit. In reality, UpdateWindow just executes the DlgProc directly. To an observer, this sequence appears as if a WM_PAINT message moves through the primary thread message queue.

```
CurrentOriginX = CurrentOriginX + HORIZONTAL_DELTA ;
CurrentOriginY = CurrentOriginY + VERTICAL_DELTA ;
if ( CurrentOriginX > HORIZONTAL_MAX )
    CurrentOriginX = 0 ;
if ( CurrentOriginY > VERTICAL_MAX )
    CurrentOriginY = 0 ;
```

Updating the upper-left corner of the bounding rectangle is the goal of these lines of code. The first two lines add the offsets HORIZONTAL_DELTA and VERTICAL_DELTA to the current locations. Each location is then checked against the limit values HORIZONTAL_MAX and VERTICAL_MAX. If either location exceeds the maximum limit, the location value wraps back to zero.

```
InvalidateRect(hDlg,NULL,FALSE) ;
UpdateWindow(hDlg) ;
```

At this point, the client area is actually empty. These two lines immediately force the execution of the paint message handler. Using the NULL value as the second argument adds the whole client area to the update region of the window. As a result, Windows draws anything inside the client area. Disabling background painting is the result of placing a FALSE value into the third argument. In combination, the last two parameters allow for a rapid redraw of the stick figure in its new location.

NOTE

Smooth, flicker-free animation results from limiting control over the amount of redrawing in the client area. During erasure, redrawing is limited to the bounding rectangle of the current location. During movement, the bounding rectangle of the new location serves as the limitation of redrawing. An application accomplishes targeted, efficient erasing and redrawing using combinations of the last two parameters of InvalidateRect followed immediately by a call to UpdateWindow.

```
void  DlgOnPaint(HWND hDlg)
{
    // Previously Discussed Lines Omitted
    // The Head
    DrawEllipseShapeAt( DeviceContext,
                    CurrentOriginX + 50, CurrentOriginY + 50,
                    CurrentOriginX + 100, CurrentOriginY + 100,
                    1 , PS_SOLID , RGB(255,0,0), GRAY_BRUSH) ;
    // The Body
    DrawLineShapeAt( DeviceContext,
```

```
                   CurrentOriginX + 75, CurrentOriginY + 100,
                   CurrentOriginX + 75, CurrentOriginY + 200,
                   1 , PS_SOLID , RGB(0,255,0) ) ;
  // The Arms
    DrawLineShapeAt ( DeviceContext,
                   CurrentOriginX + 75, CurrentOriginY + 150,
                   CurrentOriginX + 50, CurrentOriginY + 135,
                   1 , PS_SOLID , RGB(0,0,255)) ;
    DrawLineShapeAt ( DeviceContext,
                   CurrentOriginX + 75, CurrentOriginY + 150,
                   CurrentOriginX + 100, CurrentOriginY + 135,
                   1 , PS_SOLID , RGB(0,0,255)) ;
  // The Legs
    DrawLineShapeAt ( DeviceContext,
                   CurrentOriginX + 75, CurrentOriginY + 200,
                   CurrentOriginX + 50, CurrentOriginY + 215,
                   1 , PS_SOLID , RGB(0,0,255)) ;
    DrawLineShapeAt ( DeviceContext,
                   CurrentOriginX + 75, CurrentOriginY + 200,
                   CurrentOriginX + 100, CurrentOriginY + 215,
                   1 , PS_SOLID , RGB(0,0,255)) ;
     // Previously Discussed Lines Omitted
}
```

After filling the background of the client area with a white brush, the paint message handler proceeds to draw the stick figure at the current location. This method handler employs encapsulation methods such as DrawLineShapeAt from the DrawOps element discussed earlier. Arguments to the cached origin values CurrentOriginX and CurrentOriginY add precomputed offsets to ensure that the stick figure image displays correctly as a total human body. Each of the body elements utilizes a different color scheme. The head is dark gray with a red outline. A green body with blue arms composes the remainder of the stick figure.

As an example of the precomputed offsets for a specific stick body part, consider the following line of code:

```
    DrawLineShapeAt ( DeviceContext,
                   CurrentOriginX + 75, CurrentOriginY + 100,
                   CurrentOriginX + 75, CurrentOriginY + 200,
                   1 , PS_SOLID , RGB(0,255,0) ) ;
```

Recall that the first two arguments after DeviceContext indicate the start location of the line shape in virtual drawing space. To ensure that the body touches the head, the values (75,100) appear as offsets to the origin values as the start of the line shape.

```
void  DlgOnCommand(HWND hDlg ,int iID,HWND hDlgCtl,UINT uCodeNotify)
{
  switch( iID )
  {
    case IDOK:
        KillTimer(hDlg,ID_TIMER) ;
          EndDialog(hDlg , 0)  ;
    break ;
  }
}
```

Prior to completely terminating the application using EndDialog, this command message handler stops the generation of WM_TIMER messages. KillTimer is the method that the program uses for ceasing timer operations. This method requires two arguments. As the first argument, the program supplies the owner window of the virtual timer, hDlg. Also, Windows needs to know the unique integer identifier of the virtual timer, ID_TIMER. Using these two values, Windows can destroy the assigned virtual timer.

Evaluating the DrawOps Element

This program element contains a set of methods that encapsulates individual drawing operations. Each method follows the same general pattern:

1. Create the necessary drawing tools.
2. Attach the tools to the device context.
3. Perform the requested drawing operation.
4. Restore the default tools to the device context.

Because every method uses this same logic, this section analyzes only one of the methods—DrawRectangleShapeAt. This method provides all the details regarding the use of GDI tools, which are used in every one of the methods. Here is the complete listing for this method:

```
void DrawRectangleShapeAt(HDC DC, int x1, int y1, int x2, int y2,
                          int line_width , int line_style ,
                          int line_color, int fill_brush)
{
      HPEN    newPen ;
      HPEN    oldPen ;
    HBRUSH    newBrush ;
```

```
    HBRUSH oldBrush ;

    newPen = CreatePen(line_style, line_width, line_color);
    oldPen = SelectObject(DC, newPen) ;

    newBrush = GetStockBrush(fill_brush) ;
    oldBrush = SelectObject(DC,newBrush) ;

      Rectangle(DC,x1,y1,x2,y2) ;

      SelectObject(DC,oldPen) ;
    SelectObject(DC,oldBrush) ;

    DeletePen( newPen ) ;
    // Never Delete Stock Objects
}
```

Individual lines of code reveal the actual mechanics for creating GDI tools, such as pens and brushes, and using these objects in a drawing operation. For this reason, relevant sections of code appear in this detailed analysis.

```
    HPEN    newPen ;
    HPEN    oldPen ;
  HBRUSH    newBrush ;
  HBRUSH    oldBrush ;
```

Anytime a program creates a drawing tool, such as a brush or a pen, Windows GDI generates and fills an appropriate data structure. As with all system data structures, the application receives a handle to this object. This handle is a unique integer identifier, not a pointer, and is only available for use as an argument into specific methods that manipulate drawing tools. For pens, the data type of a pen object handle is HPEN. Brushes uses the data type HBRUSH to store a handle to a brush object.

The variables declared previously serve two purposes. A variable with the prefix *new*, such as newPen, stores a handle to a custom drawing tool. The program creates the tool programmatically and stores the handle to the data structure in this appropriately named variable. Any variable whose name begins with the prefix *old*, such as oldPen, serves to maintain the handle to an existing drawing tool that has been temporarily replaced in a device context.

```
    newPen = CreatePen(line_style, line_width, line_color);
    oldPen = SelectObject(DC, newPen) ;
```

By using the method CreatePen, a program can programmatically create a custom pen drawing tool. This method requires three descriptive arguments. The first argument is line_width, which is the number of pixels used to draw any point on the line. Next comes line_style, which indicates any of the legal line styles indicted by one of the predefined constants PS_SOLID, PS_DOT, PS_DASH, or PS_DASHDOT. For line_color, an application provides a red, green, and blue combination, supplying these values through the RGB macro available from windows.h. The arguments to the RGB macro indicate the concentration of red, green, and blue components in the line color.

TIP

For a detailed discussion and example of the RGB macro, see "Using Encapsulation in an Application Design," earlier in the chapter.

After creating the pen, the method stores the pen handle into a locally declared variable named newPen of data type HPEN. Using the new pen handle, this method executes SelectObject to insert the new pen into the device context, DC. SelectObject returns the handle to the default pen that was in DC, which is stored into the variable oldPen.

```
newBrush = GetStockBrush(fill_brush) ;
oldBrush = SelectObject(DC,newBrush) ;
```

Creating a custom brush uses the method GetStockBrush. A fill brush style is the only argument to this method. The fill_brush style must have a value that uniquely identifies one of the stock brushes, such as BLACK_BRUSH, DKGRAY_BRUSH, GRAY_BRUSH, LTGRAY_BRUSH, and WHITE_BRUSH.

As with the CreatePen method, GetStockBrush returns a handle to the existing stock brush. This handle resides in the variable newBrush. The program then uses SelectObject to place the new brush into the device context, DC, storing the handle to the previous brush in oldBrush.

TIP

SelectObject does not need the program to identify the kind of resource, such as a pen or a brush. Using the handle provided as the second argument, Windows is free to look into the underlying data structure, to identify the type of resource, and to replace the appropriate resource in the device context.

```
Rectangle(DC,x1,y1,x2,y2);
```

Now, the program draws the rectangle using the Rectangle method. This method receives the device context, DC, and the corner points of the rectangle in the virtual drawing space. Because the custom pen is now a member of the list of drawing tools in DC, the boundary of the rectangle appears with the attributes of the custom pen. Also, the interior of the rectangle fills using the stock brush color.

```
SelectObject(DC,oldPen);
SelectObject(DC,oldBrush) ;
```

Restoring the default pen and brush into the device context, DC, is the goal of these two lines of code. In order to restore the original drawing tools, simply execute SelectObject, providing the cached handles to the original tools. In fact, these method calls also return handles to the new tools that were previously stored. Because these handles already exist in the local variables newPen and newBrush, storing these values again is unnecessary.

```
DeletePen( newPen ) ;
```

After the drawing is completed, this method removes the custom pen whose handle is stored in newPen. Eliminating a custom pen requires that the pen handle be submitted to the method DeletePen.

Windows GDI allocates data structures for new drawing tools such as pens and brushes from a special heap owned by GDI. Using DeletePen forces the deallocation of memory from this private heap.

NOTE

This GDI heap is fixed in size and never grows. If the program does not deallocate this memory, eventually GDI heap memory will be unavailable. As a result, tool creation fails. A failure of this type may have some funny side effects, such as weird drawings.

```
// Never Delete Stock Objects
```

If the program deletes the stock brush accessed at the beginning, other programs that use the stock brush also experience some funny side effects. These effects are usually in the form of complete program failure when attempting to draw. With the process isolation supported in the Windows Kernel, this kind of failure only crashes the application and not the whole system, as occurred in earlier versions of Windows.

Analysis of the Effectiveness of the Encapsulation

Some programmers feel that all this encapsulation is simply unnecessary. In this section, however, a short analysis demonstrates the effectiveness of the use of encapsulation.

Review the code listing for the DlgOnPaint message handler. Only six lines of code are necessary in this handler in order to draw the stick figure. Now look at the encapsulating methods. On average, each method uses eight lines of code. If all this code were moved into the DlgOnPaint handler, this handler would expand to 48 lines of code.

Worse yet, because the DrawLineShapeMethod comprises five of the six method calls, 40 of these 48 lines of code would simply be cut-and-paste, modified versions of the same code. This code would be very ugly and very messy.

In reality, by reusing code in the encapsulating method DrawLineShapeAt, the stick figure uses 22 lines of code (six method calls plus two method bodies, with eight lines per method body) instead of 48 lines of code (six physical copies of the method body code, with eight lines per method body). Therefore, encapsulation reduces the size of the code to 45 percent of the cut-and-paste version. For an image significantly more complex than a stick figure, the size reduction is even greater.

The code in the DlgOnPaint method handler is extremely readable. The method names look like logical operations that are easily understood by a casual reader. Now, imagine what the 48 lines of cut-and-paste code would look like—messy and ugly. What's more, with a more complex image, the messiness and ugliness would become even worse.

Summary

This chapter introduces the mechanics of using GDI graphics within the context of an animated stick figure. Control of the animation resides in a virtual timer that is created programmatically. A DrawOps program element encapsulates the basic protocol for using custom drawing tools in a Windows application. Here are some of the key points of this chapter:

▶ After drawing operations are performed, you should return the device context to the original set of drawing tools.

▶ An application draws in a virtual drawing space that GDI clips during execution of the viewing pipeline.

▶ Windows CE contains a subset of the drawing operations of desktop Windows.

▶ Windows CE uses a fixed clipping window whose upper-left corner is at the origin of the virtual drawing space.

▶ A window can have multiple virtual timers with different timer intervals.

▶ An application can accomplish smooth continuous animation by limiting the portions of the client area involved in erasing and redrawing.

▶ Encapsulation enables an application to manage data structures or to group functionally related capabilities.

▶ Effectively using encapsulation yields programs that are faster to implement and easier to debug. They also perform better and are simpler to extend.

Sample Programs on the Web

The following programs are available at http://www.osborne.com:

Description	Folder
Desktop Simple Animation Program	SimpleAnimationProgram
Pocket PC Simple Animation Program	SimpleAnimationProgramPPC

Execution Instructions

Desktop Simple Animation Program

1. Start Visual C++ 6.0.

2. Open the project SimpleAnimationProgram.dsw in folder SimpleAnimationProgram.

3. Build the program.

4. Execute the program.

5. The stick figure should move horizontal across the client area without any flickering.

6. Click the Quit menu item on the window menu bar.

7. The application window disappears when the application terminates.

8. Modify the parameters HORIZONTAL_DELTA and VERTICAL_DELTA.

9. Build and execute the program.

10. Compare the difference in movement based on these parameter changes.

11. Click the Quit menu item on the window menu bar.

12. The application window disappears when the application terminates.

Pocket PC Simple Animation Program

1. Attach the Pocket PC cradle to the desktop computer.

2. Insert the Pocket PC into the cradle.

3. Tell ActiveSync to create a guest connection.

4. Make sure the status is "connected."

5. Start Embedded Visual C++ 3.0.

6. Open the project SimpleAnimationProgramPPC.vcw in the folder SimpleAnimationProgramPPC.

7. Build the program.

8. Make sure the program successfully downloads to the Pocket PC.

9. On the Pocket PC, open the File Explorer.

10. Browse to the MyDevice folder.

11. Execute the program SimpleAnimationProgram.

12. The stick figure should move horizontally across the client area without any flickering.

13. Tap the Quit menu item on the window menu bar.

14. The application window disappears when the application terminates.

15. Modify the parameters HORIZONTAL_DELTA and VERTICAL_DELTA.

16. Build the program.

17. Make sure the program successfully downloads to the Pocket PC.

18. Execute the program SimpleAnimationProgram.

19. Compare the difference in movement based on these parameter changes.

20. Tap the Quit menu item on the window menu bar.

21. The application window disappears when the application terminates.

Implementing a Drawing Program

T his chapter focuses on developing an application with a number of features that might appear in a full-blown application. The features in this program are similar to the ones found in any computer-aided design (CAD) program or any program with general drawing capabilities, such as Microsoft PowerPoint.

In order to show how to use new features of Windows programming, this chapter implements the drawing program incrementally. The first increment adds the ability to draw a line using rubber banding. Next, modifications to the program implement the ability to insert a single text label onto the drawing. After adding support for a text label, incorporating a menu enables the user to set the default drawing shape to a line, a rectangle, a rounded rectangle, or an ellipse.

In addition to these capabilities, this chapter also addresses a number of important design issues. The first design issue is the utilization of a class to maintain the default properties used to draw the current object. Another important design issue addressed in this chapter involves the use of a draw object class to manage the characteristics of a specific draw object. Yet another design issue characterizes the ability to partition specific functional capabilities into coherent, focused, layered classes. Finally, a state machine replaces the ugly, messy, combined mouse-and-keyboard processing of an earlier version with a clean, easy-to-use, extensible state machine.

NOTE

Proper design is the often-repeated emphasis of this book. These design issues should receive discussion and consideration early in the program development cycle. However, as these design discussions evolve, think about the effect of waiting until after tens of thousands of lines of code have been developed before attempting to address these issues. After having implemented an extensive amount of code, modifying the code to address design issues consumes extensive effort and significant schedule delay. For these reasons, always address design issues early and often.

A slightly different approach to code analysis appears in this chapter. The first section contains a complete listing of the DlgProc of the implemented program. This listing involves the fewest additions to the minimal dialog program presented in Chapter 3. However, during the remaining sections, code listings become too long to present complete listings. Therefore, these sections use a more compact approach. In these sections, code analysis proceeds for specific code organized by implementation steps and around design issue discussions.

Moreover, in many cases, analysis discussion of the code often centers around multiple lines of code rather than single lines of code. This more aggregated approach assumes a Windows programming background so that addressing individual lines of code is no longer necessary.

Drawing Objects Using Rubber Banding

In this section, modifications to the minimal dialog program from Chapter 3 enable the user to draw a line. Drawing a line involves rubber banding. Rubber-banded drawing enables the user to start the line and then drag the mouse until a desired endpoint is found. As the user searches for the desired endpoint, a line displays between the start point and the current endpoint.

TIP

The term rubber banding describes the visual image of the line shrinking and growing as the mouse is dragged, just as a rubber band shortens and lengthens when pulled on the ends.

In Figure 5-1, the graphical user interface and usage instructions appear for drawing a line using rubber banding. The numbers in the figure indicate the sequence of actions performed by your user when drawing a line. Figure 5-1 shows the line in a final location, as dictated by the start point and the final endpoint.

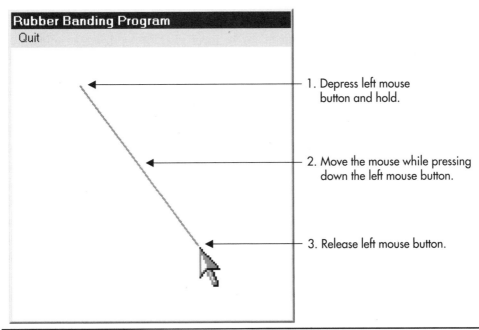

Figure 5-1   *Graphical user interface for the "rubber band" drawing application*

The user begins drawing the line by positioning the mouse cursor at a desired start location. This location becomes the anchor point of the line during all rubber-banding repaint operations. To record the start location, depress and hold the left mouse button. While keeping the left mouse button depressed, drag the mouse to a desired end location. As long as the left mouse button remains depressed, the application continues to redraw the line from the start location to the current mouse cursor location. During the redrawing of the line in response to the mouse movement, the rubber banding occurs. Once the user releases the left mouse button, the program permanently records the last endpoint and redraws the line in the permanent final position.

The algorithm and data parameters necessary to support rubber banding appear in Figure 5-2.

According to the figure, the program must maintain three data points. One data point, DragStart, stores the common start location for all rubber-banding drawing operations. At any time during the rubber-banding operation, the program needs to know the endpoints for two different lines. The first endpoint describes the line most recently drawn. The data point name for this endpoint is DragStop. In order to draw a new line, the current cursor location, indicated by the variables CurrentX and CurrentY, characterizes the end of the line.

Both DragStart and DragStop employ the data type POINT. Each POINT object provides two accessible fields, named x and y. These two values represent the locations of the point in the virtual drawing space supported by Windows and the GDI component.

As far as performing the rubber-banding operations, the program follows the steps indicated in Figure 5-2, using the data parameters previously defined:

1. Erase the old line from DragStart to DragStop.

2. Draw the new line from DragStart to (CurrentX, CurrentY).

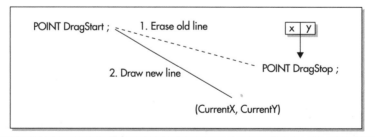

Figure 5-2 *Rubber-banding parameters and drawing algorithm*

Drawing the new line using line-drawing operations is easy to accomplish using the graphics operations described in Chapter 4.

However, recall that the program performs these operations in response to mouse activity by the user. The underlying mouse action sequence appears according to the numbers in Figure 5-3.

When the user begins rubber-banded drawing by pressing the left mouse button, a WM_LBUTTONDOWN message arrives. The dialog procedure receives this message and records the start location of the line object. As the user drags the mouse with the left button depressed, a series of WM_MOUSEMOVE messages occur. Again, these messages arrive at the dialog procedure, causing the old line to be erased and the new line to be drawn.

TIP

The number of WM_MOUSEMOVE messages that Windows emits depends on an internal sampling process to which a program does not have access. A program simply services the WM_MOUSEMOVE messages as the messages arrive at the dialog procedure.

Unfortunately, WM_MOUSEMOVE messages arrive whenever a user is dragging the mouse across the face of an application window. This situation often happens even if the user is not currently performing a rubber-banding operation. To ensure that the dialog procedure only services WM_MOUSEMOVE messages during rubber-banded drawing, a state variable distinguishes between rubber-banding and non-rubber-banding modes.

Eventually, the user releases the left mouse button. As a result, a WM_LBUTTONUP message enters into the dialog procedure. In response, the message handler method for this message executes, terminating rubber-banded drawing operations.

Message handling, data parameter maintenance, and dialog window painting all must work together to obtain the rubber-banding effect. Integration of all these elements into a single operational description appears in Figure 5-4.

User drags a mouse across the screen

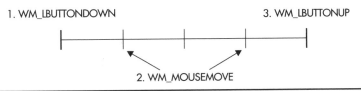

Figure 5-3 *Mouse action sequence during dragging*

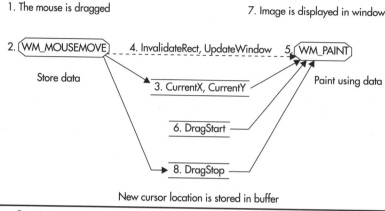

Figure 5-4   *Servicing mouse move messages during dragging*

In Figure 5-4, octagonal labels contain relevant message names. Each of these labels represents the execution of a message handler method in order to service the indicated message. Solid arrows indicate writing and reading the various points as stored data. The source of the data is at the base of the solid arrow. At the head of the arrow appears the destination of the data. The figure also contains dashed lines. These lines indicate the execution of a method. The handler at the base of the dashed arrow executes the method. Then, the handler at the head of the arrow gets executed as a result of the method generating a specific message.

Using this description of the elements in Figure 5-4 and the numbered sequence in the figure, a description of the operational actions is as follows:

1. The user performs a dragging operation using the left mouse button.

2. During this dragging, a continuous series of WM_MOUSEMOVE messages arrives. These message arrivals cause the "mouse move" message handler inside the dialog procedure to execute.

3. Inside the "mouse move" message handler body, the handler updates the data point (CurrentX, CurrentY) using the cursor location arguments provided to the handler.

4. Inside the "mouse move" message handler body, the handler successively executes the methods InvalidateRect and UpdateWindow. This sequence of method calls submits and immediately processes a WM_PAINT message.

5. The paint message handler inside the dialog procedure executes. Immediately executing the paint handler results in a smooth, continuous, flicker-free update that appears like rubber banding to the user.

6. Inside the body of the paint message handler, the variables DragStart and DragStop describe the old line. Using these variables, the handler erases the old line. Then, with DragStart and (CurrentX, CurrentY), the paint message handler generates the new line.

7. After execution of the paint message handler, the new line appears in the client area of the application window.

8. Returning from the paint message handler to the "mouse move" message handler, the "mouse move" handler updates the values of DragStop using the cursor location provided as arguments.

The process being used here is simple. This process separates the maintenance of data from the actual updating of the dialog window. In response to the WM_MOUSEMOVE message, the message handler method updates the data points and then triggers the WM_PAINT message, which causes the data points to be used to update the client area of the dialog window.

TIP

This separation of data maintenance and window updating is a direct application of the event-driven drawing model, as first described in Chapter 1.

To support drawing using rubber banding requires the following changes to the dialog procedure:

1. Add the message handler declarations and empty handler bodies for the button and mouse messages to the dialog procedure.

2. Declare the static variables to manage rubber-banded drawing.

3. Implement the message handler bodies to manage rubber-banded drawing.

4. Modify the paint message handler method to support erasing the old line and drawing the new line.

The code listings that appear in the upcoming sections correlate with the required steps just listed. By using an implementation-based analysis, correlation between the steps followed and the implemented code is a fairly easy process.

Adding Message Handler Declarations and Handler Bodies

Here is the code for the dialog procedure that demonstrates the handler declarations and the additions to the dialog procedure's message switch (note that because a detailed discussion of the handler bodies appears following the listing, the empty bodies need not appear in this listing):

```
void DlgOnLButtonDown(HWND hDlg, BOOL fDoubleClick,
                      int x, int y,
                      UINT keyFlags);
void DlgOnLButtonUp(HWND hDlg, int x, int y, UINT keyFlags);
void DlgOnMouseMove(HWND hDlg, int x, int y, UINT keyFlags);
BOOL CALLBACK DlgProc(HWND hDlg, UINT message, WPARAM wParam, LPARAM lParam )
{
    switch (message)
    {
    // Previously Discussed Lines Omitted
      HANDLE_DLG_MSG(hDlg,WM_LBUTTONDOWN,DlgOnLButtonDown);
      HANDLE_DLG_MSG(hDlg,WM_LBUTTONUP,DlgOnLButtonUp);
      HANDLE_DLG_MSG(hDlg,WM_MOUSEMOVE,DlgOnMouseMove);
    }
    return FALSE ;
}
```

Each of the required handlers appears in this listing. The WM_LBUTTONDOWN messages initiate rubber-banded drawing in the DlgOnLButtonDown handler. Actual rubber-banded drawing occurs in the DlgOnMouseMove message handler connected to the WM_MOUSEMOVE message. When the user releases the left mouse button, the WM_LBUTTONUP message initiates execution of the DlgOnLButtonUp handler, terminating rubber-banded drawing operations.

In order to understand the data available inside the handler bodies, the following discussion describes the arguments to each handler. Obviously, each handler begins the argument list with a handle to the dialog window that initiated the message; only new values in the argument list appear in the detailed discussion that follows.

```
void DlgOnLButtonDown(HWND hDlg, BOOL fDoubleClick,
                      int x, int y,
                      UINT keyFlags);
```

The first new argument in the list is the fDoubleClick flag. This Boolean value indicates when the left mouse button is clicked more than once within a predefined double-click time limit. A TRUE value signals that a double-click occurred.

TIP

Nowhere in the Windows API documentation does the value of the double-click time limit appear.

The argument pair x,y tells the location of the mouse cursor in client area coordinates, relative to the upper-left corner of the client area. Embedded in the keyFlags argument is a series of bits that yield the state of various virtual keys. These bits indicate when specific keys are pressed at the same time as the left mouse button. The keys represented by bits in this bit list include the CTRL key and the SHIFT key. A set of masks are available that allow a program to check individual bits in this list of bits.

```
void DlgOnLButtonUp(HWND hDlg, int x, int y, UINT keyFlags);
void DlgOnMouseMove(HWND hDlg, int x, int y, UINT keyFlags);
```

Both of these method handlers utilize the same argument definitions as the DlgOnLButtonDown method handler.

Declaring the Static Variables Necessary to Support Dragging

Two kinds of variables are necessary to support dragging. One variable is a simple state variable that indicates the state of the program—dragging or not dragging. The other category of variables stores specific data that characterizes the old line and the new line. Here's a complete list of the variables:

```
static BOOL   IsDragging ;
static POINT  DragStart ;
static POINT  DragStop  ;
static int    CurrentX ;
static int    CurrentY ;
```

Each of these variables uses the static storage class attribute. Applying this attribute yields a number of implications. Memory space for these variables resides in a static storage area. Data in this area persists throughout the life of the program. Therefore, this data is available to all the method handlers, regardless of the execution order or time sequence of these handlers. Maintaining this data across execution of multiple message handlers is a necessary element in providing support for rubber-banded drawing. Another effect of this storage class attribute is to hide the variables from code methods in other files. This feature is a side effect in this usage and has no benefit in support of rubber-banded drawing.

NOTE

For a more complex program, these values should be under the control of a global data manager element, as described in Chapter 3. However, for this example, these values appear within the body of the dialog procedure DlgProc so that all the relevant elements for supporting rubber-banded drawing can be viewed in context.

The state variable is the Boolean variable IsDragging. When this value is set to TRUE, the user is drawing and rubber-banded processing occurs. During any idle periods (when the user is not drawing), the program initializes this variable to a FALSE value. All code that supports rubber banding no longer executes, even if the program receives rubber banding–related messages.

In the previous conceptual discussion, definitions are available for the variables DragStart, DragStop, CurrentX, and CurrentY. The data type for DragStart and DragStop is type POINT. This type, defined in the Win32 API, is actually a record structure that contains two fields: x and y. Using this data type enables more convenient declaration of the storage variables and provides a more descriptive declaration of the purpose or functionality of the data.

Implementing the Message Handler Bodies to Manage Drawing

Support for rubber-banded drawing begins with the execution of the DlgOnLButtonDown message handler, the primary goal of which is to initialize the variables that manage drawing:

```
void DlgOnLButtonDown(HWND hDlg, BOOL fDoubleClick,
                      int x, int y, UINT keyFlags)
{
    IsDragging = TRUE ;
    SetCapture(hDlg) ;
    DragStart.x = x ;
    DragStart.y = y ;
    DragStop.x  = x ;
    DragStop.y  = y ;
}
```

Setting the IsDragging flag to TRUE activates all the code that supports rubber-banded drawing operations. Executing the Win32 API method SetCapture tells Windows to send all future mouse messages to the window hDlg. Using this method ensures that the dragging continues, even if the user drags the mouse outside the dialog window.

Once SetCapture has been executed, as the user drags the cursor outside the window, all WM_MOUSEMOVE messages still arrive at the dialog procedure. Cursor locations provided as arguments to these messages still reflect values that are relative to the upper-left corner of the client area of the window. Therefore, new lines are drawn from DragStart to a current location outside of the window. However, the clipping algorithm in the Graphics Device Interface (GDI) viewing pipeline ensures the display of only that portion of the line actually inside the client area.

```
void DlgOnMouseMove(HWND hDlg, int x, int y, UINT keyFlags)
{
  if ( IsDragging )
  {
      CurrentX = x ;
      CurrentY = y ;

      InvalidateRect(hDlg,NULL,FALSE) ;
      UpdateWindow(hDlg) ;

      DragStop.x = x ;
      DragStop.y = y ;
  }
}
```

"Mouse move" messages arrive at the dialog procedure for this application when the mouse cursor crosses the dialog window. Because this situation can occur even if the user is not performing rubber-banded drawing, the first line in this message handler checks to ensure that the IsDragging flag has been set. In other words, this line of code determines whether the program is in the rubber-banded drawing state or mode.

After the check for drawing mode, the message handler updates the values of (CurrentX, CurrentY) to reflect the desired endpoint of the new line being drawn. The sources for updating these current values are the arguments (x,y), arriving at the execution of the message handler.

The next pair of method calls that appear are to the Win32 API methods InvalidateRect and UpdateWindow. Executing these methods in this exact sequence forces an immediate repaint of the dialog window.

TIP

If the program does not immediately execute UpdateWindow, a significant time delay elapses before the update of the client area of the dialog window. This delay can cause the old and new lines to simultaneously appear as dashed lines.

A FALSE value appears as the last argument to the InvalidateRect method. This value disables repainting of the background of the client area. As a result of this disabling, only the area explicitly addressed in the WM_PAINT message handler experiences any change in delay. An optimized painting approach, such as this one, minimizes the CPU overhead required to repaint the client area, yielding a smooth, continuous, nonflickering update of the dialog window.

Once the old line is erased and the new line is drawn inside the paint message handler, the current endpoint in the arguments (x,y) becomes the endpoint of the old line. In the remaining lines of this message handler, these values become the source for updating the fields in the DragStop static variable.

```
void DlgOnLButtonUp(HWND hDlg, int x, int y, UINT keyFlags)
{
   if ( IsDragging )
   {
       ReleaseCapture() ;
       IsDragging = FALSE ;
   }
}
```

After placing the line in the desired location, the user releases the left mouse button. As a result of this release, a WM_LBUTTONUP message arrives at the dialog procedure. The message cracker then routes execution to this message handler, named DlgOnLButtonUp.

After verifying that the program is in a drawing state by checking the value of the state variable IsDragging, this handler simply needs to take two actions. Executing the Win32 API method ReleaseCapture signals to Windows to return to default mouse message routing. Under default routing, any mouse message enters the thread message queue of the window over which the cursor currently resides. As a last step, the message handler sets the IsDragging state variable to FALSE, disabling all the application code that performs rubber-banded drawing.

Modifying the Paint Handler to Support Erasing and Drawing

During "mouse move" message processing, the message handler forces processing of a WM_PAINT message. As a direct consequence of this action, the paint message handler DlgOnPaint executes. The goal of this message handler is to efficiently erase the old line and to draw the new line:

```
void  DlgOnPaint(HWND hDlg)
{
    // Previously Discussed Lines Omitted

    // Erase The Old Line
    SetROP2(DeviceContext,R2_NOTXORPEN) ;
    DrawLineShapeAt(DeviceContext,
                    DragStart.x,DragStart.y,
                    DragStop.x,DragStop.y,
                    2 , PS_SOLID , RGB(255,0,0) ) ;
    // Draw The New Line
    SetROP2(DeviceContext,R2_COPYPEN) ;
    DrawLineShapeAt(DeviceContext,
                    DragStart.x,DragStart.y,
                    CurrentX, CurrentY,
                    2 , PS_SOLID , RGB(255,0,0) ) ;
}
```

Efficient erasing and drawing utilizes a special feature of GDI called *binary raster operation*, which is a description of the manner in which binary pixel values are to be combined. In Windows, every pixel is a 32-bit value that represents a red, green, and blue combination. Therefore, a binary raster operation describes the way in which a pixel from a pen or brush combines with a pixel in the client area of the dialog window.

One example of a binary raster operation is the "copy pen" operation. This operation copies the pixel from the pen to the pixel in the client area location, replacing or ignoring the current client area pixel. Another useful binary raster operation is the "not xor pen" operation. With this operation, a new pixel that represents the inverse of a combination of the colors in the pen and in the client area location (but not in both pixels) replaces the original screen pixel.

A clearer description of the "not xor pen" operation might be as follows:

```
if   ( Client Area Pixel != Background Pixel )
    Convert Client Area Pixel To Background Pixel ;
else
    Copy Pen Pixel To Client Area Pixel ;
```

NOTE

The real benefit to "not xor pen" binary raster operations is to efficiently erase a specific image in the client area. If a drawing operation, such as drawing a line, uses this binary raster operation, pixels in the client area turn into background pixels, effectively erasing the previously drawn line. In this way, the drawing operation focuses only on the specific pixels along the line rather than erasing the whole bounding rectangle of the line or erasing the whole background of the client area.

An important drawing tool in the device context/drawing toolkit provided by GDI is the binary raster operation to be used in all pen and brush operations. The default operation is the R2_COPYPEN raster operation, which simply replaces client area pixels with pen or brush pixels. In order to erase a previously drawn object, the program resets the included binary raster operation to R2_NOTXORPEN.

Therefore, the code logic in the paint message handler employs the following sequence:

1. Use the method SetROP2 to initialize the binary raster operation in the device context to R2_NOTXORPEN.

2. Draw the old line from DragStart to DragStop, which efficiently erases the old line.

3. Use the method SetROP2 to restore the binary raster operation in the device context to R2_COPYPEN.

4. Draw the new line from DragStart to (CurrentX, CurrentY), which simply draws the new line.

Each of the drawing operations in the paint message handler uses the method DrawLineShapeAt. This method is one of the encapsulation methods for the drawing operations defined in Chapter 4.

Both the erasing and the drawing operations modify only the pixels on the actual line. All other pixels remain exactly the same. As a result of this precise focus, the erasing and redrawing yields the most efficient performance, providing the minimum possible screen refresh execution time.

Typing and Echoing Characters

The next enhancement to the drawing program is the capability to attach a text label anywhere in the drawing. A user might want to place a signature on the drawing or may need to attach labels to the axes of a graph. A drawing program can support either of these goals using the features added in this section.

For simplicity, this sample implementation retains the contents and location of a single text string. By using this simple approach, the focus is on the mechanics of supporting type and echo processing without extensive confusion resulting from other application issues.

TIP

The principles used to support type and echo processing in this program are the same approaches used for any type- and echo-based program. Samples of typical type- and echo-processing programs include terminal emulation programs and word processing programs.

Figure 5-5 displays the graphical user interface that characterizes the type and echo features to be added to the drawing program.

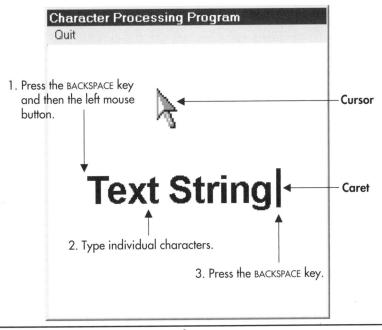

Figure 5-5   *Character-processing user interface*

The user places the interface into text-entry mode. Upon entry into this mode, the application displays a caret. As the user types characters from the keyboard, the program echoes these characters to the client area of the application window. As each character is typed, the caret moves to the right to allow room to display the typed character. The caret indicates to the user that the application is in text-entry mode. Additionally, the caret informs the user of the next available location for a character. After all characters have been typed, the user exits from text-entry mode. In response to mode exit, the program removes the caret from display.

Numbered captions in Figure 5-5 indicate the sequence of actions performed by the user during text entry. The specific sequence of actions performed by the user is as follows:

1. The user enters text-entry mode by pressing and holding the BACKSPACE key and clicking the mouse cursor at a start location in the client area. The caret appears at the indicated location.

2. As the user types characters, the caret disappears, the new character displays at the end of the string, and the caret reappears.

3. By pressing the BACKSPACE key, the user exits text-entry mode. The caret permanently disappears.

The numbers in the preceding sequence match the numbers that appear in Figure 5-5.

NOTE

This process utilizes two steps prior to text entry. The Backspace key signals entry into type- and echo-processing mode, and the left mouse button click indicates the string location. These steps must be performed in exactly this sequence. Clearly, this approach is inefficient for a user. On a desktop system, both steps could be simultaneously accomplished by clicking the right mouse button. Similarly, clicking the right mouse button could be the basis for exiting text-entry mode. However, because this application is to execute on a Pocket PC, a right mouse button is unavailable. The two-step setup is necessary to accommodate the limited user input capability of the Pocket PC hardware.

Figure 5-5 distinguishes between a cursor and a caret. Distinct differences exist between the two elements. The cursor is a graphical object that visually reveals the current location of the mouse. Windows automatically displays and moves the cursor on behalf of the user as the user drags the mouse around the desktop. A caret, however, is an entity that strictly exists under the control of an application program. A caret is a graphical object that the program employs during text-entry operations. This object shows the user the next available location for display of a typed character. When using a caret, the Windows program must specifically show the caret, hide the caret, and move the caret under the appropriate conditions. This section provides the program mechanics for using the caret during text-entry mode.

Because an application program is responsible for moving the caret each time the user types a character, data parameters and algorithms are necessary. The elements that a program employs to move the caret revolve primarily around computing the caret location after entry of a newly typed character. Figure 5-6 shows the elements that contribute to computing a new caret location.

When the user initiates text-entry mode, the program determines and stores the location of the cursor in a static variable named TextLocation. Because this variable is of data type POINT, the anchor point for the text string becomes (TextLocation.x, TextLocation.y).

After establishing the anchor point, as the user types each new character, the program determines the offset to the caret location. The key parameter used to determine the caret offset depends on the width of the text string to display, including the new character that the user typed. Every text string possesses a bounding rectangle. Typically, the size of the bounding rectangle depends on the characteristics of the font used to display the text string.

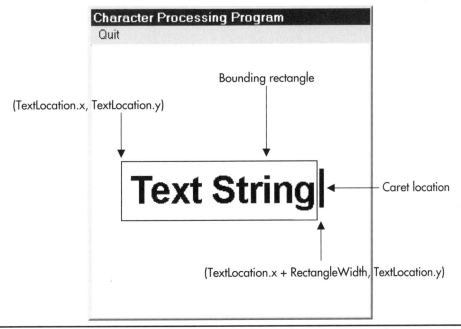

Figure 5-6   *Computing the caret location using the text-bounding rectangle*

To compute the X offset for the caret location, the program simply adds the width of the bounding rectangle. A Y offset for the caret location is unnecessary. In equation form, the caret location may be computed as follows:

```
CaretXLocation = TextLocation.x + BoundingRectangleWidth ;
CaretYLocation = TextLocation.y ;
```

TIP

When displaying a text string, a Windows program uses the Win32 API method ExtTextOut. This method assumes that the provided start location (TextLocation.x, TextLocation.y) is the upper-left corner of the bounding rectangle.

The first step in implementing the type-and-echo feature into a drawing program is to understand the mechanics of processing character keystrokes. A description of character processing appears in Figure 5-7.

Using the numbers in Figure 5-7, an operational description is available that characterizes the essence of type and echo processing, as follows:

1. After initiating text-entry mode, the user types a character.

2. In response, Windows generates a WM_CHAR message that arrives at the dialog procedure. The character message handler executes, receiving a character code for the pressed key.

3. Inside the body of the character message handler, the handler appends the character to a buffer variable named TextData.

4. After updating the buffer variable TextData, the message handler executes the InvalidateRect and UpdateWindow methods to force a redraw of the client area.

5. In response, Windows generates a WM_PAINT message and immediately executes the paint message handler.

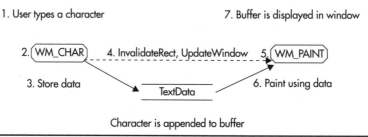

Figure 5-7   *Servicing character messages*

6. Inside the body of the paint message handler, the program uses the updated text string in buffer TextData to repaint the text string to the client area of the application window.

7. The updated text string appears in the client area of the application window with the new character appended to the end of the text string.

Every time the user presses a character key in text-entry mode, the program executes this sequence. The most recently typed character appears at the end of the displayed text string, exhibiting the type and echo capability.

TIP

This programming sequence is just another direct application of the event-driven drawing model illustrated in Figure 1-10. The preceding process, like the previous example for rubber-banded drawing, separates data maintenance and updating from client area drawing and updating.

However, this sequence fails to show the way in which caret processing works. Figure 5-8 demonstrates the character-processing sequence extended to include caret processing.

A comparison of Figure 5-7 and Figure 5-8 reveals the following additional steps after the character type and echo processing in order to move the caret:

8. Inside the body of the WM_CHAR message handler, compute the new caret location. Emit a WM_POSITIONCARET message using the Win32 API SendMessage method.

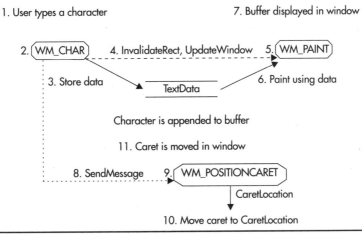

Figure 5-8   *Updating the caret using custom caret events*

9. Provide the new caret location as message arguments to the WM_POSITIONCARET message.

10. Inside the body of the WM_POSITIONCARET message handler, use the new caret location to move the caret.

11. As a result of this program-controlled caret processing, the caret disappears, moves beyond the last character that was typed and echoed, and reappears in the client area of the window.

The numbers in the preceding sequence correspond exactly to the sequence numbers employed in Figure 5-8.

A long and tedious search of the documentation for the Win32 API reveals that the message WM_POSITIONCARET does not exist. This message is actually a program-defined message specific to this application. In order to utilize a custom message, a program defines a message code and declares a message cracker for the message switch of the dialog procedure. Inside the body of the message handler for this custom message, the program uses the Win32 API methods HideCaret, SetCaretPos, and ShowCaret to move the caret to the indicated position.

TIP

Obviously, a custom message is not needed to move the caret. A special helper method could easily accomplish this same task. However, a program often needs one or more custom messages. Therefore, this specific implementation introduces the mechanics of using custom messages so that this technique is available when needed.

In Figures 5-7 and 5-8, character type and echo processing starts with the receipt of a WM_CHAR message. In this program, a WM_CHAR message never enters the primary thread message queue. Windows generates a WM_CHAR message after every WM_KEYDOWN message when the message loop executes the Win32 API method TranslateMessage as the first statement inside the message loop of a Windows main program. Because this program uses the message loop inside the DialogBox method, injecting TranslateMessage into the main message loop is impossible. For this reason, the WM_KEYDOWN message handler in this application directly executes the WM_CHAR message handler. Here's the general logic for the WM_KEYDOWN message handler:

```
convert the key into a character code ;
if the character is alphanumeric then
    if the shift key is pressed then
        convert the character from uppercase to lowercase
```

```
        end if
        pass the character to the WM_CHAR message handler
end if
```

Although this approach may seem like a clunky way to accomplish simulating WM_CHAR messages, the benefits far outweigh the losses due to the absence of WM_CHAR messages.

NOTE

Using the DialogBox method to control an application enables a developer to employ the drag-and-drop, visually immediate dialog editor to construct complex graphical user interfaces. This approach offers a significant increase in productivity, shortening the time to market. Having to simulate character messages through direct execution of the WM_CHAR message handler is the cost of this gain in productivity. Because GUI generation for the Pocket PC occurs far more frequently than supporting type and echo processing, the resultant reduction in time to market is well worth the cost of a little extra processing to support type and echo operations.

This chapter introduces another functional encapsulation—the text-processing functions. Throughout this book, text processing often requires repeated reuse of certain capabilities. An example of these capabilities is the need to compute the bounding rectangle for a text string. Stored in a file named TextFns.c is a set of text-processing functions that contains a function to compute the bounding rectangle of a text string. The prototype for this function is as follows:

```
void GetTextRectangle(HWND hWindow,
                      TCHAR * lpszInputString, int iStringSize ,
                          int iLocationX , int iLocationY,
                      LPRECT lprctRectangleArea) ;
```

Support for character type and echo processing requires the following changes to an application program:

1. Implement a text function encapsulation that provides commonly used methods for supporting text processing.

2. Add the static variables necessary to maintain the text-entry state and to buffer a text string.

3. Define a message code and message cracker for the custom WM_POSITIONCARET message.

4. Incorporate message handling for the WM_KEYDOWN, WM_CHAR, and WM_POSITIONCARET messages.

5. In the body of the WM_KEYDOWN message handler, initiate entry into text-processing mode, handle characters, and then exit from text-processing mode.

6. In the body of the WM_LBUTTONDOWN message handler, add support for marking the start location of the text string and create the caret.

7. In the body of the WM_CHAR message handler, perform the text-processing and caret-management operations described in Figure 5-8.

8. In the body of the WM_POSITIONCARET message handler, move the caret beyond the end of the updated text string.

9. In the body of the WM_PAINT message handler, display the text string from the text buffer.

The actual code necessary to implement each of these changes appears in the following sections. A step-by-step analysis shows all the required code.

Implementing the Text Function Encapsulation

Because this program as well as many others in this book utilize text strings, a number of the common operations on text strings appear in an encapsulation class called TextFns. In the following discussion, only the methods relevant to this application appear. Discussion of the remaining methods appear in other chapters when the methods come into use.

Frequently, a message handler needs to compute the bounding rectangle of a text string. The following method, GetTextRectangle, performs this calculation using several methods provided by the Win32 API:

```
void GetTextRectangle(HWND hWindow,
                      TCHAR * lpszInputString, int iStringSize,
                      int iLocationX , int iLocationY,
                      LPRECT lprctRectangleArea)
{
  SIZE TextSize ;
  HDC  hDC ;

  hDC = GetDC(hWindow) ;
  GetTextExtentPoint32( hDC , lpszInputString , iStringSize , &TextSize ) ;
  ReleaseDC(hWindow,hDC) ;
  lprctRectangleArea->top      = iLocationY ;
  lprctRectangleArea->left     = iLocationX ;
  lprctRectangleArea->right    = iLocationX + TextSize.cx ;
```

```
    lprctRectangleArea->bottom  = iLocationY + TextSize.cy ;
}
```

As the first argument, this method receives hWindow, a handle to the window in which the text string is to appear. The text string, stored in lpszInputString, and the number of characters in the input string iStringSize follow next in the argument list. Because this program is to port to a Pocket PC, the platform-portable character data type TCHAR applies to the argument lpszInputString. In order to compute the bounding rectangle, this method needs the upper-left corner of the rectangle, identified in the argument list as iLocationX and iLocationY. Once the bounding rectangle is determined, the rectangle returns to the calling method stored in the memory locations pointed to by lprctRectangleArea. This argument uses the data type LPRECT, which represents a long pointer to a RECT data structure. By definition in windows.h, a RECT data structure contains four fields: top, left, right, and bottom.

TIP

This long pointer stuff hails back to the days of 16-bit Windows, version 3.1. In order for a pointer to reference a location greater than 64KB away, the variable storing the pointer had to be explicitly declared as a long pointer. In the original Windows API, Microsoft had kindly defined a bunch of data types, such as LPRECT, that explicitly declared the long attribute. With the advent of 32-bit Windows in Windows 95, the explicit casting is no longer required. However, because all Windows programs had used these helper types, the Win32 API still allows their usage. For all practical purposes, the long property of these helper types has no meaning these days. In fact, the Win32 API defines LPRECT as RECT *, meaning a pointer to a rectangle structure.

In order to compute the bounding rectangle, this method first determines the size of the text string—width and height. This size then adds to the upper-left corner to calculate the lower-right corner of the bounding rectangle. Determining the size requires a device context. An application can acquire a device context for a window at any time—not just inside the WM_PAINT message handler—using the Win32 API method GetDC. Based on the input of a window handle (hWindow) as the argument, this method returns a device context (hDC) for the window.

Embedded within the device context is a font. This font determines the width and height of the text string to be displayed in the window using the device context. The actual calculation of the size—width and height—of the text string requires the method GetTextExtentPoint32, provided by the Win32 API. The first argument to this method is the device context (hDC) that contains the font. After this value appears the base address of the input string (lpszInputString) and the number of characters in the string (iStringSize). Inside the method, Windows computes the width and height, returning the values inside the variable TextSize. This variable is data type SIZE, declared by the Win32 API, containing fields cx and cy. The width of the text string is TextSize.cx, and TextSize.cy stores the height of the string.

After the text string extents have been computed, this encapsulating method returns the device context to Windows. Both the window, hWindow, and the device context, hDC, pass to the Win32 API method ReleaseDC. Returning the device context enables other applications to reuse it. Windows only maintains a limited number of these resources, so returning the resources is critical to the reliable behavior of all applications.

As the final logical step, this helper method fills the bounding rectangle in the provided RECT structure. The left and top values are the same as the input values iLocationY and iLocationX, respectively. Initializing the right and bottom values requires that the string size offsets be added to the upper-left corner input values. For example, the bottom side of the bounding rectangle consists of the top value iLocationY offset by the height of the text string stored in TextSize.cy.

A clever and productive programming approach is to reuse other elements of the encapsulating class TextFns to create new methods. This next method accomplishes exactly that reuse. In the method GetTextWidth, the method body first computes the bounding rectangle and then uses this rectangle to determine the width of the text:

```
void GetTextWidth( HWND hWindow,
                   TCHAR * lpszInputString , int iStringSize ,
                   int * iTextWidth )
{
  RECT rctTmpRect ;

  GetTextRectangle(hWindow,lpszInputString,iStringSize,0,0,&rctTmpRect) ;
  *iTextWidth = rctTmpRect.right - rctTmpRect.left ;
}
```

After executing the encapsulating method GetTextRectangle, this method computes the width of the text string from the temporary rectangle rctTmpRect. Obviously, text width is the difference between the right edge of the bounding rectangle and the left edge of the rectangle. By reusing the existing method, the developer does not have to retype and again debug the code that already works inside GetTextRectangle.

Adding Variables to Maintain Text Entry State and a Text String

The variables used to support text entry fall into two categories. State variables represent a series of intermediate steps that the user follows to establish the type and echo state, and numeric and string variables store actual data associated with text processing.

```
static BOOL  TypingText = FALSE ;
static BOOL  TextInitialized = FALSE ;
static BOOL  PositionSet = FALSE ;
static POINT TextLocation ;
static TCHAR TextData[50] ;
static int   CurrentChar = 0 ;
```

In this list of variables, the first three variables maintain text-processing status information. The variable TypingText indicates when the user is entering text. This variable is set upon entry into and exit from text-entry mode. In order to control the display of the text string, the program uses the variable TextInitialized. When the user enters text-entry mode, this variable is set to TRUE. The variable remains at this value, even after the user exits text-entry mode, so that the WM_PAINT handler continues to display the text string during every client area redraw. Because the user first enters text-entry mode and then clicks the mouse cursor to indicate the text location, the variable PositionSet signals that the text location has been initialized.

For storing the location of the upper-right corner of the bounding rectangle of the text string, the code segment shown earlier declares the variable TextLocation. This variable uses the POINT data type, a record structure with x and y fields. The actual text string data buffer uses the name TextData. Because this program is to port to the Pocket PC using Windows CE, the portable data type TCHAR comprises the medium for storing characters. As the user adds characters, the program tracks the next available location for new character entry into the data buffer TextData using the variable CurrentChar.

Defining the Custom WM_POSITIONCARET Message

Any Windows program can define application-specific user messages. Defining an application-specific message requires that a message code be defined and that a message cracker be generated. These steps appear in the following code segment:

```
#define WM_POSITIONCARET WM_USER + 0x100
#define HANDLE_DLG_WM_POSITIONCARET(hDlg, wParam, lParam, fn) \
                ( (fn)((hDlg),(int)(wParam),(int)(lParam) ), 0L)
```

Defining a new message code employs the Win32 API–provided symbol WM_USER. A symbolic constant named WM_POSITIONCARET uses the predefined base WM_USER plus an offset (in this case, 100 hex).

TIP

Originally, the symbolic constant WM_USER was to be the base for all user-defined messages. Microsoft had promised not to use any of the message codes above this value. Some developer at Microsoft failed to read this documentation and hard-coded the message codes between WM_USER and WM_USER + 0x100 into the message set for the common controls (to be discussed in Chapter 8). So, now all user messages must start at WM_USER + 0x100!

Implementing a message cracker for the new messages entails a bit more work. The message cracker inserts into the message switch of the dialog procedure in the following form:

```
HANDLE_DLG_MSG(hDlg, WM_POSITIONCARET , DlgOnPositionCaret) ;
```

In the header file windowsy.h, this macro already exists. Looking into the header file reveals the declaration of this macro as this:

```
#define HANDLE_DLG_MSG(hwnd, message, fn)    \
case (message): return HANDLE_DLG_##message((hwnd),(wParam), (lParam), (fn))
```

This macro expands to replace the message code in a case statement and substitutes the message symbol in the HANDLE_DLG_##message string. In order to provide a message cracker for the message WM_POSITIONCARET, the program declares a macro called HANDLE_DLG_WM_POSITIONCARET. This macro must inform Windows as to how to map the incoming message parameters wParam and lParam to the arguments of the message handler.

Repeating from the previous code listing, the specific message cracker for the WM_POSITIONCARET message is as follows:

```
#define HANDLE_DLG_WM_POSITIONCARET(hDlg, wParam, lParam, fn) \
                ( (fn)((hDlg),(int)(wParam),(int)(lParam) ), 0L)
```

According to this macro, the handler for this message takes two arguments, because the substitution argument list in the macro contains only two entries. The preceding message cracker for this message converts the wParam into an int value and passes this value as the first argument to the handler. Similarly, the lParam becomes an int value and passes as the second argument to the message handler. At the end of the macro appears the argument 0L. This value is a return value for a list-processing macro. The compiler preprocessor performs all the previous list operations (only one list entry in this case) and then returns this value. Comparing it with the definition of HANDLE_DLG_MSG reveals that this value is the return value for the specific case inside the message switch.

One element that's not clear from these definitions is the meaning of the arguments to the message handler. In reality, these two arguments can represent anything the sender and definer of the message choose for them to mean. The answer to this apparent dilemma appears in the message handler prototype:

```
void DlgOnPositionCaret(HWND hDlg, int CaretXLocation , int CaretYLocation ) ;
```

According to this declaration, the two arguments in wParam and lParam provide the desired location of the caret.

NOTE

This whole message-cracking scheme only works if the program sending the message places the desired caret location into wParam and lParam.

Incorporating the Handling of Character-Related Messages

Three messages play a role in providing type and echo features to the program. The WM_KEYDOWN message handler DlgOnKeyDown manages over all the type and echo processing. Handling for each individual character occurs within the WM_CHAR message handler DlgOnChar. Caret management is under the control of the WM_POSITIONCARET message handler DlgOnPositionCaret.

```
void DlgOnChar(HWND hDlg, UINT ch, int cRepeat);
void DlgOnKeyDown(HWND hDlg, UINT vk, BOOL fDown, int cRepeat, UINT flags);
void DlgOnPositionCaret(HWND hDlg, int CaretXLocation, int CaretYLocation);
BOOL CALLBACK DlgProc(HWND hDlg, UINT message, WPARAM wParam, LPARAM lParam )
{
    switch (message)
    {
        // Previously Discussed Lines Omitted
        HANDLE_DLG_MSG(hDlg,WM_CHAR,DlgOnChar) ;
        HANDLE_DLG_MSG(hDlg,WM_KEYDOWN,DlgOnKeyDown) ;
        HANDLE_DLG_MSG(hDlg, WM_POSITIONCARET , DlgOnPositionCaret) ;
    }
    return FALSE ;
}
```

As with every message handler, these handlers receive the handle to the dialog window hDlg of type HWND as the first argument. After the first argument, remaining arguments reflect data more appropriate to the message.

```
void DlgOnKeyDown(HWND hDlg, UINT vk, BOOL fDown, int cRepeat, UINT flags);
```

As the first argument, this handler sees a virtual key code, vk. This code represents the key pressed using a code that is independent from the bit pattern generated by the specific keyboard vendor. Using hardware-independent codes ensures that switching keyboards has no effect on the message handler code.

When a user presses a specific key multiple times before the WM_KEYDOWN message is processed by the dialog procedure, the next two arguments come into play. The argument fDown indicates whether the key was pressed once or multiple times. If this value is set to TRUE, the cRepeat argument indicates the number of presses of this specific key prior to servicing the message.

The flags argument characterizes special keyboard situations that will not be relevant for the Pocket PC. Because the Pocket PC uses a keyboard on the screen, none of these conditions will occur. Therefore, this argument may be effectively ignored during message handling for a Pocket PC–targeted application.

```
void DlgOnChar(HWND hDlg, UINT ch, int cRepeat);
```

The primary argument of interest for this message is the second argument, named ch. This argument contains the actual character that needs to be processed. For Windows programs, the data type UINT is completely interchangeable with char, WCHAR, or TCHAR. The value stored in ch represents the ASCII code for the incoming character.

TIP

An ASCII code and a virtual key code are unique and distinct values. The ASCII code set is defined by an outside agency — the American National Standards Institute (ANSI). Virtual key codes are numeric representations defined by Microsoft and translated by the keyboard device driver. Because WM_KEYDOWN receives a virtual key code, the message handler for this message translates into an ASCII character code prior to transmitting the WM_CHAR message or directly executing the DlgOnChar message handler.

Implementing the WM_KEYDOWN Message Handler

The primary message handler that manages the type- and echo-processing feature is the WM_KEYDOWN handler DlgOnKeyDown. This handler manages entry into, exit from, or continuous operations of type and echo processing:

```
void DlgOnKeyDown(HWND hDlg, UINT vk, BOOL fDown, int cRepeat, UINT flags)
{
    TCHAR Character ;
    SHORT ShiftPressed ;
```

```
    switch( vk )
    {
    case VK_BACK:
        if ( !TypingText )
        {
            TypingText      = TRUE ;
            TextInitialized = TRUE ;
            _tcscpy(TextData,__TEXT("") );
            CurrentChar = 0 ;
        }
        else
        {
          TypingText = FALSE ;
          PositionSet = FALSE ;
          HideCaret(hDlg) ;
          DestroyCaret() ;
        }
        break ;
    default:
        if ( PositionSet )
        {
            Character = MapVirtualKey(vk,2) ;
            if (IsCharAlphaNumeric(Character) || (Character == ' '))
{
                ShiftPressed = GetKeyState(VK_SHIFT) ;
                if ( ShiftPressed >= 0 )
                    Character = _totlower(Character) ;
                DlgOnChar(hDlg,Character, cRepeat) ;
            }
        }
        break ;
    }
}
```

Upon entry, the handler must first determine the kind of processing necessary. The general decision-making logic of this handler appears in the following pseudo-code:

```
if ( backspace key and not processing text ) then
    enter type and echo processing ;
else if (backspace key and processing text ) then
    exit type and echo processing ;
else
    perform type and echo processing ;
end if
```

Implementing this logic involves a switch statement with nested if statements and default processing for the final else processing. In order to determine whether the BACKSPACE key is pressed, the handler compares the incoming virtual key code in the argument vk with the value represented by the symbolic constant VK_BACK.

Entry and exit into type and echo processing are both simple to implement. Each of these operations requires that certain state and data variables be initialized. Especially important to remember is that the string data buffer TextData initializes to the empty string.

TIP

If the string data buffer TextData does not get initialized, the WM_PAINT handler displays whatever garbage is in the memory locations allocated to this buffer. This display is definitely an unpleasant side effect.

Upon termination of type and echo processing, this message handler also hides the caret and destroys the caret. Both of these operations use Win32 API methods with the obvious names HideCaret and DestroyCaret. Critical to this sequence is executing the method DestroyCaret. Windows maintains a single caret across all applications. If the program fails to perform this method, the caret resource does not return to the system. Any other application that tries to acquire the caret (which will be described shortly) fails, causing the application to behave oddly. The caret never appears in the other application.

Of greater interest is the sequence of steps performed during continuous type and echo processing. This processing converts the virtual key code in argument vk to an ASCII character code using the method MapVirtualKey. This method, provided by the Win32 API, always converts alphabetic characters into uppercase characters. If the character is an alphanumeric character or a space, the handler performs the echo processing.

Because the character begins life as an uppercase character, the handler checks the SHIFT key using the method GetKeyState and converts the character to lowercase using the method _totlower. A portable version of the conversion method appears here because this code will eventually reside on a Pocket PC. Finally, the character and the repeat count, cRepeat, pass directly to the WM_CHAR message handler DlgOnChar.

NOTE

This logic consists of precisely the core logic that would be performed by the method TranslateMessage inside the message loop of the main Windows program. Because this program is using the hidden message loop of the method DialogBox for the productivity reasons described earlier, this message handler explicitly performs the job normally performed by TranslateMessage.

Updating the WM_LBUTTONDOWN Message Handler

With this extension to the drawing program, the left mouse button serves two different roles. If the user has not entered the type and echo mode, clicking the left mouse button signals the start of rubber-banded drawing. However, if the user previously pressed the BACKSPACE key to enter type and echo operations, a left mouse click signals the location of the upper-left corner of the bounding rectangle for the text string.

Logically, some very simple pseudo-code expresses this dual usage for the left mouse button:

```
if ( not typing text ) then
    initiate rubber-banded drawing
else
    mark text location for type and echo
end if
```

All this logic exists in the WM_LBUTTONDOWN message handler DlgOnLButtonDown. In this handler, the state variable TypingText controls routing to the code specific to each of the uses of the left mouse button:

```
void DlgOnLButtonDown(HWND hDlg, BOOL fDoubleClick,
                      int x, int y, UINT keyFlags)
{
  int   TextHeight  ;

  if ( !TypingText )
  {
     IsDragging = TRUE ;
     SetCapture(hDlg) ;
     DragStart.x = x ;
     DragStart.y = y ;
     DragStop.x  = x ;
     DragStop.y  = y ;
  }
  else
  {
      if (!PositionSet)
      {
           PositionSet = TRUE ;
           TextLocation.x  = x ;
           TextLocation.y  = y ;
```

```
        GetTextHeight(hDlg,__TEXT("W"),1,&TextHeight) ;
        CreateCaret(hDlg,NULL,2,TextHeight) ;
        SetCaretPos(TextLocation.x,TextLocation.y) ;
        ShowCaret(hDlg) ;
      }
    }
  }
```

The code segment that initiates rubber-banded drawing appears in the if portion of the handler body. A discussion of this code appears earlier in this chapter. No changes are necessary for type and echo processing other than wrapping the code inside the if portion of the if statement.

In the else part of the handler body, the program establishes the data and resources necessary to support type and echo processing. After checking to ensure that the text position has not been initialized, the handler performs the data initialization and the resource allocation. The flag PositionSet initializes to TRUE, indicating that the position has now been set. After updating this state variable, the handler then initializes the fields of TextLocation using the incoming mouse cursor locations x and y. For type and echo processing, the caret is the only resource that has to be acquired and initialized.

As the first step in establishing the caret resource, the message handler uses the method GetTextHeight, supplied by the text function encapsulation TextFns, to determine a height for the caret. A good character for determining the height of the caret is *W*. This character is the largest character; therefore, using the height of this character suffices to obtain a proportionally sized caret. Because this program is to ultimately execute on a Pocket PC, the macro __TEXT surrounds the single-character string containing the *W* character.

Windows maintains a single caret across all executing applications. When an application needs to display the caret, the application reserves the caret resource using the CreateCaret method available from the Win32 API. Arguments to this method indicate the width of the caret (2) and the height of the caret (TextHeight).

After acquiring the caret resource, the message handler sets the location using the method SetCaretPos and provides the field values TextLocation.x and TextLocation.y. A final step employs the Win32 API method ShowCaret to signal to Windows to display the caret at the indicated location over the window hDlg.

When executing the method SetCaretPos, a handle to the caret resource is unnecessary. Because Windows maintains a single caret across all applications, the handle to this resource resides within Windows. Every time a program executes SetCaretPos, Windows automatically accesses the internally cached handle to the caret resource. This approach effectively encapsulates the caret, relieving you, the application programmer, of the need to maintain and manage this extraneous information.

Implementing the WM_CHAR Message Handler

Once the program enters type and echo mode, every WM_KEYDOWN message passes the typed character to the DlgOnChar message handler. This handler serves to append the character to the text buffer, display the buffered string inside the client area, and force the caret to move:

```
void DlgOnChar(HWND hDlg, UINT ch, int cRepeat)
{
    RECT TextRect ;
    int TextWidth ;

    if (PositionSet)
    {
        TextData[CurrentChar]   = ch   ;
        TextData[CurrentChar+1] = '\0' ;
        CurrentChar = CurrentChar + 1 ;

        GetTextRectangle(hDlg, TextData, _tcslen(TextData) ,
                    TextLocation.x , TextLocation.y,
                    (LPRECT)&TextRect ) ;

        InvalidateRect(hDlg,(LPRECT) &TextRect , TRUE) ;
        UpdateWindow(hDlg) ;

        GetTextWidth(hDlg,TextData,_tcslen(TextData),&TextWidth) ;
        SendMessage(hDlg , WM_POSITIONCARET ,
                    (WPARAM)TextLocation.x + TextWidth ,
                    (LPARAM)TextLocation.y ) ;
    }
}
```

This message handler body only executes if the text position has been set by the user typing the BACKSPACE key to enter echo mode and then clicking the left mouse button. Under these conditions, the variable PositionSet has the value TRUE, enabling the code of the message handler body. If this requirement were not enforced, characters would appear at random locations anytime the user typed a character at the keyboard. By using the PositionSet variable to enforce the prerequisite conditions, type and echo processing works correctly.

After verifying the prerequisite conditions, the handler adds the character stored in the argument ch to the end of the data buffer TextData in the next available location indicated by CurrentChar. Incrementing CurrentChar then points to the next location in the data buffer for the next incoming character.

Prior to displaying the text string in TextData, the handler executes the method GetTextRectangle to determine the bounding rectangle for the text string. The text function encapsulation TextFns provides this method. Arguments include the actual text string in TextData, the length of the string as computed by the target platform-independent string method _tcslen, the location of the upper-left corner of the bounding rectangle stored in the fields TextLocation.x and TextLocation.y, and a pointer to a RECT structure for receiving the bounding rectangle (&TextRect).

Forcing a repaint is the result of the consecutive method calls to InvalidateRect and UpdateWindow. The arguments to InvalidateRect include a pointer to the RECT variable TextRect and the redraw flag value being set to TRUE. This combination yields an efficient redrawing of the client area.

NOTE

By passing the bounding rectangle in TextRect and the redraw flag value of TRUE, the message handler forces Windows to paint the background only within the bounding rectangle indicated in TextRect. Limiting the background repainting to this small area enables the repaint inside the WM_PAINT message handler to be extremely efficient as well as very smooth and flicker-free. This quick repaint simply erases the old string and draws the new string, completely ignoring the remainder of the client area.

In the remaining lines of code, this message handler repositions the caret. Repositioning is a two-step process. Using the method GetTextWidth from the TextFns encapsulation, the message handler determines TextWidth, the number of pixels to offset the horizontal location of the caret from the start location of the text string. After computing this offset, the handler then uses SendMessage from the Win32 API to pack the cursor location into a WM_POSITIONCARET message and to immediately execute the message handler for this latter message. Using the formula discussed in Figure 5-6, the horizontal offset of the cursor location combines the base location of the text string, TextLocation.x, with the computed offset in TextWidth.

The Win32 API provides the method SendMessage. This method suspends processing of the dialog procedure at the current location, reenters the dialog procedure, and immediately executes the message handler for the indicated message code. This process completely bypasses the primary thread message queue. As a result, the response to executing this method is immediate and rapid. In this situation, an immediate response involves the caret moving to the new location after the newly typed character. After executing the message handler for the WM_POSITIONCARET message, execution control returns to this WM_CHAR message handler and executes any remaining code.

TIP

Another method for submitting a message to an application is the PostMessage method provided by the Win32 API. This method places the message into the primary thread message queue for the window. As a result, a perceptible delay may incur before the message works to the front of the queue. In the case of positioning the caret, this delay would be aggravating to the user, who is likely to keep typing.

Implementing the WM_POSITIONCARET Message Handler

This message handler moves the caret from a current location to a new location. Moving the caret consists of hiding the caret, setting the caret location, and then showing the caret, as shown here:

```
void DlgOnPositionCaret(HWND hDlg, int CaretXLocation , int CaretYLocation )
{
    HideCaret(hDlg) ;
    SetCaretPos( CaretXLocation, CaretYLocation ) ;
    ShowCaret(hDlg) ;
}
```

All the methods in this handler appear in previous discussions. These methods are members of the Win32 API, accessed via the header file windows.h.

Displaying a Text String in the WM_PAINT Message Handler

Displaying the text string entered by the user is the primary enhancement required in the WM_PAINT message handler. Prior to drawing the text, the paint handler sets the text background color to match the background color of the client area, as shown here:

```
void  DlgOnPaint(HWND hDlg)
{
   COLORREF   OldTextColor ;
   // Previously Discussed Lines Omitted
```

```
    if (TextInitialized)
    {
      OldTextColor = SetBkColor(DeviceContext,RGB(255,255,255) ) ;
      ExtTextOut(DeviceContext,TextLocation.x,TextLocation.y,
                 0,NULL,TextData,_tcslen(TextData),NULL) ;
      SetBkColor(DeviceContext,OldTextColor) ;
    }
}
```

After painting the complete background of the client area, this code displays the current text in the text buffer TextData. In order to display the text, the handler must first ascertain that the text has been initialized, as indicated by the state variable TextInitialized. If the text has not been initialized, the text-painting code is disabled.

Another tool inside the device context/drawing toolkit is the background color for the text. This color fills the bounding rectangle around the actual text. In order to ensure that the text melds correctly with the background of the client area, the message handler uses the method SetBkColor, provided by the Win32 API, to temporarily establish the text background color as the same RGB combination as the background of the client area. Using full concentrations of red, green, and blue yields the color white. When the method SetBkColor replaces the background color, the old color returns and resides in the variable OldTextColor.

TIP

If the background color of the bounding rectangle of the text string does not match the background color of the client area, the text appears to be inside a square box of a different color. This effect is likely to cause some confusion in the user, who is likely to interpret this label as a button and is likely to try to click the button—to no avail.

In order to display the text, this message handler uses the method ExtTextOut. This Win32 API method uses the tools in DeviceContext to place the text at location (TextLocation.x, TextLocation.y). The text string is in buffer TextData and has _tcslen(TextData) characters. After the text location arguments are the pair of values (0,NULL). The first value indicates that the clipping option is not of interest. If this value were to be set as ETO_CLIPPED, the second argument would point to a RECT structure that contains a clipping rectangle. At the end of the argument list, the NULL value can be replaced by a pointer to an array of values that allows the handler to introduce extra space between the bounding rectangle or cell of individual characters.

Subsequent to displaying the text string, this paint handler restores the default text background color to the device content. Using SetBkColor, the handler provides the device context and the original RGB combination that was cached in the variable OldTextColor.

A Short Critique of This Design/Implementation Approach

In order to utilize both rubber-banded drawing and type and echo processing in the same program, this implementation employs four state variables: IsDragging, TypingText, TextInitialized, and PositionSet. This bewildering set of variables and some very ugly code finally made this program work correctly. However, if additional features are needed for this program, the debugging effort is going to become very time consuming.

A better approach would be to use a state machine to correctly manage the user interface for this program. Adding user features to this program then requires some easily added state-processing logic with some lower-level functional processing code. Integration and debugging under this design would be far more friendly and significantly less time consuming.

In the next chapter, all the processing and functional logic appears in a state machine framework. This framework uses a layered design that is more reliable and more easily extended.

Summary

This chapter presents a drawing program that enables a user to perform rubber-banded drawing of a single line and to attach a text label anywhere in the client area. The implementation requires a number of state variables and some messy code that will be replaced by a state machine in the next chapter. A few of the important concepts you learned in this chapter include the following:

▶ Binary raster operations enable rapid erasing and redrawing of specific pixels of a graphics object.

▶ A caret indicates the location to display a new character during type and echo processing.

▶ Using a caret requires management and extra programming within an application.

▶ In order to define an application-specific message, an application defines a message code and a message cracker.

▶ Extra user steps are necessary to indicate text-entry mode and text start location on the Pocket PC due to the lack of a right mouse button.

▶ An application can acquire a device context at any time using the GetDC method.

▶ With a clipping rectangle and the redraw flag set to TRUE, a paint message handler can perform a rapid erase and redraw of a text string.

Sample Programs on the Web

The following programs are available at http://www.osborne.com:

Description	Folder
Desktop Rubber-Banded Drawing Program	RubberBandingProgram
Pocket PC Rubber-Banded Drawing Program	RubberBandingProgramPPC
Desktop Type and Echo Processing Program	CharacterProcessingProgram
Pocket PC Type and Echo Processing Program	CharacterProcessingProgramPPC

Execution Instructions

Desktop Rubber-Banded Drawing Program

1. Start Visual C++ 6.0.

2. Open the project RubberBandingProgram.dsw in the folder RubberBandingProgram.

3. Build the program.

4. Execute the program.

5. Place the mouse cursor at an arbitrary location.

6. Depress and hold the left mouse button.

7. While keeping the left mouse button depressed, drag the cursor around the client area of the window. A red line should follow the cursor around the client area without any perceptible flicker.

8. While keeping the left mouse button depressed, drag the cursor outside the window completely. The red line should follow the cursor to the edge of the client area and then be clipped outside the client area of the window.

9. Release the left mouse button. The last line drawn should remain displayed in the client area.

10. Click the Quit menu item on the window menu bar.

11. The application window disappears when the application terminates.

Pocket PC Rubber-Banded Drawing Program

1. Attach the Pocket PC cradle to the desktop computer.

2. Insert the Pocket PC into the cradle.

3. Tell ActiveSync to create a guest connection.

4. Make sure that the status is "connected."

5. Start Embedded Visual C++ 3.0.

6. Open the project RubberBandingProgramPPC.vcw in the folder RubberBandingProgramPPC.

7. Build the program.

8. Make sure the program successfully downloads to the Pocket PC.

9. On the Pocket PC, open the File Explorer.

10. Browse to the MyDevice folder.

11. Execute the program RubberBandingProgram.

12. Place the stylus tip at an arbitrary location on the Pocket PC screen.

13. Depress and hold the stylus.

14. While keeping the stylus depressed, drag the cursor around the client area of the window. A red line should follow the cursor around the client area without any perceptible flicker.

15. While keeping the stylus depressed, drag the cursor outside the window completely. The red line should follow the cursor to the edge of the client area and then be clipped outside the client area of the window.

16. Withdraw the stylus from the Pocket PC screen. The last line drawn should remain displayed in the client area.

17. Tap the Quit menu item on the window menu bar.

18. The application window disappears when the application terminates.

Desktop Type and Echo Processing Program

1. Start Visual C++ 6.0.

2. Open the project CharacterProcessingProgram.dsw in the folder CharacterProcessingProgram.

3. Build the program.

4. Execute the program.

5. Press and release the BACKSPACE key on the keyboard.

6. Place the mouse cursor at an arbitrary location.

7. Depress and release the left mouse button. The caret should appear.

8. Type a number of characters. Characters should echo in the client area, and the caret should move to the right as characters are typed. Spaces appear, but other nonalphanumeric characters, such as "!", do *not* display.

9. Press and release the BACKSPACE key on the keyboard.

10. Click the Quit menu item on the window menu bar.

11. The application window disappears when the application terminates.

Pocket PC Type and Echo Processing Program

1. Attach the Pocket PC cradle to the desktop computer.

2. Insert the Pocket PC into the cradle.

3. Tell ActiveSync to create a guest connection.

4. Make sure that the status is "connected."

5. Start Embedded Visual C++ 3.0.

6. Open the project CharacterProcessingProgramPPC.vcw in the folder CharacterProcessingProgramPPC.

7. Build the program.

8. Make sure the program successfully downloads to the Pocket PC.

9. On the Pocket PC, open the File Explorer.

10. Browse to the MyDevice folder.

11. Execute the program CharacterProcessingProgram.

12. Tap the icon on the Pocket PC that causes the keyboard to display.

13. Tap and release the BACKSPACE button on the keyboard.

14. Tap the screen with the stylus. The caret should appear.

15. Type a number of characters. Characters should echo in the client area, and the caret should move to the right as characters are typed. Spaces appear, but other nonalphanumeric characters, such as "!", do *not* display.

16. Tap and release the BACKSPACE button on the keyboard.

17. Tap the icon on the Pocket PC that causes the keyboard to disappear.

18. Tap the Quit menu item on the window menu bar.

19. The application window disappears when the application terminates.

Image Processing Using Bitmaps

In the previous chapters, programs utilize specific graphics capabilities available to Windows CE programmers. These programs employ vector graphics. Vector graphics operate using points in a two-dimensional drawing space. Each two-dimensional point is a vector. For instance, a line-drawing operation employs a start vector or location and an end vector or location. Although this approach works well for many types of user interfaces, the approach possesses a practical limitation. If a program displays a very rich graphical image, the CPU time to execute a sequence of vector-drawing commands can be prohibitively long.

For more complex images, a more efficient approach uses raster graphics. This form of graphics employs an array of pixels that a program simply copies to the screen. Windows CE provides excellent support for raster graphics through bitmaps. In fact, a bitmap is a combination of a set of metadata describing the pixels and an array of pixel values. This chapter provides a functional encapsulation for harnessing bitmaps and then demonstrates the usage of this encapsulation on three different programs.

The first program is a simple image-processing program. This program enables a user to load and display an image from a file, apply an edge-detection algorithm to the image, and then dump and store the displayed image back into a file. Applying the edge detection requires direct access to the pixels in a loaded bitmap.

The second program demonstrates the usage of a splash screen in the client area. With this program, when the application begins execution, a bitmap appears that fills the entire client area. After a certain duration, the client area changes to the normal display of the application program.

Finally, bitmap encapsulation becomes the enabling technology in the third program—an image-animation program. This program loads a background bitmap and a foreground bitmap. At the end of a specified timer interval, an update to the location of the foreground image gives the appearance of movement.

An important feature of the approach used in this bitmap encapsulation is the utilization of Windows resource bitmaps to store and to manipulate the bitmap images in memory. Most books that describe Windows bitmap programming take a radically different approach. These books typically load the bitmap into an array in memory. Then, every time the bitmap needs to be displayed, the application programmatically creates a bitmap and copies the bitmap into the client area. This approach requires continually copying the bitmap pixels prior to each display.

NOTE

An efficient and effective approach to utilizing bitmaps is to transfer the bitmaps directly from a file into a Windows bitmap resource.

Once a bitmap resides in a Windows bitmap resource, however, a number of methods are available for manipulating the bitmap using a handle to the Windows bitmap resource. By using a handle in this manner, the copying of the bitmap into a resource only occurs once, when the bitmap file is loaded, rather than reoccurring every time the bitmap requires program manipulation. For a large bitmap, the effect of this more efficient operation significantly improves the perception to the user that results from any bitmap manipulations.

All the bitmap operations performed on Windows bitmap resources occur extremely quickly, even when executing on a Pocket PC. This high performance results because of the efficiency of the Win32 API methods that support raster graphics. The primary workhorse methods are BitBlt and StretchBlt. Both of these methods operate to rapidly transfer a bitmap resource into the client area. Knowing that these methods may have to copy large numbers of pixel values, Microsoft invested significant effort into optimizing their performance.

Implementing an Image-Processing Program

Image processing is a useful technique that finds application in a number of different disciplines. The basis of image processing is an image filter. Each filter consists of a kernel that a program applies to areas in an image. Coefficients of a kernel enable an application to combine existing pixels into new pixels in a manner that reveals important features of the underlying image. In this section, a basic image-processing program implements one form of kernel called *edge detection.*

Edge detection finds visually identifiable boundaries of objects within an image. After applying edge detection to an image, a user sees a series of lines that clearly identifies the transitions between various objects in the image. For instance, when applied to an image that contains buildings, an edge-detection program clearly depicts the outlines of each of the buildings in the image.

In order to implement an image-processing program, a number of basic image operations must also be available. Some necessary fundamental functions include getting the image into memory, extracting the pixels from the image, storing the pixels that the edge-detection algorithm generates back into an image, and writing the edge detected image back out to a file.

Introducing the Graphical User Interface

In Figure 6-1 appears a graphical user interface for an image-processing program. This initial interface demonstrates the ability to select a bitmap to load.

In order to initiate the process of selecting a bitmap file, a user of this program performs two tasks. First, the user clicks the Select menu item. This action causes a popup submenu to display. From the popup submenu, the user clicks the Input

1. Click the Select menu item.

2. Click the Input submenu item.

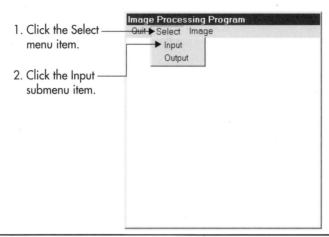

Figure 6-1 *Selecting a bitmap file to load*

submenu item. After clicking this item, a WM_COMMAND message arrives at the program dialog procedure.

Inside the WM_COMMAND message handler, the program populates and displays a File Open dialog. This dialog is one of several common dialogs available as integral elements in the Win32 API. Figure 6-2 contains the specific dialog that displays to the user.

Most users are familiar with this dialog. Many programs use the dialog, which is the reason Microsoft established a template for it. At the top of the dialog appears a navigation bar. Using the Up Folder icon and the Look In drop-down box, a user first navigates to a specific folder that contains the bitmap file. The message handler configures this dialog to only display files with the BMP extension, because the program only processes files in that format. Once the user finds the bitmap file, clicking the file name causes it to appear in the File Name drop-down field. Terminating the dialog requires the user to click the Open button.

TIP

Clicking the Open button does not actually load the file. Internally, this action simply returns the name of the selected file in a variable provided by the program.

Now that the name has been selected, the user loads and displays the selected image. Features of the user interface enabling the user to perform these operations appear in Figure 6-3.

A user begins the load-and-display process by clicking the Image menu item from the main menu bar. In response, Windows automatically displays the associated popup submenu. From the submenu, the user first selects the Load submenu item.

2. Click the desired
BMP file.

1. Navigate to
the folder.

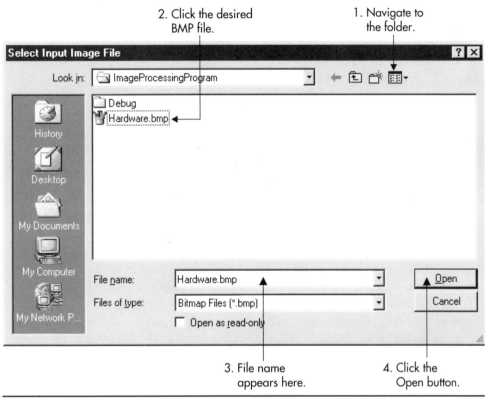

3. File name
appears here.

4. Click the
Open button.

Figure 6-2   *The File Open dialog*

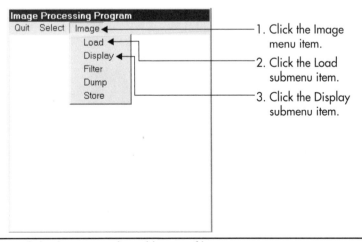

1. Click the Image
menu item.

2. Click the Load
submenu item.

3. Click the Display
submenu item.

Figure 6-3   *Loading and displaying a selected bitmap file*

Internally, the message handler for this item executes a method that loads the bitmap file into a Windows bitmap resource. Subsequent to loading the bitmap, the user again selects the Image menu item and then selects the Display popup submenu item. The message handler for the resulting WM_COMMAND message performs the actual display, copying the bitmap from the Windows resource into the client area of the application window.

NOTE

Typically, a program combines file selection, loading, and display into a single operation, initiated from a menu item. Using a step-wise approach, as indicated earlier, simply enables a developer to more easily debug individual steps.

After the user has followed the steps indicated thus far, the graphical user interface appears as shown in Figure 6-4.

Regardless of the original size of the image, the loading program scales the image to completely fill the portion of the client area below the main menu bar. If the bitmap image originally exceeds the size of the client area, Windows removes a sufficient number of pixels to fit the image within the client area. When the bitmap is smaller than the client area, Windows adds pixels using an algorithm that reasonably preserves the quality of the image. The algorithms that remove and add pixels preserve the aspect ratio of the bitmap so that the complete image appears smaller or larger.

The test bitmap that accompanies the program contains a set of hardware parts. After loading this bitmap, the user desires to determine the edges of each of the parts. Steps required to apply the edge-detection kernel to the loaded bitmap image appear in Figure 6-5.

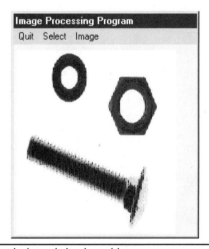

Figure 6-4   *A selected, loaded, and displayed bitmap*

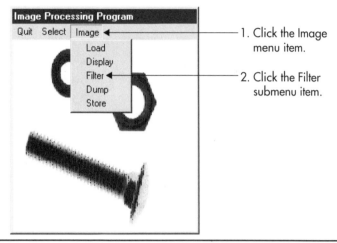

Figure 6-5   *Applying an edge-detection filter*

Two menu item selections initiate application of the edge-detection kernel. A user clicks the Image menu item. From the popup submenu, the user then selects the Filter submenu item. As usual, this action submits a WM_COMMAND message to the dialog procedure of the application. In response to this message, the DlgOnCommand message handler creates a bitmap resource for the edge-detected image and applies the kernel to the elements of the original image. Bitmap pixels in the edge-detected image now appear in a second bitmap resource. The program then maps the edge-detected image into the client area of the application window.

TIP

Using the approach promoted by other books on this subject, performing this step requires that the original bitmap first be loaded from temporary storage into a Windows bitmap resource. If the bitmap image already resides in a Windows bitmap resource, the additional execution time to copy the pixels is no longer necessary.

Figure 6-6 contains the edge-detected version of the hardware bitmap provided with the program on the web site for this book (http://www.osborne.com).

In the edge-detected image displayed in the figure, black pixels characterize the background while white pixels appear on edges of objects inside the image. At least visually, the boundaries, structures, and orientation of all objects are clearly identified. Many applications further analyze the raw pixel data in this image and construct internal representations of the objects.

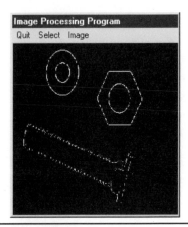

Figure 6-6   *A bitmap after edge detection*

NOTE

The bitmap utilities described in this chapter make certain assumptions about the actual data incorporated into the bitmap file. Therefore, these utilities may not work correctly for all possible bitmap files.

Analyzing Program Operations and Organization

An important first step to implementing the image-processing program is to understand the manner in which bitmaps are manipulated during program execution. These bitmap manipulations form the basic requirements that lead to implementation of a bitmap functional encapsulation.

When processed by this program, bitmaps move through a processing pipeline. This pipeline characterizes the operations and data structures used by the program in manipulating a bitmap. This processing pipeline appears in Figure 6-7.

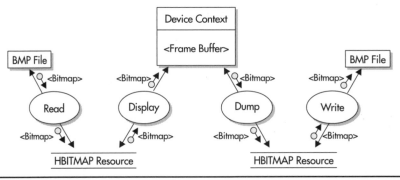

Figure 6-7   *The bitmap-processing pipeline*

In general, a bitmap moves through four phases of operation, as suggested by this figure. These phases specifically deal with the movement of bitmap data through the processing pipeline. A description of these phases appears as follows:

Phase	Characterization
Read	Moves the bitmap from external memory to internal memory
Display	Moves the bitmap from internal memory to the frame buffer
Dump	Moves the bitmap from the frame buffer to internal memory
Write	Moves the bitmap from internal memory to external memory

Think of these phases as the potential lifecycle of a bitmap during program operations. A particular phase involves the movement of bitmap data from one location to another. The overall sequence looks like this: external – internal – frame buffer – internal – external. In fact, this sequence is exactly the same sequence to which any data structure must adhere.

NOTE

When building an encapsulation for a complex data structure, the basic cycle of external – internal – local – internal – external forms the basis for all required operations and becomes the basic unit-testing sequence for the object or data type manager encapsulation.

A further definition of the phases correlates each phase to both the input and the output data structures, as follows:

Phase	Input Data Structure	Output Data Structure
Read	BMP file	Bitmap resource
Display	Bitmap resource	Frame buffer
Dump	Frame buffer	Bitmap resource
Write	Bitmap resource	BMP file

Each of these phases involves a specific movement of the bitmap data from an input data source to an output data source. For instance, the Read phase of the bitmap lifecycle consists of all the programming code necessary to translate a BMP file into a Windows bitmap resource. So, the phase or operation on the bitmap includes both movement of the bitmap data and translation into a specific internal data structure.

When the user chooses to display a bitmap, the Display method copies the bitmap resource into a portion of an internal frame buffer. This portion of the frame buffer corresponds directly to the physical area of the client area of the dialog window. The display hardware then reads these pixels from the frame buffer and draws the pixels on the physical display device.

An important feature of this set of requirements is the heavy reliance upon the Windows bitmap resource. By using this resource, the functional encapsulation controls multiple-loaded bitmaps by maintaining a handle into each of the underlying Windows system data structures. As explained earlier, this is the most efficient and effective approach for manipulating bitmaps because it minimizes the amount of pixel copying.

These four phases or basic operations form the initial set of requirements for a functional encapsulation that operates on bitmaps. As the application develops further, additional requirements emerge for adding new methods to the encapsulation.

One of the key data structures of the bitmap-processing pipeline is the BMP file. A definition of the Windows BMP file format appears in the Win32 API documentation. This format is a native Windows format, having been defined almost from the inception of the Windows product line. Figure 6-8 characterizes the organization of a Windows bitmap file.

Each BMP file contains four major areas of data. The BitmapFileHeader area identifies the file. After this area, the BitmapInfoHeader area defines the features of the bitmap. An RGBQuadTable consists of an array of RGBQUAD structures that specify the red, green, and blue intensity components for each color in a display device color palette. Finally, the raw BitmapBits contain the actual pixel values. In fact, each pixel value takes the form of a color index into the palette array represented by RGBQuadTable.

Each of the entries for these areas possesses a clear definition in the Win32 API documentation. Describing each entry here would be a bit tedious, so the following discussion focuses on a few of the critical entries. In the BitmapFileHeader, the fbType field contains the string "BM" (obviously identifying the file as a bitmap file). Another interesting field in this area is the bfOffBits entry. This field defines the offset, in bytes, from the end of the BITMAPFILEHEADER structure to the start of the BitmapBits area in the file.

A number of important entries appear in the BitmapInfoHeader region of the file. The field biWidth indicates the width of the bitmap in pixels. Similarly, biHeight defines the height of the bitmap in pixels. The field biHeight can assume a positive or a negative value. A positive value for this field indicates that the raw pixels appear in the bitmap from the bottom up, with the lower-left corner as the origin of the bitmap. A negative value defines a top-down bitmap with the origin in the upper-left corner.

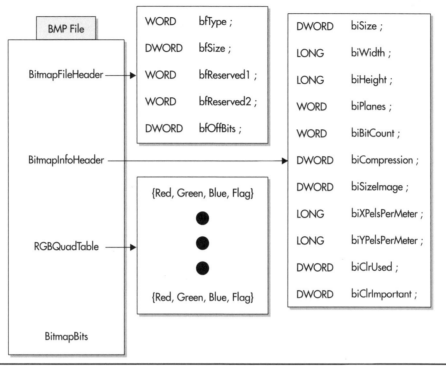

Figure 6-8   *Layout and organization of a Windows BMP file*

Normally, an application must reverse the rows in a top-down bitmap during loading and prior to displaying on the screen.

TIP

By pushing the bitmap directly into a Windows bitmap resource, the Windows code for managing bitmap resources is responsible for this interpretation and the resulting effects on pixel manipulation.

Two other key fields in the BitmapInfoHeader region of the file are the biClrUsed and the biClrImportant fields. These values indicate the number of palette entries in the RGBQuadTable. Incorrectly setting these values causes the strange behavior and potential failure of an application. If the number in these fields is larger than the actual number of entries, Windows moves beyond the end of the array, interpreting pixel values as RGB combinations. When the pixels actually display, these erroneous color combinations can cause the bitmap to display incorrectly in the client area.

Each entry in the RGBQuadTable consists of a 32-bit number that represents a specific combination of red, green, and blue. A single entry is an RGB quad. *Quad* implies that the value contains four parts, each part being 8 bits wide. Obviously, the first three parts indicate the concentration of red, green, and blue. Windows reserves the final part and requires that the application specifically initialize this value to zero. Because 8 bits represent each color concentration, the amount of a specific color can range from 0 (no color) to 255 (maximum color).

Every pixel in the rectangular area receives an entry in the BitmapBits region of the file. Entries in this area appear in row order: all the pixels in row 0, all the pixels in row 1, and so on. Every entry exists as an index into the RGBQuadTable. If this table has 256 entries, then each pixel value is in the range 0–255. In Figure 6-8, biClrUsed is declared as a DWORD. A declaration for this Windows-specific data type appears in the file windef.h, as follows:

```
typedef unsigned long DWORD;
```

This declaration indicates that a DWORD is a 32-bit unsigned integer. Based upon this declaration, the biClrUsed field can range from 0–4,294,967,295. In other words, the RGBQuadTable can represent up to 4 trillion color combinations of red, green, and blue.

As indicated earlier, the four phases of the bitmap-processing cycle form the basis for a class that encapsulates these operations. Methods in this encapsulation utilize various combinations of Win32 API calls in order to perform the action indicated by the method name. Figure 6-9 demonstrates the relationship between the BitmapUtilities functional encapsulation and methods supplied by the Win32 API.

At the upper-left side of the figure appears the functional encapsulation BitmapUtilities. A list of bitmap-related supporting methods provided by the Win32 API appear on the lower-right side. Each method in BitmapUtilities utilizes one of the methods provided by the Win32 API. A line extends directly from each of the encapsulating methods of BitmapUtilities to a specific method supported by the Win32 API. Other methods are available through BitmapUtilities. Also, each method in BitmapUtilities often utilizes more than one method from the Win32 API. However, the methods that appear in Figure 6-9 are the key methods that exist within each of the two elements shown in the figure.

As an example, consider the DisplayABitmap method provided by BitmapUtilities. This method primarily utilizes the StretchBlt method provided by the Win32 API. Upon entry to StretchBlt, the method DisplayABitmap passes two arguments. In the figure, one of the arguments is <WindowDC/Bitmap>. This formulation is necessary because StretchBlt copies a bitmap from a source device context to a destination device context.

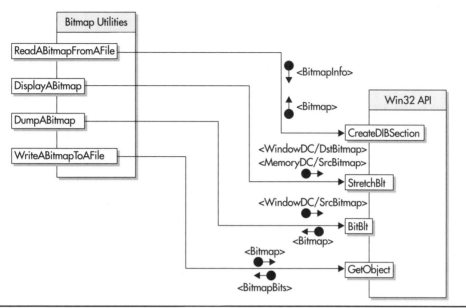

Figure 6-9   *A bitmap utilities encapsulation and the Win32 API*

NOTE

Recall that a device context is a collection of drawing tools. One of the drawing tools, not previously mentioned, is an attached Windows bitmap resource.

So, StretchBlt actually moves the bitmap attached to the source device context into the bitmap associated with the destination device context. Obviously, a far simpler approach would be for StretchBlt to copy the source bitmap directly into the destination bitmap. However, because Microsoft chose to encapsulate all the drawing tools within a single data structure—the device context—consistency requires utilizing this same approach when displaying bitmaps. Inside the method DisplayABitmap, the program creates an in-memory device context and attaches the source bitmap. Using StretchBlt, the method then copies the bitmap from the in-memory device context into the device context for the client area. Because all these involve a number of steps that utilize various methods of the Win32 API in addition to StretchBlt, hiding all this messy sequence under a single method greatly simplifies the task of displaying a bitmap from anywhere in a program.

Every method call into the Win32 API either directly or indirectly involves a Windows bitmap resource, as demonstrated in Figure 6-9. This result should come as no surprise given all the earlier emphasis on the utilization of Windows bitmap resources. Two of the methods—ReadABitmapFromAFile and DumpABitmap—receive handles to Windows bitmap resources as return values. The remaining methods—DisplayABitmap and WriteABitmapToAFile—accept bitmap handles as input arguments.

Integrating the methods of BitmapUtilities into an application is ridiculously simple. In fact, each of the bitmap-related operations defined in the user interface description earlier simply requires the declaration of a few variables and then a single method call in the command handler for each specific submenu item integer identifier.

Implementing the Image-Processing Program

In order to implement the image-processing program, a developer first implements the lowest level of utilities and support methods and then integrates these elements into the complete application. An implementation sequence that utilizes this bottom-up approach is as follows:

1. Implement a FileNameMgr element to easily utilize the File Open and File Save common dialogs.

2. Generate a KernelMgr element to maintain the properties of an edge-detection image filter.

3. Develop a BitmapUtilities element to perform the basic operations on a bitmap and to apply the edge-detection filter to a bitmap image.

4. Add the menu items to the main menu bar and attach the popup submenus to the main menu items.

5. Modify the DlgProc and the DlgOnCommand message handler to utilize methods from the BitmapUtilities element.

6. Modify the DlgOnPaint message handler to recognize and display a loaded bitmap.

In the remainder of this section, an analysis appears that lists and describes the code generated to accomplish each of these tasks.

Implement a FileNameMgr Element

Selecting a file name is a common requirement for many programs. For this reason, the Win32 API provides two file name selection dialogs—the GetOpenFileName dialog and the GetSaveFileName dialog. Using these dialogs involves filling a record structure and retrieving the selected name.

Because using this feature occurs regularly, a functional encapsulation provides even easier access to these dialogs. This encapsulation provides two methods—one for each dialog. Each method fills the required structure with a combination of arguments provided by the calling method and a set of default values.

Because both methods work approximately the same way, the following analysis only addresses the method that encapsulates the GetOpenFileName dialog. The declaration for this method is as follows:

```
void GetInputFileName(TCHAR * FileName, int NumberChars,
                      TCHAR * FilterString);
```

This method obviously enables a program to easily obtain the name of a file to open. As the first argument, the method receives FileName, a string buffer address that is to receive the selected file name. After this argument, the calling method indicates the size of the buffer as NumberChars. Finally, a filter string, FilterString, indicates the extensions of the files that the dialog is to display in the browse window.

Filter strings take a special form, as required by the GetOpenFileName common dialog. An example of the declaration of the filter string is as follows:

```
_tcscpy( FilterString, __TEXT("Bitmap Files (*.bmp)|*.bmp|") ) ;
```

In fact, a filter string contains a pair of strings for each filter extension. Each string in the pair of strings terminates with a character "|" separator. The first string of the pair displays in the Type drop-down list of the dialog. During the operation to fill the browse window, the GetOpenFileName dialog uses the second string to select specific files to display in the browse window.

TIP

A "|" terminator must follow even the last string in all the pairs of strings of a filter string. Failure to include the last terminator causes the common dialog to fail to initialize.

Inside the body of GetInputFileName, the program simply fills the required data structure using the arguments and default values and then executes the GetOpenFileName common dialog.

```
/************************************************
 * File: FileNameMgr.h
 * copyright, SWA Engineering, Inc., 2001
 * All rights reserved.
 ************************************************/
```

```
void GetInputFileName(TCHAR * FileName, int NumberChars,
                      TCHAR * FilterString)
{
     OPENFILENAME FileData ;

     ReformatFilterString(FilterString) ;

     FileData.lStructSize       = sizeof(OPENFILENAME) ;
     FileData.hwndOwner         = NULL ;
     FileData.hInstance         = NULL ;
     FileData.lpstrFilter       = FilterString ;
     FileData.lpstrCustomFilter = NULL ;
     FileData.nMaxCustFilter    = 0 ;
     FileData.nFilterIndex      = 1 ;
     FileData.lpstrFile         = FileName ;
     FileData.nMaxFile          = NumberChars ;
     FileData.lpstrFileTitle    = NULL ;
     FileData.nMaxFileTitle     = 0 ;
     FileData.lpstrInitialDir   = NULL ;
     FileData.lpstrTitle        = __TEXT("Select Input Image File") ;
     FileData.Flags             = OFN_PATHMUSTEXIST | OFN_FILEMUSTEXIST |
                                  OFN_LONGNAMES ;
     FileData.nFileOffset       = 0 ;
     FileData.nFileExtension    = 0 ;
     FileData.lpstrDefExt       = NULL ;
     FileData.lCustData         = 0 ;
     FileData.lpfnHook          = NULL ;
     FileData.lpTemplateName    = NULL ;

     GetOpenFileName(&FileData) ;
}
```

In order to use the common dialog, this method must fill an OPENFILENAME, declared with the name FileData at the beginning of the method. Additionally, prior to passing the filter string to the GetOpenFileName common dialog, a helper method named ReformatFilterString converts the filter string into a required actual format. When executed by the calling method, each string in the pair of filter strings terminates with "|". This separator is easy to type when typing from the keyboard. The common dialog actually expects each string to terminate with a "\0" terminator, the normal end-of-string terminator. ReformatFilterString performs the substitution of terminators.

A large number of the arguments are set to default values, such as 0 or NULL. An explanation for each of these appears in the online documentation. Usage of the incoming arguments is obvious and needs no further elaboration. However, some of the remaining default values bear discussion.

As the default value for the lStructSize field, the method provides the number of bytes in the record structure OPENFILENAME, computed using the sizeof operator. Windows uses this value to ensure that the provided structure is the correct version of the structure. Forgetting to initialize this field causes the common dialog to fail to initialize.

In the Flags field appears the symbolic constant OFN_LONGNAMES. This value indicates to the common dialog that long file names are to be displayed. If this flag does not appear in the Flags field, then only files that follow the DOS 8.3 file name convention display in the browse window of the dialog.

After correctly filling the contents of the OPENFILENAME structure, the encapsulating method passes the address of the variable FileData to the common dialog GetOpenFileName. Using the mouse and the navigation bar, the user browses until selecting a file name. After returning from execution of the common dialog, the selected file name resides in FileName, because this encapsulating method placed this address into the lpstrFile field of the OPENFILENAME structure.

NOTE

When the user selects a specific file name, the GetOpenFileName common dialog only returns the selected name and does not actually open the file, in spite of the name of the common dialog.

Generate a KernelMgr Element

In image processing, a filter converts one image into another image by filtering specific aspects of an image. For an image, a filter consists of a small array of coefficients that a program applies across a range of pixels. Simple filters typically consist of a 3×3 array (three rows by three columns). In image-processing terms, this small array is a *kernel*.

This small software element manages the 3×3 array of filter coefficients. The declaration for this element is as follows:

```
/***********************************************
 * File: KernelMgr.h
 * copyright, SWA Engineering, Inc., 2001
 * All rights reserved.
 ***********************************************/
void InitializeKernel(void) ;
void GetNumberRowsAndCols(int * Rows, int * Cols) ;
int GetScaleFactor(void) ;
int GetThresholdValue(void) ;
int GetKernelCoefficient( int Row, int Col ) ;
```

In addition to an array of coefficients, the KernelMgr also provides a scale factor and a threshold value. The scale factor translates the initial kernel calculations into a more appropriate range of values. A threshold value determines whether the output pixel from the filter is black or white.

TIP

The mechanics of using a kernel appear in the discussion of the BitmapUtilities, which occurs in the next section.

When BitmapUtilities executes the method InitializeKernel, this method establishes the entries of the 3×3 kernel array as follows:

```
-1      -1      -1
-1       8      -1
-1      -1      -1
```

This array of filter or kernel elements gives greatest weight to the center input pixel, with lesser weights to the surrounding pixels. Many image-processing books provide this kernel as the most effective kernel for edge detection.

Develop a BitmapUtilities Element

This functional encapsulation provides a set of methods that enable an application to easily and effectively manipulate bitmaps. As described earlier, this software element implements the basic bitmap-processing pipeline of Figure 6-7.

The first method in the bitmap-processing pipeline is the method that reads a bitmap from a file into a Windows bitmap resource. The following code listing provides the implementation mechanics for this method:

```c
/*************************************************
 * File: BitmapUtilities.c
 * copyright, SWA Engineering, Inc., 2001
 * All rights reserved.
 **********************************************/
void ReadABitmapFromAFile(TCHAR *    FileName, HDC DeviceContext ,
                        HBITMAP * Bitmap )
{
     BITMAPFILEHEADER    FileHeader ;
     BITMAPINFOHEADER    BitmapHeader ;
     RGBQUAD *           BitmapRGB ;
     int                 Size ;
     BYTE *              BitmapBits ;
```

```
    HANDLE          File ;
    DWORD           BytesRead ;
    BOOL            Status ;
    HBITMAP         WorkingBitmap ;
    int             RGBSize ;
    BITMAPINFO *    BitmapInfo ;
    BYTE *          RGBStart ;

File = CreateFile( FileName, GENERIC_READ , FILE_SHARE_READ , NULL,
                OPEN_EXISTING , FILE_ATTRIBUTE_NORMAL , NULL ) ;

Status = ReadFile(File,&FileHeader,sizeof(BITMAPFILEHEADER),
                &BytesRead,NULL) ;

Status = ReadFile(File,&BitmapHeader,sizeof(BITMAPINFOHEADER),
                &BytesRead,NULL) ;

  RGBSize = BitmapHeader.biClrUsed * sizeof(RGBQUAD) ;
  BitmapRGB = (RGBQUAD *) malloc( RGBSize ) ;
  Status = ReadFile(File,BitmapRGB, RGBSize ,&BytesRead,NULL) ;

  BitmapInfo = (BITMAPINFO *)malloc( sizeof(BITMAPINFOHEADER)+RGBSize ) ;
  memcpy( BitmapInfo , &BitmapHeader , sizeof(BITMAPINFOHEADER) ) ;
  RGBStart = (BYTE *)BitmapInfo + sizeof(BITMAPINFOHEADER) ;
  memcpy( RGBStart,BitmapRGB,RGBSize) ;

  WorkingBitmap = CreateDIBSection(DeviceContext,
                               (PBITMAPINFO)BitmapInfo,
                               DIB_RGB_COLORS, &BitmapBits ,
                               NULL, 0);

  Size = BitmapHeader.biWidth * BitmapHeader.biHeight * sizeof(BYTE) ;
  Status = ReadFile(File,BitmapBits, Size ,&BytesRead,NULL) ;

  free(BitmapInfo) ;
  free(BitmapRGB) ;

  CloseHandle(File) ;

  *Bitmap = WorkingBitmap ;
}
```

This method processes the data in a BMP file according to the organization of that file, as described in Figure 6-8. Because the file contains four major sections, this method executes the Win32 API method ReadFile exactly four times—one for each section of the BMP file.

Opening a file uses the method CreateFile. This method accepts the name of the file, FileName, and a host of other parameters. For the most part, the remaining values are all default values, so interested readers can find the meaning of these values in the online help. Execution of this method returns a handle to the open file, stored in the variable File. Every time this method reads from the file, this handle becomes the first argument to the ReadFile method. The most important arguments supplied to ReadFile include the target address for storage of the returning bytes, such as FileHeader, and the number of bytes to read. This method simply extracts the bytes from the current location in the file and then increments a file pointer to the first byte beyond the bytes just read. After all file operations are complete, the method passes the handle in variable File to the CloseHandle method, which actually closes the file.

Because the FileHeader and BitmapHeader elements are known structures of fixed size, a single ReadFile for each of these elements suffices to bring the corresponding bytes from the file into memory. Reading the color table requires some additional processing. Every BMP file has a different color table. This method computes the size of the color table in RGBSize, allocates this amount of space to store the color table in BitmapRGB, and then reads the color table into the allocated memory.

Prior to loading the actual pixel values, the method first generates the Windows bitmap resource. Generating the bitmap resource first eliminates the execution time for reading the pixels into a local storage area and then copying into the bitmap resource. This savings results because the method used to create the bitmap resource returns both a handle to the bitmap resource and the address of the memory allocated for pixel storage. Using the returned address, the ReadFile method copies the incoming pixel values directly into the allocated memory without having to perform a second copy.

Establishing the bitmap resource is a two-step process. Variable BitmapInfo of type BITMAPINFO stores the contents of BitmapHeader and BitmapRGB, which were initialized earlier. This information characterizes the bitmap and provides necessary color information to enable Windows to correctly interpret the pixel information. Once this structure has been defined and initialized, the application passes these to CreateDIBSection, a Win32 API method. This method returns a handle to a bitmap resource stored in WorkingBitmap and BitmapBits, the address of an allocated memory area sufficiently large enough to store the pixels characterized in BitmapInfo.

Now, the program uses ReadFile and the address in BitmapBits to load the pixel values directly into the allocated array. After loading the pixel values, this method returns the handle in WorkingBitmap to the calling method.

After transferring a BMP file into a Windows bitmap resource, the next step is to display all or a portion of the bitmap into all or a portion of the client area. The method DisplayABitmap accomplishes this transfer, as shown next:

```
/*************************************************
 * File: BitmapUtilities.c
 * copyright, SWA Engineering, Inc., 2001
 * All rights reserved.
 *************************************************/
void DisplayABitmap(HDC DeviceContext, HBITMAP Bitmap,
        int DstXStart, int DstYStart, int DstWidth, int DstHeight ,
        int SrcXStart, int SrcYStart, int SrcWidth, int SrcHeight )
{
    HDC     InMemoryDC ;
    HBITMAP OldBitmap ;

        InMemoryDC = CreateCompatibleDC(DeviceContext) ;
        OldBitmap =  SelectObject(InMemoryDC,Bitmap) ;
        StretchBlt(DeviceContext,DstXStart, DstYStart, DstWidth, DstHeight,
                InMemoryDC,SrcXStart,SrcYStart,SrcWidth,SrcHeight,SRCCOPY) ;
        SelectObject(InMemoryDC,OldBitmap) ;
        DeleteDC(InMemoryDC) ;
}
```

As the first argument, this method receives the DeviceContext that represents the destination for the incoming bitmap. Associated with this drawing toolkit is an embedded bitmap. The goal of this method is to transfer the source bitmap Bitmap, the second argument, into the attached bitmap for DeviceContext. Remaining arguments describe the sections of the source and destination bitmaps to transfer.

Several Win32 API methods are available for transfer of bitmaps—for example, StretchBlt is used in DisplayABitmap, and BitBlt is used in other methods of the software element BitmapUtilities. StretchBlt is the most flexible of these two methods, allowing a portion of the source bitmap to be transferred to a portion of the destination bitmap. StretchBlt also shrinks or grows the section of the source bitmap to exactly fill the indicated area of the destination bitmap.

Unfortunately, a small hitch exists in the usage of either of these two methods. These methods copy from bitmaps by referencing the device contexts to which the bitmaps are attached. Because the source bitmap is a standalone resource in this method, an in-memory device context serves as a temporary holding device context to perform the transfer of bitmaps.

Using the Win32 API method CreateCompatibleDC, a program creates an in-memory device context called InMemoryDC. After creating this temporary device context, the program then attaches the source bitmap Bitmap to InMemoryDC using the method SelectObject. As a result of executing this method, the program receives the handle to the old bitmap and stores this into the local variable OldBitmap. Using StretchBlt, the bitmap copy occurs by providing InMemoryDC as the source device context and DeviceContext as the destination context. Execution of StretchBlt causes the bitmap to display in the client area, assuming that the destination DeviceContext represents the client area of the dialog window.

After transfer of the bitmap completes, the program selects the OldBitmap back into the InMemoryDC, again using the method SelectObject. Once the InMemoryDC is restored, the final step involves releasing the InMemoryDC, using the Win32 API method DeleteDC.

TIP

Like so many of the Win32 API methods, the method DeleteDC fails to accurately describe the behavior of the method. In fact, Windows maintains a fixed number of device contexts, so DeleteDC really returns the temporarily borrowed device context rather than destroying the device context.

The method DisplayABitmap reveals the major benefit to loading the BMP file directly into a Windows bitmap resource. Once the file is loaded into a resource, displaying the bitmap involves a few lines of code—five to be exact. Dumping a bitmap, implemented in the method DumpABitmap (not listed here, but available on the book's web site at http://www.osborne.com), follows a similar pattern. This method performs some extra work to build the bitmap header and the RGB table. Then, six lines of code dump the bitmap attached to a device context associated with the client area of an application window.

A simple edge-detection algorithm appears in BitmapUtilities, implemented in the method named ApplyKernelToBitmap. This method appears in the element BitmapUtilities because the method performs operations on a Windows bitmap resource. Because BitmapUtilities exists to centralize and to encapsulate all operations on Windows bitmap resources, the method ApplyKernelToBitmap logically belongs in this software element.

A complete listing of the code for the method appears on the book's web site. A specification for this method appears as indicated here:

```
void ApplyKernelToBitmap( HDC DeviceContext, HBITMAP Bitmap) ;
```

This method takes two input arguments. The first argument, DeviceContext, indicates the drawing toolset used to apply the image filter kernel to the resource bitmap. As the second argument, the calling method provides a handle to a source bitmap, Bitmap. This Windows bitmap resource serves as both the source bitmap and the destination bitmap. When applying the edge-detection algorithm, this method retrieves a pointer to the input pixels from the bitmap resource Bitmap, applies the algorithm to a local copy of the pixels, and creates a set of output pixels. After completely filling the output pixel array, the method stores the output pixels back into the same Windows bitmap resource, Bitmap. In order to display the result, the program executes DisplayABitmap, providing the filtered bitmap.

Obtaining a pointer to the actual pixels stored in the bitmap resource Bitmap is the most efficient mechanism for accessing the source pixels. Using this approach, the method ApplyKernelToBitmap directly accesses the bitmap pixels in the memory area allocated to the Windows bitmap resource. Direct access to the storage location of the pixels saves the execution overhead of copying the source pixels into a local array.

An overview of the edge-detection algorithm describes the application of the kernel filter, as follows:

```
obtain a pointer to the bitmap pixels from the source bitmap ;
retrieve the characteristics of the kernel ;
compute a normalization value as the sum of the kernel coefficients ;
for each row in the rows of the image
begin
     for each column in the columns of the image
     begin
       compute the pixel sum by applying the kernel to the array of pixels
                             whose upper left corner is (row,column) ;
       normalize the pixel sum by dividing by the normalization value
       if the pixel sum is less than the kernel threshold
             set pixel sum to zero ;
       set output pixel of (row,column) to pixel sum ;
     end
end
store output pixels back into source bitmap ;
```

Think of the application of the kernel as sliding a small array of coefficients across the source pixel array. As the kernel overlays a small area of the source array of pixels, the kernel entries represent the coefficients in a linear combination of the covered pixels. The result of computing this linear combination is a single sum. After normalization and threshholding, the adjusted sum becomes the output pixel that replaces the pixel in the upper-left corner of the covered pixels from the source array of pixels.

By comparing the pseudo-code with the actual code listing for ApplyKernelToBitmap, a reader can easily follow the actual implementation of this method. A few additional, but minor, details are necessary for the algorithm to work correctly. These added details appear in the actual code listing. For detailed descriptions regarding any of these additional details, consult any basic text on image processing.

Add MenuItems and PopupSubmenu Elements

Adding the menu items, the popup submenus, and the popup submenu items is a task easily accomplished with the menu editor of Visual C++ or Embedded Visual C++. Because the program already uses a menu item for the Quit command, adding these elements is a simple task.

The process of incorporating all these elements into the existing main menu bar occurs in Chapter 7, which follows this chapter. For this reason, a description of the actual steps of using the menu editor does not appear in this chapter. Because the emphasis of this chapter involves bitmap processing, deferring the discussion concerning menu creation does not detract from the contents of this chapter.

Modify the DlgProc and DlgOnCommand Message Handlers

Connecting user choices from the submenu items with specific operations involves a set of variables declared in the dialog procedure combined with methods of the encapsulations developed earlier. The code that declares the variables at the top of the dialog procedure DlgProc appears here:

```
TCHAR           InputFileName[256] ;
TCHAR           FilterString[256] ;
static HBITMAP  LoadedBitmap = NULL ;
static BOOL     BitmapLoaded = FALSE ;
```

Because the user selects a BMP file to load, the variable InputFileName reserves sufficient space to store the name of the selected file. A filter string, FilterString, initialized in the method OnInitDialog ensures that only files with the extension BMP actually display during execution of the method GetInputFileName. By declaring the variable LoadedBitmap, the dialog procedure provides a location to maintain the handle of the Windows bitmap resource into which the file gets loaded. Using the Boolean variable BitmapLoaded controls the execution of bitmap-display code in the DlgOnPaint message handler.

The actual processing of user commands that utilize these variables exists in the WM_COMMAND message handler DlgOnCommand. A listing for this message handler appears here:

```
void DlgOnCommand ( HWND  hDlg , int  iID , HWND  hDlgCtl ,
                    UINT  uCodeNotify )
{
  // Previously Discussed Code Omitted
  switch( iID )
  {
```

```
        case ID_SELECT_INPUT:
              GetInputFileName(InputFileName, 256, FilterString) ;
        break ;
        case ID_IMAGE_LOAD:
              if ( _tcscmp(InputFileName,__TEXT("")) != 0 )
              {
                    DeviceContext = GetDC(hDlg) ;
                    ReadABitmapFromAFile(InputFileName,
                                       DeviceContext , &LoadedBitmap ) ;
                    BitmapLoaded = TRUE ;
                    ReleaseDC(hDlg,DeviceContext) ;
              }
        break ;
        case ID_IMAGE_DISPLAY:
              InvalidateRect(hDlg,NULL,TRUE) ;
              UpdateWindow(hDlg) ;
        break ;
    // Remaining Code Omitted For Clarity
    }
}
```

Following the thread of the earlier code analysis in this section, this listing shows limited portions of the WM_COMMAND message handler. Specific case clauses relate to requesting an input BMP file, loading the file into a Windows bitmap resource, and displaying the loaded bitmap.

Prior to this code listing, every time a device context appears, the context derives from the execution of the BeginPaint method inside of a DlgOnPaint message handler. However, in the preceding code listing, the case clause for menu item ID_IMAGE_LOAD demonstrates that a program can obtain a copy of a device context at any time, using the method GetDC. By providing this method with a window handle, a program obtains a handle to a device context. This device context contains a set of drawing tools that exactly matches those of the indicated window. After using this device context, ReleaseDC accepts the same window handle and the device context, freeing the temporarily assigned device context.

Executing the case clause for ID_IMAGE_LOAD causes the bitmap to be loaded from InputFileName. Accomplishing the file load utilizes the ReadABitmapFromAFile method provided by the BitmapUtilities functional encapsulation. Subsequent to loading the file into the Windows bitmap resource named LoadedBitmap, the handler sets BitmapLoaded to the value TRUE. This flag activates the code in the DlgOnPaint handler so that any attempts to repaint the client area force the display of the LoadedBitmap.

Once the user selects the popup submenu item identified by ID_IMAGE_DISPLAY, the case clause for this identifier executes. In response, this handler clause sequentially executes the method pair InvalidateRect and UpdateWindow. As discussed many times previously, this sequence forces an immediate repaint of the client area.

TIP

Most applications would incorporate the steps of identifying the file, loading the file into a resource, and displaying the resource into an atomic, single user command. For illustration and testing purposes, these steps are individually commanded in the sample program of this chapter.

Modify the DlgOnPaint Message Handler

Copying a loaded bitmap into a client area is the primary responsibility of the DlgOnPaint message handler. The section of this message handler that pertains to displaying a selected and loaded bitmap appears in the following listing:

```
void  DlgOnPaint(HWND hDlg)
{
   // Previously Discussed Code Omitted
      if (BitmapLoaded)
      {
           GetClientDimensions( hDlg, &ClientWidth, &ClientHeight ) ;
           GetBitmapDimensions(LoadedBitmap,&BitmapWidth, &BitmapHeight) ;
           DisplayABitmap(DeviceContext, LoadedBitmap,
                     0, MENU_OFFSET ,ClientWidth,ClientHeight,
                     0,0,BitmapWidth,BitmapHeight ) ;
      }
   // Previously Discussed Code Omitted
}
```

This handler executes at least once before the user selects any menu items. Therefore, any code that attempts to display a loaded bitmap must not execute until the user has worked through the bitmap-initialization sequence. When initialized, the BitmapLoaded flag is set to FALSE. By using this flag as an access-control mechanism, the DlgOnPaint handler ensures that the bitmap-painting code does not execute until initialization by the user. As discussed previously, the DlgOnCommand message handler sets the value of BitmapLoaded after a file name is selected and the bitmap is transferred to the Windows bitmap resource LoadedBitmap.

Once the BitmapLoaded flag is set, this WM_PAINT message handler proceeds to execute the previous code segment. This message handler obtains the size of the client area using GetClientDimensions, a method provided by BitmapUtilities (but not discussed in this chapter). Another method, also available from BitmapUtilities, named GetBitmapDimensions, retrieves the dimensions of the loaded bitmap. Using these size values, DisplayABitmap displays LoadedBitmap in the client window, represented by DeviceContext.

NOTE

Using the method StretchBlt internal to DisplayABitmap forces LoadedBitmap to scale and to display exactly within the client area, regardless of the original size of the bitmap. For instance, the CACTUS.BMP file that accompanies one of the sample programs in this chapter stores a 640×480 bitmap image. This scales perfectly into the client area on the Pocket PC.

In the preceding code segment, a symbolic constant, MENU_OFFSET, passes as the height of the upper-left corner of the client area for the bitmap destination. This constant is necessary due to semantic differences in the GetClientRect method between the desktop PC and the Pocket PC. Buried inside the method GetClientDimensions, offered by BitmapUtilities, a method call to GetClientRect asks Windows to determine the client area of a window. For desktop Windows, the upper-left corner of this client area begins at the bottom of the main menu bar. With the Pocket PC, the upper-left corner of the client area includes the main menu bar. Therefore, when executing on the Pocket PC, a program adjusts the bitmap display area to compensate for the main menu bar.

NOTE

Failing to adjust the bitmap display area to accommodate the main menu bar on a Pocket PC causes the main menu bar to overlap and to obscure a portion of the bitmap image.

Developing a Splash Screen Using BitmapUtilities

Using the BitmapUtilities encapsulation, a developer can fairly easily incorporate a variety of interesting features into an application. One such feature is the splash screen. Upon initialization, the client area of the application window displays a bitmap. Often, this bitmap contains both a company logo and a product logo. After a short duration elapses, this bitmap disappears, to be replaced by the normal client area of the program. Because the bitmap displays and then disappears, the visual effect appears to be the bitmap "splashing" into the client area.

Introducing the Graphical User Interface

Because the purpose of this program is to illustrate the usage of BitmapUtilities to quickly implement a splash screen, the user interface of the program is quite simple. When a user starts the program and the program initially loads, the user interface appears as shown in Figure 6-10.

Figure 6-10 *Displaying a splash screen*

For this program, the splash screen is a colored picture of the Bay Bridge and San Francisco skyline. This screen fills the complete client area below the main menu bar of the window.

After a short time period elapses, the user interface changes to the normal user interface for the program, as displayed in Figure 6-11.

The contents of the client area show a text string containing the title of this book. From this point onward, any operation performed by the user, such as minimizing, maximizing, dragging, or resizing the window, causes the same display. Never again during this execution of the program does the splash screen image appear within the client area of the window.

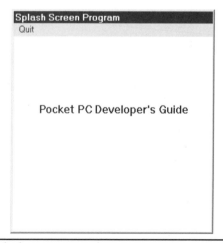

Figure 6-11 *After the splash screen completes*

Describing the Internal Operation of the Program

As with every Windows program, a drawing model characterizes the separation of data update and window update. Figure 6-12 contains the drawing model for this program.

A sequence of numbers in the figure reflects the execution and operation of the program in providing the splash screen capability. A description of the sequence is as follows:

1. From the Windows Explorer, a user executes the program. This step causes the program to load into memory and to execute a WM_INITDIALOG message.

2. Inside the OnInitDialog message handler, the program loads the BMP file into SplashBitmap, a Windows bitmap resource, using the method ReadABitmapFile from the BitmapUtilities element. Also, this handler initiates a hardware timer.

3. After transferring the bitmap file into the resource SplashBitmap, the OnInitDialog handler sets the SplashBitmapLoaded flag to indicate that the bitmap is available for display.

4. As part of the initialization process, Windows automatically executes the WM_PAINT message handler, DlgOnPaint. This handler checks the SplashScreenLoaded flag, recognizes that the bitmap is loaded, and displays the SplashBitmap resource. In order to display this bitmap resource, the handler uses the method DisplayABitmap, provided by BitmapUtilities.

5. The splash screen displays, filling the complete client area of the application window below the main menu bar.

6. Eventually, the initialized timer fires, submitting a WM_TIMER message to the dialog procedure.

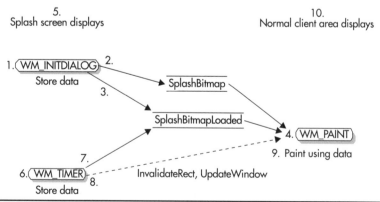

Figure 6-12   *Splash screen drawing model*

7. Inside the code body for this handler, the program kills the timer because only a single timer signal is necessary. The handler then resets the SplashBitmapLoaded flag, signaling that the bitmap is not available for display.

8. Subsequent to setting the flag, the message handler executes the pair of methods InvalidateRect and UpdateWindow, forcing a repaint of the client area. Additionally, one of the arguments to InvalidateRect completely erases the background of the client area.

9. When executing the DlgOnPaint message handler, the SplashScreenLoaded flag routes execution to an else clause that draws the normal display—the text string indicated in Figure 6-11.

A careful study of the preceding sequence indicates an interesting result. All the processing necessary to add the splash screen capability resides strictly within the dialog procedure and the message handlers.

NOTE

By reusing the methods in BitmapUtilities, an application easily incorporates a splash screen into the feature set of the program. Only two methods of BitmapUtilities play a role: ReadABitmapFromAFile and DisplayABitmap.

Implementing the Splash Screen Program

As indicated, all the changes to add a splash screen to any Windows program occur within the dialog procedure DlgProc and the associated message handlers. The required steps to add the splash screen are as follows:

1. Add a WM_TIMER message handler to the file DlgProc that hosts the dialog procedure for the application.

2. Declare the variables and symbolic constants to support a Windows bitmap resource, to control painting with the bitmap, and to manage a timer.

3. Modify the OnInitDialog message handler to load the BMP file containing the splash screen into a Windows bitmap resource, to set the flag that controls the splash screen display, and to initiate the timer.

4. Implement the body of the DlgOnTimer message handler to kill the timer, to reset the flag that manages the splash screen display, and to force a repaint of the client area.

5. Extend the body of the DlgOnPaint message handler to use the splash screen display flag to either display the loaded bitmap resource or to show the normal client area display.

All these changes specifically apply to the DlgProc software element, the dialog procedure DlgProc, and the OnInitDialog, DlgOnTimer, and DlgOnPaint message handlers. Implementation steps defined next clearly demonstrate the manner in which these steps reuse the capabilities of BitmapUtilities.

Add a WM_TIMER Message Handler

As with any message handler, three steps are necessary to add the WM_TIMER message handler. The first step is to declare the method DlgOnTimer. After declaring the handler, add the message cracker HANDLE_DLG_MSG to the message switch of DlgProc. Finally, incorporate an empty handler body at the bottom of the DlgProc software element. Use the Message Cracker Wizard to generate these pieces of code.

Declare Required Variables and Symbolic Constants

Two elements of the splash screen implementation require declarations at the top of the software element DlgProc. Several variables manage the splash screen bitmap. A couple of symbolic constants provide definitions necessary to the utilization of the hardware timer.

```
HBITMAP SplashBitmap ;
BOOL    SplashBitmapLoaded = FALSE ;

#define TIMER_ID       100
#define DISPLAY_PERIOD 5000
```

The first two declarations in the code listing support the splash screen bitmap. SplashBitmap enables the program to access the loaded Windows bitmap resource. The display of SplashBitmap depends on the value of the variable SplashBitmapLoaded.

Two symbolic constants define important elements of timer management. TIMER_ID provides a unique integer identifier for the specific timer that controls the display of the splash screen. After the duration indicated by DISPLAY_PERIOD, the user interface reverts to the normal application display, so this variable is the elapsed time until the arrival of the first WM_TIMER message.

Modify the OnInitDialog Message Handler

Once the user starts the program, Windows passes a WM_INITDIALOG message to the dialog procedure. Within this message handler, all initialization activities take place.

```
BOOL  OnInitDialog ( HWND  hDlg , HWND  hDlgFocus , long  lInitParam )
{
   HDC       DeviceContext ;
   // Previously Discussed Code Omitted
   DeviceContext = GetDC(hDlg) ;
```

```
ReadABitmapFromAFile(__TEXT("bridge.bmp"), DeviceContext, &SplashBitmap);
ReleaseDC(hDlg,DeviceContext) ;
SplashBitmapLoaded = TRUE ;
SetTimer(hDlg,TIMER_ID,DISPLAY_PERIOD,NULL) ;

return TRUE ;
}
```

This handler performs three basic steps. Using ReadABitmapFromAFile, provided by BitmapUtilities, the handler transfers the splash screen from the BMP file bridge.bmp into the Windows bitmap resource SplashBitmap. Once the bitmap resource has been initialized, the handler then sets the display control flag SplashBitmapLoaded to TRUE to ensure that the splash screen displays. Finally, the SetTimer method initiates a hardware timer with an integer identifier, TIMER_ID, that initiates the first WM_TIMER message after DISPLAY_PERIOD milliseconds have elapsed.

Because this message handler is obviously not for the paint message, the program uses the GetDC method to acquire DeviceContext. This drawing toolkit provides necessary drawing information for ReadABitmapFromAFile to correctly translate the RGB pixels during transfer. ReleaseDC returns DeviceContext to Windows after the bitmap has been transferred from a file to a Windows bitmap resource.

TIP

Any code that would force a repaint is missing and is completely unnecessary. Windows automatically passes an initial WM_PAINT message to the dialog procedure after the processing of this message.

Implement the Body of the DlgOnTimer Message Handler

After DISPLAY_PERIOD elapses, the hardware timer causes Windows to submit a WM_TIMER message to this application. The goal of this handler is to force the transition from the splash screen to the normal application user interface.

```
void DlgOnTimer(HWND hDlg, UINT id)
{
   if ( id == TIMER_ID )
   {
        KillTimer(hDlg,TIMER_ID) ;
        DeleteObject(SplashBitmap) ;
        SplashBitmapLoaded = FALSE ;
        InvalidateRect(hDlg,NULL,TRUE) ;
        UpdateWindow(hDlg) ;
   }
}
```

In response to the receipt of this message, the message handler uses KillTimer to terminate the timer. The purpose of the timer is to signal the termination of the splash screen display. Because this objective is now achieved, the timer becomes unnecessary.

After terminating the timer, the handler uses DeleteObject to eliminate the bitmap resource SplashBitmap. This object utilizes memory in the GDI heap. Unfortunately, the GDI heap is fixed in size across all simultaneously executing Windows applications. So, a program needs to release memory allocated on this heap when the resource is no longer necessary. DeleteObject removes SplashBitmap from the GDI heap, returning the memory to Windows and to GDI.

The message handler then resets the SplashBitmapLoaded flag to FALSE. From this time onward, the DlgOnPaint message handler will ignore this bitmap-display code, which appears in the next section.

Finally, the message handler executes the InvalidateRect/UpdateWindow pair of methods to force an immediate repaint of the client area. The splash screen bitmap disappears, and the normal application client area appears.

Extend the Body of the DlgOnPaint Message Handler

Inside the DlgOnPaint message handler, the flag SplashBitmapLoaded discriminates between displaying the splash screen and showing the normal user interface of the application.

```
void  DlgOnPaint(HWND hDlg)
{
     // Previously Discussed Code Omitted
     if (SplashBitmapLoaded)
     {
          GetClientDimensions( hDlg, &ClientWidth, &ClientHeight ) ;
          GetBitmapDimensions(SplashBitmap,&BitmapWidth, &BitmapHeight) ;
          DisplayABitmap(DeviceContext, SplashBitmap,
                    0 ,MENU_OFFSET ,ClientWidth,ClientHeight,
                    0,0,BitmapWidth,BitmapHeight ) ;
     }
     else
     {
          OldTextColor = SetBkColor(DeviceContext,RGB(255,255,255) ) ;
          ExtTextOut(DeviceContext,40,100,0,NULL,
                    __TEXT("Pocket PC Developer's Guide"),26,NULL) ;
          SetBkColor(DeviceContext,OldTextColor) ;
     }
     // Previously Discussed Code Omitted
}
```

As this code listing demonstrates, if SplashBitmapLoaded is TRUE, the code segment that displays the bitmap executes. Obviously, if the flag possesses the value FALSE, the else portion of the statement executes. In this clause, ExtTextOut displays the text string that comprises the normal user interface.

Prior to using the method ExtTextOut, the message handler establishes a background color for the bounding rectangle of the text string. Using the method SetBkColor, the program places an RGB combination into the background color of the bounding rectangle.

TIP

If the message handler fails to set the text background color to the same color as used to paint the client area, the color mismatch is obvious to the user. A different colored rectangle surrounds each text string.

After displaying the text at the indicated position inside of the client area, the message handler returns DeviceContext to its original state. In order to restore DeviceContext, the handler employs SetBkColor again, using the original background color that was saved in the local variable OldTextColor.

Performing Bitmap Animation Using BitmapUtilities

Another interesting and easily accomplished effect using methods in BitmapUtilities is bitmap animation. An animated bitmap slides across the client area of a window in response to WM_TIMER messages. To demonstrate the power of both BitmapUtilities and the underlying Win32 API methods, this sample program takes an additional step. In this program, one bitmap slides across another bitmap rather than simply moving across the client area.

This demonstration clearly reveals the power of StretchBlt, the workhorse of the Win32 API methods used inside BitmapUtilities. In order to move the bitmap, a program must first move the bitmap and then rapidly redraw the exposed area. Manipulating pixels in this manner can potentially involve extensive pixel manipulation, thus consuming large amounts of CPU time. However, the Win32 API method StretchBlt used inside BitmapUtilities performs all this pixel manipulation extremely rapidly.

Introducing the Graphical User Interface

The user interface for this program is really very simple. A picture of this interface that identifies the elements and their behavior appears in Figure 6-13.

Both background bitmap and foreground bitmap loaded. Timer starts after bitmaps are loaded.

WM_TIMER message handler moves the foreground bitmap.

Figure 6-13 *User interface for an animated bitmap program*

Two bitmaps appear within the client area of this program. Completely filling the client area is a picture of a bunch of cacti. This bitmap is the background bitmap. A second, smaller bitmap, called the *foreground bitmap*, overlays the background bitmap. This foreground bitmap consists of a picture of a mad hacker at a keyboard.

After each of the bitmaps loads into separate Windows resource bitmaps, a timer starts and submits a series of WM_TIMER messages. Every message causes the mad hacker (or foreground bitmap) to move to a different location in the client area.

Moving the foreground bitmap across the face of the background bitmap forces the program to resolve a number of critical issues. In order to move the foreground bitmap around in the client area, the program maintains the location of the upper-left corner of the foreground image (in client area coordinates). This foreground image location updates every time the dialog procedure handles a WM_TIMER message.

Another critical issue is the erasing of the newly exposed area that results from the movement of the foreground image. If not carefully managed, this redraw can require an excessive amount of CPU time.

A final refresh issue deals with the problem of flicker. During the redraw operation, a portion of the new image may appear in the top of the client area while a portion of the old image still exists within the bottom of the client area. If this situation occurs, the image appears to flicker during each redraw. Obviously, this effect will distract and annoy the user.

All these problems are easily managed by using a combination of methods from BitmapUtilities and a direct call to StretchBlt. Programmers often refer to this method as a "raster blaster." Execution time to display a bitmap using this method is minimal, due to extensive optimization by the developers at Microsoft.

Implementing the Bitmap-Animation Program

Performing rapid refreshes of a set of combined bitmaps uses a set of staging bitmap resources as an intermediate storage facility. Appearing in Figure 6-14 is the architecture of the staging process and the included bitmap resources.

The stages used in this refresh process move from the top of the figure to the bottom of the figure. In the first stage, read operations transfer the bitmaps from BMP files into internal bitmap resources. A background image resides in the Windows bitmap resource BGBitmap, whereas the Windows bitmap resource FGBitmap hosts the foreground bitmap.

Any time a program needs to display the combined image, the second stage comes into operation. An intermediate staging bitmap resource, MirrorBitmap, serves as the repository for the combined bitmap resources. First, the program pastes BGBitmap into the MirrorBitmap. Once this activity completes, the program then blasts FGBitmap into MirrorBitmap at a specific relative location. Because FGBitmap enters MirrorBitmap after BGBitmap, the foreground pixels completely replace or overlay the background pixels in the indicated area.

After the MirrorBitmap is created, a simple transfer moves the MirrorBitmap into the appropriate portion of the client area of the application window. This portion appears as the data store ClientAreaBitmap in Figure 6-14.

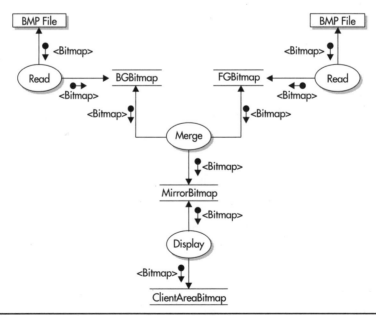

Figure 6-14   *Bitmap staging process for rapid refresh*

All the steps to implement this program occur within the dialog procedure DialogProc. The fact that the changes are limited to just this procedure demonstrates the reusability of the BitmapUtilities software element.

In order to perform the image animation, follow these steps in the dialog procedure DlgProc:

1. Declare the variables to store the input bitmaps.
2. Declare the variables to store the mirror bitmap.
3. Declare the variables to manage the foreground bitmap location.
4. Declare the variables to manage the timer.
5. Declare local methods for actually managing the bitmaps.
6. Update the message handlers to utilize the local methods.
7. Implement the local methods for managing the bitmaps.

Implementing these steps in a maintainable manner involves declaring some variables, adding some local methods, and modifying the body of the dialog procedure DlgProc to utilize the variables and local methods.

Declare the Necessary Variables and Constants

A number of variables and symbolic constants are necessary to manage the bitmap-animation process. These variables fall into four distinct categories: managing the location of the foreground bitmap, controlling the timer, maintaining the input bitmaps, and hosting the mirror bitmap. The following code listing contains the declarations for the variables and symbolic constants.

```
/**************************************************
 * File: DlgProc.c
 * copyright, SWA Engineering, Inc., 2001
 * All rights reserved.
   ********************************************/
// Declare Constants, Variables
// For Managing Location Of
// Foreground Bitmap
#define X_DELTA    5
#define Y_DELTA    5
int     CurrentXLocation ;
int     CurrentYLocation ;
// Declare Constants
// For Managing Timer
```

```
#define TIMER_ID        100
#define DISPLAY_PERIOD  50
// Declare Variables
// For Managing Input Bitmaps
BOOL    BitmapsLoaded = FALSE ;
HBITMAP BGBitmap ;
HBITMAP FGBitmap ;
// Declare Variables
// For Managing Mirror Bitmap
HDC     MirrorDC ;
HBITMAP MirrorBitmap ;
HBITMAP OldBitmap ;
```

Comments within the code listing divide the declarations into sections according to the four categories listed earlier. In most cases, the category combined with the name of the variable indicates pretty clearly the purpose of the variable or constant. However, a few of these elements bear further discussion.

A timer is the basis for events that cause the foreground image to move. Every DISPLAY_PERIOD, the timer generates a WM_TIMER message. In response to each WM_TIMER message, the foreground bitmap moves by the amount X_DELTA pixels and Y_DELTA pixels. These amounts are added to CurrentXLocation and CurrentYLocation, which describe the location of the upper-left corner of the foreground bitmap in client area coordinates.

The two-stage process for displaying the overlaid bitmaps requires two sets of bitmaps. Upon initialization, the foreground bitmap transfers into a stage one bitmap resource named FGBitmap. Similarly, the program uses a stage-one bitmap resource BGBitmap to maintain the background bitmap. In response to a WM_TIMER message, a local function executed by the DlgOnTimer message handler copies these two bitmaps into the stage-two bitmap, MirrorBitmap. Creating a memory bitmap requires that a program create a memory device context, MirrorDC, and then attach the MirrorBitmap to the MirrorDC. The program stores the OldBitmap from MirrorDC to restore this bitmap prior to returning the bitmap to Windows.

Implement the Local Support Methods

A number of important processing steps occur in response to specific Windows messages. Rather than placing the code that executes these steps directly into the message handlers, a series of local support methods manage the required processing steps.

```
void LoadTheBitmaps(HWND Window)
{
    DeviceContext = GetDC(Window) ;
```

```
        ReadABitmapFromAFile( __TEXT("cactus.bmp"),
                        DeviceContext , &BGBitmap ) ;
        ReadABitmapFromAFile( __TEXT("mad_hacker.bmp"),
                        DeviceContext , &FGBitmap ) ;

        GetBitmapDimensions(BGBitmap,&BitmapWidth,&BitmapHeight) ;
        MirrorDC = CreateCompatibleDC(DeviceContext) ;
        MirrorBitmap = CreateCompatibleBitmap(DeviceContext, BitmapWidth,
                                        BitmapHeight) ;
        OldBitmap = SelectObject(MirrorDC,MirrorBitmap) ;

        ReleaseDC(Window,DeviceContext) ;

        BitmapsLoaded = TRUE ;
}
```

The purpose of this local method is to initialize the various bitmap resources.
Using GetDC, the method obtains a device context for the current window. With
this device context, the local method employs ReadABitmapFromAFile from
BitmapUtilities to read the bitmap files into the bitmap resources BGBitmap and
FGBitmap. In the last portion of this method, the program exercises the steps
necessary to create the second-stage bitmap MirrorBitmap. These steps must be
performed in exactly this order of execution.

```
void DisplayTheBitmaps(HWND Window, HDC DeviceContext)
{
        GetClientDimensions(Window,&ClientWidth, &ClientHeight) ;
        GetBitmapDimensions(BGBitmap,&BGBitmapWidth, &BGBitmapHeight) ;
        GetBitmapDimensions(FGBitmap,&FGBitmapWidth, &FGBitmapHeight) ;

        DisplayABitmap(MirrorDC, BGBitmap,
                        0 ,MENU_OFFSET , ClientWidth,ClientHeight,
                        0,0,BGBitmapWidth,BGBitmapHeight ) ;
        DisplayABitmap(MirrorDC, FGBitmap,
                        CurrentXLocation ,CurrentYLocation ,
                        FGBitmapWidth,FGBitmapHeight ,
                        0,0,FGBitmapWidth,FGBitmapHeight ) ;

        StretchBlt(DeviceContext,0,0,BGBitmapWidth,BGBitmapHeight,
                MirrorDC,0,0,BGBitmapWidth, BGBitmapHeight,SRCCOPY) ;
}
```

When this local method executes, the FGBitmap moves to a new location in the
BGBitmap. First, the method copies the BGBitmap into the MirrorBitmap attached
to MirrorDC using the method DisplayABitmap from BitmapUtilities. DisplayABitmap
does not care whether the destination device context is in memory or associated

with a frame buffer and the actual display device. Once the BGBitmap resides in the MirrorBitmap of MirrorDC, this method then places the FGBitmap into the MirrorBitmap of MirrorDC, again reusing the DisplayABitmap method. When copying the FGBitmap into MirrorBitmap, DisplayABitmap offsets FGBitmap by the amounts CurrentXLocation and CurrentYLocation. These two steps complete stage one of the process to animate the FGBitmap. Stage two consists of directly executing the Win32 API method StretchBlt to map the MirrorBitmap attached to MirrorDC into the frame buffer managed by the window DeviceContext. As a result of these two stages of processing, the FGBitmap moves to the new location (CurrentXLocation, CurrentYLocation) in the client area of the application window.

```
void UpdateTheBitmaps(HWND Window)
{
    CurrentXLocation = CurrentXLocation + X_DELTA ;
    CurrentYLocation = CurrentYLocation + Y_DELTA ;

  GetClientDimensions(Window,&ClientWidth, &ClientHeight) ;
  if ( CurrentXLocation > ClientWidth )
        CurrentXLocation = 0 ;
    if ( CurrentYLocation > ClientHeight )
        CurrentYLocation = MENU_OFFSET ;
}
```

Executing this local method simply computes the new location of the foreground bitmap FGBitmap. Each of the location components updates by a delta amount. Before accepting these new values, a validation check ensures that each coordinate value is within the range of the client area of the application window. Using the method GetClientDimensions provided by BitmapUtilities, the width of the client area and the height of the client area appear in the variables ClientWidth and ClientHeight, respectively. If either of the newly computed FGBitmap locations exceeds these limits, the location is reset to wrap around to the top-left corner of the client area.

```
void ClearTheBitmaps(HWND Window)
{
    SelectObject(MirrorDC,OldBitmap) ;
    ReleaseDC(Window,MirrorDC) ;
    DeleteObject(MirrorBitmap) ;

    DeleteObject(BGBitmap) ;
    DeleteObject(FGBitmap) ;
}
```

This method releases the various GDI objects back to Windows in order to free the allocated space from the limited-size GDI heap. With the SelectObject method, the program returns the original bitmap to the in-memory MirrorDC. Now that MirrorDC is no longer necessary, ReleaseDC performs the actual return of this GDI object to Windows. All the bitmap resources are also GDI objects. Using the DeleteObject method causes these memory resources of these objects to be released.

Modify the Bodies of the Message Handlers

Each of the preceding local methods executes from within a specific message handler. In the following code listings, only a portion of the message handler appears. Each message handler subset illustrates the usage of the various local methods. The following message handlers appear in the order of execution over the lifecycle of the program.

```
BOOL  OnInitDialog  ( HWND  hDlg , HWND  hDlgFocus , long  lInitParam )
{
// Previously Discussed Code Omitted
      LoadTheBitmaps(hDlg) ;
      SetTimer(hDlg,TIMER_ID,DISPLAY_PERIOD,NULL) ;
    return TRUE ;
}
```

At the end of the OnInitDialog message handler, LoadTheBitmaps creates the bitmap resources utilized in the two-stage image-animation display process. Once the bitmap resources are created, this handler initiates timer operations using SetTimer. A timer message enters the message queue every DISPLAY_PERIOD.

```
void DlgOnTimer(HWND hDlg, UINT id)
{
   if ( id == TIMER_ID )
   {
        UpdateTheBitmaps(hDlg) ;
        InvalidateRect(hDlg,NULL,FALSE) ;
        UpdateWindow(hDlg) ;
   }
}
```

When DlgProc routes the timer message to this handler, this method executes. After ensuring that the timer source is TIMER_ID, this method first updates the location of the FGBitmap by executing the local method UpdateTheBitmaps. After updating and checking for client area limitations, executing the method pair InvalidateRect/UpdateWindow forces an immediate repaint of the client area. Using the FALSE flag as the last argument, InvalidateRect eliminates repainting the background of the client area. Because the BGImage fills the whole client area, the handler does not need to consume extra CPU cycles repainting the background. Additionally, if this flag were set to TRUE, the user would see a flicker as the background was repainted white and the MirrorBitmap was copied into the client area.

```
void  DlgOnPaint(HWND hDlg)
{
// Previously Discussed Code Omitted
    if (BitmapsLoaded)
        DisplayTheBitmaps(hDlg,DeviceContext) ;

}
```

As a result of executing the InvalidateRect/UpdateWindow method pair, this handler then executes. After ensuring that the bitmaps have been loaded by checking the flag BitmapsLoaded, executing the local method DisplayTheBitmaps steps through the two-stage process to animate the FGBitmap to the newly computed location. Maintaining a BitmapsLoaded flag is necessary because the WM_PAINT message handler actually executes once before the WM_INITDIALOG message handler loads the bitmaps. If this flag does not defer bitmap display until after the WM_INITDIALOG message handler actually loads the bitmaps, the program experiences a catastrophic failure.

```
void  DlgOnCommand  ( HWND  hDlg , int  iID ,
                      HWND  hDlgCtl , UINT  uCodeNotify )
{
  switch( iID )
  {
    case IDOK:
        KillTimer(hDlg,TIMER_ID) ;
        ClearTheBitmaps(hDlg) ;
        EndDialog(hDlg , 0)  ;
    break ;
  }
}
```

A user terminates this program by selecting the Quit item from the main menu bar. This action causes the DlgOnCommand message handler to execute the IDOK case clause in the message handler body. Prior to terminating the dialog, this handler stops the timer using KillTimer and employs the local method ClearTheBitmaps to return the staging bitmap resources BGBitmap, FGBitmap, and MirrorBitmap to Windows in order to release the space consumed from the fixed-size GDI heap.

Preparing ActiveSync for the Programs in this Chapter

Prior to using the applications of this chapter on a Pocket PC, a user transfers the bitmap files onto the Pocket PC. This transfer involves using Microsoft ActiveSync to accomplish the transfer. When installed, ActiveSync assumes that any bitmap being transferred converts from its original format into a 2-bit-per-pixel representation. For these programs to work correctly, the user first modifies the default settings of ActiveSync to simply perform a straight transfer of the bitmap.

Beside the fact that the programs in this chapter expect all input files to be in standard BMP file format, the user sees another important direct benefit from using the files in their original format. If an image file utilizes only 2 bits per pixel, then each pixel can only represent up to four colors. However, with the standard BMP format, each pixel can have up to 24 bits per pixel, a significantly larger number of colors, thus providing the user with a much more detailed and accurate image.

The next series of figures describe the steps to reconfigure ActiveSync to perform a simple bitmap transfer. Figure 6-15 demonstrates the first steps that the user must take.

The first step begins with the user clicking the Tools menu item from the main menu bar. This action causes the display of a popup submenu from which a user selects the Options submenu item. If a Pocket PC is not connected to the desktop machine, ActiveSync disables all the submenu items, so the user must make sure that the cradle is attached to the serial port and that a Pocket PC is in the cradle and powered on.

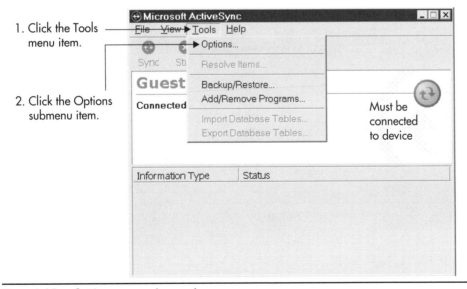

Figure 6-15   *Setting conversion options*

After the user selects the Options submenu item, the Options dialog displays, as shown in Figure 6-16.

Because the goal of this sequence of operations is to modify the conversion settings, a single action transitions past this dialog. The user uses the left mouse button to click the Conversion Settings button.

After clicking the button, a user sees the File Conversion Properties dialog, which appears in Figure 6-17.

This particular dialog allows a user to separately control conversion settings for transfers from desktop to device and device to desktop. Conversion options may be set for a number of categories of files in each direction.

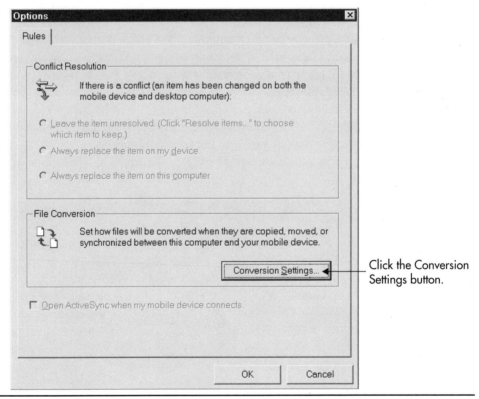

Figure 6-16   *Selecting conversion settings*

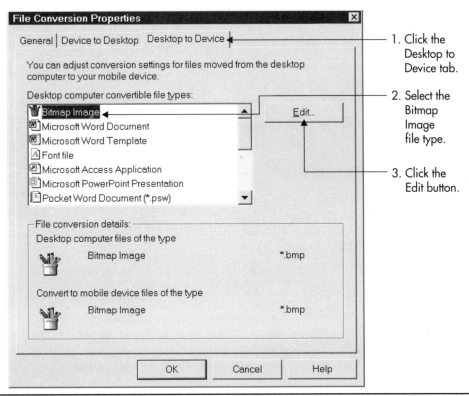

Figure 6-17   *Choosing bitmap images*

In this example, the purpose is to manage conversions of bitmap files from the desktop to the device. In order to gain access to the options for this combination of conditions, a user performs the following sequence of actions:

1. Click the Desktop to Device tab.
2. Select the Bitmap Image file type.
3. Click the Edit button.

As a result of this sequence of actions, a new dialog appears to the user. Figure 6-18 contains this dialog, called the Edit Conversion Settings dialog.

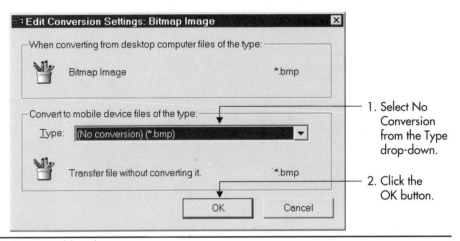

Figure 6-18 *Disabling bitmap conversion*

The important choice to be made in this dialog is the conversion option selected from the Type drop-down control. Choose the No Conversion option. As indicated in Figure 6-18, selecting this option causes ActiveSync to transfer the file without converting to the 2-bit-per-pixel format.

By selecting this option, the user ensures that all the programs in this chapter work correctly on the Pocket PC device.

Summary

This chapter emphasizes the use of detailed, rich bitmap images to improve the graphical user interface of any Pocket PC program. Because the execution sequences associated with a bitmap occur with great regularity, a BitmapUtilities functional encapsulation provides a set of methods that encompass the repeatable execution sequences. The methods in this encapsulation enable a Pocket PC programmer to write code that looks like logical operations on a bitmap resource rather than replicating tedious bitmap execution sequences throughout an application. Using the functional encapsulation BitmapUtilities, three separate programs illustrate the ease of adding realistic bitmap-processing activities to any application.

▶   All activities with bitmaps, including the methods of BitmapUtilities, operate on a Windows bitmap resource—a GDI object that already exists.

► Every complex data structure in a program follows the basic cycle of external – internal – local – internal – external during a typical program execution, which becomes the basic unit-testing sequence.

► Edge-detection algorithms apply a kernel to the pixels of a bitmap image to replace pixels by a weighted average of surrounding pixels.

► When displaying a bitmap on a Pocket PC, a program explicitly adjusts the location of the upper-left corner of the bitmap; otherwise, the main menu bar obscures the top portion of the bitmap.

► Image animation with bitmaps requires the use of an in-memory, mirror bitmap to stage the combined foreground and background bitmap prior to the actual display in the client area of a window.

Sample Programs on the Web

The following programs are available at http://www.osborne.com:

Description	Folder
Desktop Image-Processing Program	ImageProcessingProgram
Pocket PC Image-Processing Program	ImageProcessingProgramPPC
Desktop Splash Screen Program	SplashScreenProgram
Pocket PC Splash Screen Program	SplashScreenProgramPPC
Desktop Image-Animation Program	ImageAnimationProgram
Pocket PC Image-Animation Program	ImageAnimationProgramPPC

Execution Instructions

Desktop Image-Processing Program

1. Start Visual C++ 6.0.

2. Open the project ImageProcessingProgram.dsw in the folder ImageProcessingProgram.

3. Build the program.

4. Execute the program.

5. Choose the Select main menu item and the Input popup submenu item.

6. From the File Open dialog, choose the hardware.bmp file and click the Open button.

7. Choose the Image main menu item and the Load popup submenu item.

8. Choose the Image main menu item and the Display popup submenu item. The hardware image appears in the client area.

9. Choose the Image main menu item and the Filter popup submenu item. The edges of the hardware image appear in the client area. The edges are white and the remainder of the client area is black.

10. Choose the Select main menu item and the Output popup submenu item.

11. In the File Name field of the File Save dialog, enter **edges.bmp** and click the Save button.

12. Choose the Image main menu item and the Dump popup submenu item.

13. Choose the Image main menu item and the Store popup submenu item.

14. Click the Quit menu item on the window menu bar.

15. The application window disappears as the application terminates.

16. Repeat the necessary steps to select/input, load, and display the edge.bmp file to see that the edge-filtered image was successfully saved.

Pocket PC Image-Processing Program

1. Prepare ActiveSync to simply transfer the bitmap images to the Pocket PC as described in the last section of this chapter.

2. Attach the Pocket PC cradle to the desktop computer.

3. Insert the Pocket PC into the cradle.

4. Tell ActiveSync to create a guest connection.

5. Make sure that the status is connected.

6. Using the Windows File Explorer, transfer the file BLDG.BMP from the desktop to the Pocket PC. If correctly configured, ActiveSync does not convert the BMP file.

7. Start Embedded Visual C++ 3.0.

8. Open the project ImageAnimationProgramPPC.vcw in the folder ImageAnimationProgramPPC.

9. Build the program.

10. Make sure the program successfully downloads to the Pocket PC.

11. On the Pocket PC, open the File Explorer.

12. Browse to the MyDevice folder.

13. Execute the program ImageAnimationProgram.

14. Choose the Select main menu item and the Input popup submenu item.

15. From the File Open dialog, choose the hardware.bmp file and click the Open button.

16. Choose the Image main menu item and the Load popup submenu item.

17. Choose the Image main menu item and the Display popup submenu item. The hardware image appears in the client area.

18. Choose the Image main menu item and the Filter popup submenu item. The edges of the hardware image appear in the client area. The edges are white and the remainder of the client area is black.

19. Choose the Select main menu item and the Output popup submenu item.

20. In the File Name field of the File Save dialog, enter the edges.bmp file name and click the Save button.

21. Choose the Image main menu item and the Dump popup submenu item.

22. Choose the Image main menu item and the Store popup submenu item.

23. Tap the Quit menu item on the window menu bar.

24. The application window disappears as the application terminates.

25. Repeat the necessary steps to select/input, load, and display the edge.bmp file to see that the edge-filtered image was successfully saved.

Desktop Splash Screen Program

1. Start Visual C++ 6.0.

2. Open the project SplashScreenProgram.dsw in the folder SplashScreenProgram.

3. Build the program.

4. Execute the program.

5. Initially, the program displays a client area filled with a picture of a bridge.

6. After a certain amount of time passes, the picture of the bridge disappears, leaving a white client area that displays the string "Pocket PC Developer's Guide."

7. Click the Quit menu item on the window menu bar.

8. The application window disappears as the application terminates.

Pocket PC Splash Screen Program

1. Prepare ActiveSync to simply transfer the bitmap images to the Pocket PC as described in the last section of this chapter.

2. Attach the Pocket PC cradle to the desktop computer.

3. Insert the Pocket PC into the cradle.

4. Tell ActiveSync to create a guest connection.

5. Make sure that the status is connected.

6. Using the Windows File Explorer, transfer the file BRIDGE.BMP from the desktop to the Pocket PC. If correctly configured, ActiveSync does not convert the BMP file.

7. Start Embedded Visual C++ 3.0.

8. Open the project SplashScreenProgramPPC.vcw in the folder SplashScreenProgramPPC.

9. Build the program.

10. Make sure the program successfully downloads to the Pocket PC.

11. On the Pocket PC, open the File Explorer.

12. Browse to the MyDevice folder.

13. Execute the program SplashScreenProgram.

14. Initially, the program displays a client area filled with a picture of a bridge.

15. After a certain amount of time passes, the picture of the bridge disappears, leaving a white client area that displays the string "Pocket PC Developer's Guide."

16. Tap the Quit menu item on the window menu bar.

17. The application window disappears as the application terminates.

Desktop Image-Animation Program

1. Start Visual C++ 6.0.

2. Open the project ImageAnimationProgram.dsw in the folder ImageAnimationProgram.

3. Build the program.

4. Execute the program.

5. Initially, the program displays a cactus photo in the background of the client area with a mad hacker picture in the upper-left corner.

6. After a certain amount of time passes, the mad hacker picture moves to a new location in the client area. The image area exposed by this movement rapidly refreshes. A user does not see any flicker during this repaint and picture location transfer.

7. Every so often, the mad hacker picture rapidly and smoothly moves to a new location in the client area.

8. Click the Quit menu item on the window menu bar.

9. The application window disappears as the application terminates.

Pocket PC Image-Animation Program

1. Prepare ActiveSync to simply transfer the bitmap images to the Pocket PC as described in the last section of this chapter.

2. Attach the Pocket PC cradle to the desktop computer.

3. Insert the Pocket PC into the cradle.

4. Tell ActiveSync to create a guest connection.

5. Make sure that the status is connected.

6. Using the Windows File Explorer, transfer the files CACTUS.BMP and MAD_HACKER.bmp from the desktop to the Pocket PC. If correctly configured, ActiveSync does not convert the BMP files.

7. Start Embedded Visual C++ 3.0.

8. Open the project ImageAnimationProgramPPC.vcw in the folder SplashScreenProgramPPC.

9. Build the program.

10. Make sure the program successfully downloads to the Pocket PC.

11. On the Pocket PC, open the File Explorer.

12. Browse to the MyDevice folder.

13. Execute the program ImageAnimationProgram.

14. Initially, the program displays a cactus photo in the background of the client area with a mad hacker picture in the upper-left corner.

15. After a certain amount of time passes, the mad hacker picture moves to a new location in the client area. The image area exposed by this movement rapidly refreshes. A user does not see any flicker during this repaint and picture location transfer.

16. Every so often, the mad hacker picture rapidly and smoothly moves to a new location in the client area.

17. Tap the Quit menu item on the window menu bar.

18. The application window disappears as the application terminates.

PART III

User-Friendly Applications in Small Spaces

OBJECTIVES

- ▶ Employ a state machine to manage a user interface

- ▶ Utilize a layered design to separate control, data

- ▶ Employ intrinsic controls in a user interface

- ▶ Develop a drawing program with a complex interface

- ▶ Use bitmap buttons to control access to areas

- ▶ Use tab pages to control access to categories

- ▶ Use a layered design to manage program parameters

- ▶ Develop a library for storage format independence

- ▶ Target the library to multiple storage formats

Using an Effective Software Design

With the implementation of the drawing program in Chapter 5, a user can only draw a line. Admittedly, a program that can only draw a single line has limited usefulness. In this chapter, extensions to the drawing program enable the user to select from multiple drawing shapes: line, rectangle, rounded rectangle, and ellipse. In addition to allowing multiple drawing shapes, the drawing program undergoes a complete redesign. Based on the critique at the end of the chapter, this new design employs a single, encapsulated state variable managed by a state machine and an action table to manage the user interface. Additionally, a layered implementation isolates the user interface management, the logical control, and the data management into separate layers.

The simplest approach available to provide selection alternatives, such as drawing shapes, is to employ a menu. A menu presents a discrete list of predefined options. The user can then select from these options. Once the user selects a specific drawing style from the menu, the program stores the default style for later recall. In the desire to provide effective data management, the program places this style into an encapsulating class that maintains common values for all client classes. This class manages the default values and is therefore the DefaultMgr.

In essence, this program exists in one of four states: idle, drawing, pretyping, and typing. Rather than using combinations of four variables to represent these states, a single state variable suffices. This variable, when combined with state machine logic, enables the program to centralize all the decision logic into a single method. As a result, debugging the control logic of the program becomes a far easier task, improving programmer productivity and reducing the time to deliver the program to the marketplace.

As discussed at the end of the Chapter 5, the implementation of the drawing program is complicated and messy. This mess contributes to extended delays when trying to incorporate new features into the program. In this chapter, the drawing program exhibits a complete redesign that isolates the user interface management, the decision control logic, and the data management into separate layers of code. Each layer performs method calls to the next lower layer. By using this isolation, new features are easily incorporated into the program. Additionally, new features can take advantage of previously implemented code in the lower layers, contributing to programmer productivity and reducing time to market.

NOTE

In fact, design issues must take precedence over coding early in the development of any program. In order to obtain a specific feature set within a limited development period, developers must devote about 50 percent of the development period to identifying requirements and resolving design issues—before starting any coding. This approach is contrary to the approach used by most developers, who start coding on day one with the intention of making the program work during integration.

Developing the Design Rationale

The goal of this specific application is to introduce an effective design for implementing the drawing program. This design should admit to extensibility—easily adding new features, developer productivity, and performance. An evolutionary approach to this design appears in this chapter. Various aspects of the program behavior introduce specific design elements. Each new set of elements contributes to the effectiveness of the design. At the end, a layered design results that isolates the user interface, control and sequencing logic, and data management into separate, interacting layers.

NOTE

Through the use of a combination of layered, isolating software elements and data-abstraction techniques, an extensible design prevails. Each layer isolates the effect of code changes to a single layer of code. Changes in the logic and structure in one layer typically have no effect on the logic and structures of code in other layers. Encapsulating lower layers also contributes to productivity, because new elements in a layer can capitalize on methods that already exist in lower layers.

A graphical user interface that provides a user with menu-selection capabilities appears in Figure 7-1.

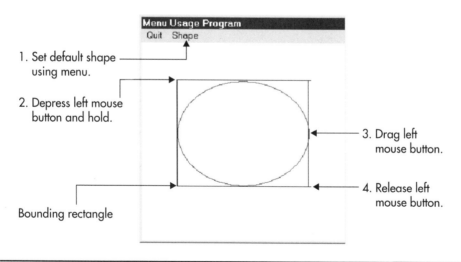

Figure 7-1   *Menu-driven user interface for the drawing program*

When the user sees the interface, in addition to the Quit menu item, the menu bar now provides one other menu item: Shape. The numbers placed in Figure 7-1 indicate the sequence of operations as performed by a user. This sequence is as follows:

1. Set the default shape to be a line, rectangle, round rectangle, or ellipse using the pop-up menu triggered from selecting the Shape menu item.

2. Point the left mouse button to an arbitrary location in the client area. Depress the left mouse button and hold.

3. Drag the mouse cursor to a second location. Based on the current endpoint, the program creates a bounding rectangle that becomes the basis for drawing the default shape.

4. Release the left mouse button. The last shape drawn by the program remains displayed in the client area.

This sequence uses the rubber-banded drawing operations implemented in Chapter 5. However, in this situation, the rubber-banding process also applies to an arbitrary drawing object rather than just a simple line.

When working with menus inside a program, a specific vocabulary identifies all the elements of a menu. The key menu elements used appear in Figure 7-2.

Across the top of the user interface appears a grayed bar called the *main menu bar*. A set of one or more labels comprises the entries on the menu bar. Each label on the

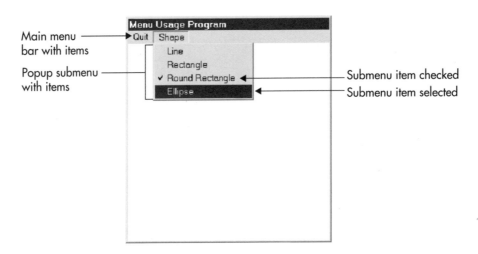

Figure 7-2   *Components of a menu*

bar is a *main menu item*. Frequently, when a user clicks a main menu item, this clicking causes the display of a *pop-up submenu*. Labels on a submenu go by the term *submenu item*.

A submenu item can lead to a *pop-up subsubmenu*. This menu then has *subsubmenu items*. In many programs, this nesting of menus can occur through a large number of levels. A program can continue this connectivity for as many levels deep as desired.

As a user drags the mouse pointer across a set of main menu items, the area around the menu item rises. This phenomenon goes by the name *selection*. Raising the area around the menu item serves as a visual cue to the user to indicate that this item is currently being considered. Submenu items may also exhibit visual cues when touched by the mouse cursor. With submenu items, selection appears as a colored (usually blue) highlighting of the area around the submenu item.

The purpose of using selection to indicate the current choice of interest is to enable a user to consider before choosing. This delay enables the user to contemplate the effect of a given selection and change to a different selection if desired.

Another useful visual cue informs the user of the chosen selection upon the previous visit to the submenu. This cue exists in the form of a *checked* submenu item. In a situation such as choosing a default line style, this cue indicates to the user the current state of the default line style. Given that dozens of selection alternatives may be available in a particular menu structure, asking the user to mentally recall each of the previously selected alternative values is quite tedious and overbearing.

NOTE

Using menus is an extremely poor approach for providing an effective graphical user interface, especially on a Pocket PC.

All the drawing shape selections could appear as menu items across the top of the main menu bar. However, this arrangement is a poor design for the Pocket PC. As new features are added to a drawing program, providing selection alternatives from a menu results in a crowded mess, with no easy way to distinguish one list of alternatives from another.

Menus do an extremely poor job in controlling the sequence that a user follows. For most applications, a user generally must execute a specific sequence of actions. For example, hardware connections may first be necessary. Attaching to parameter files may be the next required step. Moreover, everything a user needs should be available on the face of the current window. Overlaying of selections causes confusion and may hide information that a user needs to make the selection.

In fact, Chapter 8 introduces a much better alternative to creating a complex user interface. Area icons lead to category tab pages. Due to the limited screen space on the Pocket PC, this hierarchical approach with icons and tab pages leads to a much more user-friendly interface.

Menu items and submenu items are entities that enable user interaction. When a menu is displayed, a user selects a specific item on the menu. Then, the program responds to the user interaction in a clearly defined manner. Figure 7-3 characterizes the manner in which a program responds to a menu item selection.

As characterized in Figure 7-3, the response details occur as follows:

1. The user taps the stylus on a specific submenu item.

2. This interaction causes Windows to generate a WM_COMMAND message. Embedded in this message is the unique integer identifier of the submenu item. Windows routes this message to the DlgOnCommand message handler inside the dialog procedure DlgProc.

3. Inside the body of the WM_COMMAND message handler, the program responds to the chosen submenu item. This program sets the default drawing style associated with the submenu item. Setting the associated drawing style involves passing the default drawing style into a DefaultValues data structure.

4. Any time the user clicks the Shape menu item from the main menu bar, the pop-up submenu displays. Windows generates a WM_INITMENUPOPUP message prior to displaying the pop-up submenu. The message handler for this message sets the check mark for the submenu item that represents the currently selected style. By setting this check mark, the program visually cues the user as to the previously chosen submenu item.

5. To set the check mark of the selected menu item, the message handler reads the default drawing style from the DefaultValues data structure.

6. The check mark of the previously chosen submenu item is set. The user sees the check mark displayed.

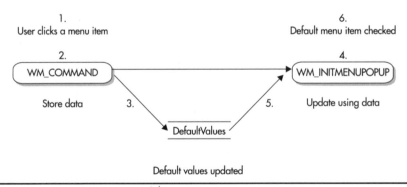

Figure 7-3   *Servicing menu item selection messages*

Interestingly enough, the program does not need to perform the actual highlighting during the selection process of dragging the mouse cursor over a list of submenu items. Once the program constructs and connects the menus, the USER component of Windows does all the selection updating work on behalf of the program.

Notice the appearance of a data structure called DefaultValues. One of these values is the drawing shape to be selected in the menu. In keeping with the encapsulating design style introduced earlier, the program maintains these default values through a default manager element named DefaultMgr. The use of the DefaultMgr in support of menu item processing appears in Figure 7-4.

The DefaultMgr element maintains a persistent, globally accessible set of values available to all other elements of the program. As an example, in response to selecting a pop-up submenu item, the DlgOnCommand message handler uses the Set access methods to register a set of defaults with DefaultMgr. For instance, this WM_COMMAND message handler inserts a default shape by executing the method SetDefaultShape and providing a code for the Shape as an argument to the method.

NOTE

Because the DefaultMgr element caches a single instance of the default style variables, this form of encapsulation qualifies as an object manager. An object manager provides a form of data encapsulation that maintains single instances of values.

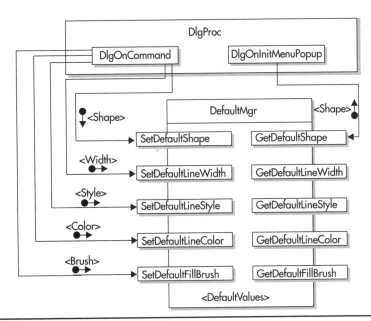

Figure 7-4   *Setting default values with a menu*

Other methods in the application access these default values through the Get access methods. With respect to submenu item processing, the DlgOnInitMenuPopup method reads the default shape to set the appropriate submenu item prior to display. This handler executes the method GetDefaultShape, receiving the currently registered shape in return. Using this returned value, the message handler can set the check for the associated submenu item.

DefaultValues appear in Figure 7-4 completely hidden from the remainder of the program but shown inside the box labeled DefaultMgr. Other methods may not access these values without going through the Set and Get access methods. This kind of hiding requires that the static storage class attribute be assigned to the variables declared inside DefaultMgr.

Once a user indicates the default drawing shape and the shape is registered with DefaultMgr, the user will likely begin drawing. Of course, this activity involves processing WM_MOUSEMOVE messages, as described in Chapter 5. However, in order to progress toward a more effective design, the program needs to manage drawing data using an encapsulation manager. From a strictly objective perspective, the program needs to manage draw objects.

Figure 7-5 shows the combined use of draw objects and the DefaultMgr when servicing WM_MOUSEMOVE messages.

As Figure 7-5 indicates, two draw objects are necessary. PreviousDrawObject tells the drawing style and endpoints of the last object drawn. The second object, named CurrentDrawObject, stores the drawing style and endpoints of the new object to be drawn. When storing the drawing style into CurrentDrawObject, the program retrieves the drawing style from the set of default values by requesting the values from

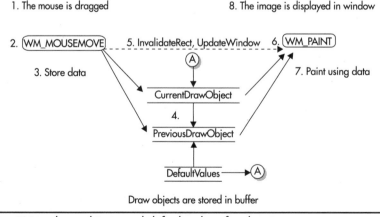

Figure 7-5 *Using draw objects and default values for drawing*

the DefaultMgr. The circled numbers indicate the sequence of execution. The circled letter shows the flow of the default drawing style from the DefaultValues managed by DefaultMgr into the draw objects, PreviousDrawObject and CurrentDrawObject.

In Chapter 5, the program utilized four variables to store the drawing data— DragStart, DragStop, CurrentX, and CurrentY. However, this implementation only uses two objects—PreviousDrawObject and CurrentDrawObject. Ultimately, the code using draw objects is less complex and less tricky than the code using the four data objects directly.

NOTE

When a program manages to use effective design to reduce code complexity, the developer is assured of getting software integrated, tested, and to the marketplace in a much shorter period of time. Managers are happy, and programmers get to work fewer hours.

A linear description of the program execution sequence characterized in Figure 7-5 follows:

1. The user drags the mouse.

2. A WM_MOUSEMOVE message arrives at the dialog procedure.

3. The primary goal of this "mouse move" message handler is to store the necessary data into the draw objects.

4. Inside the body of the "mouse move" message handler, the program copies the CurrentDrawObject into the PreviousDrawObject. This copy enables the handler to redefine the CurrentDrawObject. Values for the CurrentDrawObject come from the default drawing shape and styles, as provided by the DefaultMgr.

5. Inside the body of the "mouse move" message handler, the program then executes the method sequence InvalidateRect followed by UpdateWindow to force a repaint of the client area.

6. A WM_PAINT message causes execution of the DlgOnPaint message handler.

7. Inside the body of the paint message handler, the program reads the draw object properties from the DefaultMgr and uses these properties to erase the old object and draw the new object.

8. The user sees the previous draw object disappear, followed by the appearance of the new draw object, thus yielding the rubber-banded drawing effect.

In this sequence, the draw objects replace the individual variables. In essence, each draw object is a stand-alone entity that contains all data necessary to characterize a specific drawing situation. Placing these characteristics into a single, manageable entity enables a developer to easily modify and enhance the drawing characteristics with a minimum of effort.

NOTE

Implementing the ability to support multiple instances of a draw object requires a new type of encapsulating mechanism called a data type manager or a type manager. The first argument to every method supported by a DrawObjMgr type manager receives an instance of the data type DrawObjectType as the first argument.

Figure 7-6 contains the new type manager, named DrawObjMgr. Further, this diagram reveals the means for storing and utilizing specific instances of DrawObjectType within the drawing program.

As this figure demonstrates, the DrawObjMgr element manages a set of drawing properties, such as Shape, Rectangle, LineWidth, and others, for a specific instance of DrawObjectType. Both the methods illustrated in the figure require a specific DrawObject as their first argument. This argument appears on the arrow entering into the method. A smaller arrow with a circle at the base points toward the method, indicating that the DrawObject passes into the method.

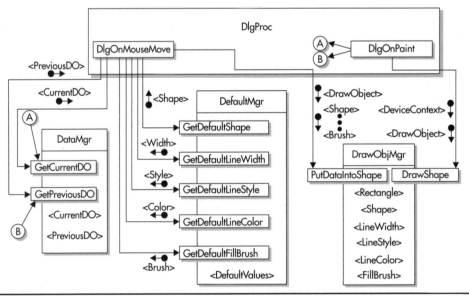

Figure 7-6 *Using draw objects for rubber-banded drawing*

TIP

For the encapsulation elements depicted in Figure 7-6, only a few of the supported methods appear. Only those methods relevant to the discussion at hand appear in the figure.

Appearing in this figure are three important encapsulation elements. The first element is DrawObjMgr. This element is the type manager for instances of DrawObjectType. Another element, discussed earlier in this chapter, is DefaultMgr. As described earlier, this element is an object manager for single instances of the default drawing styling values, indicated by user selection of a pop-up submenu item. A new element appears at the lower-left corner of the figure. A DataMgr element, described in Chapter 3 as an integral element in the minimal dialog program, serves as an object manager to house the two specific instances of DrawObjectType, named PreviousDrawObject and CurrentDrawObject.

NOTE

These three elements—DataMgr, DefaultMgr, and DrawObjMgr—compose the data management layer of the layered design, which is the lowest layer in the design. The common goal of these elements is to isolate data structure details from the remainder of the application.

Using the interactions and relationships of the software elements depicted in the figure, an understanding of the operational behavior of the program is available, as follows:

1. When dragging the mouse, the user causes WM_MOUSEMOVE messages to enter the dialog procedure.

2. These messages route to the DlgOnMouseMove message handler method.

3. The message handler first interacts with the DataMgr element to retrieve the PreviousDrawObject, CurrentDrawObject, and MouseLocation from the cache. Extraction from the cache internal to the DataMgr uses the methods GetPreviousDrawObject, GetCurrentDrawObject, and GetMouseLocation (not shown in the figure).

4. Next, the handler uses the method GetShapeBoundingRect (not shown in the figure) provided by DrawObjMgr to get the bounding rectangle from the CurrentDrawObject. Then, using the DefaultMgr, the handler extracts the current default attributes, such as Shape, LineWidth, and other features.

5. Next, the handler executes the method PutDataIntoShape to store the bounding rectangle and the default attributes into the PreviousDrawObject.

6. Finally, the method PutDataIntoShape enables the message handler to install the upper-left corner of the bounding rectangle, the mouse location, and the default attributes into the CurrentDrawObject.

7. After establishing the features of the draw objects, the handler sequentially executes the InvalidateRect and UpdateWindow methods, forcing a repaint of the client area.

8. In response, the dialog procedure executes the DlgOnPaint message handler for the WM_PAINT message.

9. In the body of this message handler, the program retrieves the draw objects from the DataMgr using the access methods GetPreviousDrawObject and GetCurrentDrawObject. (Lettered circles in the figure serve as connection points to represent these interactions. Drawing the actual interaction lines would significantly clutter the diagram.)

10. After setting the appropriate binary raster operation, the paint message handler submits the device context and each draw object to the DrawObjMgr, causing the rubber-banded drawing to work correctly.

Follow the interactions described in Figure 7-6. This sequence provides an excellent view of the manner in which data encapsulation through object managers (DataMgr and DefaultMgr) and type managers (DrawObjMgr) work to provide an extensible design.

Unfortunately, adding these program elements fails to completely resolve the extensibility requirement. As currently implemented, the program employs a number of state variables and some rather messy code logic to manage these variables. In fact, the user interface exists in a variety of states. Processing on the part of the program and the various message handlers directly correlates to these states. Therefore, an additional enhancement to the program uses a state machine–based approach to manage the user interface and the response of the program to user interactions.

An effective state machine for the drawing program utilizes four states: idle, drawing, pretyping, and typing. Figure 7-7 contains a depiction of the necessary state machine.

In this figure, a rectangle represents a specific state of the user interface. In the middle of each state rectangle is a label that identifies the name of the state. An arrow indicates a specific, allowable transition between two states. A state at the base of the arrow is the state in which the program exists before the transition. After transitioning, the user interface resides in the state after the transition that appears at the head of the arrow.

Each transition receives a label that contains information characterizing the transition. Transition labels have a numerator and a denominator. In the numerator appears the name of the "event" that causes the state transition. This event may be

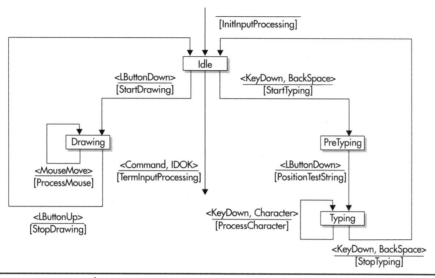

Figure 7-7   *State machine to manage user interactions*

a specific Windows message or an argument in a message. A denominator within a state transition label summarizes the details of the response action to the transition.

NOTE

States of a program indicate the history of a sequence of actions performed by the user or represent a required sequence of actions necessary to establish a specific set of operating conditions.

According to Figure 7-7, the user interface for the drawing program may exist in one of the following states:

▶ **Idle**   The program is waiting for some user input.

▶ **Drawing**   The user is performing rubber-banded drawing operations.

▶ **Pretyping**   The user wants to enter text but has yet to indicate the text location.

▶ **Typing**   The text location is defined and the user is typing characters.

In combination, the pretyping/typing state transitions force the user to follow a specific sequence of actions to ensure that the user indicates a text-display location before typing any text.

As an example, consider the transition from the idle state into the drawing state. In the label for this transition in Figure 7-7, this transition occurs when the user interface is in an idle state and a WM_LBUTTON message arrives at the dialog procedure. In response to this message, the program performs an action summarized as StartDrawing. After performing this action, the user interface resides in the drawing state.

This state machine differs from many state machines presented in other books. Every state usually possesses feedback transitions. These transitions indicate events that cause the state machine to remain in the same state but to perform processing while in that state. Often, many different messages or events can cause a program to remain in the same state after transition. Because these messages also require processing, each one needs to receive a transition with an action table entry.

An obvious example of this condition is the arrival of a WM_MOUSEMOVE message when the program exists in the drawing state. According to the state diagram in Figure 7-7, this message initiates a specific action—ProcessMouse. Clearly, this action is necessary to perform rubber-banded drawing under these conditions. Failing to incorporate this feedback transition is likely to cause a disaster.

NOTE

Omitting key feedback state transitions from a fairly complex state machine almost guarantees integration and test nightmares, resulting in longer development times and causing a significant delay of entry into the marketplace.

Notice how effectively this state machine distinguishes among the meanings of the WM_LBUTTONDOWN message in various contexts. If this message appears when the user interface is in an idle state, the state machine performs a StartDrawing action. However, if the interface is in a pretyping state, the decision logic of the state machine knows to conduct a PositionTextString action.

TIP

These state-dependent responses completely remove all ambiguity from the response to the WM_LBUTTONDOWN message and clearly indicate the manner in which state machines represent program memory of a previous sequence of interactions.

Working through the decision logic underlying the state machine, an operational execution sequence is inferred. For example, drawing operations proceed linearly through the state machine/underlying decision logic in the sequence characterized in the following table:

State Before	Event	Action	State After
Idle	WM_LBUTTONDOWN	StartDrawing	Drawing
Drawing	WM_MOUSEMOVE	ProcessMouse	Drawing
(...)			
Drawing	WM_MOUSEMOVE	ProcessMouse	Drawing
Drawing	WM_LBUTTONUP	StopDrawing	Idle

The ellipsis in the center of the table represents a series of WM_MOUSEMOVE messages. These messages arrive during the continuous dragging operations performed by the user while keeping the left mouse button depressed.

Careful evaluation of this state machine reveals a shortcoming. When in the typing state, a user could choose to transition directly to the drawing state by clicking the left mouse button. Adding another transition to recognize and respond to this situation is critical to reliable behavior of the state machine. However, notice how the state machine actually reveals this kind of shortcoming to the developer. Using the state machine not only highlights logical flaws such as this one but allows for the easy addition of this new decision rule. Just place the transition on the diagram, add the transition label, and the additional logic incorporates rapidly into the design.

NOTE

Using a state machine reveals major flaws in the decision logic of the program while simultaneously providing easy extensibility to correct these flaws.

Although the state machine is necessary to define the decision logic or rules for managing the user interface, this specification is not sufficient to completely define implementation requirements. Recall that each transition indicates an action name. Therefore, a second piece of this implementation puzzle is to define the meaning of each of the action names. For this purpose, an action table provides processing details associated with each action name.

The action table corresponding to the state machine for the drawing program appears in Table 7-1.

Each row in this table yields the gory details associated with each action name. In the first column, the action name from the state diagram appears. Contained in the second column, labeled Processing List, are the specific processing functions necessary to accomplish the action. Each unique action obtains only one row in the action table, regardless of the number of occurrences within the state machine.

Action Name	Processing List
[InitInputProcessing]	InitializeDrawingData, InitializeTextData, SetDefaultShape, SetDefaultLineColor, SetDefaultFillBrush
[StartDrawing]	SetCapture, CopyMouseLocationToCurrentDrawObject
[ProcessMouse]	PutDataIntoShape(PreviousDrawObject), PutDataIntoShape(CurrentDrawObject), InvalidateRect
[StopDrawing]	ReleaseCapture
[StartTyping]	InitializeTextData
[PositionTextString]	CopyMouseLocationToTextLocation, InitializeCaret
[ProcessCharacter]	MapVirtualKey, GetKeyState, AddCharacterToTextBuffer, GetTextRectangle, InvalidateRect, GetTextWidth, UpdateCaret
[StopTyping]	TerminateCaret
[TermInputProcessing]	TerminateDrawingData

Table 7-1   *Action Table to Define Processing for User Interactions*

NOTE

Using a combined state machine/action table significantly contributes to developer productivity. For more complex state machines, an action is liable to be reusable under a variety of conditions, eliminating the need to redevelop the same code from scratch multiple times.

Names in the Processing List column for a specific action appear in the order in which actual execution must occur. List entries consist of executing methods of lower-level abstractions (such as DataMgr, DefaultMgr, and DrawObjMgr), execution of utility methods, or calls into the Win32 API.

For instance, consider the action in the figure named ProcessMouse. The following table correlates each entry in the processing list for this action to the provider.

Action Name	Method Name	Source
[ProcessMouse]	PutDataIntoShape(PreviousDrawObject)	DrawObjMgr
	PutDataIntoShape(CurrentDrawObject)	DrawObjMgr
	InvalidateRect	Win32 API

Processing details for this action incorporate execution of methods into the data type manager DrawObjMgr and against methods provided by the Win32 API. During implementation, the processing list translates directly into a simple, readable code segment that accomplishes this action.

TIP

The combined state machine/action table further contributes to programmer productivity by yielding a readable code implementation that easily debugs because all the decision logic is clearly revealed.

The Final Layered Design

Incorporating the state machine and action table into the design integrates all the software elements into a layered design that supports extensibility and portability. This layered design appears in Figure 7-8.

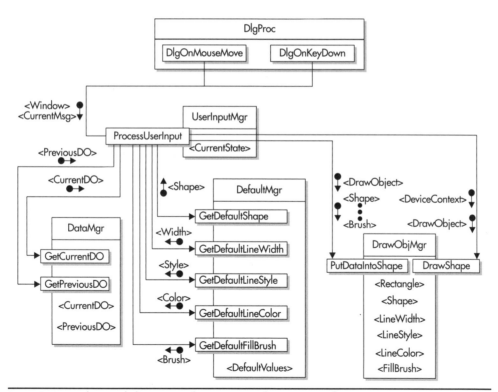

Figure 7-8   *A layered design used to manage the user interface*

This design consists of three separate and distinct software layers. Each layer focuses on specific aspects of program behavior in a manner that isolates the implementation effects on other layers. The specific focus for each layer is as follows:

▶ **User interface layer**   Handles the mechanics necessary to interact with the Windows operating system

▶ **Decision logic layer**   Implements the control logic embedded in the state machine and the action table

▶ **Data management layer**   Manages access to data through object and type managers to hide the underlying data structures

Specific software elements comprise the actual implementation of each layer. User interface layer implementation resides in the dialog procedure DlgProc. All message handlers, such as DlgOnMouseMove and DlgOnKeyDown, that require decision and control using the state machine interact directly with the decision logic layer. This layer utilizes a new software element—the UserInputMgr element. The most important method that this element provides is the method ProcessUserInput. Implemented inside this method is the combined state machine/action table that represents the decision logic. UserInputMgr serves as the data store for the state variable CurrentState. Because only the methods in UserInputMgr need to access this state variable, UserInputMgr caches the variable internally rather than asking DataMgr to house the value. Processing lists implemented inside ProcessUserInput perform all the interactions with the data management layer elements. Each of the data layer elements—DataMgr, DefaultMgr, and DrawObjMgr—exists to manipulate specific collections of data, as discussed in the previous section of this chapter.

NOTE

Using a layered design like this one enables easy transition from the state machine and action table into a single, isolated method, such as ProcessUserInput. This ease of transition reduces debugging time and increases productivity. Moreover, changes to the decision logic appear only in the single method, thus admitting a high level of extensibility.

As an example, consider the interactions that occur during dragging in support of rubber-banded drawing. Here's a linear description of the interactions:

▶ *The user interacts with the user interface layer.*   A WM_MOUSEMOVE message enters the dialog procedure DlgProc. This message routes to the DlgOnMouseMove message handler.

▶ *The user interface layer interacts with the decision logic layer.*   The handler executes the method ProcessUserInput provided by UserInputMgr, providing the message code as an input argument.

▶ *The decision logic layer interacts with the data management layer.*   Based on the value of CurrentState and the input message code, ProcessUserInput executes a code segment that implements the following action details:

> PutDataIntoShape(PreviousDrawObject) provided by DrawObjMgrPutDataIntoShape(CurrentDrawObject) provided by DrawObjMgrInvalidateRect provided by Win32 API

An important feature of these interactions is that any software element at one layer only interacts with software elements in the immediate next lower layer. DlgProc does not directly execute any methods provided by DrawObjMgr. This kind of interaction completely bypasses the decision logic layer with serious side effects.

NOTE

Limited interaction between layers reduces software complexity, thus decreasing debugging time, increasing developer productivity, and shortening time to market.

Implementation Process

In the design rationale derivation, a top-down design results in a layered set of software elements. For implementation, a bottom-up development and testing approach ensures the shortest development time.

NOTE

Implementing a top-down design by starting with the bottom layers and developing upward ensures that lower layers are debugged and reliable before the higher layers are implemented.

Utilizing the bottom-up approach for implementation leads to the following implementation steps for the drawing program:

1. Implement the data type manager encapsulation DrawObjMgr to manage multiple instances of a set of properties for a DrawObjectType.

2. Implement the object manager encapsulation DefaultMgr to manage single instances of default values for drawing, such as shape and line width.

3. Add the variables and access methods to the existing DataMgr software element that maintain a previous draw object, a current draw object, a text buffer, and a text location.

4. Add a CaretMgr functional encapsulation for performing operations on the caret during type and echo processing.

5. Implement the UserInputMgr to cache a state variable and to process messages according to the state machine and action table.

6. Modify the message handlers in DlgProc to interact with UserInputMgr instead of directly performing the rubber-banded drawing mechanics and character type and echo processing.

7. Enhance the menu to support default shape selection through a pop-up submenu.

8. Update the WM_COMMAND handler to process submenu item selection.

9. Add a WM_INITMENUPOPUP message handler to check the pop-up submenu item that corresponds to the most recently selected default shape.

Following these steps ensures that the elements of the data management layer are first implemented and working correctly. Once debugging of these elements is complete, the implementation and debugging of elements in the decision logic layer proceeds. This layer of software utilizes the data management software that has already been debugged. After the debugging the decision logic layer, integration with the user interface management layer employs the stable software from the lower layers.

One implementation step described in the preceding list needs further discussion. A CaretMgr functional abstraction replaces the application-specific Windows message WM_POSITIONCARET previously used. For manipulating a resource such as the caret, using a functional abstraction presents a more effective approach than using an application-specific message. When using a message for this purpose, the program wades back through the Windows code to reenter the dialog procedure. Execution overhead for this approach is significantly higher than directly executing a method provided by a small, directly accessible functional abstraction. Moreover, using this form of abstraction better incorporates into a cleaner, more manageable software design.

Actual Code Analysis

In this section, a detailed analysis of the code is provided that is oriented around the implementation steps described earlier. Only a subset of each step appears. Usually, the code presented represents the implementation specifics for features that were discussed during the evolution of the design rationale. These features are key to the rationale and are therefore appropriate for implementation analysis.

Implementing the Data Type Manager Encapsulation DrawObjMgr

A key element of the data management layer is the DrawObjMgr. Both the DataMgr and the UserInputMgr utilize this encapsulation. Declaration of the abstract data type occurs in two files. In the file DrawObjDecl.h, the declaration of the underlying data structure appears. A second file, DrawObjMgr.h, contains the abstract data type definition.

```
/*********************************************
 *
 * File: DrawObjDecl.h
 *
 * copyright, SWA Engineering, Inc., 2001
 * All rights reserved.
 *
 *********************************************/
typedef struct
{
    RECT        m_rect        ;
    int         m_lineWidth   ;
    ShapeType   m_shape       ;
    int         m_lineStyle   ;
    int         m_lineColor   ;
    int         m_fillBrush   ;
} DrawObjectRecordType ;
/*********************************************
 *
 * File: DrawObjMgr.h
 *
 * copyright, SWA Engineering, Inc., 2001
 * All rights reserved.
 *
 *********************************************/
    #include "DrawObjDecl.h"
    typedef DrawObjectRecordType * DrawObjectType ;
```

A DrawObjectRecordType element includes all the attributes of a specific object that needs to be drawn, such as shape (m_shape), bounding rectangle (m_rect), and others. This record describes the physical layout of the data structure for each draw object. However, the application programmer does not access this structure. Programs utilize a logical data type, declared in the second header file as DrawObjectType. This second data type provides a logical or abstract representation of a pointer to an instance of the underlying data structure. Applications perform all operations on a specific instance of the underlying data structure utilizing a variable of this abstract data type, DrawObjectType.

NOTE

In essence, this representation behaves the same as a C++ class would behave. However, this approach works in plain C and is much more reliable. With this approach, an application programmer never even knows that a pointer is involved. All pointer dereferencing occurs inside the access methods, invisible to the programmer!

In the design description of Figure 7-8, two important methods of this data type play key roles in the layered execution sequence. Declarations for these methods appear in the file DrawObjMgr.h:

```
void PutDataIntoShape(DrawObjectType DrawObject,
                 int x1, int y1, int x2, int y2, ShapeType shape,
                 int line_width, int line_style, int line_color,
                 int fill_brush) ;
```

As the first argument to this method, the programmer supplies a DrawObject. This value is an instance of the abstracted or opaque pointer to the underlying data structure. As far as the program is considered, this method performs an operation on the instance of the abstract data type. The fact that this value is a pointer and that pointer dereferencing is necessary during manipulations is irrelevant to the developer. Remaining arguments provide values for the properties or attributes to initialize within the method body.

By requiring the first argument to be an instance of DrawObjectType, this method and all other methods in DrawObjMgr.h enable a programmer to declare and utilize multiple instances of the underlying data structure. For this reason, DrawObjMgr exists as a data type manager form of encapsulation.

```
void  DrawShape(HDC DC, DrawObjectType DrawObject) ;
```

Inside this method, the actual drawing operations occur. In order to draw, the method requires a device context/drawing toolkit, DC, and a specific draw object, DrawObject. Executing this method utilizes the stored properties managed by the instance of the abstracted pointer and the device context to display the object in the

client area. Again, the program developer has no inkling that pointers are involved
in any way.

To illustrate the manner in which these methods hide both the data structure and
the existence of pointers, look at the following code listing for DrawShape:

```
void  DrawShape(HDC DC, DrawObjectType DrawObject)
{
switch (DrawObject->m_shape)
    {
    case LINESHAPE:
          DrawLineShapeAt( DC,
                   DrawObject->m_rect.left, DrawObject->m_rect.top,
                   DrawObject->m_rect.right, DrawObject->m_rect.bottom,
                   DrawObject->m_lineWidth, DrawObject->m_lineStyle,
                   DrawObject->m_lineColor ) ;
                   break;
// Remaining Case blocks omitted for clarity
    }
}
```

This scaled-down version of the method illustrates the features of interest here. Omitted
blocks exhibit the same characteristics and need not be repeated.

Upon entry to the method, a switch statement routes execution control to a specific
case block that processes the desired shape. The m_shape property of the incoming
DrawObject serves as the switch control variable. In order to access the value of the
property for the specific instance of DrawObject, this method dereferences the pointer.
Look at the switch variable: DrawObject->m_shape.

Inside the case block, the program extracts all the properties relevant to drawing a
line. Access to these properties again involves dereferencing the pointer represented
by the specific instance of DrawObjectType. These values, along with the device
context (DC), pass to the line-drawing function.

TIP

*The method DrawLineShapeAt is part of the drawing operation's functional encapsulation
implemented in DrawOps.h. Recall that this set of methods appears in Chapter 4 and is reused here.*

Reusing the DrawOps software element clearly demonstrates the value of utilizing
encapsulation. Imagine having to rewrite this code all over again, when the methods
already exist and execute reliably.

Implementing the Object Manager Encapsulation DefaultMgr

Because this encapsulation is an object manager encapsulation, type declarations do not exist. As far as a programmer is concerned, this software element appears as a list of methods. These methods operate a set of data variables completely hidden from the application programmer.

Here is a portion of the header file that declares these methods:

```
/************************************************
 *
 * File: DefaultMgr.h
 *
 * copyright, SWA Engineering, Inc., 2001
 * All rights reserved.
 *
 ***********************************************/
void SetDefaultShape(ShapeType shape) ;
ShapeType GetDefaultShape(void) ;
```

This portion of the header file displays two of the access methods available to any other portion of an application. No data types are visible, clearly indicating that only a single instance of the default shape exists inside the boundaries of the encapsulation. Typically, an object manager encapsulation serves as a data warehouse for a single instance of one or more data variables. Often, the only methods that the encapsulation provides are access methods such as Get and Set. However, sometimes a program needs to perform operations on the data members. Therefore, methods other than simple access methods can appear as part of an encapsulation.

A look inside the actual code body for this object manager reveals the following code for supporting these two methods:

```
/************************************************
 * File: DefaultMgr.c
 *
 * copyright, SWA Engineering, Inc., 2001
 * All rights reserved.
 *
 ***********************************************/
static ShapeType defaultShape     = LINESHAPE      ;
static int       defaultLineWidth = 1              ;
static int       defaultLineStyle = PS_SOLID       ;
static int       defaultLineColor = RGB(0,0,0)     ;
```

```
static int         defaultFillBrush = WHITE_BRUSH    ;
void SetDefaultShape(ShapeType shape)
{
     defaultShape = shape;
}
ShapeType GetDefaultShape(void)
{
     return defaultShape;
}
```

Initially, the cache for the stored variables assumes the form of a collection of variable declarations with a static storage class attribute. According to the language rules for the C programming language, any variable with a static attribute is visible only to code within the same C file and has memory in the global static area allocated to the application. Therefore, the only means by which an application can access these values is through the use of the access methods available.

TIP

Compile time enforcement *of the encapsulation uses static storage class access to hide the variable names and to force the use of the access methods. Programmers cannot bypass the software guards established by the encapsulation because the compiler simply refuses to compile in violating code.*

As a safety precaution, each of the private or hidden variables possesses an initial value. At the time the program is loaded, the loader assigns these values to the variables. This automatic initialization occurs only once during the initial load.

The two preceding methods are simple access methods. When a program decides to change the stored value for shape, the code executes the method SetShapeValue. In the body of this access method, the stored value defaultShape initializes using the incoming value shape. Retrieving this value utilizes the method GetShapeValue.

NOTE

This object manager plays a role similar to the DataMgr element, defined in Chapter 3, to store globally accessible variables.

In fact, the values from this object manager could easily reside in the DataMgr element. However, the values stored here represent a special usage rather than the general usage implied by DataMgr. For this reason, a separate object manager exists to maintain these default values.

Adding Variables and Access Methods to the Existing DataMgr

In the previous incarnation of the drawing program, a number of variables exist to maintain data necessary to support rubber-banded drawing and type and echo character processing. Now, these variables must be accessible throughout the decision logic layer and the data management layer. For this reason, these variables now reside within the DataMgr element.

Here is a complete listing of the new header file for the DataMgr, with a few include declarations omitted for clarity:

```
/************************************************
 *
 * File: DataMgr.h
 *
 * copyright, SWA Engineering, Inc., 2001
 * All rights reserved.
 *
 ************************************************/
void PutProgramInstance(HINSTANCE Instance ) ;
HINSTANCE GetProgramInstance(void) ;

void PutCurrentMouseLocation(int X, int Y) ;
POINT GetCurrentMouseLocation(void) ;
void CopyMouseLocationToCurrentDrawObject(void) ;
void CopyMouseLocationToTextLocation(void) ;
void InitializeTextData(void) ;
POINT GetTextLocation(void) ;
void PutTextLocation(POINT Location) ;
int GetNumberCharacters(void) ;
void PutNumberCharacters(int Number) ;
void GetTextBuffer(TCHAR * Buffer) ;
void PutTextBuffer(TCHAR * Buffer) ;
void AddCharacterToTextBuffer(TCHAR Character) ;
void InitializeDrawingData(void) ;
void TerminateDrawingData(void) ;
DrawObjectType GetPreviousDrawObject(void) ;
DrawObjectType GetCurrentDrawObject(void) ;
```

Access methods for the program instance, PutProgramInstance and GetProgramInstance, carry forward from the initial implementation of the minimal dialog program. However, all the other methods are new to this implementation.

This version of DataMgr provides two categories of methods. Simple access methods, such as GetTextBuffer and PutTextBuffer, provide the capability to store and retrieve values. However, other methods, such as InitializeDrawingData, perform complex sequences of operations on the underlying data.

In this DataMgr implementation, a number of the methods manage the current mouse location. This location enters the program through WM_MOUSEMOVE message handling. However, the use of the value occurs in a number of locations throughout the application and in various layers. As a result, the DlgOnMouseMove message handler uses the access method PutCurrentMouseLocation to cache the incoming mouse location. Other methods that use this data can then execute GetCurrentMouseLocation to retrieve the exact location values. Additionally, some methods require that this location be copied to other variables maintained internally within DataMgr. Rather than paying the execution overhead for extracting both source and target objects and then copying the values, methods such as CopyMouseLocationToCurrentDrawObject perform the data copy directly within DataMgr. Copying the data within DataMgr saves the additional extraction overhead.

TIP

For programs that ultimately execute on a Pocket PC, make every effort to reduce required CPU cycles without compromising design effectiveness.

Adding a CaretMgr Functional Encapsulation

The previous implementation of type and echo processing utilizes an application-specific message to manage the caret. This approach is a bit tedious, requiring the definition of a message code and the declaration of a custom message cracker. Additionally, using a custom message consumes extra CPU cycles to go out into Windows and to reenter the dialog procedure.

A more efficient approach is to employ a functional encapsulation. This software element provides only a few methods, as shown in the following header file:

```
/***********************************************
 *
 * File: CaretMgr.h
 *
 * copyright, SWA Engineering, Inc., 2001
 * All rights reserved.
 *
 ***********************************************/
void InitializeCaret(HWND Window, int XLocation, int YLocation) ;
void UpdateCaret(HWND Window, int XLocation, int YLocation) ;
void TerminateCaret(HWND Window) ;
```

Logically, a program only performs three operations on a caret: initialization, updating, and termination. Therefore, a single method exists for each of these logical operations. This encapsulation is functional. The code body does not maintain a single copy of any data or provide for an application to maintain multiple instances. However, the methods relate through the requirement to manage the single caret resource maintained by Windows.

In the following code listing appears the code body for the method UpdateCaret:

```
void UpdateCaret(HWND Window, int XLocation, int YLocation)
{
    HideCaret(Window) ;
    SetCaretPos(XLocation,YLocation) ;
    ShowCaret(Window) ;
}
```

This method performs the exact same sequence of operations implemented in the message handler for the custom message WM_POSITIONCARET in Chapter 5. However, this form is much more reusable across applications. A developer simply copies the .h and .c files into the project folder and then inserts the .c file into the project. After this inclusion in the project, the developer inserts method calls to UpdateCaret at the appropriate locations in the application.

Implementing the UserInputMgr to Process Messages

Adding the CaretMgr element to the project completes the implementation of the data management layer. Now, implementation proceeds up the layer chain into the decision logic layer. This layer incorporates all the decision making of the state machine and action table into actual code. Additionally, some methods in this layer serve as the controls for managing the painting of the client area.

The primary software element in this layer is UserInputMgr. Several key methods appear in this software element. These methods perform state machine and action table operations and manage graphics and text drawing within the client area. Here is a partial header file for this software element:

```
/***********************************************
 *
 * File: UserInputMgr.h
 *
 * copyright, SWA Engineering, Inc., 2001
 * All rights reserved.
 *
```

```
*********************************************/
typedef enum { Idle, Drawing, PreTyping, Typing } UserInputStateType ;
void ProcessUserInput ( HWND Window, UINT CurrentEvent ) ;
void DisplayDrawObject (HDC DeviceContext) ;
void DisplayTextString (HDC DeviceContext) ;
```

In this header file, an enumerated data type, UserInputStateType, defines the possible user-input states. When messages arrive that participate in the state mechanics, these messages pass to the ProcessUserInput method. Inside the WM_PAINT message handler, the code executes DisplayDrawObject to perform rubber-banded drawing and calls DisplayTextString to support type and echo character processing.

The second argument to ProcessUserInput is CurrentEvent, which is data type UINT. This value may be either a message code, such as WM_LBUTTONDOWN, or a Windows virtual character code that was received in a WM_KEYDOWN message. Another approach might be to pass a message code and an argument value. However, the approach that the method uses is simple and easy to implement.

Actual bodies to these methods are important to study. The code body for the method ProcessUserInput demonstrates the manner in which this method supports the state machine and action table. Additionally, this code shows the integration with the lower data management layer. Here's a scaled-down version of this method:

```
/************************************************
 *
 * File: UserInputMgr.c
 *
 * copyright, SWA Engineering, Inc., 2001
 * All rights reserved.
 *
 ************************************************/
static UserInputStateType CurrentState = Idle ;
void ProcessUserInput ( HWND Window, UINT CurrentEvent )
{
    RECT            ShapeRect ;
    POINT           MouseLocation ;
    DrawObjectType  PreviousDO ;
    DrawObjectType  CurrentDO ;
    ShapeType       Shape ;
    int             LineWidth ;
    int             LineStyle ;
    int             LineColor ;
    int             FillBrush ;
```

```
// Remaining Entries Omitted For Clarity
    if ( (CurrentState == Drawing) && (CurrentEvent == WM_MOUSEMOVE) )
    {
            // DataMgr
            PreviousDO = GetPreviousDrawObject() ;
            CurrentDO  = GetCurrentDrawObject() ;
            MouseLocation = GetCurrentMouseLocation() ;

            // DrawObjMgr
            ShapeRect = GetShapeBoundingRect(CurrentDO) ;

            // DefaultMgr
            Shape     = GetDefaultShape() ;
            LineWidth = GetDefaultLineWidth() ;
            LineStyle = GetDefaultLineStyle() ;
            LineColor = GetDefaultLineColor() ;
            FillBrush = GetDefaultFillBrush() ;

            PutDataIntoShape(PreviousDO,
                        ShapeRect.left, ShapeRect.top,
                            ShapeRect.right, ShapeRect.bottom,
                        Shape, LineWidth, LineStyle ,
                            LineColor , FillBrush ) ;
            PutDataIntoShape(CurrentDO,
                        ShapeRect.left, ShapeRect.top,
                            MouseLocation.x, MouseLocation.y,
                        Shape, LineWidth, LineStyle , LineColor ,
                            FillBrush ) ;

            InvalidateRect(Window,NULL,FALSE) ;
            UpdateWindow(Window) ;

            CurrentState = Drawing ;
    }
// Remaining Entries Omitted For Clarity
}
```

In general, the method body consists of a giant set of checks for state transition conditions. Each check, implemented as an if statement, represents a single transition in the state diagram. In order to accurately represent the combined operation of the state machine and the action table, the code inside the case alternative must perform the steps in the action table and then update the value of CurrentState to the new state. This sample code represents the feedback transition from the drawing state back into the drawing state upon the arrival of a WM_MOUSEMOVE message.

TIP

If this feedback transition was not implemented, rubber-banded drawing would never really work. Integration and test activities would be very tedious indeed.

Code implemented inside the check for a transition follows a specific logical execution flow. The following pseudocode represents this logic flow:

```
If (  CurrentState == StateValue and CurrentEvent == EventValue ) then
   Retrieve a local copy of necessary data from the data management layer
   Perform all necessary operations upon the local copies of the data
   Store the local copies of the data back to the data management layer
   CurrentState = NewStateValue
End if
```

This approach represents a clear input-processing-output form of design. Retrieving all the necessary data prior to performing the work clearly identifies the necessary inputs into the action details. After manipulation, storing the results further identifies the outputs. After the input-processing-output sequence, the implemented code updates the internal value of the state to reflect the new state, which may be the same as the old state.

TIP

Occasionally, this input-processing-output flow does not exactly match the requirements of a given situation.

For instance, in the preceding code segment, the sequence is more like input-output-processing. This variation results from the fact that the processing consists of updating the client area with the draw objects. Therefore, the draw objects need to be updated by executing the method PutDataIntoShape prior to processing (InvalidateRect, UpdateWindow).

Acquiring local copies of the data and storing output values requires interaction with the lower data management layer. Even without a reader having a detailed knowledge of the data management layer, usage of the terms *Get* or *Set* and *Put* as part of a method name clearly indicates to the reader that an interaction with a data repository takes place. Notice that the two method calls into PutDataIntoShape each take a different instance of a DrawObjectType as the first argument.

To see how the body of this code segment matches to the action table, recall the action table entry for this transition:

Action Name	Method Name	Source
[ProcessMouse]	PutDataIntoShape(PreviousDrawObject)	DrawObjMgr
	PutDataIntoShape(CurrentDrawObject)	DrawObjMgr
	InvalidateRect	Win32 API

Clearly, the sequence of three method calls in this table exactly matches the method execution sequence contained in the processing portion of the sample code:

```
PutDataIntoShape(PreviousDO,
            ShapeRect.left, ShapeRect.top,
            ShapeRect.right, ShapeRect.bottom,
            Shape, LineWidth, LineStyle ,
            LineColor , FillBrush ) ;
PutDataIntoShape(CurrentDO,
            ShapeRect.left, ShapeRect.top,
            MouseLocation.x, MouseLocation.y,
            Shape, LineWidth, LineStyle , LineColor ,
            FillBrush ) ;

InvalidateRect(Window,NULL,FALSE) ;
```

Using Figure 7-7 (the state transition diagram), Table 7-1 (the action table), and a listing of the method ProcessUserInput, the relationship among the three elements becomes clear.

NOTE

Using a control specification that includes a state diagram and an action table and then employing an implementation approach that directly maps these elements into a specific code segment significantly reduces integration and test efforts. The effect of this reduction is to shorten the amount of time to deliver a product to the market.

When this code segment performs the InvalidateRect/UpdateWindow sequence, execution control reenters the DlgOnPaint message handler for the WM_PAINT message. Inside this message handler, one line of code executes the method DisplayDrawObject. This latter method is also a member of UserInputMgr, providing a logical interaction between the user interface layer and this decision logic layer.

Here's a complete code listing for the method DisplayDrawObject:

```
void DisplayDrawObject(HDC DeviceContext)
{
    DrawObjectType PreviousDO ;
    DrawObjectType CurrentDO ;

    if ( CurrentState == Drawing )
    {
        // DataMgr
        PreviousDO = GetPreviousDrawObject() ;
        CurrentDO  = GetCurrentDrawObject() ;

        // Erase The Old Line
        SetROP2(DeviceContext,R2_NOTXORPEN) ;
        DrawShape(DeviceContext, PreviousDO) ;
        // Draw The New Line
        SetROP2(DeviceContext,R2_COPYPEN) ;
        DrawShape(DeviceContext,CurrentDO) ;
    }
}
```

This method performs rubber-banded drawing. At first glance, the method may appear to be out of place in the decision logic layer. However, close scrutiny of the first line of executable code reveals the necessity. Prior to performing any rubber-banded drawing, this method must check the internal state variable to ensure that the program is in the drawing state. In order to accomplish this check, the method needs to access the private, hidden state variable.

After determining that drawing is appropriate, the method retrieves local copies of the previous draw object, PreviousDO, and the current draw object, CurrentDO. Using these draw objects and raster binary operations, this method then performs the erase and draw activities.

In order to erase and draw, the method first sets the raster binary operation using the Win32 method SetROP2, which is discussed in Chapter 5. Then, a method call to DrawShape actually does the erasing or drawing. Recall that DrawShape is a method provided by DrawObjMgr in the data management layer. This latter method needs to know the style information embedded inside the instance of the structure managed by DrawObjectType. Therefore, DrawShape correctly resides with the data type manager encapsulation DrawObjMgr.

Modifying Handlers in DlgProc to Interact with UserInputMgr

Now that the interactions between the decision logic layer and the data management layer work correctly, the next step moves up the layer stack. This step ensures that the user interface layer and the decision logic layer interact correctly and under the proper circumstances.

The code at the user interface layer predominantly resides in the dialog procedure, DlgProc, and the message handlers. Interactions between the user interface layer and the decision logic layer relate to mouse, keyboard, and paint messages. Therefore, this section analyzes a single example of each category of handler.

As the first handler of interest, consider the following code listing for the WM_MOUSEMOVE message:

```
void DlgOnMouseMove(HWND hDlg, int x, int y, UINT keyFlags)
{
    PutCurrentMouseLocation(x,y) ;
    ProcessUserInput( hDlg, WM_MOUSEMOVE) ;
}
```

Rather than incorporating a huge amount of messy detailed code with a list of interacting state variables, this method performs two simple steps. First, the method registers the current mouse location, provided as arguments, with the DataMgr central data warehouse using the method PutCurrentMouseLocation. Next, the handler executes the method ProcessUserInput, providing the message code as an input argument.

Now, all the decision logic and action sequencing embedded in the state machine and action table take over. These elements correctly respond to the message using the mouse location stored into the DataMgr.

Recall that mouse messages enter this handler any time the mouse cursor crosses the client area. Each and every time this message arrives, the handler executes ProcessUserInput. However, unless the user has established the correct state and operating conditions, the decision logic inside ProcessUserInput simply ignores the message.

NOTE

Using a state diagram and action table with direct code implementation significantly improves the reliability and repeatable behavior of a program. This result reduces debugging time and efforts, and yields a much more satisfied user.

Now, the following code listing gives the actual implementation details for the WM_KEYDOWN message handler:

```
void DlgOnKeyDown(HWND hDlg, UINT vk, BOOL fDown, int cRepeat, UINT flags)
{
    ProcessUserInput( hDlg, vk ) ;
}
```

This implementation is ridiculously simple. The handler just passes the Windows virtual key code, vk, directly to ProcessUserInput in the decision logic layer. Assuming that the user has correctly established the typing state, this method performs all the mechanics of echoing the character and moving the cursor.

One last handler interacts with the decision logic layer. This method is the DlgOnPaint message handler for the WM_PAINT message. Here's a scaled-down version of this method handler:

```
void  DlgOnPaint(HWND hDlg)
{
    // Previously Discussed Lines Omitted For Clarity
    DisplayDrawObject(DeviceContext) ;
    DisplayTextString(DeviceContext) ;
    // Previously Discussed Lines Omitted For Clarity
}
```

This handler interacts with the decision logic layer through the methods DisplayDrawObject and DisplayTextString. As discussed earlier, these methods need to know the current value of the state variable in order to perform the intended functions. Therefore, placing these methods into the decision logic layer is entirely appropriate.

Notice the way in which using DisplayDrawObject effectively hides the gory details associated with utilizing the draw objects to perform rubber-banded drawing.

NOTE

Using functional encapsulation and data encapsulation yield extremely readable code that clearly exposes the execution logic.

Any code segment that looks more like English and high-level operations is far easier to debug. After using encapsulation, most debugging problems result from incorrect execution and sequencing logic. Burying the details of data manipulation and hiding functional sequences more clearly reveals the execution sequencing logic.

Enhancing the Main Menu Using a Pop-up Submenu

Adding the pop-up submenu and the submenu items is a task easily accomplished with the menu editor of Visual C++ or Embedded Visual C++. Because the program already uses a menu item for the Quit command, adding a pop-up submenu and individual submenu items is simple.

The process of adding the pop-up submenu and defining individual items appears in the following figures. Each figure includes a specific step in the process. Numbered labels on every figure indicate the required sequence of steps. Figure 7-9, the first figure in the series, provides the basic steps necessary to add an new menu item to the existing base menu.

Both desktop and embedded versions of Visual Studio provide tools to define and to edit menus. In order to access the menu editor, employ the following steps:

1. Click the Resource View tab of Project Explorer.

2. Click the plus sign (+) next to the Menu folder. This action expands into a list of menus.

3. Double-click the menu identifier that represents the main menu for the application. In the section to the right of the Project Explorer appears the menu editor.

4. Double-click the empty main menu item to the right of the Quit menu item.

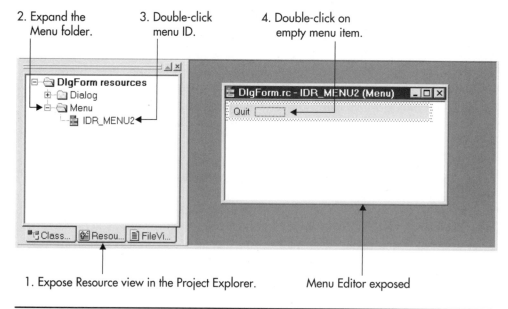

Figure 7-9   *Adding a new menu item*

The number for each step in the preceding list corresponds to the numbered labels in the figure.

After the last step, the menu item properties dialog for the new menu item displays, as shown in Figure 7-10.

Initially, the General tab of the Menu Item Properties dialog is selected. Set the properties for the new main menu item as follows:

1. Enter the label **Shape** into the Caption field. This value represents the string that the user sees on the face of the main menu.

2. Set the check mark to the left of the Pop-up option. In response, the properties dialog disables the ID field.

3. Click the close button at the upper-right corner of the properties dialog.

Pop-up dialogs do not need unique integer identifiers. A menu item uses the unique integer identifier as a message parameter when communicating the user selection to a dialog procedure. When a user clicks the menu item for a pop-up submenu, Windows automatically displays the pop-up menu. Pop-up menu items never send messages to a dialog procedure.

Once the menu item dialog closes, the menu editor displays the new menu item. The next steps necessary to define individual items in the pop-up submenu appear in Figure 7-11.

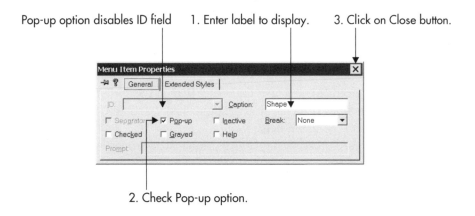

Figure 7-10   *Defining properties of the new menu item*

1. Click on pop-up menu item label.

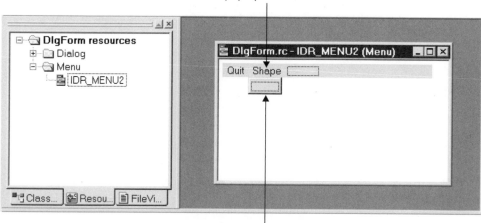

2. Double-click on empty pop-up submenu item.

Figure 7-11   *Creating menu items for a pop-up submenu*

A small number of steps is necessary to initiate the definition of a menu item for a pop-up submenu. These steps involve using the menu editor in the following way:

1. Click the label of the pop-up menu item Shape. This step reveals the empty pop-up submenu.

2. Double-click the empty menu item of the pop-up submenu.

When initiated, the first step reveals existing menu items on the pop-up submenu. If the new menu item needs to be someplace other than at the end of the list, drag and drop the blank menu item at the desired location. Then, double-click the menu item to set the properties of the menu item.

As a result of the last creation step, a new Menu Item Properties dialog appears. This Menu Item Properties dialog is shown in Figure 7-12.

Here are the corresponding steps to initialize the new menu item properties using this dialog:

1. Enter a label string, such as Line, into the Caption field.

2. Do not enter an ID because the Menu Item Properties dialog automatically creates an identifier symbol.

2. Do not select Enter An ID;
editor creates symbol for ID

1. Enter label
to display.

4. Click on
Close button.

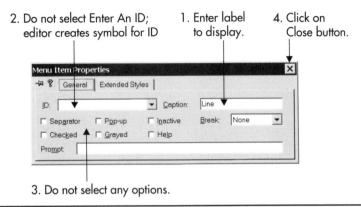

3. Do not select any options.

Figure 7-12   *Setting properties for a pop-up submenu item*

3. Do not select any options or other properties.

4. Click the close button at the upper-right corner of the Menu Item
Properties dialog.

Be especially careful to avoid any the properties on the Extended Styles tab page.
These values execute correctly on the desktop but often cause the Pocket PC program
to fail without warning or indication.

After the pop-up submenu item's properties have been defined, the submenu
items appear on the face of the pop-up dialog. An example of this display appears
in Figure 7-13.

1. Click on pop-up menu item label.

2. Double-click on
pop-up submenu
item label.

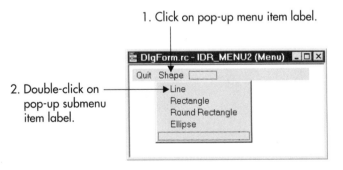

Figure 7-13   *Displaying existing items in a pop-up submenu*

A two-step process enables the review of item properties for a specific submenu item, as follows:

1. Click the label of the pop-up menu item on the main menu. Clicking this item exposes the pop-up submenu.

2. Double-click the specific menu item of the exposed pop-up submenu.

The figure shows the completely populated Shape pop-up submenu. Each menu item in this pop-up submenu has properties that were established as described earlier.

Recall that the initial setting of properties does not include setting the menu item identifier. Using the preceding steps to display the menu item properties reveals the symbol for the identifier that was created by the Menu Item Properties dialog. The dialog containing the identifier appears in Figure 7-14.

Inside the ID field, the dialog displays a symbol. This symbol represents a unique integer identifier for the menu item. The Menu Item Properties dialog creates this symbol based on the location of the menu item in the menu hierarchy.

A user selects the menu item shown earlier in Figure 7-14 by selecting the Shape item from the main menu and then clicking the Line item from the pop-up submenu. Concatenating this sequence together and prefixing with the string "ID", the properties dialog arrives at the symbol ID_SHAPE_LINE. Somewhere in the bowels of the development environment, a variable tracks the next available unique integer and assigns this value to the symbol.

As a result of all this menu item creation, Visual Studio creates two output files. The first file, named resource.h, contains the symbolic identifiers for all the menu

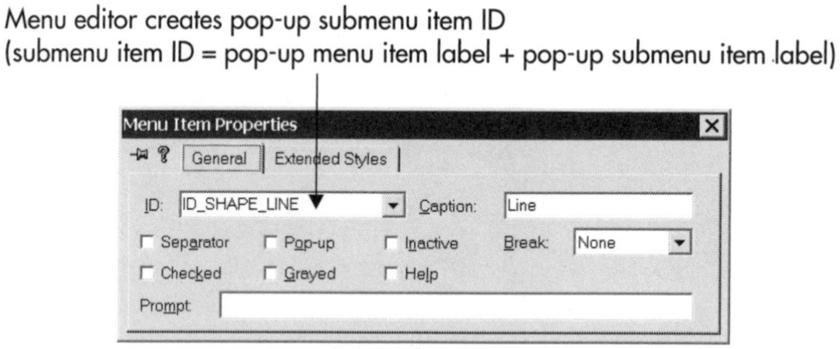

Menu editor creates pop-up submenu item ID
(submenu item ID = pop-up menu item label + pop-up submenu item label)

Figure 7-14 *A pop-up submenu item's Properties dialog*

items. Programs use these symbols to generate an appropriate response when a user selects a menu item. Here's a listing of the menu item identifiers for this project:

```
#define IDR_MENU2                       101
#define ID_SHAPE_LINE                   40001
#define ID_SHAPE_RECTANGLE              40002
#define ID_SHAPE_ROUNDRECTANGLE         40003
#define ID_SHAPE_ELLIPSE                40004
```

Visual Studio guarantees all menu identifiers form a unique set of values. Additionally, menu item identifiers reside within a separate, independent unique set of integers. Because the menu item identifiers comprise a separate unique set from the menu identifiers, the range of values that Visual Studio assigns to these entries differs.

In addition to the symbol definitions, Visual Studio generates a menu script that appears in a resource file named DlgForm.rc. This script compiles into a table that resides in the resource section of the binary signature, as explained in Figure 2-4 of Chapter 2. When the application loads the menu, the Win32 API accesses the compiled version of this script in order to generate the menu.

The following listing provides the resource script for the main menu that includes the Shape pop-up submenu:

```
IDR_MENU2 MENU DISCARDABLE
BEGIN
    MENUITEM "Quit", IDOK
    POPUP "Shape"
    BEGIN
        MENUITEM "Line",                ID_SHAPE_LINE
        MENUITEM "Rectangle",           ID_SHAPE_RECTANGLE
        MENUITEM "Round Rectangle",     ID_SHAPE_ROUNDRECTANGLE
        MENUITEM "Ellipse",             ID_SHAPE_ELLIPSE
    END
END
```

Appearing first in this script is the symbolic identifier for the menu, IDR_MENU2. Each menu item on the main menu bar then receives the entry inside the scope of the menu definition. Entries for the menu items appear in the order of display. The first entry is the Quit menu item. An entry for this item begins with the keyword MENUITEM and contains the label and the symbolic identifier for the item.

Because the second entry of the main menu is a pop-up submenu, the entry for this item begins with the keyword POPUP, followed by the label for the pop-up submenu. This entry begins a nested menu definition for the pop-up submenu. Inside this nested definition, each menu item receives a MENUITEM entry. Associated with each item is a label or caption and the symbolic identifier.

In general, a developer need not worry about resource scripts such as this one. Visual Studio and Embedded Visual Studio efficiently handle all these details.

Updating the WM_COMMAND Handler to Process Menu Items

When a user selects one of the menu items from the pop-up submenu, Windows routes a WM_COMMAND message to the dialog procedure. Embedded in the parameters of this message is the integer that uniquely identifies the selected menu item.

Generating a response to the selection of these menu items involves additional code in the WM_COMMAND handler. An abbreviated code listing shows the addition of code for one of the pop-up submenu items:

```
#include "resource.h"
void DlgOnCommand ( HWND hDlg ,     int  iID ,
                    HWND hDlgCtl , UINT uCodeNotify )
{
  // Previously Discussed Code Omitted For Clarity
  switch( iID )
  {
   case ID_SHAPE_LINE:
         SetDefaultValues(LINESHAPE, 1, PS_SOLID ,
                          RGB(255,0,0), WHITE_BRUSH) ;
       break ;
 // Remaining Code Omitted For Clarity
}
```

Each menu item receives an additional case inside the switch statement that routes execution control based on the value of the iID argument. This value represents the source of the selected menu item. In fact, this value is the unique integer created by Visual Studio. The case statement heading employs the symbolic version of this integer that is stored in resource.h. Including this header file enables the code inside the message handler to access this symbol. When the program is compiled, the C preprocessor first substitutes the actual integer for this symbol name.

For this application, the characteristic response to selecting any of the pop-up submenu items is to cache the indicated shape along with a predefined set of style values. In the next chapter, a more advanced version of this program allows the user to select individual style characteristics.

Adding a WM_INITMENUPOPUP Handler to Check the Default

When a user clicks a menu item that displays a pop-up submenu, Windows provides an application the option to modify the properties of the menu items. Windows initiates this option by sending a WM_INITMENUPOPUP message to the parent window. This message enters the dialog procedure and routes to a message handler that may exist.

This application implements a message handler that checks the menu item that corresponds to the previously selected default shape. A portion of the message handler added to this method appears here:

```
void DlgOnInitMenuPopup(HWND hDlg, HMENU hMenu, int item, BOOL fSystemMenu)
{
  if ( GetDefaultShape() == LINESHAPE )
      CheckMenuItem(hMenu,ID_SHAPE_LINE,MF_CHECKED) ;
  else
      CheckMenuItem(hMenu,ID_SHAPE_LINE,MF_UNCHECKED) ;
  // Remaining Code Omitted For Clarity
}
```

Arguments into this handler identify the source of this message. As the second argument, hMenu gives the handle to the parent menu resource. This message arrives because the user selected a menu item possessing a pop-up submenu. The value of item, the third input argument, is the position of the selected menu item on the parent menu.

The body of this handler consists of a series of queries to identify the relationship between the current default shape and a corresponding menu item. This check and response appears inside the message handler for each of the menu items on the pop-up submenu. A check consists of comparing the current default shape, requested from DataMgr through the access method GetDefaultShape, against a specific enumeration literal imported from header file DrawObjTypes.h. If the default shape matches a specific literal, the handler checks the corresponding menu item.

The Win32 API method CheckMenuItem enables a program to dynamically turn the check of a menu item on or off. Here's an example of using this method, as extracted from the DlgOnInitMenuPopup message handler:

```
CheckMenuItem(hMenu,ID_SHAPE_LINE,MF_CHECKED)
```

In order to identify the specific menu item, the first two arguments give the handle to the menu, provided by the incoming argument hMenu, and the integer identifier for the menu item. Of course, the program uses the symbolic version of this menu item identifier, ID_SHAPE_LINE. As a final input to this method, the executing program supplies a flag to indicate the operation on the check property. Using the symbol MF_CHECKED shows the check mark, whereas using MF_UNCHECKED hides the check mark.

Some Comments on the Design and the Implementation

The implementation in this chapter utilizes a state machine and an action table. Evaluating the state machine reveals only seven transitions that are the primary transitions. During testing and integration, a few more unanticipated transitions are likely to be discovered. A more complete application may have hundreds of transitions. In order for the application to work correctly, a complete and accurate state machine is necessary. The requirement for completeness presents a problem for the developer. If the implemented state machine does not encompass every feasible state and state transition, including the feedback transitions described earlier, the product is liable to experience faulty, unreliable behavior.

In order to actually develop a full and complete state machine and action table for an application, a more complete development process is necessary. This process usually involves the following steps:

▶ Identify the primary user-operations scenarios involving primary features of the application.

▶ Analyze the decision logic and functional processing needed to support the scenarios in the form of a state diagram, an action table, and data-flow diagrams.

▶ Validate the decision logic and functional processing against the user scenarios to ensure completeness and accuracy.

An important key to this process is the validation step. This step consists of a very rigorous analysis composed of simulating the behavior of the system using the scenarios and exercising the decision logic and functional processing.

Using a sequence of if statements to check for various conditions, each of which represents a combination of state and incoming message, is a marginal implementation approach for the state machine. A better approach is to embed the state machine and action machine into a table data structure and then encapsulate the data tables. This approach provides greater extensibility, because changing the decision logic involves changes to data in tables rather than modifying and debugging code.

Unfortunately, these two topics are extensive and require a complete and separate book in order to adequately provide details.

Summary

This chapter completely redevelops the drawing program from Chapter 5. Using an effectively layered design, the new implementation demonstrates a number of important conclusions:

▶ The Resource View of Project Explorer provides an easily used menu editor for adding menus to a program.

▶ In general, the use of menus is a poor means of providing a user-friendly interface when physical screen space is limited because overlapping menus hide important screen information.

▶ An object manager encapsulation controls access to a single instance of a variable or a set of variables.

▶ A data type manager encapsulation provides the means for an application to utilize multiple instances of a hidden data structure.

▶ Using a layered design isolates user interface management, decision and control logic, and data management into interacting software elements.

▶ Employing software elements in interacting layers promotes program extensibility by isolating the effects of code changes into a single software layer.

▶ An effectively layered design limits the amount of interactions among the layers, providing less execution complexity and reducing development time.

Sample Programs on the Web

The following programs are available at http://www.osborne.com:

Description	Folder
Desktop Menu Usage Program	MenuUsageProgram
Pocket PC Menu Usage Program	MenuUsageProgramPPC

Execution Instructions

Desktop Menu Usage Program

1. Start Visual C++ 6.0.
2. Open the project MenuUsageProgram.dsw in the folder MenuUsageProgram.
3. Build the program.
4. Execute the program.
5. Click the Shape menu item of the main menu. A check mark should display to the left of the Line menu item.
6. Choose a different default shape, such as Rectangle.
7. Perform rubber-banded drawing using the mouse.
8. Use the pop-up submenu to choose a different shape. Each time the pop-up submenu displays, a check mark should appear to the left of the menu item representing the previously selected shape.
9. Press the BACKSPACE key and then click the left mouse button. The caret should appear.
10. Type a string of characters. The caret should move to the next available character location.
11. Press the BACKSPACE key. The caret should disappear.
12. Click the Quit menu item on the window menu bar.
13. The application window disappears when application terminates.

Pocket PC Menu Usage Program

1. Attach the Pocket PC cradle to the desktop computer.
2. Insert the Pocket PC into the cradle.
3. Tell ActiveSync to create a guest connection.
4. Make sure that the status is "connected."
5. Start Embedded Visual C++ 3.0.
6. Open the project MenuUsageProgramPPC.vcw in the folder MenuUsageProgramPPC.

7. Build the program.

8. Make sure the program successfully downloads to the Pocket PC.

9. On the Pocket PC, open the File Explorer.

10. Browse to the MyDevice folder.

11. Execute the program MenuUsageProgram.

12. Tap the Shape menu item of the main menu. A check mark should display to the left of the Line menu item.

13. Choose a different default shape, such as Rectangle.

14. Perform rubber-banded drawing using the mouse.

15. Use the pop-up submenu to choose a different shape. Each time the pop-up submenu displays, a check mark should appear to the left of the menu item representing the previously selected shape.

16. Press the BACKSPACE key and then click the left mouse button. The caret should appear.

17. Type a string of characters. The caret should move to the next available character location.

18. Press the BACKSPACE key. The caret should disappear.

19. Tap the Quit menu item on the window menu bar.

20. The application window disappears when application terminates.

Using Intrinsic Controls in a Graphical User Interface

IN THIS CHAPTER:

A ny real Pocket PC application must provide an extensive and often complex user interface. With a desktop PC running Windows, a window can assume a rather large physical area. However, the Pocket PC severely limits the size of the physical screen space. This chapter specifically provides a set of approaches that facilitate providing a complex user interface within the physical screen space of a Pocket PC.

This chapter consists of three major sections. In the first section of this chapter appears a set of intrinsic controls. These controls enable an application to provide a user-friendly approach for entering program inputs. User interaction with one of these controls results in a Windows message being sent back to the parent application. This application provides message handlers to perform the real work of the program. The first section demonstrates the mechanics of using all the intrinsic controls.

The second section of this chapter offers a standard scroll bar control for usage in a program. Scroll bars enable the user to input a range of numbers without typing, which is subject to error, especially on the Pocket PC. Additionally, scroll bars enable an application to limit numbers to an allowable range. The standard scroll bar approach that this section provides enables a developer to implement a range-limited, validated number by implementing a small number of steps.

The final section of the chapter specifically addresses the limited physical space issue associated with user interfaces on the Pocket PC. This section employs a hierarchical scheme utilizing owner-drawn buttons and tab pages to provide maximum reuse of the limited screen space. A set of easily used libraries enable a complex user interface to be implemented with minimal programming effort.

NOTE

Starting with this chapter, emphasis is on the procedural steps necessary to utilize the libraries provided on the book's web site at http://www.osborne.com. This approach significantly differs from the previous chapters, which were heavily oriented toward simultaneously utilizing the libraries and explaining the underlying mechanics.

Using Intrinsic Controls in an Application

Intrinsic controls comprise a predefined set of user interface controls available for use by any application on the Pocket PC. Each of these controls has a standard look and feel, a standard set of properties, and a set of messages indicating user interaction as well as a set of methods for managing the behavior of the control.

TIP

The intrinsic controls available to a program are the exact same set of controls available to desktop Windows programs written in C++, Visual Basic, or Java.

Figure 8-1 shows all the intrinsic controls available to an application developer on the Pocket PC. A label on either side of the window in the figure identifies the class of each control.

Each of the controls in Figure 8-1 serves a specific purpose. The purpose of each control is as follows:

Control	Description
Static text	Represents a descriptive label that cannot be modified directly by a user
Push button	Enables a user to signal that the program is to take some action
Radio buttons	Allows a user to select from a group of mutually exclusive alternatives
Check box	Permits a user to select multiple simultaneous alternatives from a group
Single-line text	Provides a means for a user to enter a single line of text
Multiline text	Enables a user to input several lines of text
List box	Provides a list of alternatives from which a user may select one or more
Combo box	Incorporates a drop-down list box and a single-line text field to allow for a single selection from among multiple alternatives

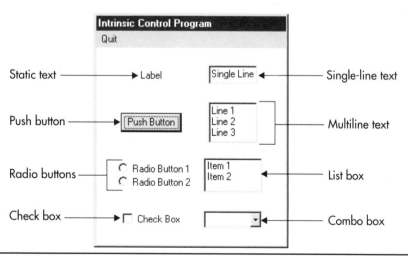

Figure 8-1   *A graphical user interface using intrinsic controls*

The most frequently used elements among these intrinsic controls are the label, combo box, and button.

NOTE

Using the minimal dialog program from Chapter 3 as the basis for a program, the resource editor and the resource toolbar of Embedded Visual Studio enable a developer to place these controls onto a dialog using a drag-and-drop operation.

In a typical user interface, the label identifies the contents of the combo box. A user taps on the arrow button of the combo box to reveal the drop-down list of items. Using the stylus, a user selects one of the items, which then appears in the single-line text field at the side of the arrow button of the combo box. Once a user has selected an entry from the combo box, tapping the button with the stylus signals the program to use the contents of the single-line text field of the combo box to perform an application-specific process.

The application provided for this section has a very simple goal. The primary purpose of this program is to demonstrate the basic program mechanics for utilizing each of these controls. In keeping with this objective, every message handler for each of these controls performs the exact same response. In Figure 8-2 appears a typical response.

This figure demonstrates the response by the sample program of this section when a user taps the button depicted in Figure 8-1. The immediate response is to display a message box. This message box provides the label "Status" in the caption bar at the top of the message window. Inside the client area of the message box is an informative message indicating the specific intrinsic control undergoing user interaction. Finally, an OK button enables a user to easily dispatch the message box from view after the user has reviewed the information in the message box.

An Overview of the Intrinsic Controls

Actually, the intrinsic controls comprise a set of predefined windows classes. During the boot-up process, Windows registers these classes with predefined properties.

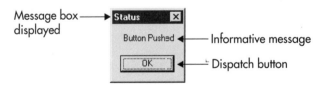

Figure 8-2   *A typical response by the message handler for an intrinsic control*

NOTE

Recall that in Chapter 3, the simple Windows program registers a window class and then creates a window in that class. Every window class possesses a set of properties, such as a window procedure that processes messages. Moreover, each window instance in the class has additional properties, such as styles.

Figure 8-3 demonstrates the exact class names associated with each of the intrinsic controls available to a developer.

Individual class names appear in the first level of the tree structure of the figure. For instance, Windows defines the button intrinsic control as the "BUTTON" class. Windows requires that the programmer use the exact class name in uppercase and surrounded in quotes, as indicated. A list box control is an instance of the Windows defined class "LISTBOX".

Associated with each control class is a set of predefined styles. These styles imply a specific look, feel, and behavior for each window instance in the control class. For instance, a specific window in the "BUTTON" class may have one of the following styles: BS_PUSHBUTTON, BS_RADIOBUTTON, or BS_CHECKBOX. Each of these exhibits a specific style when displayed within a parent window (refer to Figure 8-1).

Additionally, these styles behave in a specific manner. For instance, when a user interacts with a "BUTTON" class window declared in the BS_PUSHBUTTON style, the look of the button changes to appear as if pressed. Also, Windows submits a WM_COMMAND message to the registered window procedure for the "BUTTON" class.

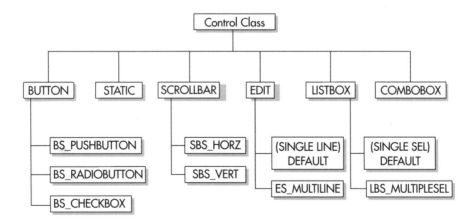

Each class has additional, *unique* style flags

Figure 8-3   *Classes and styles for intrinsic controls*

Although most of the controls require specific style properties to be explicitly declared, several of the intrinsic controls possess default styles. These control classes include the "EDIT", "LISTBOX", and "COMBOBOX" classes, as indicated in Figure 8-3. As an example, consider the "LISTBOX" control. When a program creates an instance of this control class, the window automatically possesses the single-line-style property. This property allows a user to select only a single element in the list box by tapping the stylus on that element. Once the item is selected, Windows automatically highlights that list element with a blue bar. If the user decides to select a different element, the blue selection bar moves to the most recently selected list item in the list box. A specific window instance in the "LISTBOX" control class receives this property and behavior without any additional programming effort on the part of a developer.

NOTE

After dragging and dropping a control onto the face of the dialog template in the Resource Editor of Embedded Visual Studio, a developer explicitly sets the style properties of the control. In order to modify the style of the control, the developer double-clicks the control. As a result of the double-click, the Resource Editor displays the Property dialog for the control. This dialog enables a developer to set the style properties as appropriate for the application.

When a user interacts with each of the intrinsic controls, Windows sends a message to the window procedure that was registered for the control class. This window procedure responds to the submitted message in a carefully defined way. Figure 8-4 demonstrates the complete response for a button control.

When created, each control exists within a parent window. User interaction with the intrinsic control initiates a specific sequence of interactions between the parent

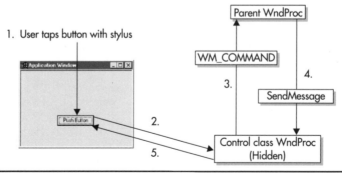

Figure 8-4   *Parent/child relationships*

window procedure and the child or intrinsic control window procedure, as show in Figure 8-4. The actual sequence of actions proceeds as follows:

1. A user interacts with the button child control by tapping the button with the stylus.

2. Windows submits a WM_COMMAND message to the registered and hidden window procedure for the "BUTTON" control class.

3. The hidden window procedure forwards the WM_COMMAND message to the window procedure for the known parent window of the control class window.

4. A WM_COMMAND message handler in the parent window procedure responds to the message in a manner appropriate to the application.

5. If the parent window needs to send a command to change the value of a property, this window procedure constructs and transmits a predefined message back to the hidden window procedure for the control class. A window procedure transmits a message to another window procedure using the SendMessage method.

6. The hidden window procedure for the control class sends the necessary commands to Windows to ensure that the requested property change takes effect.

The hidden window procedure for each of the control classes in Figure 8-3 responds to a predefined set of messages. These messages may be submitted by Windows, such as the WM_COMMAND message for the "BUTTON" class, or may be transmitted on behalf of a program using the SendMessage method. The hidden window procedures all reside within the WINDOW component of Windows, as discussed in Chapter 1. Because each hidden window procedure only responds to a specific set of messages, these messages and their arguments appear within the online help attached to Embedded Visual Studio.

A complete summary of the messages reflected from the hidden window procedure for each intrinsic control class appears in Table 8-1. This table also contains the list of messages accepted by the hidden window procedures to write and to read the properties of the control class windows.

The set of messages in Table 8-1 is by no means an exhaustive set of the available messages. A complete list of the messages that move back and forth would be rather extensive. However, the messages within this table do possess a special feature: These messages are the messages a programmer most frequently uses when employing these controls in an application. By emphasizing these messages, a programmer gains the basic knowledge necessary to become immediately productive using these intrinsic controls in an application.

Control Class	Class	Interaction Message	Write Props	Read Props
Button	"BUTTON"	WM_COMMAND	BM_SETSTATE	BM_GETSTATE
Check box	"BUTTON"	WM_COMMAND	BM_SETCHECK	BM_GETCHECK
Combo box	"COMBOBOX"	WM_COMMAND,CBN_SELCHANGE	CB_ADDSTRING	CB_GETCURSEL CB_GETLBTEXT
Edit	"EDIT"	WM_COMMAND,EN_KILLFOCUS	SetWindowText EM_SETSEL EM_REPLACESEL	GetWindowText
Static	"STATIC"	None	SetWindowText	GetWindowText
List box	"LISTBOX"	WM_COMMAND,LBN_SELCHANGE	LB_ADDSTRING	LB_GETCURSEL LB_GETTEXT
Radio button	"BUTTON"	WM_COMMAND	BM_SETCHECK	BM_GETCHECK

Table 8-1 *Control Class Messages and Property Management*

Entries in Table 8-1 describe the complete two-way interaction between a child window in a child control class and a parent window. When a user interacts with a specific window in a child control class, one of the interaction messages moves from the control's hidden window procedure to the parent's visible window procedure. At any time during execution, a parent window can obtain the value of a specific property by sending the message that appears in the Read Props column of the table. Setting the property value involves using the SendMessage method to transmit one of the messages in the Write Props column of the table. Entries in the Write Props and Read Props columns are symbolic constants that a developer can directly utilize in an application. The header file windows.h defines the constants for the application programmer.

As an example, consider the row for the "LISTBOX" control class. When a user selects a specific list entry, the hidden window procedure of the list box forwards an LBN_SELCHANGE message to the parent window procedure. In the message handler, the parent window procedure uses the SendMessage method with the message code LB_GETCURSEL to retrieve the zero-based index of the selected list item. The handler can then use this information in a manner appropriate to the application.

Unfortunately, the developers of this segment of Windows were somewhat inconsistent. Some of the classes use methods, rather than messages, to access the property values of a control window. For instance, review the row for the "EDIT" control class. Reading or writing the text for the control uses the SetWindowText and GetWindowText methods, as opposed to using a specific message. This approach is not only inconsistent but is a little confusing. These methods are normally the mechanism for accessing the caption bar title of a window. This usage applies the same methods to maintain the contents of the client area of a window rather than to manipulate the text in the caption area. However, because Windows requires this approach, the program developer simply has no choice in the matter.

Implementing with the Intrinsic Controls

Adding an intrinsic control to the graphical user interface of a Pocket PC application requires that a developer perform three important steps:

1. Add the control to the user interface.
2. Initialize the state and data associated with the control.
3. Add a message handler for processing user interaction.

By following these steps and using the tools available, a developer can easily incorporate the intrinsic controls into a user interface in a matter of minutes.

On the web site for this book, the program IntrinsicControlsProgram explicitly implements each of these steps for each of the intrinsic controls described in Figure 8-1. As a simple example, the subsequent discussion follows each of these steps for one of the controls—the list box.

Add the Control to the User Interface

Because the basis for any application is a dialog, adding a list box to the user interface is a simple task. When using the dialog editor, a floating resource toolbar displays all the available intrinsic controls. Drag the desired control (in this case, a list box) to the desired location on the dialog window. Then, drop the control into that location. Utilizing the mouse enables a developer to further refine both the location and size of this control.

NOTE

The ease with which controls may be added and moved is one of the key benefits to using a dialog-based approach for developing Pocket PC 2002 applications.

As an alternative, an application can incorporate new controls programmatically using the Win32 API method CreateWindowEx and the appropriate window class, such as "LISTBOX". However, in order to see the actual location, the developer must execute the program. After viewing the user interface, a programmer then adjusts the location and executes again. This iteration is very time consuming. A realistic user interface can consume several days or more when using this iterative approach to programmatically creating controls. Using a dialog-based application and the graphical dialog editor, the process of correctly placing intrinsic controls reduces to several minutes.

Initialize the State and Data Associated with the Control

Every intrinsic control possesses an initial state. Further, some of the controls require data initialization. Typically, an initial state reveals a certain look and feel to a user. For instance, a button needs to be in the reset state rather than the pushed state. Controls that require initial data usually involve lists, such as the "LISTBOX" and the "COMBOBOX" controls. Initialization involves placing entries into the list attached to the control.

NOTE

The correct location in which to perform intrinsic control initialization is within the WM_INITDIALOG message handler. This handler executes before the display of the main dialog window and ensures that the initial data is loaded into the control prior to actual display.

Loading the list attached to a "LISTBOX" intrinsic control involves utilizing the following code elements:

```
#include <windowsx.h>
BOOL  OnInitDialog ( HWND  hDlg , HWND  hDlgFocus , long  lInitParam )
{
   HWND       Control ;
   Control = GetDlgItem(hDlg,IDC_LIST1) ;
   ListBox_AddString(Control, __TEXT("Item 1")) ;
   ListBox_AddString(Control, __TEXT("Item 2")) ;
}
```

An additional windows header file, <windowsx.h>, provides a series of macros that wrap execution of the Win32 method named SendMessage. As explained in Figure 8-4, this method, along with special message codes and arguments, enable the parent dialog procedure to control the behavior of an intrinsic control. In the preceding code segment, the macro ListBox_AddString uses SendMessage to command a list box control to add a string to the end of the attached list of strings.

Setting the strings into the attached list requires that the handler first obtain a handle to the list box element. The Win32 API method named GetDlgItem utilizes the handle to the parent dialog window and the resource identifier IDC_LIST1 created by Visual Studio to retrieve a window handle to the control.

TIP

Every intrinsic control is a specific window object in the predefined window class for the intrinsic control. Associated with this class is a hidden window procedure registered for the class by Windows itself during initialization and loading.

After obtaining the handle to the specific list box control, the message handler places strings into the attached list. Using the macro ListBox_AddString, the handler employs the SendMessage macro to the specific control identified by the window handle stored in Control. The actual message code transmitted to the hidden window procedure of the list box control appears as the symbolic constant LB_ADDSTRING in the Win32 API. This command forces the list box control to enter the strings in the same order as received. Another macro, ListBox_InsertString, places string entries into the list box sorted in ascending or descending order, depending on a property that can be programmatically set prior to actual string submission.

Add a Message Handler for Processing User Interaction

When a user interacts with a control, the program needs to respond in an manner that reflects the effect of any selections made by the user. For the list box control, when a user selects a different member of the list, a WM_COMMAND message moves from the hidden window procedure to the parent dialog procedure. Embedded in this message, as one of the message parameters, is a notification code whose value is set to the symbolic constant LBN_SELCHANGE. This constant appears in windows.h and indicates that a new value has been selected.

NOTE

Every intrinsic control generates at least one message from the hidden window procedure to the parent dialog procedure. Sometimes the specific message requires the notification code for correct interpretation. For other messages, the notification code is irrelevant.

Processing the selection-change message indicated in the preceding paragraph involves incorporating the following code into the WM_COMMAND message handler:

```
void  DlgOnCommand  ( HWND  hDlg , int  iID ,
                      HWND  hDlgCtl , UINT  uCodeNotify )
{
  switch( iID )
  {
      case IDC_LIST1:
             if ( uCodeNotify == LBN_SELCHANGE )
             {
                 SelectedItem = ListBox_GetCurSel(hDlgCtl) ;
                 ListBox_GetText(hDlgCtl, SelectedItem, RawText) ;
                 MessageBox(hDlg,RawText,__TEXT("Status"),MB_OK) ;
             }
      break ;
}
      }
```

First, the message handler confirms that the list box is the source of the message by comparing iID with IDC_LIST1. Then, the notification code LBN_SELCHANGE serves as a filter to only admit selection-change events into the actual message-processing code. In order to determine the actual string selected by a user, the message handler queries the list box control. A handle to the control appears as one of the arguments to the message handler, hDlgCtl.

A two-step sequence is necessary to obtain the actual selected string. Using the macro ListBox_GetCurSel provided by windowsx.h, a SendMessage method call returns the index of the selected item in the attached list. Then, the macro ListBox_GetText uses this index to retrieve the actual text string selected by the user. Additional application-specific processing then utilizes this string in a manner appropriate to the application.

During the lifecycle of a program, a user may interact with these controls many times. Each time the user interacts with a control, the program responds appropriately. Often, user interaction may cause a change in the visual state of the control. The message handler is then responsible for explicitly modifying the visual state through the visible properties of the control. And, sometimes, groups of controls may be affected by user interaction with a single control in the group.

An Important Portability Issue

A review of the resource elements of the program IntrinsicControlsProgram reveals that it uses two dialog forms. Inclusion of both forms is necessary to ensure portability between the desktop versions of Windows and Windows CE.

Comparing the two dialog templates side by side in the resource editor of Visual Studio clearly identifies the major difference between the two dialog forms. Both forms contain exactly the same controls. However, controls in the dialog form named IDD_DIALOG2 are all lower on the form than the controls in IDD_DIALOG1.

NOTE

Desktop versions of Windows automatically move controls downward in the client area to compensate for the height of the menu bar. However, Pocket PC 2002 versions of Windows do not move the controls. Instead, the application developer must physically move the controls downward on the dialog form.

Therefore, in order to maintain the instant portability of a Windows application from the desktop to the Pocket PC 2002, separate dialog forms are necessary. The dialog form named IDD_DIALOG1 displays when the program executes on the desktop. When used on the Pocket PC 2002, the primary user interface is the dialog form named IDD_DIALOG2.

Portability of a Windows application between the desktop and the Pocket PC 2002 depends on the value of the flag named WindowsCE declared in the file IFiles.h.

TIP

Chapter 3 describes the occurrence and usage of the WindowsCE flag in order to obtain platform portability.

This same flag serves to control the display of the main dialog form. A simple modification to the DlgMain element of a program enables this flag to display a specific form. The actual DlgMain element for the program IntrinsicControlsProgram is as follows:

```
int WINAPI WinMain(HINSTANCE hInstance, HINSTANCE hPrevInstance,
                    LPTSTR lpCmdLine, int nCmdShow)
{
      PutProgramInstance(hInstance) ;
#if WindowsCE
      DialogBox( hInstance , MAKEINTRESOURCE(IDD_DIALOG2) ,
                HWND_DESKTOP , (DLGPROC) DlgProc ) ;
#else
      DialogBox( hInstance , MAKEINTRESOURCE(IDD_DIALOG1) ,
                HWND_DESKTOP , (DLGPROC) DlgProc ) ;
#endif
      return 0 ;
}
```

Conditional compilation statements—#if, #else, and #endif—control the actual DialogBox method call that displays the main dialog form. When the WindowsCE flag is set to a value of 1, the first alternative executes, displaying dialog form IDD_DIALOG2. If this flag has the value 0, dialog form IDD_DIALOG1 displays as the primary user interface. Flipping the software switch WindowsCE between 0 and 1 forces the appropriate user interface to display, as defined in Chapter 3.

Using a Group of Controls to Implement User-Friendly Input

One of the primary uses of a user interface is to allow a user to input numerical data into a program. For the Pocket PC, a user-friendly numerical input approach is an important design feature of the user interface of any application.

NOTE

As a result of the very small physical screen space of the Pocket PC, an application needs to enable user input of numbers without typing. The keyboard for the Pocket PC temporarily overlaps the screen area. Moreover, usage of the keyboard involves the stylus. Having a tiny overlapping visual keyboard that requires extensive stylus taps significantly increases the likelihood of user error when inputting numbers.

In addition to eliminating the typing of numbers, every program typically requires that any particular number should be within a fixed range. Therefore, any scheme that enables numerical input must also ensure that all input values are restricted to the allowable range.

For Windows applications, whether desktop or Pocket PC based, the best intrinsic control for aiding the user to input numbers is the scroll bar control. A scroll bar represents a continuous range of numbers restricted to an acceptable range. However, in order to be effective, a scroll bar control requires a number of additional controls.

Utilizing a Scroll Bar and a Text Buddy

Unfortunately, many applications that use scroll bar controls do so in a very poor manner. Typically, an application presents a scroll bar control without any identification regarding the acceptable range of values or the current value. Worse yet, the user does not have any way to refine the scroll bar input using the keyboard, if desired.

In this section, a scroll bar control forms the basis for a group of controls that more effectively allow a user to input numerical data. In addition to the user inputting a numerical value, software elements work with this group of controls to ensure that the input value is within the acceptable range limit and that any typed number is numerically valid. A text buddy accompanies the scroll bar control. This edit window displays the current value represented by the position of the scroll bar control. Additionally, the text buddy enables the user to directly input a numeric value. During processing of the keyboard input, the program also performs validation of the numeric input and correspondingly updates the position of the scroll bar control.

Figure 8-5 provides an operational view of the workings of the scroll bar–based group of controls.

According to this figure, a user can manipulate the value represented by the scroll bar via four different operations:

▶ Dragging the thumb sets the value represented by the scroll bar anywhere along the range of values. Each time a user drags the thumb, the value represented by the scroll bar control changes by some large amount determined strictly by Windows.

▶ Tapping on the shaft moves the thumb of the scroll bar by a finite but medium-sized amount, denoted as PAGE_INCREMENT units. This value may be set by the program through a specific method in the Windows API.

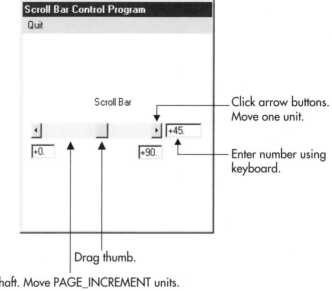

Figure 8-5 *User operations for a scroll bar control and buddies*

▶ Tapping on an arrow button at either side of the scroll bar control moves the thumb by an amount equal to one unit.

▶ Entering a numeric value into the text box at the left side of the control using the keyboard and the stylus moves the thumb to the appropriate position within the scroll bar shaft. Numbers are validated as numeric and restricted to the minimum and maximum limits associated with the scroll bar control.

The next section describes a process using a set of specially developed functions that simplify the incorporation of this scroll bar control and its buddies into an application.

Using this approach requires that a number of intrinsic controls work together. The scroll bar model in Figure 8-6 characterizes the individual controls that contribute to the preceding behavior.

Exactly five intrinsic controls combine to form the user-friendly scroll bar control. At the top of the group is a label control. This control indicates the name of the variable whose value is being determined by the control. Centered directly below this label is the scroll bar control. A user manipulates this control using the

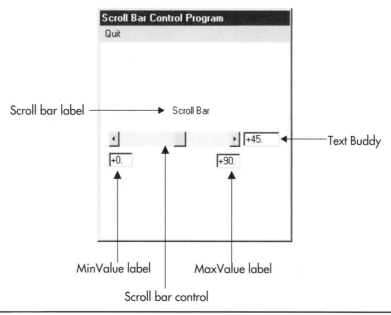

Figure 8-6   *The user-friendly scroll bar control model*

operations model in Figure 8-5. At the right side of the group is a text control. This Text Buddy serves two purposes. If a user is manipulating the scroll bar control, the value in the Text Buddy represents the current value determined by the location of the thumb of the scroll bar. Alternatively, a user may choose to employ the Text Buddy, the keyboard, and the stylus in order to directly enter a desired value. The remaining two controls are the labels that appear at the bottom of the group. These labels indicate to the user the minimum and maximum range of values acceptable to the application. The scroll bar control automatically limits the range of possible values to the values indicated in these labels. If a user enters numbers into the Text Buddy, support code enforces the range indicated in the label fields along the bottom of the group.

NOTE

A typical Pocket PC dialog that fills the whole screen area can accommodate exactly three of these groups in a single client area. If an application requires more than three input variables, a hierarchical user interface combined with a series of tab pages is necessary to collect all the input values. Techniques and library elements for accomplishing this kind of interface appear in Chapter 9.

When a user interacts with either the scroll bar control or the Text Buddy in the group, messages flow. Additionally, interaction with one of these primary elements impacts the state of the other element. Figure 8-7 demonstrates the relationships among user interaction, message generation, and multiple control status.

The numbers in the figure correspond to the order in which actions occur during the execution of a program that supports a user-friendly scroll bar control, as follows:

1. A user interacts with the scroll bar through the thumb, the shaft, or the arrows.

2. The hidden window procedure for the scroll bar control submits a WM_HSCROLL message to the parent dialog procedure.

3. Inside the parent dialog procedure, a message handler for the WM_HSCROLL message records the current value represented by scroll bar control and potentially fixes the location of the thumb.

4. Using the current value represented by the scroll bar control, the WM_HSCROLL message handler computes the current value for the variable and displays the value in the Text Buddy text window.

5. Alternatively, the user may choose to display the visual keyboard on the Pocket PC and then to use the stylus to enter a numeric value.

6. After input of every character, the hidden dialog procedure of the Text Buddy control submits a WM_COMMAND message to the parent dialog procedure. This message has a notification code set to the value of the symbolic constant EN_CHANGE, as defined by the header file windows.h.

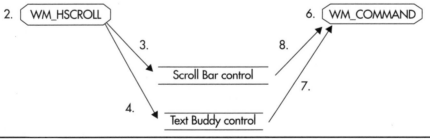

Figure 8-7   *Scroll and Text Buddy updating relationships*

7. Inside the parent dialog procedure, a message handler for the WM_COMMAND message handler reads and validates the value stored in the Text Buddy control. Validation consists of ensuring that the value is numeric and that it lies within the acceptable range.

8. If the input value passes the validation tests, the WM_COMMAND message handler uses the value to set the position of the scroll bar thumb.

Of course, a set of library methods enables all these details to be hidden away. As a result, a simple process is available that uses these methods to easily add a user-friendly scroll bar control to an application in a matter of a few minutes.

Incorporating a User-Friendly Scroll Bar Control

All the library methods that support a user-friendly scroll bar control exist within the software element GUIUtils. These methods encapsulate initialization and user interaction processing for the group of intrinsic controls that compose the user-friendly scroll bar control.

In order to employ the scroll bar control in an application, a developer performs the following steps:

1. Use the dialog editor to place all five controls onto the face of the dialog form.

2. Include the GUIUtils.h header file in the dialog procedure to provide access to the methods.

3. Declare and initialize the scroll bar–management variables that control the range and current value of the scroll bar control.

4. In the WM_INITDIALOG message handler, initialize the scroll bar control and the Text Buddy control.

5. Add a case clause to the WM_COMMAND message handler for the Text Buddy.

6. Add a WM_HSCROLL message handler method to the dialog procedure.

Using the library elements of GUIUtils.h inside the WM_INITDIALOG, WM_COMMAND, and WM_HSCROLL message handlers enables a developer to rapidly incorporate a user-friendly scroll bar into an application—using just six steps.

On the book's web site, the program ScrollBarControlProgram implements each of these steps for a single, user-friendly scroll bar. The code that actually implements each of these steps appears in the following subsections.

Use the Dialog Editor to Place All Five Controls onto the Face of the Dialog

In this step, a developer uses the resource toolbar of the dialog editor to drag and drop the individual controls onto the face of the dialog. Then, using the mouse, a developer drags the controls around until they appear in the spatial relationships described in Figure 8-6.

NOTE

The immediate visual representation of the relative spatial locations of the component controls further provides an indication as to the benefits of using a dialog-based application approach, as promoted in Chapter 3.

Include the GUIUtils.h Header File in the Dialog Procedure

Support methods for implementing the relationships defined in Figure 8-7 all appear within the following header file:

```
#include "GUIUtils.h"
```

By including this header file, all these support methods become visible and available for use within the various message handlers of the dialog procedure.

Declare and Initialize the Scroll Bar–Management Variables

All the support methods operate based on the input of a set of defining variables. These variables appear in the following code segment:

```
#define SCROLL_VALUE_MIN      0.0
#define SCROLL_VALUE_MAX     90.0
#define SCROLL_NUMBER_INCREMENTS_PER_UNIT 1
#define SCROLL_NUMBER_FRACTIONAL_DIGITS   0
double   SCROLL_CurrentScrollValue = SCROLL_VALUE_MIN ;
int      SCROLL_CurrentScrollPos = 0 ;

BOOL     SCROLL_ProcessEdit = TRUE ;
BOOL     SCROLL_BuddyInitialized = FALSE ;
```

The first two definitions, SCROLL_VALUE_MIN and SCROLL_VALUE_MAX, indicate the acceptable range of values for the input variable controlled by the user-friendly scroll bar. Because a value may have a fractional component, the symbolic constant SCROLL_NUMBER_INCREMENTS_PER_UNIT determines the number of fractional entries between each unit of the scroll bar value. For instance, declaring this constant to be 10 would allow the value to have tenths as the fractional part of the value. When the support methods display numeric values in the Text Buddy window, the constant SCROLL_NUMBER_FRACTIONAL_DIGITS determines the number of digits used to display the fractional portion of any value.

The scroll bar position ranges from 0 to 100. A variable named SCROLL_CurrentScrollPos maintains the current position of the scroll bar thumb relative to this range. During processing by the support methods of GUIUtils.h, this position translates into a value in the allowable input range dictated by the constants SCROLL_VALUE_MIN and SCROLL_VALUE_MAX. Stored in the variable SCROLL_CurrentScrollValue is the value of the thumb position translated into this allowable input range.

A very subtle relationship exists between the scroll bar control and the Text Buddy control. When the user moves the scroll bar thumb, the WM_HSCROLL message handler updates the Text Buddy field. This update causes the hidden window procedure for the Text Buddy control to generate a WM_COMMAND message. This handler then would attempt to update the Text Buddy control again, potentially causing an infinite loop between the WM_HSCROLL message handler and the WM_COMMAND message handler. By using the SCROLL_ProcessEdit flag as a common signal, these utility methods of GUIUtils.h can terminate this potential infinite loop. An application simply initializes this variable and then passes a pointer to the variable to the appropriate utility method in GUIUtils.h. All other manipulations of this variable occur within the utility methods and are of no further concern to the application.

A final variable, named SCROLL_BuddyInitialized, disables all processing of WM_COMMAND messages from the hidden window procedure of the Text Buddy control until the scroll bar control is initialized in the WM_INITDIALOG message handler. If this flag were not used, the creation of the scroll bar control would cause the initialization of the Text Buddy control based on the incorrect range of values for the scroll bar control.

NOTE

Each of the variables begins with the string SCROLL. When inserting a user-friendly scroll bar into an application, a developer can copy and paste these same values into the application. Then, a global replace allows the prefix SCROLL to be replaced with a more meaningful prefix that is specific to the application. However, this global replace should be accomplished after the remaining steps are completed, because these variables are arguments to the helper methods of GUIUtils.h.

Initialize the Controls in the WM_INITDIALOG Message Handler

In the following code segment, the method IniatializeScrollAndBuddy uses a combination of the intrinsic control identifiers and the variables to initialize the user-friendly scroll bar. After initializing all the intrinsic controls in the group, the message handler then sets the SCROLL_BuddyInitialized flag so that all WM_COMMAND messages from the Text Buddy are correctly processed.

```
InitializeScrollAndBuddy(hDlg, IDC_SCROLLBAR1,
                    SCROLL_VALUE_MIN, SCROLL_VALUE_MAX,
                    SCROLL_NUMBER_INCREMENTS_PER_UNIT ,
                    IDC_EDIT1, IDC_STATIC1, IDC_STATIC2,
                    SCROLL_NUMBER_FRACTIONAL_DIGITS,
                    SCROLL_CurrentScrollValue,
                    &SCROLL_CurrentScrollPos ) ;


SCROLL_BuddyInitialized = TRUE ;
```

In the code segment, IDC_SCROLLBAR1 is the symbolic constant that identifies the scroll bar control in the group. The identifier for the Text Buddy is the symbolic constant IDC_EDIT1. IDC_STATIC1 and IDC_STATIC2 are the identifiers of the minimum and maximum value labels.

Add a Case Clause to the WM_COMMAND Message Handler

Adding the following clause to the switch statement in the WM_COMMAND message handler ensures that direct user input into the Text Buddy control is properly processed:

```
case IDC_EDIT1:
  if ( (uCodeNotify == EN_CHANGE ) && SCROLL_BuddyInitialized )
     ProcessIntegerEditNotification( hDlg,
                    &SCROLL_ProcessEdit, IDC_SCROLLBAR1 ,
                    IDC_EDIT1, SCROLL_VALUE_MIN,
                    SCROLL_NUMBER_INCREMENTS_PER_UNIT ,
                    &SCROLL_CurrentScrollPos,
                    &SCROLL_CurrentScrollValue ) ;
    break ;
```

Both the notification code, uCodeNotify, and the scroll initialization flag, SCROLL_BuddyInitialized, determine that this is a valid signal indicating new user input into the Text Buddy. If the conditions warrant actual processing of the message, the helper method ProcessIntegerEditNotification from GUIUtils.h manages all the processing details. The current value of the flag SCROLL_ProcessEdit may have been set by the WM_HSCROLL message handler (which appears in the next subsection) to disable the actual processing, because this event may have been generated by updating the Text Buddy in response to user interaction with the scroll bar control.

NOTE

Similar methods appear in GUIUtils.h for processing unsigned integers, doubles, and unsigned doubles. Use these methods consistent with the value of SCROLL_NUMBER_INCREMENTS_PER_UNIT to ensure correct processing at the required decimal accuracy.

Add a WM_HSCROLL Message Handler Method to the Dialog Procedure

Each time a user drags the scroll bar thumb, taps on the shaft, or taps on the arrows of the scroll bar control, a WM_HSCROLL message emits from the hidden window procedure of the scroll bar control. This handler processes the message using the method ProcessScrollMessage provided by GUIUtils.h.

```
void DlgOnHScroll(HWND hDlg, HWND hwndCtl, UINT Code, int Position)
{
  HWND Scroll ;
  Scroll = GetDlgItem(hDlg,IDC_SCROLLBAR1) ;
  if ( Scroll == hwndCtl )
    ProcessScrollMessage(hDlg, &SCROLL_ProcessEdit,
                    Code, IDC_SCROLLBAR1,
                    Position, &SCROLL_CurrentScrollPos,
                    SCROLL_VALUE_MIN,
                    SCROLL_NUMBER_INCREMENTS_PER_UNIT,
                    &SCROLL_CurrentScrollValue ,
                    IDC_EDIT1 ,
                      SCROLL_NUMBER_FRACTIONAL_DIGITS ) ;
}
```

Submitting the flag SCROLL_ProcessEdit to this method enables the method to set the flag to disable the corresponding WM_COMMAND message generated by updating the Text Buddy IDC_EDIT1. After execution of the support method ProcessScrollMessage, the current value appears in the Text Buddy IDC_EDIT1 and resides in the variable SCROLL_CurrentScrollValue.

As indicated earlier, after all these changes are made, a global change and replace suffices to replace the prefix SCROLL with a more meaningful prefix. In this way, the steps implemented in the sample program are the basis for mechanically and easily inserting a user-friendly scroll bar into an application user interface with a minimal amount of code editing required.

Validating Direct User Inputs into the Text Buddy Window

One of the helper methods in GUIUtils.h is ProcessIntegerEditNotification. Recall from the last section that this method executes in response to conditions that indicate a new character has been entered into the Text Buddy control window.

```
void ProcessIntegerEditNotification(
                HWND hDlg, BOOL * ProcessEdit,
                int ScrollID , int BuddyID,
                double ValueMin, int NumberIncrementsPerUnit,
                int * CurrentPosition, double * CurrentValue )
{
  int  NewValue ;
  if ( *ProcessEdit )
  {
    *ProcessEdit = FALSE ;
    GetIntegerFromTextWindow(hDlg,BuddyID, &NewValue ) ;

    if ( NewValue >= ValueMin )
      *CurrentPosition =
      (int)((NewValue-ValueMin)*(double)NumberIncrementsPerUnit);
    else
      *CurrentPosition = 0 ;

    ValidateScrollPosition(hDlg,ScrollID,CurrentPosition) ;
    *CurrentValue =
        ((double)*CurrentPosition/(double)NumberIncrementsPerUnit)
              + ValueMin ;
    if ( *CurrentValue != NewValue )
      SetIntegerIntoTextWindow(hDlg,BuddyID,(int)*CurrentValue) ;
    UpdateScroll(hDlg,ScrollID, *CurrentPosition) ;
    *ProcessEdit = TRUE ;
  }
}
```

As the first real step of processing, this method checks the value of ProcessEdit. If this flag is set to FALSE, processing does not occur. This condition can only happen when the WM_HSCROLL message handler sets the value to FALSE prior to changing the value of the Text Buddy in response to user interaction with the scroll bar control.

On the other hand, if this flag is TRUE, this method executes because the user directly entered an input character into the Text Buddy control. In response, this helper method retrieves the value from the Text Buddy using the helper method GetIntegerFromTextWindow, also provided by GUIUtils.h. Inside the method GetIntegerFromTextWindow, an additional validation step ensures that the retrieved value is both numeric and an integer. This value represents the actual input value indicated by the user. After retrieving the value, this method converts the value into a new position for the scroll bar thumb. Using the helper method ValidateScrollPosition, which also appears in GUIUtils.h, this method constrains the value within the valid range of positions supported within by the scroll bar control. After validation, this method then converts the validated new thumb position into a new, validated input value within the range constraints imposed by the application.

If the input value has been modified, this method stores the modified input value back into the Text Buddy window. Finally, the validated new thumb position passes to the method UpdateScroll, which moves the scroll bar thumb to the indicated position.

Summary

This chapter introduces the ability to provide a graphical user interface that solicits user input. A series of intrinsic controls, such as labels, buttons, list boxes, combo boxes, radio buttons, and check boxes, provide simple, easy-to-use ways of capturing user input with little or no typing. In order to support rapid numerical input by a user within the confines of the small physical space of a Pocket PC, this chapter also defines a user-friendly scroll bar and a supporting library for easily incorporating this scroll bar into an application.

Key conclusions appearing in this chapter are as follows:

▶ Intrinsic controls are easy to use and to incorporate into your program.

▶ Each intrinsic control is a Windows-registered class with a hidden window procedure.

▶ When a user interacts with an intrinsic control, the hidden window procedure transmits a message to the parent dialog procedure.

▶ Because the primary application window is a dialog form, a visual editor enables a developer to add intrinsic controls to an application in a short period of time.

▶ A user-friendly scroll bar enables a user to rapidly enter validated numeric data on a Pocket PC in spite of the small physical display space.

▶ Because the primary application window is a dialog form, a visual editor enables a developer to add the controls that comprise a user-friendly scroll bar in a short period of time.

▶ The GUIUtils software element enables a developer to add the user-friendly scroll bar to an application in a few short steps that mostly involve cutting, pasting, and editing existing code.

Sample Programs on the Web

The following programs are available at http://www.osborne.com:

Description	Folder
Desktop Intrinsic Controls Program	IntrinsicControlsProgram
Pocket PC Intrinsic Controls Program	IntrinsicControlsProgramPPC
Desktop Scroll Bar Control Program	ScrollBarControlProgram
Pocket PC Scroll Bar Control Program	ScrollBarControlProgramPPC

Execution Instructions

Desktop Intrinsic Controls Program

1. Start Visual C++ 6.0.

2. Open the project IntrinsicControlsProgram.dsw in the folder IntrinsicControlsProgram.

3. Build the program.

4. Execute the program.

5. Click the button control. A message box should display indicating that the button was clicked.

6. Interact with the remaining controls. Each should respond with a message box.

7. Click the Quit menu item on the window menu bar.

8. The application window disappears as the application terminates.

Pocket PC Intrinsic Controls Program

1. Attach the Pocket PC cradle to the desktop computer.

2. Insert the Pocket PC into the cradle.

3. Tell ActiveSync to create a guest connection.

4. Make sure the status is connected.

5. Start Embedded Visual C++ 3.0.

6. Open the project IntrinsicControlsProgramPPC.vcw in the folder IntrinsicControlsProgramPPC.

7. Build the program.

8. Make sure the program successfully downloads to the Pocket PC.

9. On the Pocket PC, open the File Explorer.

10. Browse to the MyDevice folder.

11. Execute the program IntrinsicControlsProgram.

12. Tap the button control. A message box should display indicating that the button was tapped.

13. Interact with the remaining controls. Each should respond with a message box.

14. Tap the Quit menu item on the window menu bar.

15. The application window disappears as the application terminates.

Desktop Scroll Bar Control Program

1. Start Visual C++ 6.0.

2. Open the project ScrollBarControlProgram.dsw in the folder ScrollBarControlProgram.

3. Build the program.

4. Execute the program.

5. Drag the scroll bar thumb. New values should appear in the Text Buddy window. Incremental values should be fairly large. All values should be within the range of values indicated in the labels below the scroll bar control.

6. Click in the Shaft area of the scroll bar control. New values should appear in the Text Buddy window. Incremental values should be moderately large. All values should be within the range of values indicated in the labels below the scroll bar control.

7. Click the arrow buttons of the scroll bar control. New values should appear in the Text Buddy window. Incremental values should be very small. All values should be within the range of values indicated in the labels below the scroll bar control.

8. Enter a value directly into the Text Buddy control using the keyboard. As each character is typed, the new number should appear in the Text Buddy control. As each character is typed, the scroll bar thumb should move to reflect the latest value entered into the Text Buddy control.

9. Click the Quit menu item on the window menu bar.

10. The application window disappears as the application terminates.

Pocket PC Scroll Bar Control Program

1. Attach the Pocket PC cradle to the desktop computer.

2. Insert the Pocket PC into the cradle.

3. Tell ActiveSync to create a guest connection.

4. Make sure the status is connected.

5. Start Embedded Visual C++ 3.0.

6. Open the project ScrollBarControlProgramPPC.vcw in the folder ScrollBarControlProgramPPC.

7. Build the program.

8. Make sure the program successfully downloads to the Pocket PC.

9. On the Pocket PC, open the File Explorer.

10. Browse to the MyDevice folder.

11. Execute the program ScrollBarControlProgram.

12. Drag the scroll bar thumb. New values should appear in the Text Buddy window. Incremental values should be fairly large. All values should be within the range of values indicated in the labels below the scroll bar control.

13. Tap in the Shaft area of the scroll bar control. New values should appear in the Text Buddy window. Incremental values should be moderately large. All values should be within the range of values indicated in the labels below the scroll bar control.

14. Tap the arrow buttons of the scroll bar control. New values should appear in the Text Buddy window. Incremental values should be very small. All values should be within the range of values indicated in the labels below the scroll bar control.

15. Expose the keyboard in the screen area of the device.

16. Enter a value directly into the Text Buddy control using the keyboard and the stylus. As each character is typed, the new number should appear in the Text Buddy control. As each character is typed, the scroll bar thumb should move to reflect the latest value entered into the Text Buddy control.

17. Tap the Quit menu item on the window menu bar.

18. The application window disappears as application terminates.

Developing a Complex User Interface

While providing excellent software support for an application's capabilities, the Pocket PC does suffer from one very important limitation—the physical screen size. A typical Pocket PC device provides 240×320 color pixels in the physical display area. Actual usable space is about 10 percent less than this amount, due to window borders and menu bars. Therefore, an important design issue deals with the way in which an application presents a complex user interface.

In order to compensate for the very limited screen space, a developer must use two very specific techniques. The user interface should consist of a hierarchy of windows through which a user navigates in order to access specific features of the application. At the bottom level of the hierarchy, a set of tab pages enables the application to effectively overlay groups of related controls within the small physical footprint of the device.

This chapter presents a simple drawing application that utilizes these two specific interface-design techniques. Employing these techniques requires that the developer use several special software elements. An additional aspect of this chapter presents a series of procedures for employing these software elements in a specific application. Using the code from the simple application, specific code segments illustrate the process of following the indicated steps.

A Drawing Program with a Complex User Interface

The drawing program appearing in this chapter is a more sophisticated version of the program developed in Chapter 5. This program allows the user to set a variety of drawing tool properties. After setting these properties, a user draws using the initialized drawing tool properties.

When the program begins execution, the user sees the interface in Figure 9-1.

Because the interface exhibits significant complexity, this first window provides initial entry into the top level of a hierarchy. This top level enables the user to enter specific areas of interaction. A simple picture or icon controls access to a specific area of user interaction.

NOTE

An area of user interaction represents a large group of logically related capabilities. Specific areas of interaction should be chosen carefully and should correlate well to the specific steps a typical user would follow to perform a specific major task.

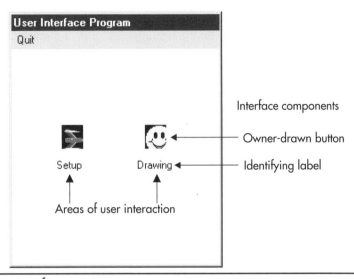

Figure 9-1   *Complex user interface*

In order to develop an effective user interface, a developer must actually become trained as a user—at least to a basic level of competence. For example, if the program is to collect reports on product problems and upload them, at least the key developers should obtain training and some measure of experience in actually analyzing product problems. By the developer learning the way in which a user approaches a job, the areas of the user interface are easily chosen in a manner that facilitates the user's ability. Sadly, most programmers do not want to learn the user's job. This short sightedness was easily but incorrectly overlooked for desktop applications due to the large physical screen space and the extensive physical memory. However, with the smaller physical space of the Pocket PC, insight into the user's needs is critical to the effective selection of areas at the top level of a hierarchical user interface.

From a programming perspective, each area requires two components, also indicated in Figure 9-1. As the primary link to a specific area of the user interface, an icon is available that a user can tap in order to transition to the next lower level of the interface hierarchy. As the figure shows, an owner-drawn button composes this element of the interface. An owner-drawn button consists of a button with an arbitrary bitmap on its face. This type of button requires special handling inside the program.

Unfortunately, these days, icons are more often nonexpressive rather than communicative. Therefore, in order to avoid any confusion, each owner-drawn button possesses an identifying label. This label clearly describes the capabilities available to the user within the area of the interface hierarchy.

The specific interface shown in Figure 9-1 identifies two specific areas: Setup and Drawing. Notice that the Setup area appears first, at the left side of the interface. In fact, a user usually performs the setup of the drawing tools prior to performing drawing.

NOTE

By thinking about the sequence of actions a user performs when using a drawing program, the selection of areas and their sequencing in the first level of the user interface are almost obvious. This result further confirms the need to become trained as a user — at least to a rudimentary level of capability.

If a user taps the Setup picture, the interface transitions to the next level in the user interface hierarchy. Upon entry to this level, a user views the interface that appears in Figure 9-2.

For this application, the window in this figure represents the lowest level in the user interface hierarchy. However, at this level, additional interface design issues are of concern. Due to the small screen size and the large number of input variables, the interface uses tab pages to organize the input variables. As the figure illustrates, tab pages represent a simple and elegant approach to reusing the very limited screen space of the Pocket PC.

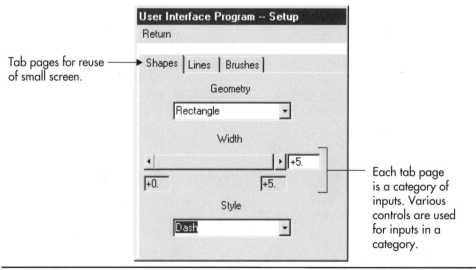

Figure 9-2   *Managing sets of parameters for setup*

Each tab page in this user interface represents a category of inputs. During the design of the user interface, specific choices are necessary to divide the large group of input variables into categories. Each category includes a number of logically related input or output variables.

NOTE

Again, the need to be trained as a user rears its ugly head. By being trained as a user, the collection of variables into categories is an obvious process dictated by the way in which a user thinks about the job at hand—in this case, setting drawing tools.

At the top of each tab page appears a label. This label indicates the name of the category and suggests the logical basis for grouping the input variables into the category.

TIP

Due to the limited screen space, a developer really should restrict category names to one word.

In the remainder of the tab page appears the intrinsic controls needed to enable the user to manipulate the data variables assigned to the category of inputs. A text label precedes each user input, identifying the name of the input. If the input variable is constrained to a discrete set of alternatives, a "COMBOBOX" intrinsic control represents the preferred input mechanism. For numerical inputs, employ the user-friendly scroll bar described in Chapter 8, as shown in Figure 9-2.

After setting all the input variables in the Shapes category, the user taps the next tab page, labeled Lines in Figure 9-2. This tap forces the user interface to transition to the next tab page. Prior to this transition, an application saves the default values into a globally available storage location. For most applications, the DataMgr element serves as the global repository, as demonstrated in Chapter 3. After all input variables have been initialized (or left at their default values), a user taps the Return item on the main menu bar. After this tap, the user views the top-level area interface.

Now, a user taps the Drawing button. In response, the program transitions to the drawing page. Employing the stylus, the user performs a rubber-banded drawing operation. An example of the drawing user interface appears in Figure 9-3.

This figure illustrates the effect of using the parameters established in Figure 9-2. Looking back at that figure reveals that the drawing geometry is a rectangle and that the line width is set to 5. This setting means that the lines along the border of the drawn object are 5 pixels wide. As Figure 9-3 reveals, the rectangle drawn by the user does indeed have thick borders.

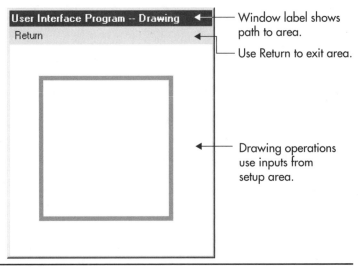

Figure 9-3   *Performing actual drawing*

Figure 9-3 also contains another very important aspect of providing a complex user-friendly interface on a Pocket PC. Because the user has to traverse through a complex hierarchy, the program always informs the user as to the current location in the interface hierarchy. The most clearly visible location in which to place the current location is in the caption area of the window.

NOTE

Placing the interface hierarchy path in the caption area makes the information available without consuming any of the limited and very valuable client area of the application window.

In Figure 9-3, the caption area contains the hierarchy path "User Interface Program – Drawing." This path gives the root node in the hierarchy, which is the program itself, followed by the individual steps in the path leading to the current location in the hierarchy. In a more complex interface hierarchy, the root node is often unnecessary when displaying a pathname. As this figure reveals, the root node consumes way too much physical space in the caption area. Additionally, a single word usually represents each step in the path, again due to the limited space in the caption area for actually displaying the path.

In the previous discussion, extensive reference to an interface hierarchy occurs on a regular basis. Figure 9-4 exhibits the complete interface hierarchy for this simple application.

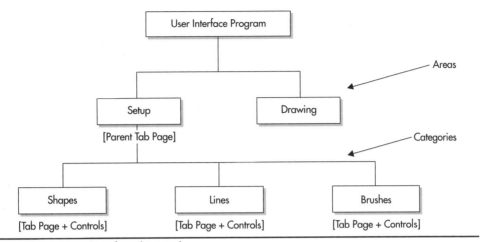

Figure 9-4   *User interface hierarchy*

Although this program provides a fairly simple set of capabilities, its interface hierarchy contains three levels. Obviously, a more complex set of capabilities requires more levels.

NOTE

When establishing an interface hierarchy, a developer must balance the number of levels in the hierarchy against the available screen space at each level. Having too many levels requires extensive navigation in order to perform simple tasks; having too few levels results in an interface that cannot fit within the physical screen space. This necessary balance further reinforces the need to become trained as a competent user of the software. By organizing the user interface around the way in which a user does the real job supported by the software, the required balance usually becomes obvious.

Level one of the interface hierarchy for this program is simply the program. Two entries appear at the second level: the Setup and Drawing areas of the interface hierarchy. At the bottom or third level appear the Shapes, Lines, and Brushes categories, which control specific input variables.

In addition to the hierarchy, Figure 9-4 contains information regarding the coding implementation requirements. Below the Setup area appears the requirement that this portion of the interface utilize a parent tab page. Individual categories need a specific tab page and intrinsic controls to enable the user to view and input data variables.

Using Bitmap Buttons to Support Areas of the Hierarchy

In order to implement the bitmap buttons approach for controlling access to logical areas of the user interface, a developer can use owner-drawn controls. Unfortunately, using these controls involves an extensive amount of coding, which consumes a bit of time and effort. Therefore, a BitmapButtonMgr software element makes a lot of sense from a reuse perspective. By providing a BitmapButtonMgr software element with methods that encapsulate most of the mechanics, bitmap buttons easily become the area managers for the interface hierarchy.

Steps for Using the Bitmap Buttons Software Element

After adding the BitmapButtonMgr.h and BitmapButtonMgr.c to a project, incorporating bitmap buttons into the area level of an interface hierarchy requires the following steps:

1. Using the resource editor, add a bitmap resource to the list of resources.

2. Using the dialog editor, add the button and label to the dialog form that displays the bitmap buttons.

3. In the dialog procedure, include the BitmapButtonMgr software element.

4. Declare an object of BitmapButtonType.

5. In the WM_INITDIALOG message handler, create the object using the bitmap resource.

6. In the WM_COMMAND message handler, destroy the object in the IDOK clause.

7. Add a WM_DRAWITEM message handler to display the bitmap on the face of the button.

Using some judicious cutting and pasting from the sample programs, these steps enable a developer to incorporate the area interface controls into an application.

An Example of the Steps for Using Bitmap Buttons

For the sample program in this chapter, named UserInterfaceProgram, only two bitmap buttons are necessary. This section follows the implementation of the bitmap button for controlling access to the Setup area of the interface hierarchy.

Add a Bitmap Resource to the List of Resources Using the Resource Editor

One of the tools available with the resource editor of Visual Studio is a bitmap resource editor. Using this editor, a developer stores a 32×32 pixel bitmap into the resource portion of the program, as described in Chapter 2. An example of a resource editor that contains two bitmap resources for the sample application appears in Figure 9-5.

Inserting the bitmap resource is simple to accomplish using the menu bar for Visual Studio. If the bitmap has been drawn by someone else, the menu bar of Visual Studio allows a developer to import an existing bitmap file into the project. Just make sure the bitmap is 32×32 pixels. The number of colors available to each pixel depends on the color depth of the target Pocket PC. Each Pocket PC hardware type supports a different color depth.

After importing or drawing the bitmap, a bitmap editor is available for viewing and for editing the raw pixels on the bitmap. Double-click the bitmap resource in the resource editor. In response to the double-click, Visual Studio launches the bitmap editor with the raw pixels displayed to the developer.

NOTE

Extra care is necessary to select bitmaps that reflect the capabilities of the area controlled by this bitmap. Again, getting trained as a user ensures the usage of an image that is meaningful to the user.

Appearing in Figure 9-6 is the bitmap image for the Setup area bitmap button. This bitmap uses only 16 colors and displays well on any Pocket PC that supports any number of colors.

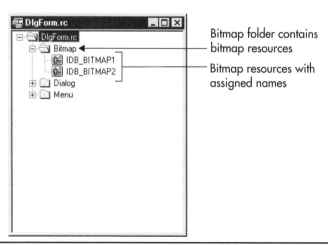

Figure 9-5 *A resource editor containing two bitmap resources*

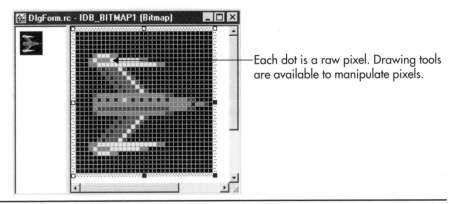

Figure 9-6 *The bitmap editor showing raw pixels*

When drawing a bitmap image, the more colors used, the sharper the displayed image. Lines are cleaner and more accurate. Colors appear brighter. But, assuming too many colors limits the specific display devices that can support the bitmap buttons. Rendering the image requires a balance between the potential capabilities of the target Pocket PC display hardware and the need to use an image that is meaningful to a real user of the software.

Add the Button and Labels to the Dialog Form

Every bitmap button utilizes two intrinsic controls, as demonstrated earlier in Figure 9-1: an owner-drawn button and a label for the button. Using the resource toolbar in the dialog editor of Embedded Visual Studio, a developer simply drags the controls to the face of the dialog form or template. Figure 9-7 demonstrates the results of using drag-and-drop operations to place the intrinsic controls for the sample program UserInterfaceProgram.

Each of the button controls in Figure 9-7 is a 16×16 button (in standard dialog units). A dialog unit is Windows' way of describing sizes with units that are independent of the physical screen characters. The labels use static controls. When placing the labels, center them below their corresponding owner-drawn button controls. Select a label that accurately describes the functional capabilities of the area of the user interface. Given the small physical display size of the Pocket PC 2002 device, a label should consist of a single word with a small number of letters.

A careful view of the button controls in Figure 9-7 reveals that these controls possess some unique styles. Double-clicking a button control causes Embedded Visual Studio to display a Push Button Properties dialog for the intrinsic button control. Using the

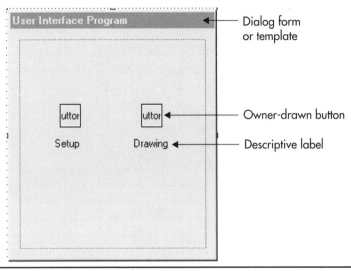

Figure 9-7   *Dialog template with intrinsic controls*

mouse, click the Styles tab of the Properties dialog. In response to this click, Visual Studio reveals this tab, as shown in Figure 9-8.

As shown in this figure, only two style properties are necessary. Setting the Owner Draw style property forces Windows to send a WM_DRAWITEM message to the application. This means the application is accepting responsibility for drawing the face of the button. Using a Flat style property eliminates the three-dimensional

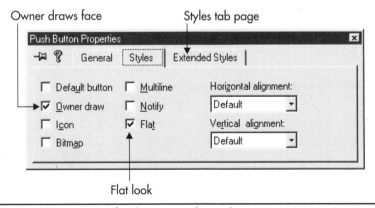

Figure 9-8   *Button properties for the owner-drawn button*

feature and any borders. Keeping the button flat enables an application to place a bitmap on the face of the button, which is certainly the desired goal here.

Ensure that checks do not appear next to any of the other style properties. If any other properties are active, undesirable side effects occur when displaying the bitmaps on the face of the buttons.

Include the BitmapButtonMgr Software Element

```
#include "BitmapButtonMgr.h"
```

Including this header file causes the methods of the BitmapButtonMgr to become visible for usage within the dialog procedure.

Declare an Object of BitmapButtonType

```
BitmapButtonType SetupBitmapButton ;
```

BitmapButtonMgr provides a data type abstraction. Any program may have multiple instances of this abstraction. For each bitmap button, declare an object of data type BitmapButtonType. Use a meaningful name that indicates the purpose of the button. When a bitmap button controls a specific functional area of the user interface, simply prefix the name of the area (as used in the corresponding label) to the string "BitmapButton". As this example demonstrates, using this approach clearly reveals both the purpose and class of the variable.

These objects do not need to be declared with a static storage class attribute. Using this attribute hides the object within the dialog procedure. The main goal with this declaration is to provide an object that is accessible from within any of the message handlers of the dialog procedure. Placing the declaration of this variable within the scope of the dialog procedure file but outside of every message handler accomplishes this global visibility.

Create the Object Using the Bitmap Resource

```
SetupBitmapButton = CreateBitmapButton(hDlg, IDB_BITMAP1) ;
```

Because the bitmap button is an application-controlled object, the WM_INITDIALOG message handler creates the instance of the object. The method CreateBitmapButton, provided by BitmapButtonMgr, gives a program the capability to create a bitmap button.

When creating a bitmap button, two arguments are necessary. As the first argument, the creator provides a handle to a window. The second argument consists of the integer identifier of the bitmap button resource that is to appear on the face of the button.

Destroy the Object in the IDOK Clause

```
DestroyBitmapButton(SetupBitmapButton) ;
```

Prior to termination of the program, the program explicitly destroys the bitmap button. The method to accomplish this task is DestroyBitmapButton, provided by BitmapButtonMgr. As the single argument, the destroyer gives the bitmap button object returned by the method CreateBitmapButton.

Add a WM_DRAWITEM Message Handler

```
void    DlgOnDrawItem(HWND hDlg, const DRAWITEMSTRUCT * DrawItem)
{
    UINT ControlID ;

    ControlID = DrawItem->CtlID ;

    if ( ControlID == IDC_BUTTON1 )
    {
        DisplayBitmapButton(SetupBitmapButton,DrawItem->hDC,32,32) ;
    }
}
```

Because the bitmap button possesses the Owner Draw style, a WM_DRAWITEM message arrives at the registered dialog procedure anytime Windows is going to draw the button. The primary argument to this handler is a pointer to a DRAWITEMSTRUCT, containing information that identifies the bitmap button that requires drawing.

Embedded in the DrawItem argument is a CtlID field that gives the integer identifier for the intrinsic button control that needs drawing. For clarity and ease of programming, the message handler first stores this identifier into a local variable, named ControlID. Because every button with the Owner Draw style requires processing through this message handler, an if clause routes execution to the specific drawing commands for the incoming button.

In order to draw a bitmap on the face on an owner-drawn button control, the message handler uses the method DisplayBitmapButton, provided by BitmapButtonMgr. This method requires a handle to the device context of the button that is stored in the hDC field of the incoming DrawItem argument. Size information, in pixels, provides the width and height to draw the bitmap on the face of the button control.

These few, very easy steps are all that are necessary to incorporate bitmap buttons into an application. All the messy details appear within the body of BitmapButtonMgr.

An Overview of the BitmapButtonMgr Implementation

BitmapButtonMgr provides an abstract data type for usage by an application developer. With this abstract data type, a developer can employ multiple instances of a BitmapButtonType.

The following code segment shows the declarations for BitmapButtonType:

```
typedef struct
{
     HDC MemoryDC ;
} BitmapButtonRecordType ;


typedef BitmapButtonRecordType * BitmapButtonType ;
```

Associated with each button is an HDC. This device context handle identifies an in-memory device context that stores the bitmap for the button. A simple structure serves to store this handle. Using a structure enables the developer to further expand the data associated with a bitmap button at a later date.

After declaring a structure that holds the bitmap button–specific data, a second declaration describes the abstract data type as a pointer to the structure. This declaration hides the fact that a pointer is involved in any way. Every time a method is called to operate on a specific bitmap button, a thinly disguised pointer is the first argument. By hiding the pointer, all operations appear to be performed on an abstract object, thus adding to the reliability of the application.

The following code listing shows the way in which the method CreateBitmapButton actually generates the entries of the BitmapButtonRecordType just described:

```
BitmapButtonType CreateBitmapButton(HWND Window, int BitmapID)
{
   // Variable Declarations Omitted - See Code On Web Site
   BitmapButton
       =(BitmapButtonType)malloc( sizeof(BitmapButtonRecordType)) ;

   Bitmap = LoadBitmap(Instance,MAKEINTRESOURCE(BitmapID)) ;

   DeviceContext = GetDC(Window) ;
   MemoryDC = CreateCompatibleDC(DeviceContext) ;
```

```
    SelectObject(MemoryDC,Bitmap) ;
    ReleaseDC(Window,DeviceContext) ;

    BitmapButton->MemoryDC = MemoryDC ;

    return BitmapButton ;
}
```

The first step is to use malloc to create memory space for the record structure itself. After reserving memory, the method LoadBitmap retrieves a handle to the bitmap resource stored in the resources area of the loaded program, as described in Chapter 2. Actually, LoadBitmap is a misnomer for what this method really does. In reality, the bitmap already exists in memory as part of the loaded binary image. This method actually retrieves a handle to an already loaded bitmap.

After obtaining the handle to the loaded bitmap, the next steps create an in-memory device context with the loaded bitmap attached and ready for display. This step is necessary because copying a bitmap to the display requires a device context, as described in Chapter 6.

In the WM_DRAWITEM message handler, the method DisplayBitmapButton performs the actual display of the corresponding bitmap. The following code segment shows the body for this method:

```
void DisplayBitmapButton(BitmapButtonType BitmapButton,
                   HDC ButtonDC , int Width, int Height)
{
    BitBlt(ButtonDC,0,0,Width,Height,BitmapButton->MemoryDC,0,0,SRCCOPY) ;
}
```

As the first argument, the client method provides an instance of BitmapButtonType, described earlier. The device context of the button, ButtonDC, represents the destination drawing surface of the button control being drawn.

In drawing the bitmap on the face of the button, this method employs the Win32 API method BitBlt. This method simply copies the bitmap attached to the MemoryDC for the BitmapButton to the destination DC of the face of the button. By using BitBlt, an exact copy occurs. In order to scale the bitmap onto the face of the button, replace this method with the StretchBlt method, as described in Chapter 6.

The BitmapButtonMgr provides the technology to easily support access to a number of areas in a user interface hierarchy. After obtaining the category level of a particular area within the interface, tab pages enable a developer to reuse the limited physical screen space by overlapping groups of controls.

Using Tab Pages to Support Categories of the Hierarchy

Every category represents a group of logically related input variables. Each category utilizes a tab page. Tab pages provide a very natural way for users to enter values, because most users are familiar with the concept of card catalog operations. Using tab pages is similar in concept to using a card catalog.

Implementing tab pages requires two types of dialogs. A parent dialog serves as the container for a tab control. Each tab page further requires a tab page dialog. For example, consider a tab dialog with three overlapping tab pages. This implementation uses one tab parent dialog and three tab page dialogs. Because four dialogs are involved, four dialog procedures are necessary. A dialog procedure for the tab parent dialog handles the construction of the individual tab pages and the transition among the tab pages. Each tab page further needs a tab page dialog in order to process user interactions with intrinsic controls on the face of the tab page. In the Reusable Components folder of the code available for downloading from the web site (http://www.osborne.com), templates are available for both the tab parent dialog procedure and the tab page dialog procedures.

According to the Win32 API documentation, the mechanics for building tab pages on a tab page control and for managing transition among tab pages are onerous, time consuming to implement, and just plain intimidating. This chapter presents a software element, TabPageMgr, that encapsulates all this tedium and provides a mechanical process for rapidly and easily utilizing the TabPageMgr software element in an application.

Steps for Using the TabPageMgr and Tab Templates

In order to use the TabPageMgr in any application, first add the TabPageMgr software element to your project. After adding this software element, perform the following sequence of steps:

1. Create the dialog procedures from the dialog templates.
2. Create a tab control on the parent dialog form.
3. Create borderless dialog forms for each tab page.
4. Modify the parent dialog procedure to create and manage the tab pages.
5. Modify the tab page dialog procedures to manage the intrinsic controls.

6. Add the methods PutTabPage and GetTabPage to the DataMgr software element.

7. Configure the project to use tab controls.

These steps are very simple and easy to follow. After performing the steps once, the process becomes mechanical. Once these steps are learned, a programmer can add working tab pages to an application in a very short amount of time.

An Example of the Steps for Using TabPageMgr

This section demonstrates the steps for adding tab pages to the UserInterfaceProgram of this chapter. The code examples show only the modifications necessary to implement specific tab pages into an application. Tab page mechanics that are automatically incorporated into a template and that do not require modification by a developer do not receive any discussion in the following examples.

Create the Dialog Procedures from the Dialog Templates

Performing this step involves creating the parent and tab page dialog procedures for the application. To create these dialog procedures, perform the following sequence of actions:

1. Copy the file \ReusableComponents\TabParentDlgProc.c into the project folder. Rename this file to something more meaningful to the application, such as SettingsDlgProc.c.

2. For each tab page, copy the file \ReusableComponents\TabDlgProc.c into the project folder. Rename this file to something more meaningful to the applications, such as LinesDlgProc.c, ShapeDlgProc.c, or BrushDlgProc.c.

3. Add the parent dialog procedure and the tab page dialog procedures to the project.

When changing the name of the file containing the parent dialog procedure, use a name that reflects the area of the user interface that controls access to the categories. For individual tab page dialog procedure files, the best name includes the one-line description of the category that appears on the tab index.

These steps create the required dialog procedures in the project. However, the files are not ready for compilation until all the following changes are made in these files. Any attempt to compile the project or any of the added files at this point leads to a huge number of compilation errors.

Create a Tab Control on the Parent Dialog Form

Add a parent dialog form or template to the project using the resource editor. In the resource toolbar, click the left mouse button on the miniature tab control. Then, use a rubber-banding drawing operation to place the tab control onto the dialog form.

After placing the tab control onto the dialog template, drag the lower-right corner of the tab control to size the control to 148×136 dialog base units. Then, center the tab control in the dialog form, leaving an equal amount of empty space around all sides of the dialog. When the tab control is properly located and sized, the parent dialog form should appear as shown below in Figure 9-9.

The recommended size of the tab control uses almost all the dialog face, enabling a developer to maximize the size of each tab page and to provide efficient use of the limited display area of the Pocket PC.

Create Borderless Dialog Forms for Each Tab Page

Every tab page uses a dialog form as a container for the controls on the face of the tab page. These forms have a special characteristic—individual tab page dialogs do not display borders. This approach enables the tab page dialog to blend seamlessly

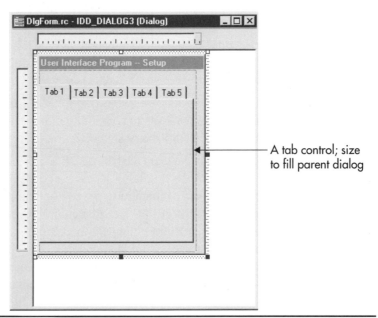

Figure 9-9   *A parent dialog with a tab control*

with the tab page control. Using borders on a tab page dialog would result in a very ugly effect on the tab pages when displayed within the tab control.

Figure 9-10 contains a borderless tab page dialog for the Lines tab page.

Intrinsic controls on the face of the tab page provide the user with a means to input data variables. As the user inputs these values, the underlying tab page dialog procedure saves the values into the DataMgr software element and serializes the values into a configuration file in the RAM storage area of the Pocket PC.

Setting the properties of a tab page dialog involves the display of a properties dialog, such as the one shown in Figure 9-11.

Double-clicking the tab dialog form in the dialog editor causes Embedded Visual Studio to display this Dialog Properties form. Clicking the Styles tab reveals the properties of the tab page. Set the style to Child using the Style drop-down list in the Dialog Properties form. After clicking the arrow of the Border drop-down list, choose not to use a border by selecting the drop-down list entry None. Finally, uncheck all the remaining style check boxes to ensure that the tab page does not exhibit any odd features.

Modify the Parent Dialog Procedure

Once the visual elements of the tab page are created, a number of code changes are necessary. These code changes modify the various dialog procedure templates to

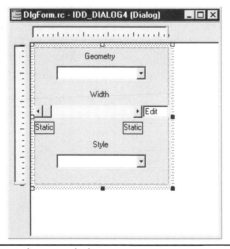

Figure 9-10   *A borderless tab page dialog*

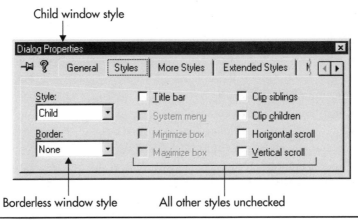

Child window style

Borderless window style   All other styles unchecked

Figure 9-11   *Dialog properties for a tab dialog*

create code that actually compiles, executes, and correctly implements the tab pages for an application.

```
BOOL CALLBACK ChildYDlgProc(HWND hDlg, UINT message,
                            WPARAM wParam, LPARAM lParam ) ;
```

The parent dialog procedure template contains a single statement that declares an arbitrary child dialog procedure. Copy and paste one instance of this statement for each tab page managed by the parent dialog procedure. Then, modify the prefix of each declaration to reflect the real name of the dialog procedure. Use the same prefixes as those used in renaming the tab dialog procedure files. For example, replace ChildY with Lines for the tab page dialog procedure in LinesDlgProc.c.

```
BOOL CALLBACK ParentXDlgProc(HWND hDlg, UINT message,
                             WPARAM wParam, LPARAM lParam )
{
    switch (message)
    {
        // Handler Declarations Omitted For Clarity
        HANDLE_DLG_MSG( hDlg , WM_NOTIFY , ParentXDlgOnNotify ) ;
    }
    return FALSE ;
}
```

In the template for the parent dialog procedure, the prefix ParentX appears everywhere that an application-specific name is required. Using the global find-

and-replace feature, substitute a meaningful name for the prefix ParentX. As with the tab page dialog procedures, use the same prefix as the area name of the interface hierarchy that was used to rename the file that contains this parent dialog procedure. In the sample program for this chapter, UserInterfaceProgram, the prefix Settings replaces ParentX for the parent dialog procedure stored in file SettingsDlgProc.c.

```
BOOL  OnInitParentXDialog  ( HWND  hDlg , HWND  hwndFocus ,
                            long  lInitParam )
{
//  Some Code Omitted For Clarity
   TabPage = CreateTabPage(3,IDC_TAB1) ;
   PutTabPage(TabPage) ;
//   AddTab(TabPage, hDlg, IDD_DIALOGY,
              __TEXT("Velocities")) ;

   return TRUE ;
}
```

In the WM_INITDIALOG message handler of the parent dialog procedure template, some of the code uses methods from the TabPageMgr to create a tab page object named TabPage. This object stores all the information about the tab page control and its tab pages. A developer modifies this code to construct the actual tab page control for an application.

The first necessary changes involve the arguments to the CreateTabPage method supplied by TabPageMgr. As the first argument, provide the number of tab pages that the tab control hosts. When the tab control is added, Embedded Visual Studio creates a numeric identifier for the tab control. This identifier provides the second argument to CreateTabPage.

After creating the TabPage object for the tab control, the message handler adds individual tab pages to the tab control using the AddTab method provided by TabPageMgr. Inside the message handler for the parent dialog procedure template is a commented example of using the AddTab method. Copy and paste an instance of this method for every tab page in the tab control. Replace the dialog identifier IDD_DIALOGY by the identifier of the borderless tab page dialog. The text that is to appear in the tab itself is the final argument to this method. Remember to use the __TEXT macro to ensure portability from the desktop to the Pocket PC 2002 device.

```
VOID WINAPI ParentXOnSelChanged(HWND hwndDlg)
{
     // Code Omitted For Clarity
     Selection = TabCtrl_GetCurSel(TabWindow);
     switch( Selection )
```

```
        {
        case 0:
//              OnTabSwitch(TabPage, 0, hwndDlg,
                            IDD_DIALOGY,ChildYDlgProc) ;
                break ;
        }
}
```

When the user taps the stylus of the Pocket PC on one of the tab pages, the hidden
dialog procedure for the tab control generates a WM_NOTIFY message. This message
arrives at the parent dialog procedure. The primary argument to the WM_NOTIFY
message handler is a pointer to an NMHDR structure—a notify message header.
Embedded within this structure is a code field. When this field is set to the flag TCN_
SELCHANGE, the message handler routes execution to the OnSelChanged method
of the parent dialog procedure. Code for handling this transfer of control already
exists in the parent dialog procedure template. Because this code does not require
any modification by the developer, discussion of the transfer code is unnecessary.

Using the macro TabCtrl_GetCurSel implemented within windowsx.h, the message
handler OnSelChanged determines the index of the tab page tapped by the user. A
switch statement transfers execution control to the correct handler. A developer adds
a case statement for each tab page contained in the tab control. Based on the index of
the selected tab page, the case handler for the selected tab page executes the method
OnTabSwitch, available from the TabPageMgr software element.

A commented example of the execution of this method already appears in the
template for the parent dialog procedure. Replace the dialog identifier IDD_DIALOGY
by the identifier of the borderless tab page dialog displayed on the new tab page. As
the last argument to this method, substitute the real tab dialog procedure name for the
placeholder ChildYDlgProc that appears in the sample invocation.

Modify the Tab Page Dialog Procedures

Once the parent dialog procedure is modified, further changes are necessary for each
of the tab dialog procedures. A portion of the tab dialog procedure template appears
in the following code segment:

```
BOOL CALLBACK TabXDlgProc(HWND hDlg, UINT message,
                            WPARAM wParam, LPARAM lParam )
{
    switch (message)
    {
        HANDLE_DLG_MSG( hDlg , WM_INITDIALOG , OnInitTabXDialog ) ;
        // Code Omitted For Clarity
```

```
    }
    return FALSE ;
}
```

Incorporated into the tab dialog procedure template is the placeholder string TabX. Using the global find-and-replace feature, substitute a meaningful expression for this placeholder. In the parent dialog procedure, the single word representing the category replaces the ChildY prefix in the declaration of the tab page dialog procedures. Use this same replacement for the TabX placeholder in the tab page dialog procedure file. For instance, in the preceding parent dialog procedure, the string Lines replaces the ChildY prefix, thus yielding LinesDlgProc. Globally replace TabX in file LinesDlgProc.c with the string Lines. As a result of this one global replacement, the file LinesDlgProc.c becomes a correctly defined file and will compile and link into the program.

Default code that already exists within the tab page dialog procedure handles all of the mechanics associated with transitions to and from the tab page managed by this tab page dialog procedure. The only other code that the developer must add to each tab page dialog procedure is the code needed to create, initialize, service, and destroy any intrinsic controls on the face of the tab page.

Add the Methods PutTabPage and GetTabPage to the DataMgr

As the user transitions among the tab pages by tapping the stylus on each tab page, the TabPageMgr handles all the transition mechanics. Support for the transition mechanics requires access to the TabPageType object created by the parent dialog procedure using the method CreateTabPage. As with all other global variables, the DataMgr serves as the central repository for the TabPageType object that characterizes all the tab pages.

```
#include "TabPageMgr.h"

static TabPageType CurrentTabPage ;

void PutTabPage(TabPageType TabPage)
{
    CurrentTabPage = TabPage ;
}
```

The preceding code segment implements storage for the TabPageType object. This code provides visibility to the TabPageMgr, uses the static storage class attribute to provide persistent storage for the object, and implements access methods—put and get—for managing access to the declared storage.

This code is essentially a boilerplate and can be pasted into the file DataMgr.c of any application without further modification. Declarations for the access methods must also appear within DataMgr.h in order for the modified templates to work correctly.

Configure the Project to Use Tab Controls

One final step is necessary to make the project link correctly. The tab control is a member of the common controls library. This library is not automatically part of the list of libraries linked as part of the Win32 API.

In order to link the project to the common controls library, perform the following sequence of steps:

1. Choose the Project menu item from the main menu of Embedded Visual Studio.
2. Choose the Setups popup submenu item from the Project popup submenu.
3. Click the Link tab on the right side of the Project Settings dialog.
4. Click the Object/Library modules text box.
5. Type the name **comctl32.lib**, followed by a space, in this text box.
6. Click the OK button.

Now, the program can be compiled and executed. All the transitions between tab pages work correctly at this point.

An effective development approach is to get these modifications working first. Once these updates allow the tab pages to correctly display and transition, a developer can then concentrate on implementing support for the controls of the face of a single tab page dialog. In fact, different programmers can work on each tab page independently and then return the modified tab page dialog procedure and support code to the project baseline, further shortening the development cycle and time to market for the application.

An Overview of the Tab Pages Templates Implementation

The TabPageMgr software element encapsulates a data structure that manages all the relevant information regarding the a tab control and its associated tab pages. In the following code segment appears the declaration for this data structure and the TabPageType stored in DataMgr:

```
typedef struct
{
    int                 TabPageID ;
    RECT                DisplayRect;
```

```
    DLGTEMPLATE **          TabTemplates ;
    int                     NumberTabs ;
    int                     MaxNumberTabs ;
    HWND                      CurrentTab ;
} TabPageRecordType ;

typedef TabPageRecordType * TabPageType ;
```

Just like the BitmapButtonMgr element discussed in the previous section of this chapter, TabPageMgr implements an abstract data type. This form of implementation is necessary because an application certainly may require more than one of these objects to exist at any point during program execution.

As with all the abstract data types in this book, a two-phase declaration is necessary. The first step declares the underlying record structure. After the structure is defined, a second step uses a typedef to hide a pointer to the structure from the remainder of the application.

```
TabPageType CreateTabPage(int MaxNumberTabs, int TabPageID)
{
    TabPageType TabPage ;

    TabPage = (TabPageType) malloc(sizeof(TabPageRecordType)) ;

    TabPage->MaxNumberTabs = MaxNumberTabs ;
    TabPage->NumberTabs = 0 ;
    TabPage->TabPageID = TabPageID ;
    TabPage->TabTemplates =
    (DLGTEMPLATE **) malloc(MaxNumberTabs * sizeof(DLGTEMPLATE *)) ;
    TabPage->CurrentTab = NULL ;
    return TabPage ;
}
```

In fact, the underlying data structure contains a table of information about all the tab pages displayed by the tab control. After all the tab pages are added, this table contains a pointer to each of the tab page dialog templates in memory. Notice that the TabTemplates element stores a pointer to a dialog template that is of data type (DLGTEMPLATE **). This notation indicates that an array of pointers to dialog templates eventually appears within this array or table of pointers.

```
void AddTab(TabPageType TabPage, HWND Dialog, int TabID, LPTSTR TabTitle)
{
    TCITEM Item;
    // Some Code Omitted For Clarity
```

```
Item.mask = TCIF_TEXT | TCIF_IMAGE;
Item.pszText = TabTitle ;
TabCtrl_InsertItem(TabWindow, TabPage->NumberTabs, &Item);
}
```

This code shows the body of the AddTab method. In order to add a tab page to a tab control, a program first creates an instance of TCITEM. Then, some required flags are set in the mask field of this item. Also, the title of the tab goes in the pszText field. Finally, the program adds the tab page to the tab control by executing the TabCtrl_InsertItem macro provided by windowsx.h.

Two important arguments are necessary for this macro. This first argument is the tab index number. This number is the value of TabPage->NumberTabs, which is computed within the omitted code. Finally, a pointer to the TCITEM structure containing the mask and tab title comprises the other final argument to this macro.

A Final Consideration for Developers

Several times within this chapter, great emphasis has been placed on the value of learning the job of the user in order to develop an intuitive user interface hierarchy. Many programmers do not want to expend this effort, preferring to sit in an office and code in a vacuum. This attitude leads to unfriendly, nonintuitive user interfaces and to shoddy, bloated code. If a developer takes this head-in-the-sand approach, the result is also likely to be poor performance and possibly even an application that simply does not execute within the available memory space.

One final consideration—think how much fun learning another person's job can be. As a result pursing a fundamental knowledge of the user's job, a programmer often obtains experiences that are not offered to many people.

Summary

This chapter describes the procedures for using two software elements—BitmapButtonMgr and TabPageMgr—to construct a user interface on the Pocket PC. The following key points appear throughout the chapter:

▶ Limited physical screen space requires the usage of a hierarchical user interface.

▶ In order to effectively design this interface hierarchy, a developer needs to learn how the user performs the real job supported by the interface.

▶ At the top level of the hierarchy, broad areas control access to logically related capabilities.

▶ At the lower levels of the hierarchy, narrow categories control access to specific data input and output variables.

▶ Owner-drawn buttons and labels are the visual representations of areas within the hierarchy.

▶ Tab controls and tab pages are the visual representations of categories within the hierarchy.

▶ Tab controls and tab pages enable a developer to reuse the limited physical screen space of the Pocket PC, similar to the common card file.

Sample Programs on the Web

The following programs are available at http://www.osborne.com:

Description	Folder
Desktop User Interface Program	UserInterfaceProgram
Pocket PC User Interface Program	UserInterfaceProgramPPC

Execution Instructions

Desktop User Interface Program

1. Start Visual C++ 6.0.
2. Open the project UserInterfaceProgram.dsw in the folder UserInterfaceProgram.
3. Build the program.
4. Execute the program.
5. Click the Settings bitmap button. This action should transition to the Settings dialog and should display the tab controls with the Lines tab page exposed.
6. Interact with the Lines features on this page.
7. Click the other tab pages and set the various drawing properties using the controls on the faces of the tab pages. Each time a tab page is clicked, the program should hide the previous tab page and should expose the selected tab page.
8. Click the Return menu item on the Settings dialog menu bar.
9. Click the Drawing bitmap button.
10. Perform rubber-banded drawing with the mouse. Any displayed graphic object should reflect the properties set through the tab pages of the Settings dialog.

11. Click the Return menu item on the Drawing dialog menu bar.

12. Click the Quit menu item on the window menu bar.

13. The application window disappears as the application terminates.

Pocket PC User Interface Program

1. Attach the Pocket PC cradle to the desktop computer.

2. Insert the Pocket PC into the cradle.

3. Tell ActiveSync to create a guest connection.

4. Make sure the status is connected.

5. Start Embedded Visual C++ 3.0.

6. Open the project UserInterfaceProgramPPC.vcw in the folder UserInterfaceProgram PPC.

7. Build the program.

8. Make sure the program successfully downloads to the Pocket PC.

9. On the Pocket PC, open the File Explorer.

10. Browse to the MyDevice folder.

11. Execute the program UserInterfaceProgram.

12. Tap the Settings bitmap button. This action should transition to the Settings dialog and should display the tab controls with the Lines tab page exposed.

13. Interact with the Lines features on this page.

14. Tap the other tab pages and set the various drawing properties using the controls on the faces of the tab pages. Each time a tab page is tapped, the program should hide the previous tab page and should expose the selected tab page.

15. Tap the Return menu item on the Settings dialog menu bar.

16. Tap the Drawing bitmap button.

17. Perform rubber-banded drawing with the mouse. Any displayed graphic object should reflect the properties set through the tab pages of the Settings dialog.

18. Tap the Return menu item on the Drawing dialog menu bar.

19. Tap the Quit menu item on the window menu bar.

20. The application window disappears as the application terminates.

Maintaining Application Parameters

E very program uses a specific set of parameters. When a user enters the program, the program usually returns the values of these parameters to the values that were set at the most recent usage of the program. The goal of this chapter is to introduce the code necessary for maintaining the values of application parameters across successive executions.

Although this goal is important, this chapter introduces several other design considerations. In order to obtain parameter maintenance, a reusable library appears in this chapter. With minimal recoding, this library enables a developer to incorporate parameter maintenance into an application in a very short time. Providing the capability for easily tailoring the library requires the use of a layered software design. As the application-specific data passes across the software layers, the layers translate the data into a platform-independent format and then target the data to a specific storage format.

Sample code demonstrates the way in which a developer can target the bottom layer to three specific storage media: text files, the registry, and the Pocket PC database system. Guidelines indicate the conditions under which each storage format is an appropriate selection for an application.

Although the chapter uses three separate sample programs, each of the programs employs the same, common user interface. Figure 10-1 contains the common user interface for all the programs.

When a user executes this program, a single window appears and provides the complete interface for the program. This program manages a register that stores a floating-point value. Each register has an owner name and a value. Additionally, the parameter database possesses a version number, set by the program during the initialization of the database.

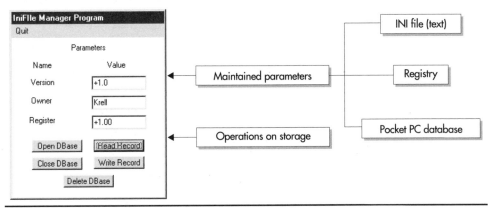

Figure 10-1 *User interface for parameter-maintenance programs*

Within the user interface of Figure 10-1, two distinct areas appear. At the top of the window, a user sees the data-management area. In this area, the user sees the complete current state of the parameter database. In the lower portion of the interface window, a set of buttons enable the user to perform operations on the database.

In the data-management area, two columns exist for providing support to the user. In the left column appears a series of parameter names. On the same line in the right column is a corresponding text area that enables a user to modify the value of the specific parameter identified by the label on the left. For example, in Figure 10-1, the Owner parameter is set to Krell.

When the interface first appears, the text areas are empty. In order to actually manipulate the parameters in the database, the user performs operations by employing the buttons in the bottom portion of the interface window. A typical sequence of user operations might look like the following:

1. Tap the Open DBase button to connect to the database.

2. Tap the Read Record button to retrieve the current values of the parameters.

3. Use the stylus and the keyboard to change the values of the Owner and Register fields.

4. Tap the Write Record button to store the updated values of the parameters.

5. Tap the Close DBase button to disconnect from the database.

6. Tap the Open DBase button to connect to the database.

7. Tap the Read Record button to retrieve the current values of the parameters.

This sequence clearly demonstrates that the storage and retrieval mechanism works correctly.

When implementing the ability to maintain application parameters, a number of storage media are available to a developer. This chapter contains three separate versions of the software to maintain application parameters. These versions target the most common storage media available to an application, as shown in Figure 10-1. An INI file maintains the data as raw text. Inside the system registry, data appears as binary data that can be reviewed with a special registry editor. Finally, the Pocket PC possesses an intrinsic database that stores the data through indexed records in a binary format that is not human readable. Guidelines for selection from among these alternate storage media appear in "Choosing a Target Storage Format."

Using a Layered Design for Managing Parameters

In order to achieve a measure of target storage independence, a layered software approach is necessary. At the application level, the parameter database appears to be a set of indexed locations. Each uniquely indexed location number contains a name and a value of a specified data type. Once a parameter database is created, the program simply stores and retrieves values via a set of type-specific methods, giving the position or index number and sending or receiving the name and value stored into that indexed location of the parameter database.

For the sample programs of this chapter, the parameter database contains the following set of parameter values:

Index	Name	Data Type
1	DBVersion	Double
2	Owner	String
3	Register	Double

As the first entry into the database, DBVersion serves to allow the parameter database manager software to remove and replace an older parameter database with a newer parameter database. By assumption, every parameter database managed by the software presented in this chapter provides a version number in the first indexed location of the database. Remaining parameter values are specific to a given application.

Figure 10-2 displays the layered design approach employed by the software developed for this chapter.

This figure traces a single interface method through the software layers that control access to the physical storage format. Each layer serves as an intermediate step in transforming the data from the device-independent format accessed by the application to the specific format required by the target storage format.

An application interfaces directly to the ParameterDBMgr software element, as shown in Figure 10-2. As a simple example, the figure starts with an application request to the parameter database for an integer record using the method GetDoubleValue. The primary input into this method is the index position of the desired record containing an integer value. In response, this access method returns the name and integer value stored in the indicated position.

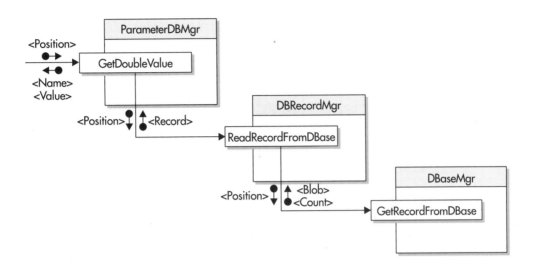

Figure 10-2 *Layered design for access to storage*

NOTE

Because the parameter database can also support doubles and strings, two other methods are available from ParameterDBMgr for access to the database: GetIntegerRecord and GetStringRecord. When a developer utilizes the services of ParameterDBMgr, the responsibility for using the proper access method against a specific indexed location is the total responsibility of the developer.

Upon receipt of the request for an integer value at Position, ParameterDBMgr relays the position to the method ReadRecordFromDBase, provided by the DBRecordMgr software element. The primary goal of this element is to translate the raw data to and from a standard application record format. So, the method ReadRecordFromDBase accepts the position number and returns the record in the standard application format. regards

Actually, DBRecordMgr passes the request to DBaseMgr. This software element interfaces directly to the specific store mechanism. Its primary goal is to encapsulate or to hide all the specific details regarding interaction with the storage format.

NOTE

A different version of DBaseMgr exists for INI/text files, the registry, and the Pocket PC intrinsic database. However, the upper layers do not change in any way as a result of using a different storage format.

The method executed to retrieve data from the actual storage format is GetRecordFromDBase, supplied by DBaseMgr. In order to make the implementation of this method as simple as possible, the DBaseMgr software element employs a standard storage format. This format requires little programming to implement. Moreover, every storage format easily supports this format. As shown in Figure 10-2, this format consists of a blob of data and an accompanying count of the number of bytes in the blob.

In order to retrieve data from the storage format, the layers work together in the following manner:

▶ GetRecordFromDBase of DBaseMgr retrieves a blob of data.

▶ ReadRecordFromDBase of DBRecordMgr converts the blob of data into a record.

▶ GetDoubleValue of ParameterDBMgr extracts the float value from a record.

These operations on the data enable a developer to easily initialize, read, and write to the parameter database with a minimal amount of programming necessary for a specific storage format.

Figure 10-3 depicts the various data formats at each software layer defined in Figure 10-2.

Each software layer appears by name in Figure 10-3. At the right side of each layer is a layout of the data structure managed by the layer. An arrow connects the software layer name to the layout of the data format.

An application interfaces to the parameter database through access methods supported by ParameterDBMgr. As explained earlier, separate access methods exist for each data type. When a program interacts with one of these access methods, the interface specifies a record position (starting with location 0) and a name and value for the program parameter.

Methods supported by DBRecordMgr are somewhat more generic. Each access method uses an application record. This record contains a name, a data type indicator code, and a value. Records at this level are self-sufficient. Records appear as a set of completely numeric fields containing all the necessary information to completely characterize the program parameter.

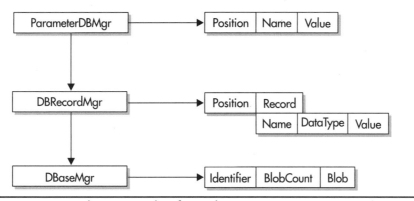

Figure 10-3 *Data translation in each software layer*

When passed to the DBaseMgr layer, the collection of bytes exists strictly as a blob of data. (A *blob* is a set of data bytes without specific fields or other characterizing information.) In this layer, each blob is just a big bag of data bytes. Using blobs at this layer provides several important benefits. Every storage format available to Pocket PC program developers is capable of managing a blob of data bytes. Implementing this layer for a specific storage format is an easy task, because reading and writing blobs of data requires the least amount of programming.

Three sample programs accompany this chapter. Each of these programs differs strictly in the implementation of the DBaseMgr layer of the program. One program, the INI File Manager, targets DBaseMgr to read and write from text files. Another program, the Registry Manager, uses DBaseMgr to read and write the data from and into the system registry. A final implementation implements DBaseMgr for access to the intrinsic Pocket PC database system.

Choosing a Target Storage Format

A Pocket PC application has three primary storage formats in which program parameters may be stored—INI or text files, the registry, and the intrinsic Pocket PC database. Each alternative has different strengths and weaknesses.

Using INI or text files has one very important benefit: A user or a developer can edit these files using any text editor, either on the desktop or on the Pocket PC device.

For a developer, reviewing the contents with a text editor improves the ability to rapidly create test inputs and to debug outputs, thus reducing development time. To a user, the ability to edit program parameters using text editors provides an extra measure of flexibility if the user chooses to sidestep portions of the program's graphical user interface.

However, placing program parameters into one or more INI or text files can lead to significant configuration control and installation problems. During installation, every one of these files needs to accompany the application, potentially causing a failed installation if accidentally omitted. Another issue with text-based files is processing speed. Text files are linear in nature. In order for a program to access the last parameter in the file, access must proceed through all preceding parameters in the file. For a large program parameter file, this sequential access can take quite a bit a time, thus degrading program performance.

Employing the registry for storing program parameters provides a number of benefits. Values are stored in the registry in an indexed form, making access to the values significantly faster than sequentially parsing a text file. A special editor, called the Registry Editor, is necessary to directly access this data independently from a program.

An important reliability issue relates to using the registry in order to store program parameters. The registry is the system database for Windows CE. If a program incorrectly programs the data in the registry, Windows CE may cease to execute correctly.

As the final alternative, the intrinsic Pocket PC database is available for storage of program parameters. This database is indexed so that access to specific parameters is direct, requiring the shortest response time. For many applications, this format is probably the ideal format, because the indexing of the intrinsic database provides the best speed.

However, this database is a binary database that resides strictly on the Pocket PC. Direct access to program parameters stored in this database is not possible without writing some special programs. Worse yet, if a program writes erroneous data into this database, no mechanism exists for fixing the corrupted data, short of rebooting the Pocket PC completely and destroying all data and installed programs. Additionally, if a program uses this format, desktop testing is difficult unless both versions of the layered access software are conditionally compiled into the program.

NOTE

For a Pocket PC program, the best approach is usually the INI or text file. Using either of these provides the most portable and debugging friendly approach, since the files are text readable.

For the most part, access to the database occurs only twice during interactions with a single window of the user interface. When the user enters a specific window of the user interface, the first access to the parameter database loads the parameter database from the storage format into a global data area managed by a DataMgr, such as described in Chapter 3. Upon exit from the window into another window of the user interface, the second access to the parameter database stores the values maintained by DataMgr back out to the store format.

During manipulations of the controls on the face of the window by the user, updated parameter values simply replace the values stored in DataMgr. Attempting to update the parameter database back into the storage format in response to the manipulations of the controls on the face of the window would result in very sluggish response times. Since performance dictates that access to the parameter database should occur only upon entry to and exit from a specific window, all access to the parameter database will be sequential. The indexing capabilities of the registry approach and the intrinsic database approach are unnecessary. Given the lack of need for indexing and the debugging friendliness, the INI text-based approach is usually the best for maintaining a set of application parameters.

Steps to Tailor a Parameter Database Manager

Prior to actually tailoring the parameter database manager software to a specific application, a developer performs several specific steps:

1. Select a specific target storage format.

2. Configure DBaseMgr.c to the selected target storage format.

3. Add the files DBaseMgr.h, DBaseMgr.c, DBFieldMgr.h, DBFieldMgr.c, DBRecordMgr.h, DBRecordMgr.c, ParameterDBMgr.h, and ParameterDBMgr.c to the project.

4. Add any files used to tailor DBaseMgr.c to the selected target storage format, such as StrMgr.h, StrMgr.c, PortabilityUtils.h, and PortabilityUtils.c.

These steps configure the project so that after performing the tailoring steps indicated next, the program interacts directly with the target storage format.

In order to tailor the database manager software elements for a specific program, perform the following steps:

1. In the file ParameterDBMgr.h, define the record organization of the parameter database.

2. In the file ParameterDBMgr.c, define default records for each of the parameters.

3. In various parts of the program, use the methods of ParameterDBMgr.h to interact with the parameter database.

If these requirements seem ridiculously simple, this very simplicity further demonstrates the value of using the layered software approach described in this chapter. Once the DBaseMgr element has been tailored to the target storage format, all the hard work is over. The upper layers work perfectly, independent from the translation, transformation, and management tasks of the lower software layer, DBaseMgr.

An Example of Tailoring a Parameter Database Manager

In this section, sample code demonstrates each step in the tailoring process. Because actual reading and writing of the database can occur in a variety of situations within an application, only a single example of database access occurs. The steps that appear in the sample code are the exact same steps that appear in all three of the applications for this chapter.

Define the Record Organization of the Parameter Database

Defining the record organization consists of declaring a set of symbolic or manifest constants for use throughout the program. For the sample programs of this chapter, the following code listing gives the declaration for the required constants that appear in file ParameterDBMgr.h.

```
#define CurrentDBVersion              1.0
#define NumberParameters              3
#define DBVersionRecordNumber         0
#define OwnerNameRecordNumber         1
#define RegisterValueRecordNumber     2
```

As the first constant, every application provides a constant named CurrentDBVersion. Using this constant, one of the lower layers decides whether the organization of the database has changed. If the current version number differs from the version in this constant, the software deletes the old version of the database and creates a new version with the new record organization and default values defined in the next section.

For looping through database records, the lower layers of software need to know the actual number of parameters being stored in the parameter database. The constant that provides this piece of information is NumberParameters.

After defining NumberParameters, a developer creates a symbol representing an index for each of the records in the parameter database. By convention, the first record has the index 0 and the symbol name DBVersionRecord. Lower layers use this record number to store the version number into the database and read this record to determine whether the parameter database organization has changed.

Remaining records contain the actual parameters used by the application. A developer is free to use any name that accurately reflects the content of the parameter. Typically, these constants all contain the suffix RecordNumber. Later in the application, the program passes these constants to the access methods provided by ParameterDBMgr to read from and write to specific records in the parameter database.

Define Default Records for Each of the Parameters

As explained earlier, the lower layers of the software automatically manage the creation and configuration of the parameter database. If the database does not exist at all, the software automatically creates the database. A change in the version number of the database causes the old parameter database to be deleted and the new parameter database to be created. In order for these two operations to work correctly, the tailored software provides default record definitions for the parameter database. An example of creating a set of default records for the parameter database appears in the following code listing:

```
void SetDefaultValues(void)
{
    SetDoubleRecordIntoParameterDBase(DBVersionRecordNumber,
        __TEXT("Version"),      DoubleValue,      CurrentDBVersion ) ;
    SetStringRecordIntoParameterDBase(OwnerNameRecordNumber,
        __TEXT("Owner"),     StringValue,      __TEXT("Krell")  ) ;
    SetDoubleRecordIntoParameterDBase(RegisterValueRecordNumber,
        __TEXT("Register"),      DoubleValue,      1.0 ) ;
}
```

In this code listing, every record in the database receives a default declaration. The software element ParameterDBMgr provides the preceding access methods. Two access methods—Set and Get—are available for each data type that may appear as a parameter in the database. Obviously, this example only demonstrates some of the Set methods.

Every access method supplied by ParameterDBMgr involves three arguments. As the first argument, the client program supplies a record number. In the preceding code listing, the record numbers use the symbolic constants defined earlier. The remaining arguments indicate the name of the parameter, a numeric code for the data type of the parameter, and a value for the parameter. This value must be the same data type as indicated in the name of the access method. For instance, if the access method is SetDoubleRecordIntoParameterDBase, the last argument is a double value.

The first default value always inserts the version number into record DBVersionRecordNumber. As the value for this parameter, the last argument to the access method is the symbolic constant CurrentDBVersion defined earlier.

Use Methods to Interact with the Parameter Database

Throughout the application, various user interactions require access to the database. When the program displays a window for soliciting inputs, read operations are necessary. Part of the response to modifications of the input values by the user involves write operations to the parameter database. Typically, these operations appear as close as possible to the support code for the user interaction. The following code section exists as part of the dialog procedure for all three applications attached to this chapter:

```
void  DlgOnCommand  ( HWND  hDlg , int  iID ,
                        HWND  hDlgCtl , UINT  uCodeNotify )
{
  switch( iID )
  {
    case IDC_BUTTON1:
          GetValuesFromParameterDBase(hDlg) ;
      break ;
    case IDC_BUTTON3:
          OpenParameterDBase() ;
      break ;
    case IDC_BUTTON4:
          CloseParameterDBase() ;
      break ;
  }
}
```

In general, an application performs four basic operations on a parameter database: opening the database, reading parameter records, writing parameter records, and closing the parameter database. Each of the case alternatives in the preceding switch statement performs the required operations. When a user clicks the associated intrinsic button control, the WM_COMMAND message handler performs the required operation on the parameter database. This code segment is the same for all three sample programs, regardless of the target storage format.

Two of the methods executed in the preceding code segment, OpenParameterDBase and CloseParameterDBase, are available from the first software layer, ParameterDBMgr. When a user performs a read operation, the handler for IDC_BUTTON1 executes a local utility method. Source code for this utility method appears in the following listing:

```
void GetValuesFromParameterDBase(HWND hDlg)
{
    GetStringValueFromParameterDBase( OwnerNameRecordNumber,
                                      Owner ) ;
    GetDoubleValueFromParameterDBase( RegisterValueRecordNumber,
                                      &Register ) ;

    SetStringIntoTextWindow(hDlg,IDC_EDIT2,Owner) ;
    SetDoubleIntoTextWindow(hDlg,IDC_EDIT3,Register,2) ;
}
```

This utility method uses methods provided by ParameterDBMgr to extract parameter data from the parameter database. Because the Owner parameter is a string value, the method GetStringValueFromParameterDBase retrieves the owner name from record number OwnerNameRecordNumber in the parameter database. Obtaining the Register value, which is a double value, requires using the method named GetDoubleValueFromParameterDBase. This code is entirely independent of any knowledge about the underlying storage format.

After retrieving the values into local variables, this utility method passes the data into intrinsic edit controls for manipulation by the user. Another software element, GUIUtils, provides methods to make this data transfer a simple task. For example, SetDoubleIntoTextWindow enables the utility method to place the Register value from a local variable into the actual text window. This method accepts the handle of the parent window (hDlg), the identifier of the text control (IDC_EDIT3), the value of the register, and the number of digits to the right of the decimal point (2) as input arguments.

A Code Walk Through the Layers

This section takes a guided tour through the layers of software elements that manage the parameter database. The walkthrough proceeds through the layers in the same sequence as demonstrated in Figure 10-2.

Entry into the software layers begins with a message handler, such as the WM_COMMAND message handler, executing a method provided by ParameterDBMgr. The following code segment provides an example of this starting point:

```
GetDoubleValueFromParameterDBase( RegisterValueRecordNumber,
                                  &Register ) ;
```

Inside ParameterDBMgr, this method expands into the following code segment:

```
static DBRecordType Record;
void GetDoubleValueFromParameterDBase( int Position, double * Value )
{
     if (DBaseIsOpen)
     {
          Record = CreateRecord() ;
          ReadRecordFromDBase(Record,Position) ;
          GetDoubleValueFromRecord(Record,Value) ;
          DestroyRecord(Record) ;
     }
}
```

First, the method checks to ensure that the parameter database is open. The flag DBaseIsOpen is set elsewhere within ParameterDBMgr when the client program executes the method to open the parameter database.

The primary data structure for the next software layer is the record. Once this method establishes connectivity to the database, the method creates an instance of the abstract data type DBRecordType. A static global variable named Record maintains the contents of this instance. By executing the method ReadRecordFromDBase, this method fills the data type with the values that are stored at the requested position. After filling the record with real data, this method uses an access method, GetDoubleValueFromRecord, to extract the real parameter value from the record. Finally, the method destroys the working record by executing the method DestroyRecord.

Review the simplicity and clarity of this method. The method almost reads as if written in English. Even an unsophisticated reviewer can look at this code segment and easily understand the logical flow of execution. These features all represent the benefits that accrue due to effective use of layered, abstracted software. The primary goal is to push implementation-specific details to the lowest possible layer. Meeting this goal achieves simplicity and clarity of coding style. The long-term impact of these benefits is to reduce programming errors and debugging time, thus leading to shorter development periods.

```
void ReadRecordFromDBase( DBRecordType Record, int Position )
{
     RecordSize = GetDBRecordSize() ;
     Buffer = CreateEmptyRecordBuffer() ;
     GetRecordFromDBase(Position,Buffer,RecordSize) ;
     CopyRecordBufferIntoRecord(Record,Buffer) ;
     DestroyRecordBuffer(Buffer) ;
}
```

This method, operating at the lowest software layer DBaseMgr, uses a buffer record as temporary storage. In this situation, the buffer record is simply a blob or bag of bytes. The method retrieves a blob of bytes into a buffer record through a utility method named GetRecordFromDBase. Then, another local method called CopyRecordBufferIntoRecord transfers the blob of bytes into an actual data record as expected by the calling method.

The method GetRecordFromDBase interacts with the selected physical storage format and reflects the characteristics of the format. The code body for this method appears in the following code segment:

```
void GetRecordFromDBase( int Index, BYTE * Data , int Count )
{
     Counter = 0 ;
     while (Counter <= (Index - 1))
     {
          ConvertIntToString(Counter,CurrentName) ;
          RemoveCharactersFromFront(CurrentName,1) ;

          ReadIntPropertyFromFile(CurrentDBase,CurrentName,&BlobSize) ;
          ReadBlobFromFile(CurrentDBase,BlobData,BlobSize) ;

          Counter = Counter + 1 ;
     }

     ConvertIntToString(Index,IndexName) ;
     RemoveCharactersFromFront(IndexName,1) ;
     ReadIntPropertyFromFile(CurrentDBase,IndexName,&BlobSize) ;
     ReadBlobFromFile(CurrentDBase,BlobData,BlobSize) ;
```

```
        if (Count < BlobSize )
              memcpy(Data,BlobData,Count) ;
        else
              memcpy(Data,BlobData, BlobSize) ;

        SetFilePointer(CurrentDBase,0,0,FILE_BEGIN) ;
}
```

This code body represents the software necessary to interact with an INI file that contains the parameters as ASCII text. In order to obtain a specific parameter record, this method cycles through all the records until the record with the indicated index is encountered.

Cycling through the records in the file involves reading the record, converting the incoming index from the record into an integer, and checking to determine whether the correct number of preceding records has been successfully processed and eliminated. Once the linear sequence of records has been correctly positioned, this method then retrieves the bytes from the current record. After retrieving the bytes, the method transfers the data into the buffer provided by the client method.

Targeting the Bottom Layer to a Destination

The last method in the preceding section demonstrates the way in which methods of DBaseMgr are configured to accommodate the unique linear, sequential characteristics of INI files. By way of comparison, this section reveals the implementation of the same method, GetRecordFromDBase, for accessing data stored a different storage format.

Appearing in the following code segment is the method body for GetRecordFromDBase when the target storage format is the system registry of Windows CE:

```
void GetRecordFromDBase ( int Index, BYTE * Data , int Count )
{
     DWORD       BlobCount ;
     BYTE        BlobData[MAX_BLOB_BYTES] ;

     ConvertIntToString(Index,IndexName) ;

     RegQueryValueEx( CurrentDBase, IndexName, NULL, &Type,
                      BlobData, &BlobCount);
```

```
     if (Count < (int)BlobCount )
          memcpy(Data,BlobData,Count) ;
     else
          memcpy(Data,BlobData, BlobCount) ;
}
```

This process really contains three simple steps. First, the method converts the desired record number, named Index, into the string IndexName. Using the Win32 API method RegQueryEx, the next step simply employs IndexName as a key to quickly retrieve the blob of bytes from the registry. Finally, this method copies the retrieved data from the temporary BYTE buffer BlobData into the buffer Data, provided by the upper client layer.

Compare this implementation with the previous implementation. Far fewer lines of code are necessary. Furthermore, data stored in the registry is correctly and automatically keyed for rapid access. DBaseMgr utilizes the key feature of data by employing the index or record number as the key value. Employing the record number as the index value is a clever trick to enable DBaseMgr to avoid the need to create an arbitrary key value.

Summary

The purpose of this chapter is to demonstrate the way in which software layers may be effectively used to encapsulate access to a specific target storage format for program parameters. Key concepts discussed in this chapter include the following:

▶ Several storage media are available to Pocket PC programs for maintaining program parameter values across separate user accesses.

▶ Each storage format has strengths and weaknesses.

▶ A layered design approach provides an easy way to tailor a program to a specific storage format.

▶ Each software layer transforms, converts, or manages a specific representation of the data necessary to obtain storage format independence.

▶ The lowest software layer treats data as a blob of raw data bytes.

▶ Using blobs at this lowest layer makes implementation quick and easy.

Sample Programs on the Web

The following programs are available at http://www.osborne.com:

Description	Folder
Desktop INI File Program	IniFileManagerProgram
Pocket PC INI File Program	IniFileManagerProgram PPC
Desktop Registry File Program	RegistryManagerProgram
Pocket PC Registry File Program	RegistryManagerProgram PPC
Desktop Intrinsic Database Program	Not applicable
Pocket PC Intrinsic Database Program	DBaseManagerProgram PPC

Execution Instructions

Because all three programs execute in exactly the same way, only one set of instructions appears in this section. Simply replace each project and program name with the appropriate names, as indicated in the list of programs.

Desktop INI File Program

1. Start Visual C++ 6.0.
2. Open the project IniFileManagerProgram.dsw in the folder IniFileManagerProgram.
3. Build the program.
4. Execute the program.
5. Click the Open DBase button to open the database. If this is the first execution, the program creates the parameter file with the default values. The name of the file is ParameterDB.
6. Click the Read Record button to read the records of the database. If this is the first execution, the edit fields should contain the same default values as those appearing in Figure 10-1.
7. Modify the Owner and Register values.
8. Click the Write Record button to write the records of the database.
9. Click the Close DBase button to close the database.

10. Click the Quit menu item.

11. The application window disappears as the application terminates.

12. Execute the program again.

13. Click the Open DBase button to open the database.

14. Click the Read Record button to read the records of the database. The edit fields should contain the same values as those entered into the fields when the records were last written.

15. Click the Close DBase button to close the database.

16. Click the Quit menu item.

17. The application window disappears as the application terminates.

Pocket PC INI File Program

1. Attach the Pocket PC cradle to the desktop computer.

2. Insert the Pocket PC into the cradle.

3. Tell ActiveSync to create a guest connection.

4. Make sure the status is connected.

5. Start Embedded Visual C++ 3.0.

6. Open the project IniFileManagerProgram PPC.vcw in the folder IniFileManagerProgram PPC.

7. Build the program.

8. Make sure the program successfully downloads to the Pocket PC.

9. On the Pocket PC, open the File Explorer.

10. Browse to the MyDevice folder.

11. Execute the program IniFileManagerProgram.

12. Tap the Open DBase button to open the database. If this is the first execution, the program creates the parameter file with the default values. The name of the file is ParameterDB.

13. Tap the Read Record button to read the records of the database. If this is the first execution, the edit fields should contain the same default values as those appearing in Figure 10-1.

14. Modify the Owner and Register values.

15. Tap the Write Record button to write the records of the database.

16. Tap the Close DBase button to close the database.

17. Tap the Quit menu item.

18. The application window disappears as the application terminates.

19. Execute the program again.

20. Tap the Open DBase button to open the database.

21. Tap the Read Record button to read the records of the database. The edit fields should contain the same values as those entered into the fields when the records were last written.

22. Tap the Close DBase button to close the database.

23. Tap the Quit menu item.

24. The application window disappears as the application terminates.

Systems Programming

OBJECTIVES

- ▶ Learn the threading model of Windows CE

- ▶ Demonstrate the effect of thread priorities

- ▶ Understand the synchronization problem

- ▶ Design a multithreaded architecture

- ▶ Implement the architecture using events

- ▶ Understand the COM architecture

- ▶ Develop a COM component using ATL

- ▶ Implement a COM client

- ▶ Register a COM server on the Pocket PC

CHAPTER

11

Multithreaded Applications and Synchronization

IN THIS CHAPTER:

The Use and Abuse of Threads

An Introduction to the Synchronization Problem

Implementing Threads with Synchronization

Summary

Sample Programs on the Web

A common interpretation of multithreaded execution is that threads allow pieces of a program to execute in parallel. This statement is false. Certainly, on the outside, these pieces appear to execute in parallel. From the user perspective, the software pieces appear to execute in parallel. In reality, something quite different happens below the surface. One of the goals of this chapter is to explain the details of multithreaded execution.

Consider the motivation for using threads in a program. A user would like to print a file. This file is a large file. If a program concentrates only on printing the file, the user is not going to be very happy. Writing a program that single-mindedly prints a file prevents the user from interacting with the program during the print cycle. If the print output is large enough, the printing can take several hours. Imagine how a user would feel if this freeze out happens!

Upon reflection, the problem is simple. A program needs to service two external interfaces simultaneously—the user and the printer. If a developer can organize a program to appear to be servicing these interfaces at the same time, the user will think that the two pieces are executing in parallel.

This need to service multiple interfaces simultaneously arises over and over again. Examples of using threads to manage interfaces include servicing network ports, commanding hardware devices such as lasers or manufacturing control systems, downloading databases from hard disks to embedded controllers, and probably millions of other uses. Sometimes a program needs to perform a complex set of calculations simultaneously while servicing a user and at the same time handling other hardware interfaces.

The Use and Abuse of Threads

A *thread* is a code element independently scheduled for CPU cycles by the Kernel component of Windows CE. By using threads, a program can service multiple interfaces. However, this effect does not mean that the pieces of a program are executing in parallel.

NOTE

The Kernel element of Windows CE is a somewhat scaled-down version of the same component of Windows 2000 and Windows XP.

Figure 11-1 demonstrates the execution timeline of two threads in a hypothetical program.

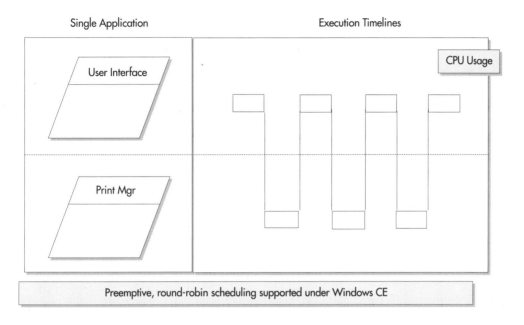

Figure 11-1 *Threads and parallel execution timelines*

This figure assumes that that a program executes two threads. The User Interface thread services commands from a user. A second thread shown in Figure 11-1, named Print Mgr, controls simultaneous printing of a large file. To the right of these threads appears an area called Execution Timelines.

An execution timeline indicates the time periods in which a thread is using the CPU. Figure 11-1 reveals that each thread uses the CPU for a period of time. After using the CPU for a period of time, the thread then relinquishes the CPU to another thread. The act of relinquishing the CPU is a *context switch*. This switching and CPU sharing is the cause of the apparent parallel execution.

NOTE

Threads do not execute in parallel. Although the threads appear to be supporting multiple interfaces simultaneously, only one thread at a time actually executes using the CPU. After all, a Pocket PC has only a single CPU. However, from a user's perspective, the threads appear to be executing simultaneously.

By devoting a number of cycles to each thread, each thread has some time devoted toward servicing a particular interface. The User Interface thread can interact with the user when using the CPU during assigned CPU cycles. A little more of the file prints each time the Print Mgr thread gains control of the CPU. Therefore, neither interface becomes starved. The user does not grimace every time a program ignores a stylus tap. The User Interface thread never misses stylus taps, because this thread usually experiences a context switch frequently and acquires the CPU.

Under Windows CE, threads execute until a finite time quantum has elapsed or until an input/output request is issued. At the expiration of the time quantum, the Kernel component of Windows CE forces a context switch. This forced switching is *preemptive multitasking*. By forcing each thread to relinquish the CPU, the Kernel ensures that each thread (and each interface or algorithm managed by the thread) receives a fair share of the CPU.

States of a Thread

Every thread used in an application exists in a variety of states. The state of a thread affects the behavior and the performance of the application. In Figure 11-2, a state-transition diagram describes the states of a thread.

Each box in the figure represents a specific state of the thread. Text inside the box provides a name for the state. An arrow between two state boxes indicates a transition from the state at the base of the arrow to the state at the arrow's head. Each transition possesses a text string label that reveals the condition that caused the transition.

One of the most interesting states is the Running state. In this state, a thread owns the CPU and receives all the available CPU cycles. Three arrows proceed from this state. Each of these arrows indicates a condition under which a thread exits in this state. If a thread reaches the end of its CPU-scheduling quantum or gets preempted by a higher-priority thread, then the thread returns to the Ready state. Recall the discussion of preemption and its purpose earlier in this chapter. When a thread reaches the end of its executable body, a move into the Terminated state occurs. Finally, any statement that causes a thread to wait for synchronization with another thread causes the thread to enter the Waiting state.

An area in Figure 11-2 of special importance is the section involving the transitions between the Ready, Standby, and Running states. According to this sequence of states, once a thread becomes ready, two actions must occur before this thread gains access to the CPU. First, a thread must be selected from among all the Ready threads for execution. Then, the present thread that owns the CPU must exit the Running state. Because these two factors can take some time, a thread may experience extensive time delays. A developer can help reduce these delays by the correct use of threading in an application.

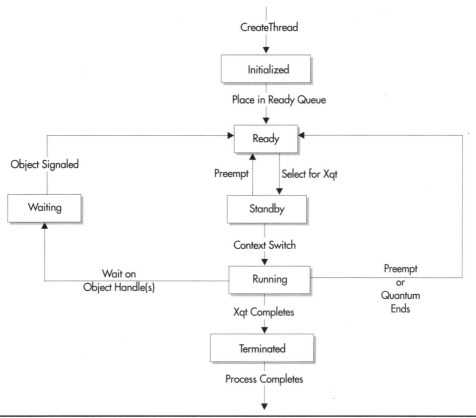

Figure 11-2   *Thread states and transition conditions*

NOTE

Much of the delay from scheduling disappears if the number of threads in an application remains as small as possible. Experience with multithreaded architectures indicates that a developer can help to reduce these scheduling delays by designing an application to use at most seven to ten carefully selected and designed threads.

Typical uses for threads include the monitoring of hardware interfaces, decision-making controllers, algorithm managers, and user interface managers. If a program employs threads in these ways, some form of messaging or signaling is necessary to support interthread communication.

Scheduling a Thread for Execution

When a thread enters the Ready state, the Kernel component of Windows places the thread into a ready queue. The structure and organization of this queue appears in Figure 11-3.

This queue contains a number of bins. Each bin represents one of the possible thread priorities. If a thread appears in bin 0, that thread has the lowest possible priority. Additionally, each thread assigned a priority of 31 has the highest priority and obviously enters the queue in the top bin.

When selecting a thread for execution, the Kernel component of Windows uses a two-step process. First, a search conducted through the bins, starting at the top priority of 31, finds the first nonempty queue. Once this queue is determined, the thread at the head of the queue becomes the thread selected for execution. All this means that a thread cannot execute until all the bins of higher priority are emptied.

Recall from the previous discussion that a thread may return to the ready queue after completing a time quantum or by being preempted by a higher-priority thread. Upon returning to the ready queue, a thread appears at the tail end of its priority bin.

TIP

The term that describes this scheduling approach is round-robin, first-come, first-served (FCFS) priority thread scheduling.

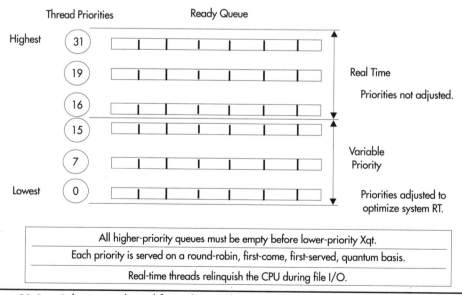

Figure 11-3 *Selecting a thread from the ready queue for execution*

By moving a thread from the front of the queue to the rear of the queue after execution, the Kernel creates a round-robin effect on a thread.

The Kernel component of Windows divides thread priorities into two major categories. Priorities in the range 16–31 exist in the Real Time category. If a thread has a priority between 0–15, that thread belongs to the Variable Priority category. For performance purposes, the category to which a thread belongs is important. If a thread exists in the Real Time category, the thread priority remains at the same value throughout execution unless explicitly modified by code within the thread. However, suppose that a thread is a member of the Variable Priority group. In this case, the thread's priority actually changes because the Kernel regularly modifies the thread priority to improve overall system response time (RT).

Thread Priorities and Priority Management

Appearing in Figure 11-4 is a characterization of the thread priority–adjustment process.

This figure reveals that a variable-priority thread actually possesses a priority that ranges above and below a base value.

When a variable-priority thread begins execution, the Kernel component of Windows CE assigns an initial thread priority. This priority is the process-base priority defined as a default value in Windows CE. Initially, a thread priority automatically rises to some higher level, usually about four levels higher than the

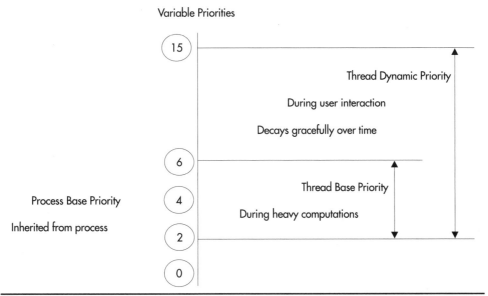

Figure 11-4   *Variable thread priorities*

base priority. As a thread uses more and more CPU cycles, the priority of a thread gradually decays until reaching a value somewhat below a base priority. Typically, this lowest priority level is about three levels below the base priority. At this point, a thread priority returns to the highest level, and the decay cycle begins anew.

In using this decaying-priority algorithm, the Kernel basically penalizes a thread for accumulating more and more CPU cycles. The justification for the decaying priority is simple. Early in the consumption of cycles, a thread is probably interacting with the user to collect inputs. As a thread accumulates more and more CPU cycles, that thread is probably taking these user inputs and beginning to perform some complex calculations. By lowering a thread's priority, extensive calculations take longer to complete, but other threads with higher priorities can interact with users.

NOTE

When using threads, an application should employ a multithreaded architecture that is priority neutral. In other words, threads should operate in such a way that the thread priority is not modified programmatically.

No matter how a developer tries to modify thread priorities, the likelihood of success in using thread priorities to the advantage of an application is extremely small. The Kernel is simply going to move all the priorities around, regardless of the values of the thread priorities.

Of course, a program can always set a thread priority up in the Real Time level. Unfortunately, this approach is likely to end up freezing out every other thread in every other executing application. Sooner or later, somebody is bound to complain. Once anyone realizes that an application is the CPU hog, users are likely to register extensive complaints.

Demonstrating the Effect of Thread Priorities

Nothing provides better insight into a problem than a picture. In an attempt to provide effective visualization about the effect of thread priorities, a sample program, called the Bouncing Square program, is available from the book's web site at http://www.osborne.com. As with all other programs that accompany this book, both desktop and Pocket PC versions of this program are available.

The concept behind this program is very simple. A user creates a series of bouncing squares in the client area of the program window. Each square bounces up and down within the client area of the program window. As the square bounces, the vertical position decays, ultimately causing the square to disappear. When a user creates a bouncing square, an independent thread manages the decaying vertical position and display of the square. Every thread possesses a user-determined thread priority. By varying the priorities of the threads controlling the bouncing squares, a user visualizes the effect of priority management by the Kernel component of Windows CE.

Figure 11-5 demonstrates the user interface for the Bouncing Square Program.

Two options appear in the main menu bar of this application. At the right end of the main menu bar is the Priority menu item. Prior to starting one or more threads, a user taps this menu item. In response to the stylus tap, Windows CE displays the Priority popup submenu containing a list of priorities.

The available priorities fall into two major groups, indicated by a separator bar inside the popup submenu. Priorities that appear above the separator bar of the submenu represent numerical values defined as symbolic constants by the Win32 API library. At the bottom of the submenu, a friendly priority appears. When a thread is created with this priority, the thread has an obligation to voluntarily relinquish the CPU after performing a single update of the controlled bouncing square. Within the thread control body, if this property is set the control code executes a Sleep statement with a delay of 0 milliseconds. The direct effect of this statement is to force the thread to the rear of the ready queue, relinquishing the CPU to the next thread selected by the Kernel component of Windows CE. Using the stylus, an operator selects one of the priorities displayed in the popup submenu. From this point on, each time the user creates a bouncing square, the controlling thread receives the most recently selected priority.

A user adds bouncing squares to the client area using a stylus tap. Figure 11-6 shows a typical view of the user interface during execution of the Bouncing Square Program.

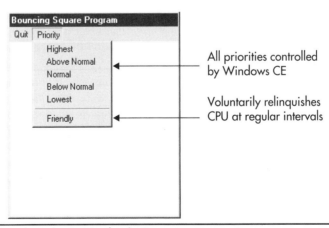

Figure 11-5   *Setting thread priorities for the Bouncing Square Program management threads*

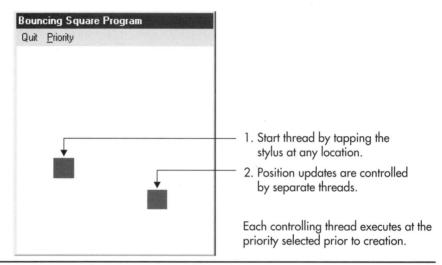

Figure 11-6   *Viewing performance impact of thread priorities*

The user interface in this figure shows two bouncing squares. A user creates various squares of differing priorities by selecting a different priority from the menu prior to starting a new square. By choosing different combinations of priorities, a developer can see the effects of thread priority. During execution, the varying of the priority levels by the Kernel component becomes obvious. As a specific thread has its priority reduced, the update speed of the managed bouncing square gets slower and slower. Any thread that receives a priority speed updates the position of the bouncing square more frequently. Threads at the Highest priority level starve the remaining threads for CPU cycles, causing the remaining squares controlled by other threads to practically freeze in place.

NOTE

The best way to view the promotion of thread priorities is to give one thread a Normal priority and to allocate a Below Normal priority to several other threads.

An Introduction to the Synchronization Problem

Using threads helps a program to serve multiple masters (interfaces). However, this support does not come without some aggravation. Threads can have a problem when accessing shared data. This special problem has several names. Typically, programmers call this problem the *synchronization problem* or the *thread-safe problem*. Regardless of the term used, the problem remains the same. When threads share data under a round-robin, preemptive scheduling system, the shared data can become quite corrupted. If a program is going to share data among threads, a design is necessary to avoid this potential corruption.

As an example of how this problem occurs, consider a simple program. In this program, two threads execute. The first thread, Thread A, writes some data into a shared memory structure. The name for the shared memory structure is RawData. Now, a second thread, Thread B, has the thankless job of reading the data placed into RawData and increasing its value.

Thread A uses a loop to generate the input values. The value placed into the RawData structure is the index of the loop multiplied by 10. Each time Thread B reads the data, the code multiplies the value by 20, and the data is returned to RawData. If all threads are working correctly, the main thread of an application should read a set of values from RawData that are simply multiples of 200.

Although this example may seem contrived, the characteristics of the problem are similar to many faced when implementing a multithreaded application. For instance, a thread might sit in a loop and read data from a hardware interface. As data is found, the thread reads this data, placing the data into a buffer. When a controller thread finishes processing the last piece of data retrieved from the buffer, the thread retrieves a new piece of data and responds accordingly. This description compares favorably with the sample problem description. This sample problem is a simplified version of the real-world hardware-monitoring problem.

On the surface, a developer might like to write code for the two threads that looks like the following:

```
// Thread A
for ( Index = 0 ; Index < 20 ; Index  =  Index + 1)
          RawData[Index]  =  10 * Index ;
// Thread B
for ( Index = 0 ; Index < 20 ; Index  =  Index + 1)
          RawData[Index]  =  10 * RawData[Index];
```

Although this little bit of code might look like the solution to the problem, take a look at the virtual machine code that these threads might generate, as shown in Figure 11-7.

In this figure appears the data structure RawData. To the left of this structure, Thread A is writing data into RawData. On the right of the structure, Thread B is reading the data out of the structure before Thread A can update the data.

Of interest is the typical machine code that appears below each thread. Consider Thread A first. Thread A begins by multiplying the index j by 10 and storing the result in a register (reg). The next line of code determines the target address of the

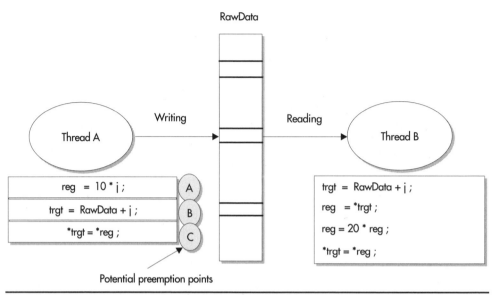

Figure 11-7   *An example of the synchronization problem*

data (trgt). This target address consists of the base address of RawData added to an offset to index location j. Finally, the contents of the target address (*trgt) are replaced by the contents of the register (*reg). A similar machine code characterization appears for the reading operation aspect of Thread B.

Look carefully at this code. The single line of code that computes and writes the data into RawData translates into three lines of machine instruction. Thread A can experience a forced context switch to relinquish the CPU after the execution of any one of these three machine instructions. These three lines of code are potential preemption points, labeled with the characters A, B, and C.

If a program creates two threads and executes this code about 20 or so times, some funny results occur. Sometimes, the correct multiples of 200 appear. Other times, only multiples of 10 appear, demonstrating that Thread A wrote an initial value into a location of RawData after Thread B wrote a value into the location. When this phenomenon happens, this clearly reveals the side effects from unsynchronized preemption.

In order to fully characterize the effects of preemption at these three points, look at the analysis provided in Table 11-1.

(A)	10 * j not yet written by Thread A Thread B reads garbage, multiplies by 20 Thread B writes 20 * garbage Thread A writes 10 * j
(B)	10 * j not yet written by Thread A Thread B reads garbage, multiplies by 20 Thread B writes 20 * garbage Thread A writes 10 * j
(C)	10 * j written by Thread A Thread B reads 10 * j, multiplies by 20 Thread B writes 200 * j

Table 11-1   *Analysis of Preemption Points*

At the left side of this table, the labels represent the possible preemption points in Thread A. Next to each label appears an analysis of the effect that occurs if Thread A is preempted at the labeled point. These analyses also assume that Thread B gets to execute all of its instructions from Figure 11-7.

Compare this analysis with the instruction sequence for Thread A from Figure 11-7. Consider, for example, the possible preemption point labeled A. At this point, Thread A has computed the target value of 10 times the index j. Yet, the value stays in a register temporarily. Now, a context switch occurs. This switch causes the register contents to be stored away temporarily into some tables maintained in the guts of the Kernel.

Thread B becomes the executing thread. Under the assumption stated in the preceding paragraph, this thread gets to execute all the machine instructions from Figure 11-7. As a result, the target location in RawData now contains a nonsense value. At this point, because Thread A has no chance to write the value, Thread B simply reads a garbage value. As everyone in programming undoubtedly knows, garbage in yields garbage out. Now, the Kernel decides to interrupt Thread B. A context switch occurs that restores Thread A, including the previously saved register value.

After being context-switched into life, Thread A simply resumes at the next line of code, which is possibly preemption point B. With a little luck, Thread A completes both steps B and C.

If the program prints the value in the indexed location of RawData at this point, the value equals only the index multiplied by 10. Because Thread B was preempted in the middle of the data-generation and writing sequence, the desired sequence of operations fails to execute in the desired manner.

This example demonstrates the possible corruption of data known as the *preemption problem* or the *thread-safe problem*. The proper way to avoid this corruption is to find a way to make the data-generation and writing sequence into an atomic action. An *atomic action* consists of any set of activities that may not be broken into smaller pieces but must be accomplished at once. Providing atomicity to this sequence prohibits access by Thread B to a location in RawData until Thread A has a chance to fill the data correctly.

Imagine the extent of grief that can result from preemption in a real application. Recall the earlier example of the hardware interface–monitoring thread that passes data into a buffer. Suppose the monitor places half a message into the buffer and then preemption occurs. If the controller thread reads the data from this location, the retrieved message consists of half the old message and half a new message. This concoction certainly sounds like a garbled mess that can cause an application to choke in midstream.

A Solution to the Synchronization Problem

The key to controlling the potential data scrambling from context switching is to synchronize access to the shared data in RawData. However, providing synchronization is not necessarily a simple task. In order to operate correctly, the multithreaded application must correctly apply synchronization.

Appearing in Figure 11-8 is a synchronization-based, multithreaded architecture that solves the preceding synchronization problem.

This figure contains three threads. At the top of the architecture, a thread has the label WinMain. This thread is the primary thread the Kernel component of Windows creates for every program. A program receives this thread for free. At the bottom of the figure are two threads that actually do the work of the sample problem—Thread A and Thread B. WinMain, the primary thread, creates both Thread A and Thread B. These threads then become child threads of the parent thread WinMain.

In addition to the threads themselves, the figure depicts thread interactions, indicated by dashed arrows. These arrows signify synchronization between the two threads. A thread at the base of a dashed arrow signals the thread at the head of the arrow. Thus, the thread at the head of the arrow waits for the signal from the sender. Programmatically, a synchronization object enables two threads to synchronize using a wait/signal construct.

Look at the multithreaded architecture carefully. This architecture employs six synchronization objects. Perhaps this number of objects is a surprise. Most programmers think that a single synchronization object effectively controls access to the data structure RawData. In this situation, because of the characteristics of the problem, all six synchronization objects are absolutely necessary to ensure correct sequencing.

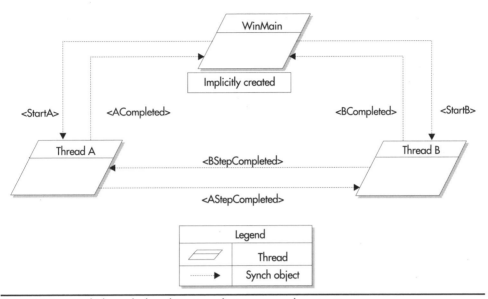

Figure 11-8 *Multithreaded architecture that uses synchronization*

Consider the way in which the threads work together with the synchronization objects. At the start of execution, the thread WinMain creates the two threads: Thread A and Thread B. These threads wait until signaled by WinMain to begin execution. WinMain uses StartA and StartB to signal the threads to begin execution. After signaling the two threads to begin execution, WinMain waits for the two threads to complete execution.

Thread B waits for Thread A to signal that the current indexed location of RawData has been written. Thread A informs Thread B using AStepCompleted. Once Thread A apprises Thread B, Thread A waits for Thread B to complete the work on the current indexed location of RawData before proceeding to the next indexed location of RawData. Thread B signals Thread A using BStepCompleted.

After each thread completes all the work on all the locations in RawData, both threads inform the WinMain thread that the work is finished. These threads use ACompleted and BCompleted to inform WinMain that the work is finished. Of course, WinMain has been sitting and waiting for the confluence of these two signals.

All these signals are necessary. Thread A needs to start the data-generation and data-writing process first. Unfortunately, documentation for the Win32 API does not indicate any preferred order for thread initiation. Therefore, the StartA and StartB synchronization objects ensure that Thread A begins processing before Thread B. In order to guarantee this desired sequencing, WinMain issues the start signal StartA to Thread A first.

Another problem for the developer involves holding the primary thread WinMain in memory until all the child threads have completed execution. This requirement is another area where the Win32 API documentation appears to be deficient. If WinMain reaches the end of its executable body before the child threads complete execution, then the Kernel component of Windows CE is free to remove WinMain and terminate the child threads. Clearly, this approach makes little sense. To avoid a possible problem, two synchronization objects, such as ACompleted and BCompleted, from the child worker threads force WinMain to wait for completion signals.

Obviously, the step-completion signals control direct access to the shared data structure RawData. Each worker thread behaves like a good neighbor. Thread A works on an indexed location of RawData and then signals availability to Thread B. Thread B interacts with Thread A using the same good manners.

Some Detailed Design for a Review

When implementing synchronized access to shared data, a number of implementation approaches are available to a developer. In the following code implementation, a number of special software elements provide a framework for controlling access to the shared data. These elements and an example of their usage appear in Figure 11-9.

This example demonstrates the usage of the framework elements from the perspective of Thread B alone. A similar diagram would detail a corresponding set of relationships of Thread A to these packages.

The first element in Figure 11-9, SynchMgr, appears on the left side. This element serves as a repository or manager of the synchronization objects. The objects named AStepCompleted and BStepCompleted are maintained as static storage class variables, limited to the inside of the body of the element. Access to these private fields is available strictly through the property-access methods indicated on the element diagram, such as WaitForAStepCompletedSignal.

Figure 11-9 also contains the element DataMgr. This element serves as a manager to control access to the data structure RawData. Inside the element rectangle, the private field RawData actually stores the indexed set of shared data values. The property-access methods GetRawDataAt and PutRawDataAt are the means by which an application thread gains access to the data stored in the hidden structure.

Some developers may feel that placing all the synchronization objects and wait/signal methods inside an element is a bit of overkill. However, by using this approach, the program accrues an additional benefit.

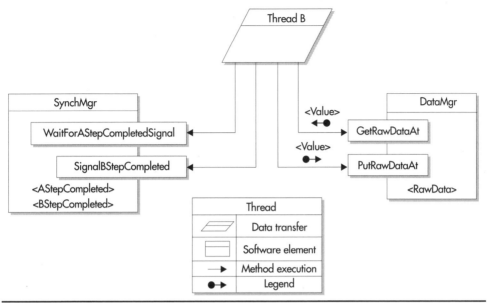

Figure 11-9   *Implementing thread-safe access to shared data*

NOTE

Encapsulating all the synchronization-specific elements of a program inside an encapsulating software element rigidly enforces synchronized access to the hidden data structures. If several programmers are independently developing and are individually responsible for synchronization, a great likelihood exists that at least one programmer will forget.

Using the DataMgr software element meets several important objectives. Because the data structure RawData needs to be globally accessible, this element serves as the global data repository. Wrapping the data in access methods establishes the framework to ensure that synchronization objects treat the data access as an atomic, indivisible operation. Finally, hiding the data structure prohibits any element of a program from knowing the organization of the structure RawData. Currently, RawData uses an array structure. Arrays are statically sized at creation. If the program needs to shrink and grow the data structure dynamically, a programmer eventually will have to convert the data structure from an array into a linked list. Because all the data structure details are hidden inside DataMgr, code to update the RawData structure has no impact on the remainder of the code in the program.

By inference from Figure 11-9, a sequence of method calls appears necessary to ensure synchronized access to the data in RawData. This execution sequence appears as pseudocode:

```
SynchMgr.WaitForACompletedSignal() ;
Value = DataManagerElement.GetRawDataAt(CurrentIndex) ;
// Multiply Value By 20
DataManagerElement.PutRawDataAt( CurrentIndex, Value ) ;
SynchMgr.SignalStepBCompleted() ;
```

All the accesses to RawData use the access methods provided by DataMgr. Surrounding the data-access methods with methods declared in SynchMgr forces the total access to RawData to become an atomic action. Access to the shared data by Thread A is just as effectively prohibited as if a user had turned off the electrical current in the circuits between Thread A and the memory occupied by RawData.

Implementing Threads with Synchronization

The remainder of this chapter contains an analysis of the actual implementations of the solution to the preceding synchronization problem. This implementation analysis follows a specific sequence of steps, as follows:

1. Creating the threads.
2. Implementing the main thread.
3. Implementing a child thread.
4. Creating the synchronization objects.
5. Waiting for step completion.
6. Signaling step completion.
7. Waiting for the child threads.

The order of the steps in this sequence represents the way in which the pieces of code execute during actual operations.

Additionally, all the code analyses demonstrate the implementation from the perspective of Thread B. A code analysis by tracing through the corresponding sequence of steps for Thread A is symmetric and reveals the same comments.

Creating the Threads

```
ThreadBHandle = CreateThread(
            0,0,
            (LPTHREAD_START_ROUTINE )ThreadBProcedure,
            0,0,&ThreadBID) ;
```

A program creates and initiates a new thread using the method CreateThread, supplied by the Win32 API. The primary argument to this method is the address of a routine that implements the thread body, such as ThreadAProcedure. The thread body of every thread appears defined as a method in an element named ThreadMgr. The object ThreadBHandle, returned by CreateThread, is an instance of a thread object created by the Kernel component of Windows CE in response to this method execution.

Implementing the Main Thread

```
WaitForThreadsToSetup() ;
StartThreads() ;
WaitForThreads() ;
```

This code segment coordinates the initiation and termination of the main thread of WinMain with the worker threads using a number of methods provided by other software elements. The method WaitForThreadsToSetup suspends WinMain until the worker threads signal that the initialization is completed and is waiting to proceed. After being signaled by the worker threads, WinMain initiates the real operations of the worker threads by signaling them to begin execution. The method StartThreads issues the start signals so that Thread A begins execution first. After starting the threads, the WinMain thread sits and patiently waits for the two child threads to signal completion. Waiting on these two signals occurs inside the method WaitForThreads.

Implementing a Child Thread

```
void ThreadBProcedure(void * Parameter)
{
          WaitForBStartSignal() ;
          SignalBStepCompleted() ;
```

```
    NumberEntries = GetNumberArrayElements( ) ;
    for ( i = 0 ; i < NumberEntries ; i = i + 1 )
    {
        WaitForAStepCompletedSignal( ) ;
        CurrentValue = GetRawDataAt( i ) ;
        CurrentValue = 20 * CurrentValue ;
        PutRawDataAt( i , CurrentValue ) ;
        SignalBStepCompleted( ) ;
    }
    SignalBCompleted( ) ;
}
```

In this code listing for ThreadBProcedure, the entry-point declaration requires a specific signature. A required signature indicates the names and data types of the arguments as well as the return data type. This thread function returns a void data type with a pointer to an undetermined data type as the primary argument. If a program needs initialization parameters for this thread, the incoming pointer may yield an application-defined data structure that contains relevant initialization data.

Upon entry to the thread body, execution suspends until the StartB signal is received. Once this signal is received, the thread signals Thread A to initiate data-generation and storage activities. This thread then enters a loop. This loop performs the atomic data management described by pseudocode presented earlier in this chapter that ensures the proper sequencing of access to RawData in DataMgr. After all indexed locations in RawData have been updated, this thread signals the primary thread in WinMain that work is completed.

Creating the Synchronization Objects

```
static HANDLE BStepCompleted ;
BStepCompleted = CreateEvent(0,FALSE,FALSE,__TEXT("BStepCompletedEvent") ) ;
CloseHandle(BStepCompleted) ;
```

These three elements appear with the software element SynchMgr. Each of these elements plays an important role in the lifecycle of the synchronization object BStepCompleted.

The mechanism for enabling threads to signal each other using the Win32 API is a synchronization object called an *event*. Each event object that a program creates can be in one of two states. If the state is *signaled*, the event is available to a waiting thread. A *non-signaled* event is not available, and any threads waiting for the event enter the private wait queue maintained for each and every event object.

Two types of events are available: manual reset events and automatic reset events. With the manual reset event, a thread that acquires the event object explicitly executes a method to set the event into a non-signaled state. Automatic reset events are entered automatically into the non-signaled state when allocated to a waiting thread. A thread does not have to do any extra work here. This application uses only automatic reset events.

A program creates an automatic reset event using the Win32 API method named CreateEvent. The first argument to this method enables a program to set access permissions for the event object. For Windows CE applications, this argument is always set to 0 because Windows CE does not support the sophisticated security model provided by Windows 2000. The second argument is a manual reset flag. Initializing this value to FALSE indicates that the program does not want a manual reset event. As a result, this event operates as an automatic reset event. In the third argument, the initial state of the event appears. A FALSE value here says to the Kernel that the program wants this event to start in a non-signaled or non-available state. Any thread that attempts to access this event then blocks until some line of code in another thread explicitly sets the event into a signaled state. In the last argument, a string becomes the global name of the event object. Using this name, any thread in the world, even in another application, can gain access to the event object.

After all the threads in an application have finished executing, the Win32 API method CloseHandle tells the Kernel that the synchronization object is no longer useful. This method decrements a reference count created and initialized when the program created each synchronization object. The Kernel component of Windows CE uses this count to know how many outstanding users currently have a handle to the object. When the reference count of any handle falls to zero, the Kernel destroys the synchronization objects.

Waiting for Step Completion

```
void WaitForAStepCompletedSignal(void)
{
    DWORD Status ;

    Status = WaitForSingleObject(AStepCompleted,INFINITE) ;
    if ( Status != WAIT_OBJECT_0)
    {
    }
}
```

Waiting for a signal from another thread using an event is simple programmatically. A program uses the method WaitForSingleObject. The primary argument to this method is a handle to the specific event object that the program wishes to acquire. The second argument indicates the maximum duration a program is willing to wait. Using the symbol INFINITE informs the Kernel that the program is willing to wait forever.

If the desired event object is non-signaled or unavailable, the thread enters the Waiting state, indicated earlier in Figure 11-2. The Kernel places the suspended thread into a special queue maintained for the event object.

Encapsulating or hiding the synchronization mechanism in this manner avoids another problem that often occurs with multithreaded architectures. If two threads attempt to synchronize against a pair of event objects but in reversed order, then both threads can potentially deadlock waiting for the other thread to signal an event while each thread holds the event required by the other thread. If all synchronization waits are hidden in a method, every thread would use the sequence pair in exactly the same order. This forced sequence is exactly the correct approach for avoiding this deadlocked situation.

Signaling Step Completion

```
void SignalBStepCompleted(void)
{
     SetEvent(BStepCompleted) ;
}
```

When a thread owns a synchronization object, the thread releases the object by executing the method SetEvent. In response to this method, the Kernel component causes the event object to become signaled or available.

Once the event object becomes signaled or available, the Kernel selects the thread at the head of the wait queue for the object. This thread moves into the Ready state that appears in Figure 11-2. Because this is an automatic reset event, the Kernel automatically sets the event object back into a non-signaled state. Now, the new thread temporarily owns the synchronization object.

Waiting for the Child Threads

```
void WaitForThreads(void)
{
#if !WindowsCE
    ThreadHandles[0] = ACompleted ;
    ThreadHandles[1] = BCompleted ;
    Status = WaitForMultipleObjects(2,ThreadHandles,TRUE,INFINITE) ;
    if ( Status != WAIT_OBJECT_0 )
    {
    }
#else
    Status = WaitForSingleObject(ACompleted,INFINITE) ;
    if ( Status != WAIT_OBJECT_0)
    {
        WaitForSingleObject(BCompleted,INFINITE) ;
        if ( Status != WAIT_OBJECT_0)
        {
        }
    }
#endif
}
```

At the end of the primary thread WinMain, program execution waits until all the child threads signal completion. Separate implementations are necessary to wait for the child threads on the desktop and on the Pocket PC. Conditional compilation, controlled by the WindowsCE flag in IFiles.h (introduced in Chapter 3), ensures that the correct implementation compiles into the target executable.

The first clause of the conditional compilation supports the desktop version of the program. The Win32 API contains a convenient and simple mechanism for waiting for the simultaneously signaling of multiple event objects. This mechanism is the method Win32.WaitForMultipleObjects.

To use this method, a program loads an array with handles to the event objects of interest. This array passes to the method WaitForMultipleObjects along with a maximum time limit. In the third argument to this method, a TRUE value indicates that the program wants to want until all the event objects are available.

Unfortunately, the method WaitForMultipleObjects is not supported by the Kernel component of Windows CE. In order to ensure that multiple worker threads have completed, this method utilizes a series of nested if statements that employ WaitForSingleObject. Each statement ensures that one more worker thread has signaled completion.

Summary

This chapter provides a detailed introduction to the support for threading and synchronization under Windows CE. Key concepts defined in this chapter include the following:

▶ Threads share the CPU and provide simultaneous service to multiple interfaces.

▶ Thread context switching may cause shared data to become garbled.

▶ Signals enable a program to synchronize among threads to control access to shared data.

▶ Every application receives a primary thread automatically.

▶ A threading architecture indicates thread interactions using signals.

▶ The Kernel component of Windows CE does not support the desktop method WaitForMultipleObjects.

▶ Hiding the synchronization objects in a software element ensures that synchronization occurs correctly and reliably.

Sample Programs on the Web

The following programs are available at http://www.osborne.com:

Description	Folder
Desktop Bouncing Square Program	BouncingSquareProgram
Pocket PC Bouncing Square Program	BouncingSquareProgram PPC
Desktop Synchronization Program	SynchronizationProgram
Pocket PC Synchronization Program	SynchronizationProgramPPC

Execution Instructions

Desktop Bouncing Square Program

1. Start Visual C++ 6.0.

2. Open the project BouncingSquareProgram.dsw in the folder BouncingSquareProgram.

3. Build the program.

4. Execute the program.

5. Select the Below Normal priority from the Priority popup submenu.

6. Click the left mouse button several times anywhere in the client area. This action should cause bouncing squares to start moving vertically.

7. Select the Normal priority from the Priority popup submenu.

8. Click the left mouse button anywhere in the client area. This action should cause a new bouncing square to start moving vertically. The new square should initially have priority over the lower-priority squares. Eventually, however, the Normal priority square experiences priority degradation to the point where the Below Normal priority squares get more CPU cycles.

9. Click the Quit menu item.

10. The application window disappears as the application terminates.

Pocket PC Bouncing Square Program

1. Attach the Pocket PC cradle to the desktop computer.

2. Insert the Pocket PC into the cradle.

3. Tell ActiveSync to create a guest connection.

4. Make sure the status is connected.

5. Start Embedded Visual C++ 3.0.

6. Open the project BouncingSquareProgramPPC.vcw in the folder BouncingSquareProgramPPC.

7. Build the program.

8. Make sure the program successfully downloads to the Pocket PC.

9. On the Pocket PC, open the File Explorer.

10. Browse to the MyDevice folder.

11. Execute the program BouncingSquareProgram.

12. Select the Below Normal priority from the Priority popup submenu.

13. Tap the stylus several times anywhere in the client area. This action should cause bouncing squares to start moving vertically.

14. Select the Normal priority from the Priority popup submenu.

15. Tap the stylus anywhere in the client area. This action should cause a new bouncing square to start moving vertically. The new square should initially have priority over the lower-priority squares. Eventually, however, the Normal priority square experiences priority degradation to the point where the Below Normal priority squares get more CPU cycles.

16. Tap the Quit menu item.

17. The application window disappears as the application terminates.

Desktop Synchronization Program

1. Start Visual C++ 6.0.

2. Open the project SynchronizationProgram.dsw in the folder SynchronizationProgram.

3. Build the program.

4. Execute the program.

5. Click the left mouse button anywhere in the client area. This action should cause numbers in multiples of 200 to appear in the client area of the program window.

6. Click the Quit menu item.

7. The application window disappears as the application terminates.

Pocket PC Synchronization Program

1. Attach the Pocket PC cradle to the desktop computer.

2. Insert the Pocket PC into the cradle.

3. Tell ActiveSync to create a guest connection.

4. Make sure the status is connected.

5. Start Embedded Visual C++ 3.0.

6. Open the project SynchronizationProgramPPC.vcw in folder SynchronizationProgramPPC.

7. Build the program.

8. Make sure the program successfully downloads to the Pocket PC.

9. On the Pocket PC, open the File Explorer.

10. Browse to the MyDevice folder.

11. Execute the program SynchronizationProgram.

12. Tap the stylus anywhere in the client area. This action should cause numbers in multiples of 200 to appear in the client area of the program window.

13. Tap the Quit menu item.

14. The application window disappears as the application terminates.

CHAPTER
12

Utilizing COM Components

IN THIS CHAPTER:

Component Object Model Architecture

Creating COM Components with ATL

Analyzing the ATL COM Component

Creating a COM Client

Registering a COM Server on a Pocket PC

Summary

Sample Programs on the Web

Software programmers want to obtain as much reuse as possible from the software they develop. Reuse enables a programmer to generate new products rapidly. Because these new products are constructed by reusing existing, extensively tested components, the new software products are also fairly reliable.

With the Windows product line, the keys to developing reusable products are the Component Object Model (COM) and ActiveX. In general, the COM philosophy applies to the development of components that do not exhibit a graphical user interface. ActiveX enables a program to incorporate visual elements into a COM object so that user interaction is available.

Distinguishing between COM objects as nonvisible binary components and ActiveX controls as visible binary components is a slight simplification. In fact, ActiveX controls are also COM objects.

Although this distinction is somewhat artificial, for the purposes of the discussion in this chapter, characterizing binary objects in this way helps to clearly define the programmatic differences between implementing visible and nonvisible binary objects.

Initially, this chapter provides a conceptual introduction to COM. The discussion in this initial section provides a programmer with enough knowledge to be able to comprehend the remainder of the chapter, which describes implementation details.

NOTE

All the code examples in this chapter are in C++. Although COM objects can be implemented in vanilla or ANSI C, using C is ill advised. Implementations of COM in C are messy and difficult to debug. C++ is a natural implementation language because of the inherent support for function pointers, which are critical to the implementation of COM interfaces. However, the difficult parts of C++ reside in a set of templates that most developers will never see.

Component Object Model Architecture

A COM object is a binary component that can be used as a part of any program. The chief benefit to using COM objects is that an application can reuse a binary component independent of the physical location of the binary object. An important aspect of COM objects is that a program attaches to the objects dynamically during execution. Dynamic linking differs from the normal reuse policy with which a programmer may be familiar. Typically, a program reuses a binary component by linking the object statically to an application during compilation. When a program links statically, the binary object becomes an integral and permanent part of the application. With dynamic linking of binary objects, a program connects to the object after execution begins.

To link a binary object dynamically during execution, both the program and the operating system cooperate to find the actual binary object. The Component Object Model (COM) defines all the elements that both the program and the operating system use in cooperation to ensure that the dynamic linking process works correctly.

Figure 12-1 shows the elements that participate in the dynamic linking process to attach a binary object to a program.

Every COM control that resides on a Pocket PC must register with the Windows CE operating system. Registration information appears in the Windows CE registry. In the registry, a COM object places a class identifier (ClassID) that supposedly identifies the control uniquely across all machines and forever in time. In the COM/ActiveX literature, the name of this class identifier is a *globally unique interface identifier* (GUID).

When a control client wants to link dynamically to a registered COM control, the client program uses the ClassID to identify the binary object. Windows CE has a special component whose primary function is to translate a ClassID into a binary object loaded in memory. This component, shown in Figure 12-1, goes by the name Service Control Manager, or SCM for short (typically pronounced *scum*).

Once the SCM receives a ClassID, this Windows SCM component searches a special area of the registry to find this ClassID. This special registry section is a hive named HKEY_CLASSES_ROOT. Hives comprise the major categories of data stored in the Windows CE system registry. Data stored inside the hive under the requested ClassID indicates the disk location of the dynamic link library that hosts the control. The SCM loads the library and returns an interface pointer to the object. This interface pointer contains pointers to the methods that an object supports.

A program typically interacts with the dynamically linked binary control object by executing methods listed in the interface pointer. If the control needs to initiate interaction with a client program, the program registers event handler methods with the control. Under appropriate and well-defined conditions, the control emits events that the registered event handler methods service.

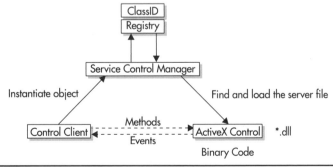

Figure 12-1   *COM elements used to support dynamic linking*

In order to make this dynamic instantiation process work correctly, a COM object or server satisfies a number of different masters. Three elements interact with a COM object. A client application utilizes the services of a COM object. The programmatic mechanics for utilizing a COM object require that the object is implemented within a specific programming language. Finally, the operating system/SCM manages a COM object utilizing information placed into the registry.

Figure 12-2 demonstrates the separate views of a COM object and the implications of these views.

From the perspective of an application programmer, a COM object appears to be an interface (ISimpleCOMServer) that provides one or more application-specific methods (DisplayString). By defining access to the COM object as an interface with supporting methods, a program obtains several important benefits. Application programmers use a uniform access mechanism (interfaces/methods) that reduces the learning time necessary to utilize a COM object. Moreover, this uniform approach enables an application programmer to utilize objects that may reside on a physically separate machine. The mechanics of accessing the services of a COM object on a separate machine exist beneath the interface to the object, encapsulating the connection and disconnection details.

The implementation of access to a COM object is through a specific programming language. Programmatic access to an object through interfaces and methods requires the use of a table of function pointers. In Figure 12-2, the function pointer interface appears as an arrow that extends from the DisplayString method underneath the Programming Language view. In essence, a table of function pointers is a simple table of integer values. This representation is the most compiler-independent mechanism available and allows COM support to be easily integrated into any programming language.

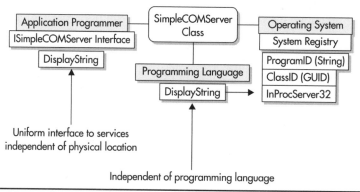

Figure 12-2   *Views of a COM object*

When a program initiates access to a COM object, the Windows CE operating system and the SCM component utilize data that the program places into the system registry to identify and locate an object. The most important information that the SCM uses in the location of a COM object appears in Figure 12-2. ProgramID is a string name for the COM object. A program associates a unique identifier with this name, called a *globally unique interface identifier* (GUID). This identifier distinguishes a COM object from all objects on all machines and ostensibly forever in time, with some limitations. Finally, the SCM needs to know the server type and the physical location of a COM object's binary code. The InProcServer32 element provides both of these pieces of information to the SCM.

A COM object provides access to services through one or more interfaces. An *interface* is nothing more than a collection of related methods. A client program obtains access to the methods provided by the interface by obtaining a pointer to the interface. In fact, the client program is obtaining a pointer to a table of function pointers. Each function pointer enables a program to access a single method provided by the interface.

When a client application accesses the interfaces of a COM object, the client program is actually writing code that uses the pointers in the corresponding function pointer table. A compiler for a language such as C++ reserves space for the function pointer table and then points to the location in the table each time a client program invokes the method. However, the actual contents of the function pointer table remain empty. Entries are placed into the function pointer table using special methods at the time the client program actually executes and instantiates the COM object.

Figure 12-3 contains a simple COM server named SimpleCOMServer, represented as an interface.

This server provides a single public method named DisplayString. Encapsulated within this object is a private data member named ServerCount. This simple counter maintains a reference for the number of currently attached client applications.

In order to make this COM object and its single method accessible to client applications, the implementation includes a COM class, SimpleCOMServer, and defines a single interface, ISimpleCOMServer. This interface contains a single function pointer to the DisplayString method.

According to Figure 12-3, a COM object actually needs two GUIDs. A GUID for the COM server, called a CLSID (class identifier), uniquely identifies the COM object from among all available COM objects. However, the object also needs a second GUID, called an IID (interface identifier), for uniquely distinguishing among all the interfaces supported by a single COM object. In fact, the naming convention used for these GUIDs is to attach either the CLSID or IID prefix to the GUID. In this way, the client program knows whether the GUID is being used to access an overall COM object or to access a specific interface supported by a COM object.

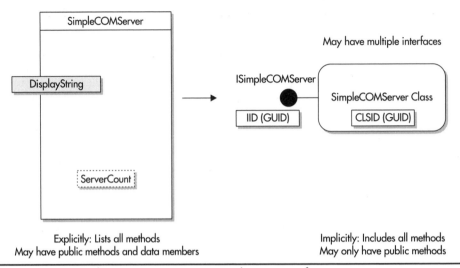

Interface: A collection of related methods provided by a server

Figure 12-3   *A simple COM server represented as an interface*

Most books on COM use the electronic component representation for COM objects that appears on the right side of Figure 12-3. A rounded rectangle represents the COM object class. Extending from the object symbol, a line that ends with a circle represents each interface supported by the object. This symbolic representation mimics the notation used in electronic hardware to represent an electrical interconnection.

Showing only the interfaces supported by a COM object provides an efficient mechanism for representing the role of a COM object within a software design. Simply connecting a client to the specific interfaces used results in a clear picture of the interconnection of clients and COM objects that comprise a software design. Imagine the clutter and confusion in a software design diagram if a program shows all the relationships to specific methods.

A number of implications of using COM objects via interfaces appear in Figure 12-3. A COM object/server may have multiple interfaces. By enabling multiple interfaces, the COM server provides a mechanism for grouping functionally related methods together, making the use of a COM object easier for a client program. Additionally, because the actual implementation of an interface is a table of function pointers, a COM object can only provide methods to client applications. This mechanism requires that a program use methods to modify the contents of private data members.

As a result, a COM object enforces encapsulation of internal data structures, hiding the data-structuring details from a client application. A client application does not require significant modifications if the underlying data structures change, as often happens in an ongoing development.

When implementing a COM object, a minimum of two interfaces are necessary. One interface is predefined by Microsoft and requires a program to implement methods used in controlling the lifetime of a COM object. This interface goes by the name IUnknown. Consider this to be a default interface because all COM objects must support this interface and its methods. In addition to this default interface, at least one additional interface provides application-specific methods representing services supported by the COM object.

A characterization of the default interface, IUnknown, and its associated methods appears in Figure 12-4.

The default interface contains three methods that must be implemented in a COM object. The method QueryInterface provides a mechanism for a client program to access any of the interfaces supported by a COM object. In reality, the client program uses QueryInterface to convert a pointer from one interface into a pointer for another interface. In this respect, QueryInterface acts as a type-conversion operator, where interfaces play the role of data types.

Encapsulated within a COM object is a reference counter. This private data member serves to track the number of connected client applications. The remaining methods, named AddRef and Release, operate on the reference counter. Because the COM

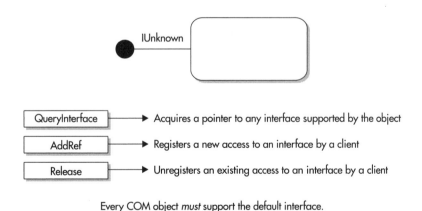

Every COM object *must* support the default interface.

Figure 12-4 *IUnknown, the default interface*

object knows the number of attached clients, these methods provide additional lifetime management, terminating the COM object when the client reference counter drops to zero.

By definition, every COM object must implement the IUnknown interface. If an object fails to implement these methods, a client application is likely to experience some rather bizarre behavior. Without the QueryInterface method, a client program might have to load multiple copies of a COM object, thus leading to poor performance in the overall operating system environment. Using the methods AddRef and Release ensures that a COM object does not self-destruct while multiple clients are utilizing the provided services. The resulting instability of the client application would seriously affect the marketability of a product that is implemented using a COM object.

Each COM object and the specific interfaces supported by that COM object receive a unique identification stamp using a GUID. As discussed previously, this identifier is unique over all machines and forever in time, with some limitations.

A detailed characterization of a GUID and its construction appears in Figure 12-5.

A GUID actually exists in two formats. A string format appears in the various locations in the operating system registry. A numeric representation of a GUID is necessary when using the GUID within client applications and within the actual COM object implementation.

As shown in Figure 12-5, the numeric representation of a GUID is 128-bits wide. An unsigned long field named Data1 is 32 bits. The fields named Data2 and Data3

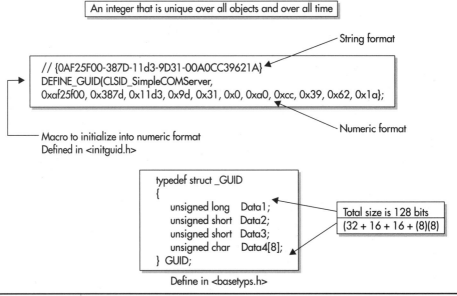

Figure 12-5 *Globally unique identifiers (GUIDs)*

are unsigned short values, each consuming 16 bits. Eight unsigned char values each require 8 bits. Adding these lengths together reveals that the numeric representation of a GUID consists of 128 bits.

When using the numeric representation within a COM object, a variable and a specific macro initialize the variable to the associated numeric value. The macro that initializes the numeric value of the GUID has the name DEFINE_GUID and appears in the header file initguid.h. Typically, the variable name that a COM object uses internally begins with the prefix CLSID or IID. As related earlier, these prefixes indicate whether the GUID refers to a COM object or to an interface supported by a COM object.

GUID generation is not a problem. Embedded Visual Studio has an integrated tool for generating GUIDs. In order for this tool to generate unique GUIDs, a network card must exist on the development computer. If a network card is not installed, the GUID-generation tool simply generates the same GUID over and over and over.

When a COM object installs onto a machine, the installation places descriptive data into the registry on that machine. Earlier discussions in this chapter indicated some of the required registry data. However, this information is not the complete picture.

Figure 12-6 contains a complete description of the location and data entries required for a typical COM server.

Windows CE organizes the registry into a number of sections called *hives*. The hive named HKEY_CLASSES_ROOT contains all the entries for COM objects. Contents of each hive exist in a hierarchical structure in much the same fashion

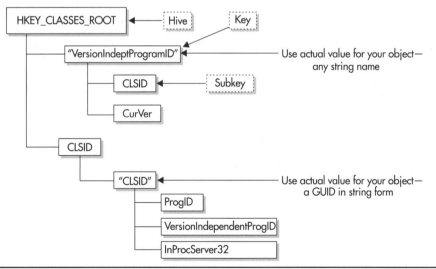

Figure 12-6 *Registering the COM object*

as a directory structure on a hard disk. A *path description* is the manner in which a program navigates to any location in the registry, similar to the way in which a program moves through a disk directory structure.

COM object registration requires that a COM server provide registration data in two separate areas of the registry. These two areas appear as subordinates to the hive HKEY_CLASSES_ROOT in Figure 12-6. Immediately subordinate to the hive HKEY_CLASSES_ROOT is a key value that represents the string name of the COM object. This string name is a version-independent program identifier. Associated with this string name, a subkey explicitly named CLSID indicates the GUID for a COM object in its string format. A path representation for this entry looks like the following:

```
HKEY_CLASSES_ROOT\SimpleCOMServer\CLSID =
                        {0AF25F00-387D-11d3-9D31-00A0CC39621A}
```

By using a method named CLSIDFromProgID, a client application converts the string name "SimpleCOMServer" into the preceding string form of the GUID. This method uses a string name to construct the path indicated, traverses the registry, and then reads the GUID. By executing this method, the client application retrieves a COM object GUID without having to actually enter the numeric or string version of the GUID explicitly into the client program.

The second area of the registry where a COM object places registration data is under the predefined key CLSID. Data entered into this area enables the SCM to locate and load a COM object into memory. Subordinate to the key CLSID, a subkey appears that is the string form of a COM object GUID. To this subkey, the registering COM object attaches three subsubkeys: ProgID, VersionIndependentProgID, and InprocServer32. The most important subsubkey is the InprocServer32 entry. The value for this subsubkey provides a path to the physical location of the binary code that implements a COM object. An example of this entry is:

```
HKEY_CLASSES_ROOT\CLSID\
    {0AF25F00-387D-11d3-9D31-00A0CC39621A}\InprocServer32 =
                        c:\SimpleCOMServerCPP\ SimpleCOMServerCPP.dll
```

As this code snippet reveals, the COM object implementation in this example takes the form of a dynamic link library, or DLL file. Using a dynamic link library enables a client to initialize the function pointer table during client execution rather than during static linking immediately after compilation. Additionally, multiple clients share a single instance of a dynamic link library, thus providing more efficient use of local machine resources.

Once the GUID is obtained using the method CLSIDFromProgID, a client application submits the GUID to the operating system/SCM for loading and retrieval of an interface pointer. The method used by the client application to perform this operation is named CoCreateInstance. As a first step, this method inserts the GUID into the path shown in the preceding code snippet. The method then reads the registry using the path and retrieves the physical location of the binary code for a COM object.

A detailed operational analysis of COM object creation that results from executing the method CoCreateInstance appears in Figure 12-7.

This sequencing diagram shows the elements involved in the COM object–creation process. Across the top of the diagram appear specific entities involved in COM object creation. The sequence of interactions among the participating entities proceeds from the top of the diagram to the bottom of the diagram.

A client application requests access to a specific interface supported by the COM object using the method CoCreateInstance. This method accesses the System Control Monitor (SCM) requesting that the COM object be loaded. The SCM queries the registry along the indicated path, obtaining the path to and the name of the InprocServer dynamic link library (DLL). After obtaining this information, the SCM then passes this information to the Windows CE operating system using the LoadLibrary method. Inside this method, the operating system physically loads the DLL into memory and returns a handle to the loaded COM object. Using the handle to the object, the SCM constructs a pointer to the method DLLGetClassObject. This method is part of the

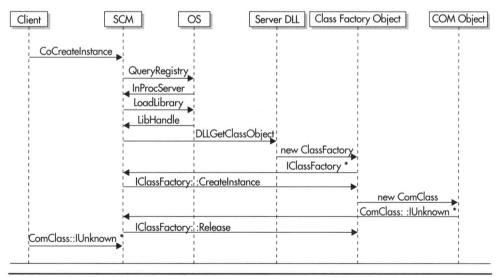

Figure 12-7 *COM object-creation sequence*

COM object's dynamic link library support framework. The SCM then executes this method through the constructed function pointer.

Inside this method, the COM object instantiates a class factory object implemented as part of a COM support environment. A pointer to the class factory interface (IClassFactory *) then propagates all the way back up to the SCM. Using this interface pointer, the SCM executes the method named CreateInstance, supported by the class factory object. An implementation of this method creates an instance of the COM class that actually provides all the methods that may be accessed by a client application. The act of creating this class enters the function pointers in an interface table so that a client application can actually execute the supported methods. A pointer to the default interface (IUnknown *) returns to the SCM. When the SCM receives this interface pointer, the SCM executes the Release method of the class factory object. This object unloads itself from memory, leaving the actual COM object loaded in memory. After releasing the class factory object, the SCM returns the default interface pointer (IUnknown *) to the client application. This pointer now references a table of function pointers for supported methods, enabling the client to execute the methods provided by the COM object.

The entity interaction sequence just outlined only occurs in its entirety the first time a client instantiates a COM object. If another client wishes to utilize methods supported by this same COM object, an interface pointer to the same COM object is returned to the new client. Two clients can share the same COM object when the implementation of the COM objects utilizes a DLL housing, because the Windows operating system natively supports shared DLL clients.

An actual COM control may exist within several host or execution environments, depending on the ultimate physical location of the binary object file. When implementing COM objects, the selection of an execution environment has several important implications.

A COM server can potentially execute with three hosting environments. Depending on the implemented hosting environment, a COM object may operate as an in-process server, a local server, or a remote server.

Figure 12-8 summarizes the characteristics and implications of using each of these execution environments.

An in-process COM server executes within the same process address space as the client application. Because the COM object resides in the same address space, an in-process COM server exhibits the fastest response time. A shorter development time occurs for an in-process COM object because less code is necessary for integrating with the execution environment. However, with this server, a program must register a copy of the COM object on every machine that maintains a copy of the client application.

Local COM servers reside on the same machine as the client application. However, these COM objects execute in a different process address space. As a result, extra

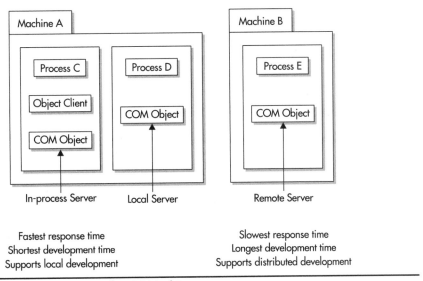

Figure 12-8   *Execution contexts for COM objects*

code is necessary to ensure that the arguments into a method transfer across process boundaries from the client process to the COM server process. The activity of transferring data across process boundaries comprises the *marshaling of interfaces*. Because some extra code executes to marshal data across processes, a local server COM object is going to take a little longer to respond to method calls. Developing the extra code to pass argument data across process boundaries does require a bit more coding effort, which lengthens development time somewhat. Because the COM object executes on the same machine as the application client, a program must also store and register a copy of the COM object on every executing client machine.

As a final option, a COM object can execute on a remote machine. When adopting this approach, a client program must also marshal arguments to each method call. Moreover, in this case, using a method provided by the server requires a transfer of data from the client machine to the server machine across some sort of network. Obviously, response times for executing server methods are going to be much longer. Executing a method across a network connection is likely to experience a nondeterministic response time. Every time a client program performs a remote method invocation of the same method, the client application experiences a completely different response time. If the network is clogged with traffic, some very long response times occur. The code that supports the marshaling of method arguments for a local server also supports the marshaling of method arguments for a remote server. However, cross-machine debugging is often necessary, thus causing development times to be radically lengthened. Cross-machine debugging is the most time-consuming form of debugging. With a remote COM server, only a single copy of the COM server needs to be loaded and registered on the actual server machine. This makes updating a remote COM server a relatively painless, low-effort process.

In fact, the act of marshaling data between client and server is a key issue when implementing a COM object or server. Depending on the relationship between the client and the server, a program uses different programming technologies to accomplish the marshaling of argument data during method calls from the client application to the server COM object.

Table 12-1 identifies the programming technologies employed to perform marshaling of data for performing method calls on a COM object, and shows the types of marshaling, the boundaries across which a program marshals the data, and the specific approach for marshaling the data.

When a COM object is hosted as an in-process server, the COM object resides in a dynamic link library (DLL). All the methods appear to a client application as entry points in a global function pointer table. Passing data from the client application to the COM object does not require any special programming technologies. Essentially, the marshaling of argument data is completely unnecessary.

For the local and remote server execution environments, marshaling argument data is necessary in order to move arguments across process boundaries or between computer nodes on a network. When accomplishing this data transfer, standard marshaling becomes the mechanism of choice. In order to perform standard marshaling, an Interface Definition Language (IDL) with an accompanying compiler allows a program to generate code that transfers the data across process or computer boundaries to a COM object. The code that this special compiler generates consists of two separate pieces: a proxy and a stub. The proxy attaches to the client application; a COM server uses the stub. These two pieces of software handle the mechanics of moving data between the client application and the COM object server across process or computer boundaries.

Another marshaling approach enables client applications written in a different language, such as Visual Basic, to access a COM object that is written in C++. *Dispatch*

Marshaling/Unmarshaling	Transferring Data Across Boundaries

Type of Marshaling	Boundaries	Approach
No marshaling	Dynamic link library	Global addressing
Standard marshaling	Process/node	Interface Definition Language
Dispatch marshaling	Programming language	Automation marshaler
Custom marshaling	Process	Special Sofware, protocol

Table 12-1   *Marshaling Technologies for Data Transfer to COM Objects*

marshaling is the act of transferring argument data across computer language boundaries. A predefined marshaler, called the *automation marshaler*, is an integral component of the Windows CE operating system. In order to use this marshaler, both the client application and a COM object must package the data into a standard data format called a VARIANT data type. This marshaler also provides a single entry point, the Invoke method, which accepts a numeric operation code for the method name and the input data arguments packaged into this standard VARIANT data format. Every COM object that supports dispatch marshaling implements this single, standard entry point. Inside this method, a COM server extracts the data from its standard VARIANT data format and executes the requested method.

Creating COM Components with ATL

A significant portion of the code for creating a COM object consists of boilerplate overhead. Visual Studio provides a program with an easily tailored approach for generating COM objects—the ActiveX Template Library (ATL)—that handles all the tedious details necessary to implement COM objects. By using templates to automatically generate the underlying boilerplate code, a developer is free to concentrate on the application-specific methods that perform the real work of a COM object/server.

In addition to providing a template-based library, Embedded Visual Studio has integrated wizards that make using ATL as a development framework a very simple job. However, a few hidden snags do exist when using ATL. These snags are identified in the following discussion.

CAUTION

A word of caution is necessary before proceeding further on this topic. For the most part, a developer simply uses the wizards integrated into Visual Studio in order to develop a COM object using ATL. However, from time to time, a compilation error leads a programmer into the source code for one of the templates. For this reason, a developer needs to be somewhat familiar with the concepts underlying C++ templates (or, at least have access to someone who does). Without some basic knowledge of the way in which templates work, debugging efforts are likely to be difficult and frustrating.

When creating a COM object using ATL, use Embedded Visual Studio to perform the following steps:

1. Create an ATL COM object using the ATL COM AppWizard.
2. Insert a new ATL object using the ATL Object Wizard.
3. Add application-specific methods using the Add Method to Interface Wizard.
4. Generate the bodies of application-specific methods.

The remainder of this section follows these steps to use ATL to construct a simple COM object. This COM object, called the COMServerProgram, supports a single interface named ICalculatorMgr. This interface provides a series of methods that perform operations on a hidden register, such as set, clear, add, subtract, multiply, and divide.

Create an ATL COM Object Using the ATL COM AppWizard

This first step creates an ATL COM object for a COM server. In order to perform this step, employ the ATL COM AppWizard using the following sequence of steps:

1. On the File menu, click New. Then click the Projects tab.

2. Along the left side of the New dialog box appears a list of project categories. Click the ATL COM AppWizard project category.

3. In the Project name box, enter the name **COMServerProgram**.

4. At the lower-right corner of the New project dialog box, click OK (see Figure 12-9).

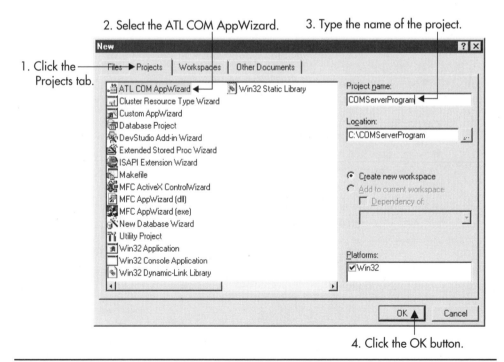

Figure 12-9   *A New project dialog box properly configured*

5. In the ATL COM AppWizard Step 1 dialog box, click Dynamic Link Library (DLL) to create an in-process server.

6. In the lower-right area of the ATL COM AppWizard dialog box, click Finish (see Figure 12-10).

7. After verifying the entries in the specifications text box, click OK in the lower-right area of the New Project Information dialog box (see Figure 12-11).

These steps create the DLL host environment for an in-process server COM object. Another result from these steps is to create all the code necessary to actually register a COM object in the system registry. This type of COM object is therefore self-registering.

Insert a New ATL Object Using the ATL Object Wizard

Now that the hosting environment has been defined and configured, entering an actual COM object is the next required creation step. Use the ATL Object Wizard of Embedded Visual Studio to perform this task:

1. On the Insert menu, click New ATL Object.

2. Along the left side of the ATL Object Wizard dialog box is the Category list. Click Objects in the Category list.

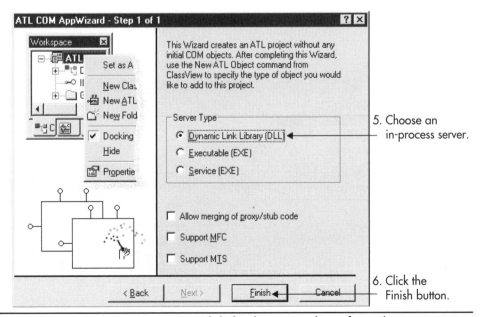

Figure 12-10   *An ATL COM AppWizard dialog box properly configured*

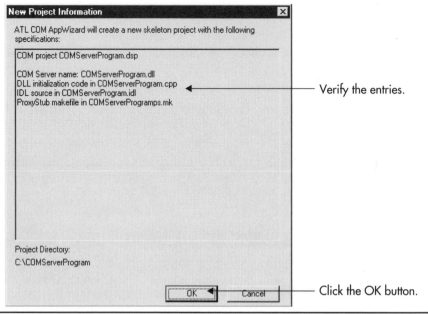

Verify the entries.

Click the OK button.

Figure 12-11 *A New Project Information dialog box describing generated files*

3. The right side of the ATL Object Wizard dialog box now contains an Objects list. Click the Simple Object icon in the Objects list.

4. In the lower-right area of the ATL Object Wizard dialog box, click Next (see Figure 12-12).

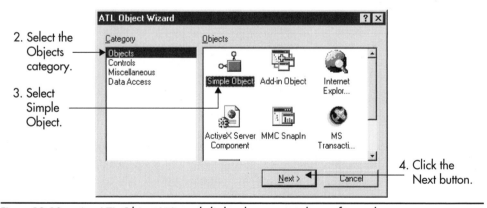

Figure 12-12 *An ATL Object Wizard dialog box properly configured*

5. Visual Studio displays the ATL Object Wizard Properties dialog box. If necessary, click the Names tab.

6. In the Short Name box, type the name of the server class, **CalculatorMgr**. All remaining fields automatically update based on the contents of the Short Name box.

7. In the ATL Object Wizard Properties dialog box, click the Attributes tab (see Figure 12-13).

8. In the Attributes tab, set the following attributes:

   ▶ Under Threading Model, click Single.

   ▶ Under Interface, click Custom.

   ▶ Under Aggregation, click No.

   Leave all remaining entries unchecked. The dialog box should look like Figure 12-14.

9. From the View menu, click Workspace and then click the ClassView tab (see Figure 12-15).

   After these steps are completed, the COM server receives an application class, CCalculatorMgr, and an interface, ICalculatorMgr. With the application class, the server acquires a templated version of a class factory, used to create a COM object

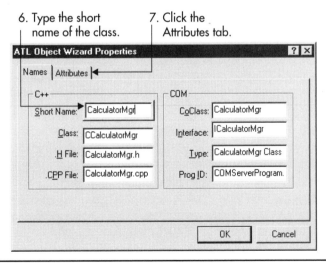

Figure 12-13   *An ATL Object Wizard Properties dialog box with the Names tab*

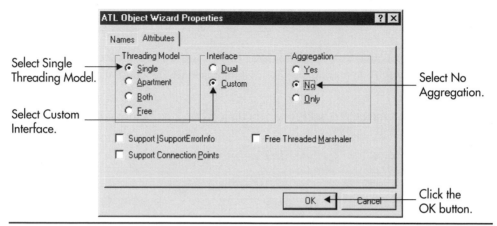

Select Single Threading Model.

Select Custom Interface.

Select No Aggregation.

Click the OK button.

Figure 12-14   *An ATL Object Wizard Properties dialog box with the Attributes tab*

when first instantiated. The server also inherits default implementations for the IUnknown methods QueryInterface, AddRef, and Release, which manage client access to interface pointers and control the lifetime of a COM object.

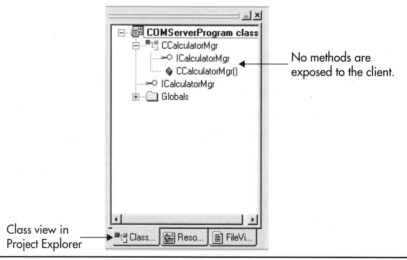

No methods are exposed to the client.

Class view in Project Explorer

Figure 12-15   *A Project Workspace view showing the ClassView tab*

Add Application Methods Using the Add Method to Interface Wizard

Once the server possesses the host environment, a class factory, and the IUnknown methods added to a COM object, the next step in the development process is to insert application-specific methods. A client application executes these methods in order to utilize the services of a COM object. When adding a method to a COM object, use the Add Method to Interface Wizard, as demonstrated in the following steps:

1. In the ClassView tab of the Project Workspace view, right-click the interface ICalculatorMgr.

2. On the shortcut menu, click Add Method.

3. In the Return Type box, select HRESULT.

4. Type a method name, such as **Add**, into the Method Name box.

5. Insert the following code snippet into the Parameters box (see Figure 12-16):

```
[in] double Argument
```

Most application methods return an HRESULT. When specifying parameters for a method, provide the parameter list in the same format as the Interface Definition Language. This format requires that a program indicate the direction of data transfer. By indicating the direction [in], the argument definition establishes that the data passes into the method but is not modified by the method.

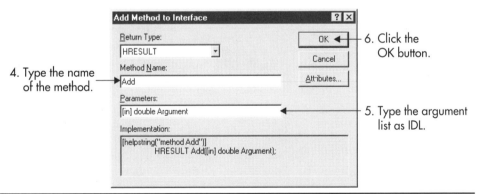

Figure 12-16 *An Add Method to Interface dialog that defines an Add method*

In the Implementation box of the Add Method to Interface dialog box, the wizard shows a complete listing of the method signature based on the data that a programmer has input.

6. At the upper-right corner of the Add Method to Interface dialog box, click OK.

Using the entered descriptive information, the wizard places an entry into the Interface Definition Language file of a project. The wizard also automatically generates a method into the server class, CCalculatorMgr.

Generate the Bodies of the Application-Specific Methods

After defining the application-specific methods in a COM object, enter the actual code bodies for these methods. Using the Project Workspace window, open a text edit window into the body of the COM server class using the following steps:

1. From the View menu, click Workspace and then click the ClassView tab.

2. Click the "+" icon at the left of the CCalculatorMgr entry to expand the contents of this class.

3. Click the "+" icon at the left of interface ICalculatorMgr below the class CCalculatorMgr to expand the contents of this interface, as shown in Figure 12-17.

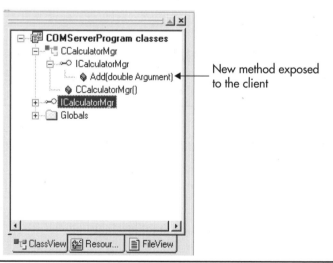

Figure 12-17   *A ClassView tab expanded to reveal the Server methods*

4. Double-click the Add method underneath the interface ICalculatorMgr subordinate to class CCalculatorMgr. This action opens a text edit window into the body of the method Add within the file that contains class CCalculatorMgr.

5. Inside the body of method Add, insert the following code snippet:

```
Register = Register + Argument ;
```

This line of code updates the value of the register that is declared as a private data member in class CCalculatorMgr declared in the file named CalculatorMgr.h (see Figure 12-18).

6. From the Build menu, select Build COMServerProgram.dll.

In response to this selection, Visual Studio compiles and links the COM server object. If a successful compile and link results and the target machine is a desktop,

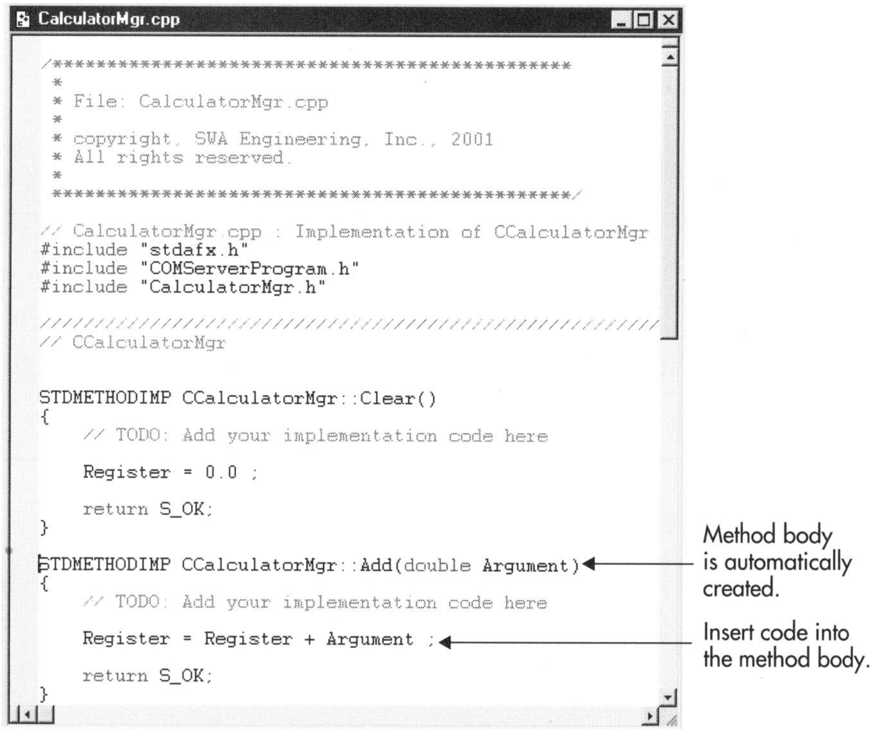

Figure 12-18 *Inserting code for the method body*

Visual Studio goes one step further, registering a COM object on the local machine. Client applications can now use the services of the COM object. However, if the target machine is a Pocket PC, extra steps are necessary to download and register the server on the Pocket PC. Later in this chapter, the section "Registering a COM Server on a Pocket PC" explains the methods for accomplishing registration on the Pocket PC.

Analyzing the ATL COM Component

This section walks through the various pieces of code associated with a COM object. Most of this code consists of wizard-generated output. Specific code reviewed includes a class declaration, a class body, the global methods and objects, an interface definition file, and the registry script.

A Class Declaration

The declaration for the server class appears in the file CalculatorMgr.h. This declaration is a standard C++ class specification that uses multiple inheritance.

```
#ifndef __CALCULATORMGR_H_
#define __CALCULATORMGR_H_
#include "resource.h"        // main symbols
// CCalculatorMgr
class ATL_NO_VTABLE CCalculatorMgr :
    public CComObjectRootEx<CComSingleThreadModel>,
    public CComCoClass<CCalculatorMgr, &CLSID_CalculatorMgr>,
    public ICalculatorMgr
{
public:
    CCalculatorMgr()
    {
        Register = 0 ;
    }
DECLARE_REGISTRY_RESOURCEID(IDR_CALCULATORMGR)
DECLARE_NOT_AGGREGATABLE(CCalculatorMgr)
DECLARE_PROTECT_FINAL_CONSTRUCT()
BEGIN_COM_MAP(CCalculatorMgr)
    COM_INTERFACE_ENTRY(ICalculatorMgr)
END_COM_MAP()
// ICalculatorMgr
public:
```

```
        STDMETHOD(get_Register)(/*[out, retval]*/ double *pVal);
        STDMETHOD(put_Register)(/*[in]*/ double newVal);
        STDMETHOD(Divide)(/*[in]*/ double Argument);
        STDMETHOD(Multiply)(/*[in]*/ double Argument);
        STDMETHOD(Subtract)(/*[in]*/ double Argument);
        STDMETHOD(Add)(/*[in]*/ double Argument);
        STDMETHOD(Clear)();
private:
        double Register ;
};
#endif //__CALCULATORMGR_H_
```

A COM server class inherits from three base classes: CComObjectRootEx, CComCoClass, and ICalculatorMgr. Two of these classes are actually template classes. Template parameters within the parameter delimiters (< . . . >) indicate which base classes are the template classes. The remaining class is an interface that has been declared as an abstract base class. Under the rules of C++, the derived class must implement the bodies of each of the methods in this base class. Because these methods are the specific services that were defined for a COM server, requiring the server class to implement the bodies is appropriate.

The class CComObjectRootEx provides a default implementation for the IUnknown interface methods QueryInterface, AddRef, and Release. When a COM object derives from this class, a client can use QueryInterface to acquire an interface pointer to any interface that the COM object supports. The methods AddRef and Release perform reference counting to hold a COM object in memory while multiple clients are using interface pointers.

Deriving from the base class CComCoClass provides a default implementation of a class factory. The class factory creates an instance of the server class in the memory space of a DLL environment. In order to create an instance of the server class, the COM object code provides the name of the server class, CCalculatorMgr, and a GUID for the server object, CLSID_CalculatorMgr. The variable CLSID_CalculatorMgr contains a numerical representation of the GUID for the COM object. Both the GUID and the numerical representation are created for the server during automatic code generation by Embedded Visual Studio.

Another important element of the class declaration is the COM map. This map contains a list of the interfaces that the COM object supports. An entry in the COM map uses the macro COM_INTERFACE_ENTRY. When this entry appears in the map, the template expansion creates a table with interface GUIDs and interface pointers. This map is then used by the default QueryInterface method inherited from templated base class CcomObjectRootEx. Whenever a client application executes the QueryInterface method, the default implementation searches this map for a matching interface GUID. If a match is found, the default method returns the corresponding interface pointer.

Near the end of the class declaration appear declarations for the methods that perform operations on the hidden register, such as Add, Subtract, Multiply, and Divide. These methods appear as publicly visible methods and use the COM calling conventions defined by the macro STDMETHOD. By declaring the methods to be publicly visible, the COM object ensures that the methods can be executed by a client application.

A private clause at the end of the class declaration declares an encapsulated Register Data Member. All the previous methods perform operations on this data member. Within the constructor for CCalculatorMgr, initialization of this data member occurs.

The Class Body

The code for the class body of the COM server resides in the file CalculatorMgr.cpp. This class body code contains only the application methods added using the Add Method To Interface Wizard. Bodies for all other methods, such as QueryInterface, exist within the template that provides this method.

```
/************************************************
 * File: CalculatorMgr.cpp
   * copyright, SWA Engineering, Inc., 2001
  * All rights reserved.
   ***********************************************/
// CalculatorMgr.cpp : Implementation of CCalculatorMgr
#include "stdafx.h"
#include "COMServerProgram.h"
#include "CalculatorMgr.h"
// CCalculatorMgr
STDMETHODIMP CCalculatorMgr::Add(double Argument)
{
     Register = Register + Argument ;
     return S_OK;
}
// Remaining Methods Omitted For Clarity
```

This code contains several COM-specific features automatically added to the method on behalf of the Add Method to Interface Wizard.

As the return data type, this method uses the macro STDMETHODIMP. This macro appears in the header file BASETYPS.H. Using this macro enables a COM server to implement two important COM-related features. One aspect of this macro causes the method to return an HRESULT, the normally preferred return code. Additionally, the macro informs the C++ preprocessor as to the COM-required method-entry sequence for managing parameters on the call stack.

Because the return value is to be an HRESULT, the wizard automatically inserts a line of code to return the constant S_OK. This manifest constant meets the data structure format of an HRESULT and contains a success return code embedded within that structure.

Global Methods and Objects

In the ClassView tab of the Workspace View resides a folder named Globals. If this folder is expanded, several global methods and a single global object appear. The wizards insert these elements into a project in order to harness some additional critical pieces of the ATL. These elements appear in file COMServerProgram.cpp.

```
// COMServerProgram.cpp : Implementation of DLL Exports.
#include "stdafx.h"
#include "resource.h"
#include <initguid.h>
#include "COMServerProgram.h"
#include "COMServerProgram_i.c"
#include "CalculatorMgr.h"


CComModule _Module;

BEGIN_OBJECT_MAP(ObjectMap)
OBJECT_ENTRY(CLSID_CalculatorMgr, CCalculatorMgr)
END_OBJECT_MAP()

extern "C"
BOOL WINAPI DllMain(HINSTANCE hInstance, DWORD dwReason,
                    LPVOID /*lpReserved*/)
{
    if (dwReason == DLL_PROCESS_ATTACH)
    {
        _Module.Init(ObjectMap,hInstance,&LIBID_COMSERVERPROGRAMLib);
        DisableThreadLibraryCalls(hInstance);
    }
    else if (dwReason == DLL_PROCESS_DETACH)
        _Module.Term();
```

```
        return TRUE;      // ok
}
STDAPI DllCanUnloadNow(void)
{
    return (_Module.GetLockCount()==0) ? S_OK : S_FALSE;
}
STDAPI DllGetClassObject(REFCLSID rclsid, REFIID riid, LPVOID* ppv)
{
    return _Module.GetClassObject(rclsid, riid, ppv);
}
STDAPI DllRegisterServer(void)
{
    return _Module.RegisterServer(TRUE);
}
STDAPI DllUnregisterServer(void)
{
    return _Module.UnregisterServer(TRUE);
}
```

Near the head of the file containing these elements exists a declaration of a single object named _Module, which is an instance of class CComModule. This module is a set of methods that keep track of all the COM objects hosted in this DLL. The methods in this module access the list of COM objects maintained in a table called the Object map.

A server places entries in this table using the ObjectEntry macro. For each COM object that resides in this DLL, the COM server places two values into a single entry of the Object map. The first entry consists of the GUID that uniquely identifies the COM object. As the second value, the server gives the name of the class that implements the COM object. Using this information, the macro expansion fills an entry in the underlying table with all sorts of useful information, such as the address of the CreateInstance method of the class factory used to create the object in memory.

When loading a DLL into memory, the SCM/COM executes the DllGetClassObject method. This method executes the CreateInstance method of the class factory and returns an interface pointer to a COM object. The default implementation of global method DllGetClassObject accomplishes this job by executing the method GetClassObject provided by the global entity _Module. Inside the method GetClassObject, access to the Object table described earlier yields a pointer to the CreateInstance method of the class factory. So, the method GetClassObject retrieves this pointer, uses the pointer to create a COM object, executes the QueryInterface provided by a COM object, and returns the interface pointer to the SCM/COM.

An Interface Definition Language File

An Interface Definition Language (IDL) file is used for one of several purposes. If an object is an out-of-process server, Visual Studio uses the IDL to create a proxy/server stub DLL. This DLL provides marshaling of data from the client process into the COM server process. Another use for the IDL file is to create a type library (TLB). This file is necessary if a COM server wants to make interfaces accessible to Visual Basic programmers. Finally, one of the outputs from the midl compiler that processes a IDL file is a header file that contains the object and interface GUIDs as well as the interface declarations used by client applications. This header file is the file that a COM object provides to a client application that wants to access the methods supported by interfaces of a COM object.

For this simple COM server, hosting occurs within an in-process server. In this situation, the only usage of the IDL is to generate a header file with the object and interface GUIDs. This file also contains an interface declaration. An interface declaration creates a function pointer table that C++ clients can use to access an interface and its methods. By including the header file, a client application reserves space for a table of function pointers. The client application compiles successfully, leaving space in the function pointer for the method addresses. These addresses are filled during execution when the client instantiates a COM object.

```
import "oaidl.idl";
import "ocidl.idl";
    [
        object,
        uuid(3E1DCD2F-4A21-4EDF-BE0E-FE247B5AB317),
        pointer_default(unique)
    ]
    interface ICalculatorMgr : IUnknown
    {
        HRESULT Clear();
        HRESULT Add([in] double Argument);
        HRESULT Subtract([in] double Argument);
        HRESULT Multiply([in] double Argument);
        HRESULT Divide([in] double Argument);
        [propget]HRESULT Register([out, retval] double *pVal);
        [propput]HRESULT Register([in] double newVal);
    };
  [
    uuid(E677B4AE-937B-40CC-A2B8-6587015722DC),
    version(1.0)
  ]
```

```
library COMSERVERPROGRAMLib
{
        importlib("stdole32.tlb");
        importlib("stdole2.tlb");
        [
                uuid(20A02FF0-88BD-468B-8C26-286DFA163655
        ]
        coclass CalculatorMgr
        {
                [default] interface ICalculatorMgr;
        };
};
```

In an IDL file, definitions exist for interfaces, coclasses, and libraries. An interface consists of a list of specific methods. Usually, these interfaces are functionally related in a general category. Additionally, each interface gets a unique GUID that was automatically generated by the Visual Studio wizards. A COM object can have multiple interfaces. If a server supports multiple interfaces, then the server declares each of these interfaces and the associated methods in an IDL file.

A coclass statement provides a listing of the supported interfaces for a component object. If a COM object supports multiple interfaces, a list of all the interfaces appears inside the coclass. The combined coclass/interface organization provides a hierarchical structure for the definition of the interface to a COM object. The coclass also receives a GUID generated by the Visual Studio wizards. A coclass GUID appears in a string format in the registry.

Appearance of the library keyword causes the midl compiler to generate a type library. VB uses this library in combination with a dispatch interface to make object methods programmatically accessible to the VB programmer. A type library must also have a GUID. Again, the Visual Studio wizards kindly generate this GUID for a program.

A Registry Script

When a client application attempts to load a COM object, the SCM/COM looks into the registry for specific information. Visual Studio creates a registry script that contains the necessary information. This information appears in the registry hive HKEY_CLASSES_ROOT (HKCR).

The registry script for this simple COM object exists in the file CalculatorMgr.rgs.

```
HKCR
{
        COMServerProgram.CalculatorMgr.1 = s 'CalculatorMgr Class'
        {
                CLSID = s '{20A02FF0-88BD-468B-8C26-286DFA163655}'
```

```
        }
COMServerProgram.CalculatorMgr = s 'CalculatorMgr Class'
{
        CLSID = s '{20A02FF0-88BD-468B-8C26-286DFA163655}'
        CurVer = s 'COMServerProgram.CalculatorMgr.1'
}
NoRemove CLSID
{
        ForceRemove {20A02FF0-88BD-468B-8C26-286DFA163655} =
                s 'CalculatorMgr Class'
        {
                ProgID = s 'COMServerProgram.CalculatorMgr.1'
                VersionIndependentProgID =
                        s 'COMServerProgram.CalculatorMgr'
                InprocServer32 = s '%MODULE%'
                {
                }
                'TypeLib' =
                        s '{E677B4AE-937B-40CC-A2B8-6587015722DC}'
        }
    }
}
```

This registry script primarily places data into the registry in the HKCR hive under a predefined key named CLSID. A subkey under this key is the GUID of the coclass of the COM object, entered in string format.

Below the subkey that represents a COM object's GUID appears a subsubkey named InprocServer32. This subsubkey has a value indicated in the script by the script value %MODULE%. When this script is processed by the midl compiler, the actual name of the project executable replaces this script variable. As a result, the real script entry looks like the following code snippet:

```
InprocServer32 = "C:\COMServerProgram\debug\COMServerProgram.dll"
```

When the SCM/COM attempts to load a COM object, this entry in the registry takes the SCM directly to the location of the executable code.

Creating a COM Client

This chapter describes a COM client for the simple COM server, COMServerProgram. This program provides a graphical user interface for a simple calculator. In response to user interaction with the interface, the message handlers interact with the lower-level COM object.

NOTE

Many applications use lower-level COM objects in this manner. A typical usage for lower-level COM objects is to have these objects implement a standard interface for managing a piece of hardware. The methods provided by the COM object encapsulate access to the hardware device as logical operations.

The graphical user interface for the Calculator client program appears in Figure 12-19.

This user interface contains two areas. Data entry occurs in the text windows at the top of the user interface. Commands to the calculator COM object are the purpose of the buttons along the bottom of the user interface.

Figure 12-19 actually provides the concept of operations for the user interface. When setting the register value, a user performs the following steps:

1. Type a numeric value into the Register data window.

2. Tap the Set button at the bottom of the window.

After initializing the register, the user can perform operations on the current value of the register by performing a different sequence of actions:

3. Type a numeric value into the Argument data window.

4. Tap any of the command buttons at the right side of the bottom of the window.

This user interface is intentionally kept simple in order to focus on the code necessary to interface to the COM object.

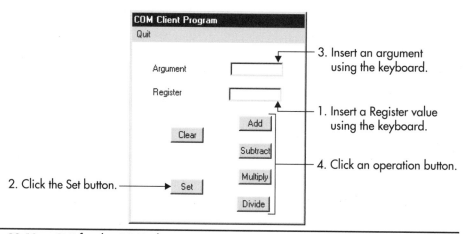

Figure 12-19 *GUI for the COM client*

NOTE

The client program that resides in the folder COMClientProgram uses the standard dialog application of Chapter 3. However, all files now possess the .cpp extension. This change is necessary to ensure that the COM function pointer tables maintained for the COM server interface work correctly.

Establishing the COM Object Interface

When the COM server code was compiled, one of the compilation steps includes processing the IDL file by the midl compiler. This compiler produces a number of important outputs. Two of the outputs from this compilation are necessary for the COM client program to have access to the COM object, the interfaces, and the methods supported by the COM object.

Prior to implementing any coded access to the COM server within a client application, copy the files COMServerProgram_i.c and COMServerProgram.h into the project folder of the client program. The file COMServerProgram_i.c declares all the GUIDs for the COM object, the interfaces, and the type library. In addition to the GUIDs, a client application needs a table to maintain the function pointers for the interfaces and methods supported by the COM object. Declarations inside the file COMServerProgram.h provide these table declarations.

Programming the COM Object Interface

Using a COM server from a client application is a fairly simple process. This process includes the following steps:

1. Import the necessary GUIDs and function pointer tables.
2. Declare an interface pointer variable.
3. Create an instance of the object.
4. Use the methods of the object.
5. Destroy the instance of the object.

The following subsections provide code examples that demonstrate each of these steps. These examples come from the sample client program in the folder COMClientProgram.

Import the Necessary GUIDs and Function Pointer Tables

```
#include <initguid.h>
#include "COMServerProgram_i.c"
#include "COMServerProgram.h"
```

Including these three files in a COM client program provides access to the capability the client program needs to use a specific COM server object. Using the file initguid.h, the client program gains access to a number of macros necessary to support initialization of any GUID when used in program code.

The file COMServerProgram_i.c declares all the GUIDs for the specific COM object that will be used by the client program, the interfaces, and the type library. In addition to the GUIDs, a client application needs a table to maintain the function pointers for the interfaces and methods supported by the COM object. Declarations inside the file COMServerProgram.h provide these table declarations.

Declare an Interface Pointer Variable

```
static ICalculatorMgr * Calculator ;
```

In fact, the variable Calculator, which is an interface pointer for ICalculatorMgr, is the table that hosts the function pointers for the interface supported by the COMServerProgram COM object. Without this variable, the client program would not have a storage area available to store the function pointers after loading the specific COM object into memory.

Create an Instance of the Object

```
#if !WindowsCE
   CoInitialize(NULL) ;
#endif
CoCreateInstance(CLSID_CalculatorMgr,NULL,
                CLSCTX_INPROC_SERVER,
                IID_ICalculatorMgr,(void **)&Calculator) ;
```

In order to create an instance of the COM object, the client program performs two steps. If the client program executes on a desktop computer, then the client program first loads COM support. Executing the method CoInitialize loads COM support if necessary. Apparently, this step is unnecessary when the client executes on the Pocket PC.

Once COM services are loaded, the client creates an instance of the desired COM object using the method CoCreateInstance, provided by the Win32 API. As the first argument, the client program gives the class GUID for the object,

CLSID_CalculatorMgr. For most applications on the Pocket PC, the second argument will always be NULL. The symbol CLSCTX_INPROC_SERVER indicates that the server is an in-process COM object. This constant tells CoCreateInstance to find InProcServer32 in the registry in order to determine the physical path to the executable server DLL. In addition to a GUID for the object class, the next argument indicates the GUID for the interface. This GUID must match the specific interface for the pointer variable previously declared. Finally, the client application provides the address of the interface pointer variable as the location in which the function pointer table resides.

Once CoCreateInstance interacts with the Windows CE SCM, as shown earlier in Figure 12-7, this method can fill the function pointer table with pointers to the method entry points of the COM server object.

Use the Methods of the Object

```
case IDC_BUTTON3:
     GetDoubleFromTextWindow(hDlg,IDC_EDIT1,&Argument) ;
     Calculator->Add(Argument) ;
     Calculator->get_Register(&Register) ;
     SetDoubleIntoTextWindow(hDlg,IDC_EDIT2,Register,2) ;
break ;
```

When the user taps the Add button on the face of the user interface, the WM_COMMAND message handler executes this case clause. First, this clause retrieves the value of the argument from the edit window identified by IDC_EDIT1. Using the interface pointer, the next step in the response is to invoke the Add method of the COM object. By dereferencing the interface pointer, the client moves through the function pointer table to execute the actual method provided by the COM object.

After performing the Add method, this message handler retrieves the current value of the hidden register by executing the property access method get_Register. This current value then displays in the Register data window.

The methods GetDoubleFromTextWindow and SetDoubleIntoTextWindow are members of the software element GUIUtils. For this application, these utility files also acquire the .cpp extension. This extension allows them to compile and execute in the C++ namespace without further modification.

Destroy the Instance of the Object

```
Calculator->Release() ;
#if !WindowsCE
```

```
        CoUninitialize() ;
#endif
```

When created using CoCreateInstance, the COM object increments a reference pointer. In order to enable the object to self-destruct, the client application executes the Release method provided by the COM object. This method decrements the reference counter. If the counter value becomes zero, the object knows that no clients are active. In this situation, the COM object self-destructs.

After releasing the object, the client program executes CoUninitialize. This method signals to the SCM that one less application needs any kind of COM support. As with COM service initialization, using this method is only necessary when the client program executes on a desktop PC.

Registering a COM Server on a Pocket PC

A few special steps are necessary to register a COM server on a Pocket PC. A special program must reside on the Pocket PC in order to register and to unregister COM objects on the Pocket PC.

NOTE

Using Asynch Manager, download the program regsvrce.exe into the root folder of the Pocket PC. Usually this program is available in the folder named C:\Windows CE Tools\wce300\MS Pocket PC\ target\mips. The last element in the path reflects the actual target platform.

After downloading this registration program to the Pocket PC, a developer only has two ways in which to execute this program. One alternative is to use an INF file and an installation program. This approach enables a batch approach that does not involve human interaction.

For testing purposes, an interactive approach is more appropriate. Unfortunately, the program regsvrce.exe does not have a user-friendly interface. For this reason, the files associated with this book (available for download at http://www.osborne.com) have a program that provides a user-friendly interface for regsvrce.exe.

Figure 12-20 provides the graphical user interface for the RegistrationMgrProgram that accompanies this book (available for download at http://www.osborne.com).

Using this interface involves a three-step process. When tapped with the stylus, the Browse button at the top displays a File Open dialog. With this dialog, a user can navigate the whole storage area of the Pocket PC to find the desired DLL server. Once this server is selected, the name of the server appears in the edit control in the

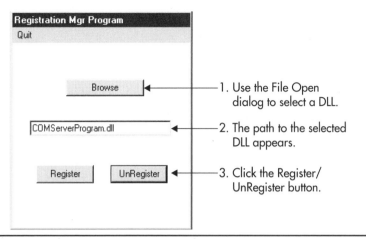

Figure 12-20   *Registering the COM server on a Pocket PC*

middle of the client area. Alternatively, the user can simply type the path to the server object DLL directly into this edit control. Finally, the user taps either of the command buttons to register or unregister the COM object DLL.

NOTE

This program creates a separate process to execute the regsvrce program and then waits to be signaled regarding the status of the commanded operation.

Summary

This chapter emphasizes the use of COM objects and COM servers on the Pocket PC under Windows CE. Lessons learned in this chapter include the following:

▶   The simplest approach for creating a COM server is to use the ATL wizards.

▶   Creating the COM server using the ATL wizards requires creating the COM ATL DLL housing and then inserting an ATL object into the housing.

▶   Using an in-process COM server provides the fastest response time of all the COM execution contexts.

▶   Multiple clients can share a loaded COM object more effectively using the limited memory resources of the Pocket PC.

▶ A COM client uses an interface pointer that provides a table for a set of function pointers that provide access to the methods supported by the COM object.

▶ Entries are dynamically bound into this table of function pointers during execution when the COM object is loaded into memory.

▶ Registering a COM object on a Pocket PC requires an INF file and regsvrce.exe when being performed without human interaction.

▶ Registering a COM object on a Pocket PC requires a special GUI program and regsvrce.exe when being performed interactively by a human.

Sample Programs on the Web

The following programs are available at http://www.osborne.com:

Description	Folder
Desktop COM Server Program	COMServerProgram
Pocket PC COM Server Program	COMServerProgramPPC
Desktop Registration Mgr Program	RegistrationMgrProgram
Pocket PC Registration Mgr Program	RegistrationMgrProgramPPC
Desktop COM Client Program	COMClientProgram
Pocket PC COM Client Program	COMClientProgram PPC

Execution Instructions

Desktop COM Server Program

1. Start Visual C++ 6.0.
2. Open the project COMServerProgram.dsw in the folder COMServerProgram.
3. Build the DLL.

Pocket PC COM Server Program

1. Attach the Pocket PC cradle to the desktop computer.
2. Insert the Pocket PC into the cradle.

3. Tell ActiveSync to create a guest connection.

4. Make sure the status is connected.

5. Start Embedded Visual C++ 3.0.

6. Open the project COMServerProgram PPC.vcw in folder COMServerProgramPPC.

7. Build the DLL.

8. Make sure the program successfully downloads to the Pocket PC.

Desktop Registration Mgr Program

1. Start Visual C++ 6.0.

2. Open the project RegistrationMgrProgram.dsw in the folder RegistrationMgrProgram.

3. Build the program.

4. Execute the program.

5. Click the Browse button at the top of the client area.

6. This action should cause the File Open dialog to display.

7. Use the Explorer window of the File Open dialog to navigate around the disk to find the COMServerProgram.dll file.

8. Click the Register button in the bottom of the client area.

9. Click the Quit menu item.

10. The application window disappears as the application terminates.

Pocket PC Registration Mgr Program

1. Attach the Pocket PC cradle to the desktop computer.

2. Insert the Pocket PC into the cradle.

3. Tell ActiveSync to create a guest connection.

4. Make sure the status is connected.

5. Download the program regsvrce.exe to the root folder of the Pocket PC. Usually this program is available in the folder C:\Windows CE Tools\ wce300\MS Pocket PC\target\mips. The last element in the path reflects the actual target platform.

6. Start Embedded Visual C++ 3.0.

7. Open the project RegistrationMgrProgram PPC.vcw in the folder RegistrationMgrProgramPPC.

8. Build the program.

9. Make sure the program successfully downloads to the Pocket PC.

10. On the Pocket PC, open the File Explorer.

11. Browse to the MyDevice folder.

12. Execute the program RegistrationMgrProgram.

13. Tap the Browse button at the top of the client area.

14. This action should cause the File Open dialog to display.

15. Use the Explorer window of the File Open dialog to navigate around the disk to find the COMServerProgram.dll file.

16. Tap the Register button in the bottom of the client area.

17. Tap the Quit menu item.

18. The application window disappears as the application terminates.

Desktop COM Client Program

1. Start Visual C++ 6.0.

2. Open the project COMClientProgram.dsw in the folder COMClientProgram.

3. Build the program.

4. Execute the program.

5. Enter a numeric value into the Register data-entry window.

6. Click the Set button.

7. This action should cause the numeric value in Register to become permanent.

8. Enter a numeric value into the Argument data-entry window.

9. Click any operation button.

10. This action should cause the contents of the Register data-entry window to be updated, consistent with the commanded operation and the Argument value.

11. Click the Quit menu item.

12. The application window disappears as the application terminates.

13. Execute the RegistrationMgrProgram to unregister the COM server.

Pocket PC COM Client Program

1. Attach the Pocket PC cradle to the desktop computer.

2. Insert the Pocket PC into the cradle.

3. Tell ActiveSync to create a guest connection.

4. Make sure the status is connected.

5. Start Embedded Visual C++ 3.0.

6. Open the project COMClientProgram PPC.vcw in the folder COMClientProgram PPC.

7. Build the program.

8. Make sure the program successfully downloads to the Pocket PC.

9. On the Pocket PC, open the File Explorer.

10. Browse to the MyDevice folder.

11. Execute the program COMClientProgram.

12. Enter a numeric value into the Register data-entry window.

13. Tap the Set button.

14. This action should cause the numeric value in Register to become permanent.

15. Enter a numeric value into the Argument data-entry window.

16. Tap any operation button.

17. This action should cause the contents of the Register data-entry window to be updated, consistent with the commanded operation and the Argument value.

18. Tap the Quit menu item.

19. The application window disappears as the application terminates.

20. Execute the RegistrationMgrProgram to unregister the COM server.

Index

INTERNATIONAL CONTACT INFORMATION

AUSTRALIA
McGraw-Hill Book Company Australia Pty. Ltd.
TEL +61-2-9417-9899
FAX +61-2-9417-5687
http://www.mcgraw-hill.com.au
books-it_sydney@mcgraw-hill.com

CANADA
McGraw-Hill Ryerson Ltd.
TEL +905-430-5000
FAX +905-430-5020
http://www.mcgrawhill.ca

**GREECE, MIDDLE EAST,
NORTHERN AFRICA**
McGraw-Hill Hellas
TEL +30-1-656-0990-3-4
FAX +30-1-654-5525

MEXICO (Also serving Latin America)
McGraw-Hill Interamericana Editores S.A. de C.V.
TEL +525-117-1583
FAX +525-117-1589
http://www.mcgraw-hill.com.mx
fernando_castellanos@mcgraw-hill.com

SINGAPORE (Serving Asia)
McGraw-Hill Book Company
TEL +65-863-1580
FAX +65-862-3354
http://www.mcgraw-hill.com.sg
mghasia@mcgraw-hill.com

SOUTH AFRICA
McGraw-Hill South Africa
TEL +27-11-622-7512
FAX +27-11-622-9045
robyn_swanepoel@mcgraw-hill.com

**UNITED KINGDOM & EUROPE
(Excluding Southern Europe)**
McGraw-Hill Education Europe
TEL +44-1-628-502500
FAX +44-1-628-770224
http://www.mcgraw-hill.co.uk
computing_neurope@mcgraw-hill.com

ALL OTHER INQUIRIES Contact:
Osborne/McGraw-Hill
TEL +1-510-549-6600
FAX +1-510-883-7600
http://www.osborne.com
omg_international@mcgraw-hill.com

(continued)

GENERAL: This License Agreement constitutes the entire agreement between the parties relating to the SOFTWARE. The terms of any Purchase Order shall have no effect on the terms of this License Agreement. Failure of SWA-ENG to insist at any time on strict compliance with this License Agreement shall not constitute a waiver of any rights under this License Agreement. This License Agreement shall be construed and governed in accordance with the laws of the State of California. If any provision of this License Agreement is held to be contrary to law, that provision will be enforced to the maximum extent permissible and the remaining provisions will remain in full force and effect.

ACKNOWLEDGEMENT: By downloading the SOFTWARE from the McGraw-Hill website or the SWA-ENG website and using the SOFTWARE, you signify your acceptance of the terms of this license agreement. If you do not agree to the terms of this license agreement, do not download or use this SOFTWARE.

CONTACT INFORMATION: Dr. Bruce Krell, SWA-Engineering, Inc., PO Box 3821, Beverly Hills, CA 90212, BKrell@SWA-Engineering.com